FOREIGN STRANDS

Also by Stephen Alexander

Sweet Kwai Run Softly

FOREIGN STRANDS

A British Council Journey

Stephen Alexander

Merriotts Press

First published in 2003 by

MERRIOTTS PRESS

174 Long Ashton Road, Bristol BS41 9LT
Tel: 01275 392 347

Printed and bound in Great Britain
by J W Arrowsmith Ltd, Bristol

A CIP catalogue record for this book is available
from the British Library

ISBN 0 9526763 1 1

Breathes there the man, with soul so dead,
Who never to himself hath said,
This is my own, my native land!
Whose heart hath ne'er within him burned,
As home his footsteps he hath turned
From wandering on a foreign strand!

Sir Walter Scott, *The Lay of the Last Minstrel,* 1805

I am so convinced of the advantages of looking at mankind instead of reading about them, and of the bitter effects of staying at home with all the narrow prejudices of an Islander, that I think there should be a law amongst us to set our young men abroad for a term among the few allies our wars have left us.

Lord Byron to his mother, 14th January 1811

Contents

Illustrations

Acknowledgments

My grateful thanks to Ruth Alexander and Caroline Taylor for their indispensable help and encouragement. My thanks also to HMSO for quotations from Michael Swan's *British Guiana,* to Ian McDonald and Frank Thomasson for those from *Kyk-Over-Al*, and to the Hakluyt Society for those from *Robert Bargrave's Travel Diary.* I have tried without success to contact the copyright owner of Walter Dupouy's edition of *Sir Robert Ker Porter's Caracas Diary 1825-42*, published 'under the sponsorship of the Foundation Instituto Otto y Magdalena Blohm' in 1966, and would welcome guidance on the expression of my debt to this fascinating book.

Foreword

FOR MANY YEARS the British Council, irked that the British public in general – and the Daily Express in particular – saw its priority as teaching Morris dancing in the Galapagos Islands, solemnly issued a booklet entitled *What is the British Council?* In this it sought to clarify its role as exporter of British education, arts and developmental practice, and promoter of any kind of cultural interchange with an overseas country that would, hopefully, prove of mutual benefit.

The definition of that role has varied with the years. Conceived in 1934 as 'The British Committee for Relations with Other Countries', the new body was christened by the Foreign Office 'The British Council' for short, and its aim was set out in 1935 as 'promoting abroad a wider appreciation of British culture'(through language, literature, music, fine arts, sciences, philosophic thought and political practice) and effecting regular educational interchange (especially of staff, students and operatives in universities, technical institutes and factories). Since then there has been ample cause for confusion between multiple aims and changing national priorities, and by the 20th century the impenetrable language of globalisation has added its obfuscations. 'What does the British Council do?' asks a recent Council circular plaintively; it gives a fashionably threefold reply of 'purpose (to win recognition abroad for the UK's values)', 'brand statement for use on web-sites (to connect people worldwide with learning opportunities)' and 'strategic objectives (to strengthen engagement with the diversity of UK culture, good governance and human rights).'

To explain such a sea change from the original launching, the public might well have expected a softening-up process to have operated in the intervening years. Yet it was not until the 1970s that the Council hired a professional PRO. When it did so, it chose a journalist so careless of verifying his sources that in his inaugural address he attributed (without contradiction) to Hilaire Belloc the familiar verse on his kind by Humbert Wolfe.

You cannot hope
To bribe or twist
(Thank God!) the British
Journalist;
But seeing what
The man will do
Unbribed, there's no
Occasion to.

No wonder the newspapers have had such fun with the Council! It is not its successes that make good copy but its flops; not the great but 'resting' actor's first triumphant one-man show in Mbongo-Mbongo but his second, when he was half-seas-over.

Most of the real work of the Council – educational exchange, consultancy, English teaching, community development and the provision of libraries (latterly 'information centres') – is not headline-grabbing. Moreover, the Council man on the spot may not be able to demonstrate Britain at her best (quality is expensive) and London HQ is susceptible to fashions for which foreign countries may not be ready; they often admire Britain for reasons disapproved of by the current establishment. Fortunately the parts of Council life and work are greater than its whole – at least they have been in the past and this will increase in importance as the parts and whole of a once Great Britain are unravelled and reassembled in a new form.

Britain's shop window, unlike that of her rivals in the field, tends to be a bit of a muddle. She spends far less on disseminating her cultural image than comparable countries and has never been clear on how it should be done – or indeed what cultural image it is she wishes to convey. As a result her man, or increasingly woman, on the spot is often left to interpret his or her role as best he or she may. Indeed, because of the unenlightening title and all-encompassing (though variable) role of the British Council its 'officer' overseas is regularly mistaken for the British Consul. Our cultural competitors are at least saved from such 'Council/Consul' confusion. (The Alliance Française is a good catch-all title, and the Italians and Germans use the distinctive names of Dante Alighieri and Goethe for their institutes, which are primarily cultural and linguistic; schools, scholarships and aid work are the province of their embassies. The Americans – in theory – split cultural and educational responsibilities between their Information Services and the State Department, while cultural propaganda from Russia throughout the Cold War period remained strictly diplomatic.) A more effective name for the British Council is not easy to find; naming it after Shakespeare, for instance, might well be resented by three parts of our increasingly disunited kingdom.

It is also open to argument what kind of person Britain's representative should be – populariser, specialist, academic, manager, artist, writer? The Betjemans have not stayed long with the Council ('I cannot read this, it is too dull!' was John's contribution to some carefully composed minuting) and well-known names in the arts were not often a success. There have been colourful figures, but on the whole earnestness has prevailed, and the importance of being earnest is not generally appreciated by press or public (unless they have cause to rely on it).

Perhaps after three and a half years as a prisoner of the Japanese* I was too conscious of the extremes of life overseas to be properly earnest. This book shows what the British Council – over thirty-three chameleon years – was for me and also what, for better or worse, I contributed to the image of Britain abroad.

* Described in *Sweet Kwai Run Softly*, Merriotts Press, 1995.

1
Culture Shock

'WHEN I GO TRAVELLING,' said Mac, 'I often stay in brothels. They're cheaper than hotels – and cleaner.'

It was May 1946 and my first night in Colombia (at the top left-hand corner of South America, as I'd learned when I looked it up on the map four months before). I was twenty-six. After three and a half years as a Japanese prison of war in the Far East I had felt alienated by life in England. The British Council had come up with the offer of a job in the Far West, and with a mixture of curiosity and resignation I had accepted it. So, after a rudimentary training and a few Spanish lessons, I found myself a 'lecturer Latin America' and once more an exile.

We were sitting in El Gato Negro, Barranquilla's most superior alfresco nightspot, drinking Cuba Libres. It was a charming scene. The white walls and palm-fringed patio gave it the air of a P C Wren fort – though perhaps a film version rather than the real thing. Round the walls were rooms which the girls opened, when required, with keys hanging from their waists. A small band was playing *Soy, soy, soy Tolimense!* (I'm from Tolima).

'These girls,' Mac explained, 'have to work pretty hard for their living; people mostly come for the atmosphere rather than for anything else. It's more fun than the Prado Hotel and more comfortable than the *cantinas* in town. In Colombia they roll up the sidewalks at about seven, and you won't see any respectable women about after that. In Medellín you'll see the girls sitting at their bedroom windows and their *novios* (suitors) serenading them through the *rejas* (bars), or bombarding them with the sort of innuendoes you or I wouldn't dream of using with our girlfriends. Then they go and sublimate their feelings in the *barrio* – the red light district.'

Certainly there was a disarmingly domestic air about the Black Cat, enhanced by the presence outside of the only British car in Barranquilla, its first post-war Austin. Bill MacLaughlin, a former ship's purser and a wartime Director of the local Instituto Cultural Colombo-Británico, had met the three of us British Council recruits at the airport on our way through to Medellín. Ozzie Pope and I had left our fellow lecturer, Margery Hall, at the hotel, talking at cross purposes about the Direct Teaching Method to a libidinous oilman. We had given her a chance on the *Gripsholm*, which carried us from Liverpool to New York, and also on the plane south. She had been offered cigarettes (she didn't smoke), cocktails (she didn't drink) and even a dance (she didn't dance), and seemed to us elderly in the extreme (she turned out to be thirty-six). She countered her absence of make-up and greying hair with an effusive manner and instant smile, but at heart she was clearly a no-nonsense Yorkshire woman to whom social niceties were unimportant. She might well disapprove of our frivolous attitude to post-war opportunities compared with her own missionary zeal but she need not have actually said that she was worth her eight hundred pounds a year to the British Council, compared to our five or six, because she had 'spent the war gaining experience by teaching while we had only been fighting'. She was certainly put out by the ebullient, unassuming and disconcertingly deaf Mac.

'Mr MacLaughlin, do you use the Eckersley books for all your classes or only for beginners?'

'Practically all our classes *are* for beginners. Most of them are girls and only matriculate so that they have an alibi for staying out in the evenings. They don't often come to classes but, as long as they pay their fees each year, who am I to complain? It helps to pay the rent.'

'Good gracious! What a situation! Isn't it time for a rethink?'

'A wee drink? You're right, why not? Let's see if there's enough in the petty cash to go out and get one.'

It was obvious that Mac, in spite of his irreverent ways, had much affection for Colombia. In Barranquilla, where Spanish culture is strongly tinged by the black influence of the coast, life in general is more easygoing than in the inhibited societies of the inland cities. But to us the place seemed very hot and squalid and as we boarded the Avianca plane for Medellín we said goodbye with some relief. I was to work with Mac many years later; he was completely unchanged – except in having a wife and a fearsome hearing aid that whistled and clicked all round the office.

Miss Hall – I still think of her as Miss Hall since it was thus we addressed her in retaliation for her calling us Mr Pope and Mr Alexander – did indeed prove to be a dedicated and competent teacher. But in Medellín she was to flower in other ways. No doubt the heavy gallantries of her more mature and perennial pupils had their effect for her hair took on a new bloom, her dresses took the eye and her hats got bigger and bigger. She made up, she smoked, she danced a spirited *bambuco* and – after a drink or two – would oblige at the piano with a rendition of *The Lass with a Delicate Air.*

Medellín lies about halfway in distance and height between Barranquilla and Bogotá, 9000ft up in the cold and wet of the Chibcha country. Medellín has a perennial spring or coffee-friendly climate but the rugged mountains round it, which appeared alarmingly at the cabin windows as we came in to land, can be very chilly at night; the wise traveller in them carries a flask of *aguardiente*, with its attendant lemon and pinch of salt. The town had prospered in the war and its pretty 'colonial' patio houses were giving way to blocks of flats. The outskirts, except on the smart Poblado side with its country club and airport, were becoming a free-for-all of factories, football pitches, riding stables, the bullring and a cockpit – not to mention the huge red-light district conveniently signposted at night by a neon cross on its church spire. The only modern hotel was the American-run Nutibara, which towered like a grey beached whale over the two-storey shops of the Parque Berrio, with its vaguely baroque church of La Candelaria, its regulation statue and dozens of bootblacks.

The city was rarely quiet. From dawn to dusk church bells jangled, ancient trams rocked through the narrow streets, ear-splitting horns were sounded on American cars, newspaper and lottery ticket sellers cried their wares and bus conductors bawled their destinations; and even at night, when families locked themselves safely away behind their patio walls, taxi drivers at the kiosks continued shouting to each other into the small hours, and *cantinas* and barbers' shops blared out their music – local dance tunes, American hit-songs and, to add to the confusion, the odd Beethoven symphony.

The Instituto Cultural Colombo-Británico rented a fine patio house belonging to a British businessman in the quiet Plazuela de San Ignacio and opposite the Jesuit university. It housed not only the library and classrooms but also the director, Jack Harriman, and his family – and a small swimming pool. We three new recruits settled into the Pension Rumania, run by amiable and hard-working German Jews, near the modern and not very attractive cathedral. Why should a small town in Colombia, whose global notoriety lay far in the future, merit three teachers and a director paid for by the British Council?

I knew little about the British Council when I was demobbed after a war service distinguished only in its longevity. Being unqualified to work in business or colonial government, I thought that in the Council I might be able to fight for Britain overseas more effectively than I had in my imperialist role.

It had, however, been the imperial fervour of Lord Lloyd which had been the impetus for inaugurating the Council in 1936, in order to counter the cultural propaganda of the Axis powers. Germany and Italy were fast overtaking France in 'manifestations' (as cultural showpieces were named) and had been busy providing subsidies for schools as far afield as South America, while Britain had long left such airy-fairy matters to her colonial governments.

Lord Lloyd could at first only extract enough from the Foreign Office grant to fund a few exhibitions and salaries for teachers of English, mostly in the 'soft underbelly of Europe' and the Middle East. However, as the war progressed and Britain lost her footing in many long-held parts of the world she became frightened into expanding her influence in neutral countries elsewhere – in Spain and Portugal and their former Latin American empires, in which many more Axis than British immigrants had settled. In Latin American capital cities some English teachers working locally became the British Council 'Representative' with overall responsibility for others appointed as 'directors' of teaching institutes in the provinces and also in the capital (where they could be in the same building as the Representative's office). The Institutes themselves were Anglophile societies or *culturas* managed by a Board of Directors (the *Junta Directiva*) composed of friendly nationals and local British residents. Some of their teachers were – like me –

recruited by the Council and had extra-mural duties such as lecturing at universities and radio stations, or introducing film shows or travelling exhibitions; others were 'locally-engaged' and usually British businessmen or wives. The Council supplied books for the *Cultura* libraries (backed up by a 'London-appointed' librarian in the capital), sponsored visitors each way, and funded scholarships and academic exchanges. Tuition and membership fees allowed the *Culturas* to provide social as well as cultural activities. The *Culturas* burgeoned during the war, partly from national sympathies, partly because commerce with the United States demanded English but people preferred to learn it from the British, for whom a romantic attachment was still a legacy of the Wars of Independence. Moreover they had never forgiven the United States for helping Panama secede from Colombia in order to control the canal. In the more feudal and priest-ridden countries *Culturas* also opened a chink to a liberal education or, to be honest, were simply places where girls could go unchaperoned and meet men.

It all sounded very neat. The Council got wide coverage on the cheap and the *Culturas* got glamorous 'native' teachers and official status, distinguishing them from commercial schools of English. But delegation has its pitfalls. After the war national sentiments changed, and not least in Britain; in South America Germany and Italy became our allies against the Red Menace, the United States launched their own lavishly subsidised *Culturas*, national colleges were liberalised and the convenience of *Culturas* as dating agencies declined. But just when Anglophile societies began to feel the draught and asked for more support the Council was least able to oblige; it was busy expanding elsewhere in the 'free world', including the countries of its own new Commonwealth. India alone soon had the lion's share of its budget. Other problems arose as vested interests took root; entrenched membership of a *Junta* encouraged the abuse of patronage and nepotism, control of finance became sketchy, and long-serving local staff lost dynamism. At the same time the experienced long-term Council Director often fell victim to the chopping and changing on the promotional ladder of the Council's post-war career service. The disengagement of the Council from many autonomous institutes – from the enormously wealthy but corrupt to the virtually bankrupt – was to prove a long and painful process.

But of all this I was unaware when I went to 3 Hanover Street and signed a year's contract as a Temporary Teacher Grade IV at an annual salary of £420 with an overseas allowance of £340. These were modest sums but most of us had modest expectations and did not aspire to expensive commitments like cars – or wives.

I was nonplussed by the colleagues I met in the London office; they were certainly not all of a piece. Up at the top there were old colonials (like the avuncular A J S White), retired diplomats and colonels (the Adjutant General, Sir Ronald Adam, was shortly to take over as both Chairman and Director General), and proponents of the adult education now popular with the Attlee government. It was evidently the helpful, capable and (to my eyes) mature ladies in the lower echelons who ran the show while we new recruits were a mixture of ex-service people and of the woolly-sweater brigade, with a polo neck here, a shirt collar outside the jacket there, and the odd beard to bolster artistic pretensions.

The word 'Culture' was not bandied about in Hanover Street, and John Betjeman, the Council's intellectual odd man out, was able to lie on his stomach to direct a Books Department outposted to Blenheim Palace in comfort as well as security. During our sketchy induction course, far from any common staff characteristics emerging, it became clear that the Council was divided between those who had intellectual interests of some sort and those who, however worthy in other ways, had not. Over the years the balance between the two was to change inexorably.

In the happy days when travel was cheaper by sea than by air it was general practice by even the most niggardly employer to send staff overseas by boat, and particularly so when heavy baggage was involved and speed was not of the essence. As a 'British Council Officer' some of the happiest days of my life – counted as duty, not leave – were spent at sea, and at the expense of HMG. All my sea travel hitherto had been similarly subsidised, but that was in troopships. In 1946 I was in a mood of some gloom at leaving England so soon after being repatriated from the Far East at the end of the war. On the other hand, I was relieved to have settled an uncertain future, even for a short-term contract with such an unknown quantity as the British Council. I was to take the Swedish liner *Gripsholm* from Liverpool to New York and fly south to the port of Barranquilla, where our man there would put me on a local plane to Medellín.

There is nothing, absolutely nothing, like watching a ship's wake as it changes colour in the twilight. The ups and downs of life drop peacefully astern in an ebb and flow that yet drives confidently forwards, and one rides the waves in majesty and power and with no effort at all. (I never could maintain my sympathy for the Flying Dutchman once he had abandoned the wheelhouse for the spinning wheel.) In my teens my romantic idea of the sea was fired by *Treasure Island* and *Peter Simple* and C S Forrester, and later I came across Patrick O'Brien's biography of 'Foul-Weather Jack' and embarked on his Jack Aubrey and Stephen Maturin saga. In 1978 I attended a Council course to brief overseas staff on the latest cultural fashions, and the speaker on the Novel – A S Byatt, not yet the ubiquitous pundit she was to become – reeled out the usual icons (Virginia Wolfe, D H Lawrence, Orwell, Lessing, Naipaul, Angela Carter, Martin Amis). When I suggested that some of them were not very digestible to foreign readers and that genre writers like Le Carré, P D James and especially Patrick O'Brien surely deserved a mention, there was a puzzled silence.

The *Gripsholm* was very civilised after the discomforts of the wartime troopships *Sobieski*, *Mount Vernon* and *Corfu*, and in the matter of romantic wakes it more than lived up to my expectations. My companions in the second class cabin were a publisher, a jeweller, and Ozzie Pope. Our fellow lecturer, Miss Hall, shared a cabin with a Council wife going out to join her husband in Bogotá, who lent me Somerset Maugham's *Then and Now*. Dipping into it, in order to postpone studying Spanish, I learned that 'when a woman feels with every nerve in her body that you want her she can resist only if she's passionately in love with another'. Ozzie and I debated whether we should put this apophthegm to Miss Hall, our senior in years and – in teaching at least – in experience, but decided to save it up to use as a gambit with the two attractive Dutch girls we had spotted in the bar.

I was attracted first by the younger prettier one, Friedje Beyen, who was going to join her father who was at the International Bank in Washington. Germaine van der Wyck, at twenty-six, was to be his secretary. When I first saw her she was reading *Brideshead Revisited* and refusing invitations to dance in order to go on reading it. By the time we landed I had found that she was a better dancer and conversationalist that Friedje and that as she was proposing to marry a Swiss businessman in New York as soon as he got his divorce she 'didn't know whether she was free or not'.

I pondered this as we saw Friedje's eighteen pieces of luggage through customs. Germaine remained part of the blur of my first impressions of New York. She wrote a note from Scarsdale which caught me as I left to catch the plane to Barranquilla; her admirer had rung up and noticed her lack of enthusiasm – she was thinking of my face with its faint smile; would it be better not to write any more? She would be with me on my way to Colombia.

An early correspondent in Medellín was John Betjeman, bringing a wave of homesickness and an indication of the hardening image of the Council.

XXVIII	Farnborough
VI	Wantage
MCMXLVI	Berkshire

I have now left the Council because what with it and the reviewing in the *Daily Herald* I found I couldn't do the two things. So I am sticking to the one and find myself very poor now as my income is halved.

Blenheim to me, high upon these rainy Berkshire downs looking across to Hants and Wilts, seems almost as far off as it must to you in Colombia.

I have just done a church tour in Lincs with Jack Yates – 46 churches in 2 days and only about 5 locked. One, Radbourne, was a knockout – enamelled windows c.1812 and a big east one of J Martin's Sodom and Gomorrah being destroyed. Another church, Hannah, alone on the marsh, was untouched 1753 inside with 3-deckers, box pews and communion rails in this form.[Here came a sketch of the chancel and 'HOLY TABLE'.] Don't you think the seats at the side must have been for communicants? How pleasantly trivial this must all seem in Colombia. I am sorry my reply is so short. My wife is away as my mother-in-law – a splendid old girl with a positive faith in lack of faith – died this afternoon. I have been running things here single-handed.

In Colombia the Director we were relieving was a former schoolmaster, Jack Harriman (or John K H Harriman as he announced himself on his letterhead). Harriman had been in Medellín for five years. 'I was unfit for military service,' he said, 'but it hasn't been all cakes and ale here. It gets claustrophobic after a bit. But it's not as bad as Popayan. Poor Peter Gibbs has been stuck there with his wife for the whole war!' I expressed the sympathy proper from a recent joy rider on the Burma-Siam railway and was surprised to hear how thick on the ground the Council was. There was another Institute at Cali, and up in Bogotá there was a staff of eight expatriates under another pre-war teacher, Jack Bruton, who doubled as British Council Representative and Director of the Institute – a common but not always compatible coupling of responsibilities.

It was clear that in Medellín Jack and his imperturbable wife Brenda had been popular and successful. Their farewell presents were a solid gold bracelet and a block of shares in Colteger, the local textile firm which went from strength to strength. Three hundred people attended their farewell party and a hundred, many in tears, saw them off at the airport.

Jack had been posted to Peru and there – uniquely in Council history – he remained for the rest of his service. Over the next twenty years attempts by the Personnel Department to tidy its promotional snakes and ladders by a Harriman transfer were firmly resisted by his *Junta Directiva.* Even on retirement Jack remained in Lima, going into publishing there. It is interesting to speculate on the effect of such local loyalty – like that in the old Levant Consular Service which produced so much regional expertise – had it been encouraged in the Council rather than thought inimical to a fair career structure which was also safe from the staff 'going native'. At any rate Jack, whom I ran into thirty years later in Caracas, proved to be a wise old bird, and I only wish I had paid more attention to his words of advice to me in Medellín. 'Never say "no". Never refuse point blank. Always let time elapse before giving any answer that cannot be "yes".'

Of course Medellín had its British colony. Without it there would have been no Institute and no library. Council libraries have been criticised for catering both too much and too little for British readers but local circumstances dictate local policies. In Latin America we needed the support, introductions and local knowledge of British residents, and in exchange offered a library that extended far beyond the requirements of English teaching. Of course we hoped that sophisticated Colombians would use it too, but the choice of books has always been a problem. For me, as for some of the other Council employees, I suppose the biggest perk of Council service overseas has been its libraries, however quirkily stocked (and often it was I who was stocking them). In Medellín a Colombian's English wife soon introduced me to its pitfalls:

'My husband says there's a book in this library that's not fit to be here. He says it's scandalous and will cause great offence. I think it's by Aldous Huxley.' It turned out to be *Brave New World.*

Colombia seemed to be in many ways a brave *old* world, and engaged in a hopeless battle with *Yanqui* influences. Unlike its neighbours – Venezuela, Brazil, Argentina, Chile – it had resisted immigration from Europe and had been immune to change and to revolution for fifty years. As in 18th-century Britain, government had alternated between Liberals and Conservatives of *alta sociedad* families, with Medellín positively *godo* (gothick) in its priest-ridden conservatism. One of my students (at the Liberal University of Antioquia, not the Jesuit Bolivariana where I did my broadcasting) summed it up:

Los Liberales tomamos
Cerveza, ron y aguardiente
Los Conservadores toman
Agua bendita caliente.
(We Liberals drink beer, rum and aguardiente.
Conservatives drink warm holy water.)

The Medellinenses were largely of Basque stock – Echeverria, Ochoa, Ibarra were common names – and their enterprise had made the town the textile capital of Colombia. Jack Harriman said that the average number in a family was twelve (which I could well believe) and in a darker moment that forty per cent of the population were prostitutes (which I took with a pinch of salt). The well-to-do had immense charm, couched in ornate courtesy phrases long outmoded in Spain. Such emollients as 'Be so good as to...', 'I should be beholden to you if...', 'God bless your Honour', 'I am always at your service' and 'It's a great honour to know you' took a bit of getting used to but were useful gap-fillers – as long as they were not presumed upon. Going home one night from the Institute I walked down the street with the President of the Board, the rotund lawyer Dr Lazaro Tobón. It had been an excellent lecture, he said, a good audience; I would like Colombia; the people were very hospitable – especially to the British because of their help in the War of Independence; Colonel Jaime Rooke ... Admiral Cochrane ... and now my Winston Churchill; if there was anything I wanted, anything at all, I must let him know; and now here we were at his house; I must treat it as my own.

'Bueno, Mr Alexander,' he concluded as he opened the front door, 'always remember that "*esta es su casa*". Thees ees yourr 'ouse!' He shut the door behind him, and that was as much of 'ees 'ouse' as I was to see.

Entertaining at home, except among the very rich, was not in fact the custom, and when a special occasion demanded it – a wedding or funeral, or perhaps a returned British Council scholar returning hospitality to a British 'specialist tourist' – the niceties that had to be observed did not make for conviviality. At a sit-down meal, for instance, one's plate was remorselessly filled, decline as hard as one might, with second and further helpings. The only way to stop the flow was to leave a substantial portion uneaten, not an easy habit to adopt after war-time deprivation. Even buffet suppers were slow to warm up; for half an hour no drinks were served since this might suggest guests had only come for the victuals. After that, however, the drinks never stopped until many of the men were half seas over. From a taxi in Bogotá I once saw a midday wedding party with a line of immaculately dinner-jacketed guests vomiting into the gutter. Our own parties were complicated by Colombian vagueness about time; guests might not come at all or arrive one or two hours late or stay two or three hours too long.

Dress habits, considering the mildness of the climate, were strict. Indeed the climate itself was treated with suspicion, with *la gripa* considered to be ever lying in wait for the careless. Cinema audiences after a show did not at once emerge into the street but stood about in the entrance for five minutes with handkerchiefs held to their noses to get acclimatised. Passing a cinema one evening I recognised one of the jollier of my students hiding behind her handkerchief and gave her a wave; I was ignored as though I had trespassed upon some intimate ritual. Other rituals were, for women, not sitting down in a bus seat until it had been left to cool after its previous occupant, and not washing during the menstrual period, while, for men, it was not shaving for the duration of a cold and – less forgivably – not lifting the seat in a WC.

The formal manners and ornate courtesies of everyday life also covered a multitude of sins and were exploited in 'sophisticated' confidence tricks, known locally as *paquetes chilenos*. One is very vulnerable if one is trained never to give offence, and the clever con man knows this and knows also that a foreigner in a semi-diplomatic job and aping the manners of his hosts is doubly vulnerable. Later on in Bogotá three of us were caught by the taxi fare trick.

I was walking up the path to the office one morning when someone called 'Mr Alexander'. Turning round I saw a neatly dressed man, his face shining with innate goodness and a black band on his arm. Seizing my hand he said in rapid Spanish how lucky he was to see me, having just been up to the office to see Ponton who was out. Did he mean Humberto Ponton? Yes, indeed, because Humberto had been at the funeral too, sharing the taxi but forgetting to pay it, and here he was without a peseta on him. It was so embarrassing! I knew Humberto was away from the office that day so he might very well have been at the funeral. How much was the fare? Two pesos fifty. I only had a twenty peso note. Oh, that was alright, he'd bring me the change. Next day I asked Humberto if he could remind his bereaved friend of his debt, but he had been in bed all day and knew nothing about any funeral. How the man had learned my name I don't know; the porter denied having given it him.

Extraordinarily enough I was accosted again a year later by my old friend still sporting the black armband. I suppose as I was, unusually, emerging from a smart hotel he thought I was a newcomer. His pleasant features once again gave an impression of a friendly and familiar face I couldn't quite place. Then as he rattled away it all came back. I said nothing and he began to run out of steam. I asked a few questions and he looked apprehensive. Then I seized his arm – Colombians are small people – and cursed him in my lowest Spanish. He wrenched himself out of my grasp and disappeared in the crowd, leaving his jacket in my hand.

In my early days in Medellín I did not experience these sins of the big city. On the contrary, to judge by appearances, butter would not melt in the Medellinense mouth, especially the female one.

I felt something of a Peeping Tom at my first Corpus Cristi procession. It was a big occasion. First, schools in their different uniforms marched by; then philanthropical societies bearing aloft their banners and separated by bands dressed like musical comedy hussars; then groups of community nuns and holy women of one sort or another moving their lips in prayer; then the cathedral canons, choir and lesser fry bearing the sarcophagus, crucifixes, chandeliers and censers; and at last – heralded by the Departmental Band booming out the notes of *Colonel Bogey* – the Archbishop himself with not a little but a very big button on top and riding in a palanquin. Bringing up the rear was the *Alcalde* (Mayor) in a morning coat and all the great and the good with their wives and daughters in severest black. It was clearly not a good idea to wave to such faces as escaped anonymity on a solemn occasion like this.

At other times deep mourning was worn with considerable gaiety and style. With such large families and so much intermarriage, many girls were hardly ever out of mourning and could hardly be expected to prevent cheerfulness from breaking in for ever.

However, men never wore shorts and slacks for women were unheard of; even shirtsleeves were strictly for workmen. One sweltering afternoon at the Colegio Mayor I took off my jacket the better to reach the blackboard and was summoned after the class to the principal's office.

'*Señor* Alexander,' said Doña Teresita Gonzalez de Santamaría, one of a family famous for breeding fighting bulls, 'I saw you take your coat off in class today. Why did you do that?'

'Because it was very hot.'

'That is no reason to take your coat off in my classroom.'

'But I cannot teach well if I am uncomfortable.'

'Then you must teach badly and remain uncomfortable.'

'Ah! But suppose I die of heat stroke?'

'Then you die of heat stroke, but you do not take off your coat in front of my young ladies!'

If I had known as much about her young ladies then as I knew later I might not have knuckled under so cravenly. One of them was the young wife of Clarence Finlayson, an engaging Anglo-Chilean lecturer of philosophy whose name, and study at Notre Dame University in the States with W H Auden and Robert Speight, belied the sketchiness of his spoken English. His charm did not always survive a party and at our Institute dance a fight broke out and noses bled when he accused a fellow dancer of flirting with his wife. I was not altogether surprised as she had caused me no little embarrassment earlier when, purely from a sense of duty, I had asked her to dance. 'So fold thyself my dearest, thou, and slip into my bosom and be lost in me...' I had unwisely written Tennyson's lines on the blackboard (in my shirtsleeves) in my literature class and she had taken them all too literally. Presuming on this acquaintance, she talked me into holding an exhibition of paintings by a protégé of hers. Assuming that a university wife was a reliable sponsor I omitted to vet the pictures, which turned out to be virulent sub-Orozco primitives. Brawny peons wielded honest spades, raised honest families, led honest marches, saluted with honest fists the red, red sky while in the background fat capitalists and leering priests were smothered in their own moneybags and despatched with their own crosses. They brought the Institute no kudos at all but gave me my first lesson in the perils of promotion in modern art. Clarence, too, was no ascetic. He had once challenged his Rector to a dual and been gaoled for it, and I myself saw him in a very unacademic state one night in the *barrio.* It was like a scene from the Rake's Progress yet the next day he appeared in class looking as sober as a judge.

I suppose at heart we felt like missionaries. The classroom was our church where we dispensed our message, and we did not expect the faithful, who sat so becomingly at our feet, to kick against the pricks extramurally. Intramurally, too, some illusions were soon dispelled. It is sometimes said that Latin America is a melting pot where intermarriage has dispelled racial prejudice. It has certainly refined it, and since racial prejudice is endemic the world over and as natural as the air we breathe Medellín was well placed – midway between the Caribbean coast and the highlands – to display some unusual refinements.

The Chibcha Indians round Bogotá have hair growing low on their foreheads. Some of my students shaved their foreheads into high widows' peaks to dispel such simian traits. In the office one day I came upon Ligia, our secretary, rubbing oil into her legs. This was, she explained, to encourage the growth of hair. Black girls from the coast had hairless legs, and she didn't want to be suspected of *costeña* blood. This explained something that had puzzled me, coming from a country where legs were either veiled in opaque lisle stockings or bare and depilated. In Medellín girls wore the sheerest of nylons, proudly revealing the longest and blackest of hairs.

Frivolities of this sort should have been beneath me as I got down to the serious business of teaching, but at that time the teaching of English as a foreign language was at a primitive stage and Longmans Green, with their series of books by Eckersley, had a stranglehold on the curriculum. For the lazy teacher they were not a bad 'tool', and in a small way they beat the drum for Britain, featuring a group of foreign students registering in carefully graded English their admiration of our history and tourist facilities. But oh, those jokes! How they palled when explained for the hundredth time! Eckersley himself came out on a lecture tour and proved to be a simple soul whom we could well credit with them. I was soon teaching thirty hours a week, divided between the Institute, the University of Antioquia and the Colegio Mayor.

2
Medellinenses

FLUENT IN SPANISH and French, Ozzie Pope, who was to be our Acting Director until James Besant came out in September, was a tall man of great charm and saturnine good looks. A Channel Islander with a Spanish mother, he had read Modern Languages at Oxford and he looked after me patiently until my own Spanish, after three months, suddenly gelled. He was a marvellous person to introduce me to local life, sensitive enough to have a deep insight into Colombian habits but liberal enough to be amused by them. He was also a knowledgeable guide to bullfighting and is much quoted in a poor travel book by Christopher Isherwood called *The Condor and the Cows*. ('There's a chap called Christopher Isherwood downstairs who wants to see me,' said Dermot Milman, then in the Bogotá office. 'Does anyone know him?')

My first *corrida* in the dusty Macarena ring was hardly auspicious. The main attractions were Velasquez and Mendoza II but Velasquez was also presenting for his baptism of fire a *novillero* called, inappropriately enough as it turned out, *El Terremoto* (the Earthquake). The opening parade and *paso doble* before the *Presidente* cannot but thrill the first-time spectator – even without the panoply so impressive in Spain. It is all so ancient, so familiar from pictures, and so uniquely sacrificial. And the bulls are so magnificent that it seems churlish to grudge them the glory of their sacrifice. But my excitement ceased to be pleasurable when El Terremoto's turn came; he had lost his nerve. Grey with fear he took to leaning against the barrier, burying his face in his arms, deaf to the howls of execration from the crowd, then trying to return to the battle and prove himself. The scene became ever more pathetic and frightening – but finally ludicrous when he had the seat of his *traje de luces* ripped as he clambered over the barrier.

As if to make up for this, Velasquez – though tossed once but escaping with split pants – gave the crowd some treats.

'Oh, no!' cried Ozzie, as we watched him kneel between the barrier and the bull and whisper into its ear, 'he's not going to do the Telephone!' But he did, to immense applause, and just below our seats he placed a hat on the bull's head and sat in front of it stroking its horns.

Mendoza, a more stolid but competent fighter, split the bull's windpipe in his attempted kill. As the animal stood there, looking puzzled and licking its lips to staunch the flow of blood from its mouth before it died, its reactions reminded me of fellow prisoners under torture by the Japanese. At a certain stage there is an awful sameness of suffering for man and beast; there is only a creature struggling unconsciously for life where before was, distinctively, a man or a beast.

On the walls of a local bar posters of Christ jostled those for *corridas*. 'I invite you,' He said in one, 'to my great procession on the 23rd.' In another, His face bleeding from its crown of thorns and pale eyelids closed, He was flanked by Dorothy Lamour and Betty Grable.

Ozzie was less knowledgeable about women, and the previous Christmas had advertised for a wife in the *Matrimonial Times*. However with his charm, height, good looks and excellent Spanish he was much in demand and good manners, if nothing else, led him to accept invitations to sticky teas in antimacassared chairs set round veloured walls in some of the older patio houses. Sometimes he would take me along as a chaperone; on the girl's side a brother or aunt would be at hand throughout. Papa would enter for a brief formal salutation, confirming his admiration of Britain by pointing to a bas-relief of the Houses of Parliament with a real clock in the face of Big Ben, or to a picture of a moonlit Scottish castle outlined in mother-of-pearl. But all too soon would come the confidential aside at a party – backing for a school, perhaps; a place in the firm to build up the British import side; a settlement of some sort – and Ozzie would run for the barrier. One of the nicest, and plainest, of his students was Olga Posada, whose father had the Everfit tailor's shop in the Parque Berrio.

'I was going to see Olga yesterday,' said Ozzie, 'and I was going to propose to her. But as I walked through the park I found myself looking for omens. And then I thought "Good heavens! If I have to look for favourable omens I must be absolutely mad to think of marrying at all." So I turned round and went home and sent a note saying I felt ill.'

Later on, when he was in Bogotá, Ozzie was made much of by the British librarian. She was a warm-hearted soul but exceedingly plain, and so tall that cheeky little Colombians beside her at the bus stop would point upwards, blow on their fingers and cry 'Ay! It must be cold up there.' When asked how he could bear to make love to someone so off-putting, Ozzie replied 'If I don't, who will? She is such a good sort.'

Not all his illnesses were diplomatic, nor were all his reactions, and it was soon clear that an initial impression of strength and urbanity concealed an uncertain constitution and temperament. One stifling night in August Ozzie had an attack of angina which was severe enough to make him think he was dying. Afterwards he remembered trying to say, 'I want to be cremated,' but not knowing why. He recuperated in the warm climate of the Frontino gold mines in Segovia, returning a week later much revived but glad to get away from the Somerset Maugham atmosphere there. On arrival he had had, as he thought, an unnoticeable evacuation behind the garden hedge of the Manager's house before going in to join an At Home. After being introduced all round by the manager's wife he noticed one man's eyes travel downwards and avert themselves, and following their direction found not only his fly buttons undone but a piece of his shirt hanging out. But this experience was far outweighed by a new interest – the Cholo Indians. For some years after that he would vanish from time to time with a sack of beads and mirrors and return with bows and arrows, basketware and pottery and extol the virtues of the noble savage and a simple life free from afternoon teas and classes of English.

There was a business man teaching at the Institute called Alf Smith. He had married a placid Colombian wife who had presented him with three daughters. But his chief concern was to acquire status in the Institute, where he had become Chairman of the Social Committee. In Ozzie's absence Smith had not been idle. Going through the files I was shocked to find a letter, signed by the secretary, to Bruton in Bogotá saying that Pope was 'abnormal'. The Institute, she wrote, needed two more teachers but not a Director; it was going to pieces and Smith was the only man who could put things right. Smith later admitted that it was he who had written the letter. He was a big man around here, he said, and we must learn to toe the line with him or we should be sorry. And it was into this little imbroglio that the new Director arrived at the end of the month.

A few weeks later Ozzie switched places with Eric Pierce, a teacher in Bogotá. (At the end of his probationary period Ozzie's contract was not renewed and it was as a freelance that he stayed on in Colombia.) His first impressions of Bogotá were mixed:

> It is always nearly fine, you are always waiting for it to clear up. The streets are always shiny, the poor shabby, dirty and downtrodden; you get back to lots of things you have forgotten about: shabby lounge suits of the clerks, awful false teeth like tomb stones, and the down-at-heel look of people trying on $100 to look as if they were rich – and failing. There is a steady characteristic smell about the place; sweet, dirty and repellent. But there are a lot of things to make up for it. The churches are really beautiful, they are old and there are lots of them. You can go and hear a debate in the congress whenever you like. There are hourly papers on sale on the street all day long. The cafés are big, clean and comfortable. Now I have moved to the Savoy. The smell in the bathroom in the morning after all and sundry have performed during the night without a light is absolutely appalling.
>
> I don't know exactly what it is. It may be the altitude that makes you feel things worse when they go wrong, or it may be – and I think this is more like it – that the people are not fundamentally as nice as in Medellín. There is none of that rigmarole about *como amaneció?* (how did you meet the dawn?) when you meet the servants in the morning, which seems to me the only way to deal with them, with a lot of set phrases.
>
> The other day I went to the open air theatre which functions on Sunday mornings. Of course all the usual shambles: important-looking young men strutting round on the stage, going up to the singer in the middle of his act and altering the position of the mike. Boys selling peanuts at the tops of their voices and, when they tired of that, going

> in front, resting their baskets on the stage and leaning on them while the people whose view they blocked pelted them with orange peel. It came on to rain and a general, his daughter and members of the *alta sociedad* were ushered across the stage with the act going full blast, to a shelter at the back. That was too much for the bootblacks, etc. and a terrific surge began towards the stage. A policeman came up and opened up a way for us to get a glimpse of the actors. Then the producer grabbed the mike and made this pronouncement. 'The audience is requested to clear off the stage.' And they did.
>
> I have moved up in this world. I know a bullfighter and shake hands with him in the street and get told all the scandal of the ring, who is fighting next week and who are the *banderilleros*, how Pepe who got gored last week is coming on. And all this is sheer honey to me.

I am sorry not to have seen Ozzie again. It was he who cushioned the culture shock of the Council (I never had to teach thirty hours a week again) and of my first experience (apart from Thailand) of living in a country never subject to British rule. Like Jack Harriman, he taught me how to say 'no', first to the endless beggars – employing instead of a straight 'No' the qualified: *'Hoy no'* ('Not today'); then, to the won't-take-no-for-an-answer pourer of drinks, the only acceptable refusal: *'Me duele el hígado'* ('I have a bad liver').

Eric Pierce could scarcely have been a greater contrast to Ozzie. He was short and fair and amiable and uncomplicated. A bad crash in the RNVR had left one of his eyes with an unnatural stare that gave an unnatural intensity to his remarks which they did not always deserve, couched as they were in the thickest of public school and RAF slang and liberally laced with shaggy dog stories. Eric had had his troubles in Bogotá, resulting from the 'them and us' feelings which tended to vary directly with the size of a Council office: the still strong wartime sensitivity between combatant and non-combatant; the unspoken grammar versus public school distinction; and the love-hate relationship of Council and Embassy.

Some of his lessons must have taxed his students' comprehension. 'Do you know the story,' he would say, 'of the jolly old Colombian chappie who went into a shop in London to buy socks? But his English was even worse than my Spanish, so the chappie behind the counter couldn't make out what he wanted. He brought out shirts, and then pants, then vests and ties, and suspenders and stockings and, at last, socks. "Ah," cried the Colombian chappie, "*Eso si que es!*" And the chappie behind the counter said, "S.O.C.K.S? Why didn't you say so in the first place?"'

Eric was not adept in the finer points of literary analysis with his students. But neither was I. Bogotá liked to call itself the Athens of South America and the weekend papers had pages of poetry and literary criticism in them, including translations of foreign poets; on one Sunday there were two translations of Keats's *Ode to a Grecian Urn*. The Spanish version of Kipling's *If,* done – and distributed – by our flamboyant wartime Ambassador to Uruguay, Sir Eugen Millington-Drake, hung in many classrooms. But there were really only two literary figures from Britain who were universally acknowledged – Shakespeare, because of Laurence Olivier, and Oscar Wilde, because of *The Portrait of Dorian Gray*. Byron was also popular, both for his life style and because some of his poems were very short. ('Byron is very disappointed of the love business. He prefers to be quite. He is very tired.') It was difficult to inject an equally pleasing innuendo into the works of sobersides like Milton or Wordsworth. ('Dorothy Wordsworth was sister of Wordsworth that help him in the confections of many poems. She was very good with the poet who lived with her after the diet of his wife.') I still have a Colombian translation of *The Ballad of Reading Gaol* and remember the agonies of hair-splitting discussions I went through whenever the Bogotano translator managed to nobble me.

Students at the Institute in the mornings were mostly ladies of leisure, some with excellent English, who came to be entertained rather than instructed. Many were married, but one I presumed was not, both from the length of the essay she handed in and from its tone – a fine Madeleine Bassett pastiche:

> I like lotus because I've noticed how the dewdrops tremble on their corollas as life trembles in the huge heart of everlasting hours. I like to indulge in daydreams and to think that the wind is wild, the water is disturbed and that the night is dark, because I know that my ship is anchored in a safe place where the pains of life don't arrive. I like the monotony of pathways bordered by trees like solemn shades that pray; the music of the mountains that in the sleepless night patrols the wandering scents, with its naked little bodies weaving its garlands ... Mr Alexander there is a note for you on the next page. Please write your answer.

And on the next page:

> My name is Angela. I like very much to have you as my teacher. I would like to teach you Spanish. Will you come with me and we will have a nice time. Angela.

I did not go with Angela but I did enjoy hospitality from others, including a private student named Raúl Montoya. He was an edgy poor little rich kid and must have been one of the few only-sons in that philoprogenitive town; otherwise he would not have been so lonely and bored – and so anxious to take me out in his new Ford convertible. I tried to avoid pushing a hole through the floorboards of the Ford as we rocketed and skidded through the 220 bends in the road to Rionegro. Apart from driving, he seemed at a loss. When we arrived somewhere, he had no idea what to do except drive on somewhere else or go back to where we had come from. He did once borrow a Canadian canoe from Alejandro Echevarría and four of us – I, Raoul, Emilio Cardona, a fellow student, and Alan Mackintosh of ICI – paddled seven miles down the river. But it was not a successful outing, and after shipping enough water to soak everything, we were caught at midday naked in an icy storm. We landed, frozen and miserable and, while the others sat about drinking *aguardiente*, it was Alan and I who got a fire going to barbecue sausages.

Alejandro Echevarría's family – his father, Guillermo, had been governor of Antioquia in 1936 and lived in a fine white ranch-type villa in Poblado – entertained me in a quite different way. It was his sister, Margot, in my university class who invited me to an evening 'at home', and I found myself in a Chekhovian gathering of young intellectuals of the *alta sociedad* – Ozzie's '*altas*'. The parents left them to it, and they sat round sparkling in Spanish and French as I strove to keep up with them, periodically raising their voices to be heard through recordings of Sibelius, Saint-Saëns or Berlioz played on an enormous HMV. How elegant it all was! Instead of spindly Victorian chairs set stiffly round the walls, deep sofas were dotted about and beckoned through inviting archways. Instead of the *Light of the World* or *Windsor Castle*, the artfully lit walls displayed Picasso, Dufy and Diego Rivera. How elegantly, too, everyone was dressed!

A light-hearted but affectionate survey of the vagaries of the Roman Catholic church from a young lawyer who had recently been on a Retreat with the Jesuits soon spread to secular subjects. Had anyone read Van Loon? Or been at Cocteau's film *La Belle et la Bête* when the Colombian national anthem and the Marseillaise had been played simultaneously from different amplifiers? Why, in last week's *Blithe Spirit,* had Madame Arcati become Monsieur Arcati? Was it because the Mexican company lacked a character actress or because the Latin race simply did not produce characters like Margaret Rutherford? Had Grigor Piatigorski been right to shoulder his 'cello as he strode off the platform? The Fu Man Chu show had really been very clever; did we realise that Fu Man Chu himself came from Southport in England?

The men were the entertainers; the girls were charming and appreciative, dropping remarks in to keep the men on their toes. There was no suggestion of flirting. We were all very prim. 'You can't neck whores,' Raúl Montoya had complained when feeling at a particularly loose end, 'and the *altas* won't neck!' At 2am people at last started to leave; and I went home and took a couple of Veganin.

An English girl whose parents worked in the Frontino mines gave me a graphic description of life in the convent school of La Presentación at the time. The girls were seated alternately, 'good' and 'bad', so that the good ones kept the bad ones upright in spirit and posture. Dancing was considered a sin for the evil intentions it encouraged. Men were to be assumed uniformly wicked, and she had left at eighteen still ignorant of the means of reproduction. When the girls bathed they wore turn-of-the-century swimsuits with double layers of protection down to the knees, and a huge stone Virgin stood beside the pool to guard them from evil thoughts engendered from the caresses of the water. At their weekly shower they wore long 'Mother Hubbards' and the nuns toured the showers to make sure none of the girls put their hands inside their chemises to touch their 'dishonest' parts. Only the face and neck would be washed with the hands. Science and maths were hardly touched upon, and embroidery – but not dressmaking – was taught at great length. So affected was this girl by her schooling that she avoided boys with horror and had only recently been able to shake off the awful feelings of guilt relating to anything to do with her own body or bodily sensations.

Perhaps such polarisation was not surprising in a society where men had equally distorted views of women, though it was a chicken and egg situation. No doubt foreign bachelors should have set a good example, but I doubt if the British Council would have renewed my contract had they read some of my diary at that time.

In September the new Director, James Besant, arrived. He had not only to sort out the Alf Smith imbroglio but also to pick up the loose ends left by Ozzie. They resembled each other only in speaking Spanish and French and being invalided out of the Navy. James Besant was a forthright Glaswegian and his wife, Colette, a forthright Parisienne, and I don't think either of them felt at home with the mercurial Medellinenses. Critical though Ozzie and I were at times of our Medellinense hosts, we had probably enjoyed more hospitality (and more confidences) than we would have done if we had been married. Margery Hall, too, who had distanced herself from office politics, was much liked by her students, not least by the two charming old pillars of the Institute, Don Raimundo Salazar and Don Ramón Guendica. These two, who came to classes year after year with no noticeable improvement in their English, were glad to act as chaperones to the girls who came on *paseos* on fiesta days. These outings could be wearing because of the frequent bus stops at cantinas and increasing drunkenness of the men, but they could also be spectacular. On *puentes*, the long weekend 'bridges' between a fiesta week day and a weekend proper, we could go up to the bracing climate of Sonson or down to the tropical Puerto Berrio on the Magdalena River. Colombians visited Sonson to see the great rock of El Peñol, which reared up out of the plain nearby and justified the existence of a reasonable *pension* in town. Foreigners liked the little market town for its colonial atmosphere, unspoilt by the usual clutter and squalor of development. But what I particularly remember about neat little Sonson was the contrast between *el barrio* on Good Friday night, when it was as dark and silent as the grave, and on Easter Saturday, when it was like Piccadilly Circus. A new colleague, Harold Norminton, who had succeeded Marjorie Hall and Eric Pierce, came on the Sonson trip. Our *pension* had only one communal washbasin on the top landing, and Harold realised that he had left his toothbrush there. Hastily remounting the stairs, he found another guest busily brushing his teeth with it. To Harold's remonstrations he replied *'Perdóneme, yo creí que apartenecía al hotel'* (sorry, I thought it belonged to the hotel).

The trip to Puerto Berrio involved a wild west kind of train which took twelve hours to do the 100 kilometres. At the stations the men jumped off to buy rum and beer, so by the time we arrived the rot had already set in. The hotel overlooked the river and its rubbish was thrown into what had once been a garden. Paddleboats made their way up to La Dorada, the port for Bogotá, and we crossed over to Santander, where the local drink was maraschino. In the evening a band came in and everyone danced, pouring with sweat, until its members – one by one as in Haydn's *Surprise Symphony* – passed out. I was sharing a room with a moustachioed ex-RAF type who worked in the *Banco de Londres*. One moment he was saying, 'God, look at this! What a body! Couldn't you do her, Steve? All these bloody beauties in Colombia, and they don't know what it's for! Wouldn't it bite your bloody arse?' The next moment he blacked out, and woke up seven hours later with a fearful hangover.

I tried to convince myself how much more I had enjoyed the *conversaziones* at the Echevarrías than this rumbustious weekend, but there is something uniquely relaxing in the change from the formalities of a temperate climate – and even more from a cold one – to a hot one where everything is scruffy and life goes at half the speed.

The British bank manager was a bookish man, as well he might be, for his Colombian wife after twenty years of marriage spoke little English. The vice consul, whose wife was horsy and more voluble, had less literary taste. He rang up the local bookshop one day to order a set of bound classics he'd seen in the window and was asked which set he wanted – the Dickens or the Scott? He wanted the set with the blue covers. British residents were mostly highly respected. *Palabra Inglesa* – the word of an Englishman – was still common currency in the shops. There were however other British residents besides Smith who could cause trouble. Alf Smith's orchestrated campaign against the Council ended in his expulsion, but Ashworth too could be awkward. Fattish and fortyish, he resembled a bespectacled Mr Toad, whose temperament he shared if not his party spirit. 'I speak better Spanish than anyone in the British colony,' he informed me, 'and I'm probably the best-read man in Medellín. How much do you know of Schopenhauer?' He was one of the few members to borrow poetry from the library. 'You're supposed to be a cultural chap,' he said, 'but do you know how to recite poetry properly? It's an art which you have to cultivate with care and application. I have taken the trouble to do it.' And he recited *Home Thoughts from Abroad* quite beautifully. So beautifully, in fact, that I think if we'd had an amateur dramatic group he could have been its temperamental star and a much happier man. As it was he could be quarrelsome, as he was at the country club one night. (I was too poor to be a member – either of that or of the even smarter Cantaclaro cockfighting club.) Irked when his partner broke up a bridge four to go home to his wife, he exploded. 'You chaps have only got yourself to blame. Look at me, a free agent, my own master!'

He soon found himself more of a free agent than he might have wished. He must have been lonely and was probably homesick. So I was shocked but not altogether surprised when word went round that he had attempted suicide by cutting his throat. 'A pity he didn't make a good job of it,' was one comment, 'especially as he always claimed to be so bloody good at everything!'

Lying in bed, with a great double chin of bandages, he looked more like Mr Toad than ever. He sounded like him too, seeming proud of himself for having come through a testing experience.

'I felt fed up with everything. I was sick of the life here, but there's nothing for me back in England. I don't enjoy my work. Nobody likes me. So I sat looking at myself in the mirror for a couple of hours, hoping that the phone would ring or someone would ring the bell. But nobody did. And then I decided to do it. And d'you know, a most extraordinary thing happened. I'm not a religious man, but as soon as I made my decision I felt engulfed in the Old Testament. Biblical characters I'd forgotten all about appeared over my shoulder and started to gibber at me. So in a sort of panic I took the razor – and did it... Then I realised it hadn't worked and I tried to get across the room to the telephone. Oh, it was a mess! I opened my bowels, you see.'

It was the primness of this final expression that surprised me most in Ashworth's fearful tale. Again like Mr Toad, he was a reformed character – for a time; people made a point of asking him out and he made a point of asking, rather ostentatiously, for 'soft drinks only, if you don't mind'. But before I left Medellín I heard of another fracas at the club. He had been offensive to an American, who invited him to take his glasses off and take what was coming to him.

'My dear chap, civilised people don't fight in clubs. I have no intention of taking my glasses off!'

'Civilised people don't talk crap in clubs. So keep your glasses on and be my guest!' And he hit poor Ashworth, glasses and all.

3
Family Ties

I SAY 'POOR' ASHWORTH because I myself had begun to feel that Medellín was a bad place in which to be friendless. In a way life was stranger than it had been in the Far East, where East was East and West was West. Here the fusion of Spanish and Creole life was very strong and one had to take part in it wholeheartedly or hang on firmly to one's European roots.

Being on one's best behaviour all the time, always formally dressed, relentlessly cheerful and unfailingly polite, and the effort of speaking either in Spanish or in carefully articulated English all built up a head of steam. Sometimes, with Ashworth's awful warning in mind, I let this off by going out with other bachelors – mostly British, an Italian, a Swede and the American pilot of the local Catalina. We hired ancient nags near the bullring and clattered along the banks of the Rio Medellín through the still outlying villages of Robledo and América. We went to one or two cockfights and remained curiously neutral about them. It was difficult to equate this tatty sport with elegant 18th-century sporting prints, but anyone who has seen the fervour with which fighting cocks go at each other cannot but wonder whether it isn't better to go under with, as it were, the blood up than by having the neck wrung or failing to cross the road and get to the other side. It was a relief to go out with the gang like this and behave like schoolboys, but at other times I felt at too low an ebb even for company. What was I doing in Medellín? Was the job a dead end? Were Colombians worth teaching, let alone marrying? Was teaching itself something I was good at? Would it get more interesting, or repetitive and boring? Would I ever find stimulating colleagues? Could I stay in Colombia and remain *me*? Should I make a grand gesture and resign?

To postpone having to make a decision (always my weak point) I would take myself off for a walk through the slums of Sucre and up the old mule track – three and a half hours up but only an hour or so coming back – to the Santa Helena pass. Muleteers and small boys toiling up it with their bundles gave me their cheerful and surprised greeting. Far below, the Avianca planes were coming in up the valley to land. I was so high up that they were noiseless and the moment of their landing only came to me as a spurt of dust, then another, and another, and a long tail of it at the end of their run. Over on the right the road which Raul Montoya enjoyed cutting down to size zigzagged up through scrubby red soil, islands of rhododendrons and terraces of green grazing.

The mud track I was on had stretches of stone paving which led to daydreams of older civilisations – Chibcha, perhaps, or by extension Iberian, Roman, Moorish; perhaps I was not so far away from Europe after all. Descending through the lengthening shadows, I left the evening chill behind me and the stodgy warmth of the city came up to reclaim me. I rewarded myself with a beer at the first *cantina* I came to.

A more unusual escape came when I and the Anglo-Irishman, Harold Norminton, accepted an invitation from one of our library members to visit him at home. George Mathieson was a stout pipe-smoking Yorkshireman and 'at home' meant the cement works where he worked as a chemist. We flew down with my Catalina pilot and landed slap-bang-flop-flop on the River Nare, which flows into the Magdalena 30 kilometres above Puerto Berrio. It is virgin jungle and the boat trip through the gorge and the climb up the cliff path to the top of the generator falls was as spectacular and wild as one could wish. It was an extraordinary contrast to return in the sunset to the cement works themselves, with hundreds of birds sitting warming their bottoms above the revolving kilns (as usual, the older ones were made in Britain and later models in the States). And George's quarters, at least for an urban visitor, were a delight. Perched over the river, defended by mosquito screens, air-conditioned and with a fridge full of drinks, his hut was transformed into a palace by his splendid gramophone. To sit on the verandah watching life on the river in the fading light, appreciating the well-built and jolly black girls from the coast packing up their laundry as the lights came on in the village, absorbing the damp heat as it dissolved the inhibitions and dissimulations of Medellín, with George saying, 'Put those Pielroja cigarettes away and open one of those tins of Gold Flake, and you'll find more beer in the fridge' was the acme of relaxation. But to have Beethoven pealing out across the river as well was the ultimate joining of body and soul – the blessed state that Indian swamis wrecked their lives to achieve.

'The Ninth, isn't it?' asked Harold, pouring out.

'Yes,' said George, puffing away. 'Pity he had to spoil it with all that caterwauling at the end!'

'I absolutely agree with you!' said Harold, once a chorister at Westminster Abbey. I kept quiet; it was never until the caterwauling started that I recognised the symphony as the Ninth.

Trips of this kind eased some of the tensions building up in Medellín but were no use in the major quandary which had emerged after only two months at post. The *Gripsholm* still had me struggling in her wake, and I had sought advice with conflicting results.

Farnborough, Wantage, Berkshire
X.VIII.MCMXLVI

… Roy Campbell's *Talking Bronco* has much good poetry in it. Whether the old-fashioned leftists of Books Dept will send it out of the country remains to be seen….

I have just come out of a three-day Retreat with the Cowley Fathers at Oxford, and your letter made me think how very different the Anglican old-fashioned Tractarians are from RCs. The smell of O'Cedar-polished passages, the unstained oak and grim altar frontals, the plainsong singing of offices, the rough food, the silence, not to speak of the bitter gall of using Father Langridge's *Ignatia Retreats* with meditations on Death, Hell, Sin and the Judgment for its first day and a half, then the gradual, beautiful unfolding of the illuminative way. By the end of the Retreat I was in a state of mortified ecstasy and quiet which, I like to think, still hangs round me. And a piece of advice my Retreat gave to me I pass on to you when you are feeling, as I do, full of self-pity or misery with your lot. At the end of each day list events in it, whether trials or pleasure, which you can count as blessings and things to be thankful for, and say the General Thanksgiving. It certainly works….

My dear fellow, don't get married unless you are in love – <u>love</u> – <u>LOVE</u>.

Yours, John Betjeman

For me the love, love, love that Betj advocated had not yet acquired underlining, let alone capital letters, but I had gone so far as to put my dilemma to my sisters:

> What about this Dutch girl? I wrote her a rather florid letter in the first pangs of separation and t'other day received a marconigram from Washington: 'Darling, your letter found. Am terribly happy.' I wonder exactly what I said in that letter, and how much of it I really meant? Germaine is sensitive, intelligent, extremely efficient and speaks four languages. I like her very much, tho' I suspect she is rather intense and she is terribly <u>OLD</u>; she is only a fortnight younger than me! Meanwhile the vampires of Medellín crowd round me with their curvaceous figures, lush black hair, great sumptuous mouths turning down at the edges and big white teeth. It is providential that they are such ardent Catholics.

For the next five months, as our letters blew hot and cold, I continued to dither and, like poor Ozzie with his omens, to bombard family and friends for reassurance one way or the other. Ozzie himself strongly approved of marriage but by that time may have thought any change in our circumstances one for the better. Jack Bruton said that if I waited till I 'could afford to marry' I'd never marry. Albert Dothée, a Belgian architect who had married locally and unhappily, told me either to go ahead or 'get out of Colombia and the Council because the salary was absolutely ludicrous'.

My army chaplain brother Hugh was as usual not short of moral prevarication:

> Whatever happens we shall all rally round when you and she appear in England and make her welcome. But, speaking in the dark:
> a) The fact that she wants to marry you does not necessarily mean she would make you a good wife.
> b) The pleasure of having a bed partner does not extend to much more than once a week, while someone you like being with and like talking to always is a continuous joy. The latter is 'being in love'.
> c) The body makes a b..... nuisance of itself but it won't really hurt you to keep it down till you are thirty.
> d) The best thing is to have a lot of girl friends and keep them all on the hop about you.
> e) You are a good match because you are English. Make sure it's little Stevie she wants before you accept her.
> f) Think of your delicious freedom now!
> g) In other words DON'T.

My doctor brother, Bim, appeared equally doubtful; my unmarried sister Margie was noncommittal; David, perhaps on the rebound from India, was gloomy; my mother aired her usual anxieties:

> Joan said she and Rachel were very thankful they were not young at the time of the return of ex-POWs, having their hearts warmed and glowing with longing to make up to them for what they had lost and wanting to help them, and then find their ideals crashing to the ground by their faithlessness.

And Robin, in the Malayan Civil Service and having been interned by the Japanese in Singapore, as usual forbore to comment on a mere love affair:

> I hope you're finding things enjoyable. Don't overwork. A lot of our young ex-internee police have been packed off home after a few months. However, I don't expect you to pack up. Many of the older people had violent reactions after release. Tony Churchill said he would have finished himself off if it hadn't been for his old mother.

It may seem feeble of me to have invited advice at all, but with seven elder brothers and sisters to support or refute the Victorian certainties of my parents it was natural to sound out both generations. The thousands of miles between us only strengthened the link, for in the ebb and flow of family relationships absence certainly makes the heart grow fonder. How often is not a reunion a disillusion? The sibling is smaller, worse-dressed or sillier than one remembered. Nevertheless, it is the silliness, the irreverence, the lack of self-consciousness that one values. We were all energetic letter writers so when the richness and strangeness of Colombia no longer concealed its vulgarity and squalor – and, I was bound to admit, the goodwill of Council work the fuzziness of its purpose – I aired my uncertainties all the more frankly to the family, and especially to my sister Joan.

> Are you engaged to this Germaine? I think your two objections are pretty feeble on the whole, I mean age and passion. Thank God she isn't a young girl! You've no idea how middle-aged a man quickly becomes once he is married – a woman becoming simply more open like a flower until death finishes her off (my favourite bitter remark – 'a man only wants a mother he can sleep with'). As for passion, if you get along even moderately, well you're lucky; that's good enough; and see that she has a good time. And as for her being too good – look at me. I was as good and simple as grass, oh I was *full* of patience and helpfulness and loving kindness and generosity and forgiveness and all those *detestable* virtues but I assure you I lost them, and now only love goodness when I see it elsewhere and any that I have except for the children comes from the mind not the heart.

Stuart Simmonds, a regimental friend who had had the strength of mind to postpone a return to Asia or escape elsewhere and was reading English, wrote enviously from Oxford: 'All success with the Dutch girl – how nice to be able to have multilingual children and bring them up in the sunshine – born supra-nationalists.' The fact that I had been asking so many people to make up my mind for me hardly suggests a white-hot burning passion, but at twenty-six I was beginning to tire of my own company and that of other aimless bachelors. Germaine combined the glamour of a foreigner with shared European roots. I thought she was a typical continental – sophisticated, vivacious and tolerant; she thought I was a typical Englishman – hearty, conventional and reliable. We were both wrong, but not nearly so wrong as thousands of other couples who have lived happily together. At any rate on Friday 13th December 1946, after refusing with a last twinge an invitation from Margot to a cocktail party, I flew up on a cut-price charter flight to Washington.

Germaine was living in the apartment of Nancy Drance, a young secretary at the Admiralty. In the evenings, Nancy would mix herself a Manhattan, undo her suspender belt, roll her stockings down round her ankles, light a cigarette and tell us about the affairs she was having with two elderly admirals and a fiftyish British businessman.

After a couple of days Nancy said that perhaps it wasn't a good idea for me to go on sleeping on the sofa. After all, Germaine and I weren't even engaged yet and what would people think?

We were helped out by Herb, a neighbour of hers, who looked sixty but was seventy-five, drew two pensions (from Spanish-American war service and the National Parks), and when he felt like it served at the corner store for $20 a week. He lived in a row of neat mini White Houses and offered to put me up, refusing any payment. 'The wife's in Florida for the winter, Steve, and I'd be glad of the company.' From time to time he would abandon the corner store to run a poker school from home. He did this shortly after I moved in and the school ran for ten days. When I went with Germaine to New York I left the school comatose in the lounge. Only Herb roused himself to bid me, very slowly and carefully, a courteous farewell.

Perhaps it was Germaine's power to inspire Herb's generosity and her patience with Nancy (if she could put up with her, she could put up with me) that tipped the balance in the Prince George Hotel. After an evening at the Met she had been telephoned by her father. I heard a disjointed crackle on the line.

'What was all that about?'

'He said, "Has he proposed yet?"'

'Oh! Well. What about it?'

'What about what?'

'Getting married. I think we'd better, don't you?'

'Yes.'

She rang back to tell her father the news, and he gave me his blessing in that deep gravelly voice many of the Dutch have. Those were the only words we spoke, for he died of cancer before the wedding, but in January he sent me a letter of welcome.

My father too wrote expressing his approval. His writing, though extraordinarily neat, was always extraordinarily illegible, and we used to wonder what risks his patients ran whose fate depended on his prescriptions. Even now I can scarcely decipher the reaction from Bristol.

> You have done well, I think, to make your solution ... Do not wonder if, alone and far away from all of us, you begin to question all you have done ... In changes of life we try often a wrestling with the Angel; we not only struggle with our fellow men, we battle with our destiny and do not know that its name is 'Love'.

That spring of 1947 was a bad one for both of us. Germaine had to return to The Hague to help nurse her father. In Medellín there was no rain, and physical discomfort aggravated mental uncertainties. There was no water for baths, laundry came back from the river covered in gravel, and the heat was so bad that, as the local wits said, 'hens were laying fried eggs, flies were diving into the Flit to cool off, and mosquitoes carried little bottles of DDT to prevent that sinking feeling'. I now had all too much time to ponder the future.

We had seriously considered getting married immediately in Washington but thought our families deserved more notice. I also wanted to see which way the wind was blowing in the Council; my contract would be up for renewal in August.

As spring merged imperceptibly with summer, my missionary zeal was steadily blunted by my teaching load. But, worse than that, I began to doubt whether we were still the worthy successors to *La Legión Británica,* which we liked to think ourselves, in the development of South America. Family letters deplored the squalors of austerity in Britain and the inefficiencies highlighted by the hard winter. In Colombia factories complained of orders not fulfilled, parts not available, new machines that were faulty. The few British cars in town broke down. British films were rare, in spite of the runaway success of *The Seventh Veil.* But in American newsreels Britain had plenty of publicity, with the evils of mandate in Palestine and the pains of overdue independence in India. (South Africa was not yet on their agenda – as I could well understand, having been moved firmly from the back to the front of a Greyhound bus in Virginia.)

Jack Bruton was succeeded as Representative in Bogotá by Dr Neil Mackay, former principal of Markham College in Peru. A fiftyish-seeming son-of-the-manse type who turned out to be only thirty-seven, he was shocked at my lack of qualifications and thought I should go back to Cambridge and add a proper degree to my two years chopping and changing there before the war. No doubt he was right, but now didn't seem the time to do it.

If I wasn't sure about the British Council, the Council now seemed a bit surer about me and, by renewing my contract, tempted me to stay on. Domestic events also discouraged a new venture at this time. My prospective father-in-law died in The Hague and Germaine was anxious to join me. I suspect that it is not only the woman who feels the nesting instinct; at a certain age – and twenty-seven seemed to be about that age – the man, too, feels the urge to 'settle down'. It is largely a proprietorial urge; he longs not only to possess his girl but also to show her off and move up a rung in society. She is his status symbol, like a new car – and in those days one more easily acquired. (Nobody in the Council except the Representative had a new car, and few could even afford an old banger.)

Feminine society in Colombia had been upsetting, and on the rebound from Anglo-Saxon stodginess and Latin American flightiness it is not surprising that a Dutch compromise had its appeal. It was romantic – was not Holland a cradle of the arts? – but also practical (and certainly so in religious terms); and Germaine's adaptability to life in North America augured well for a rougher life in the South.

When she at last visited the family in England, their reaction was unequivocal. 'The question is not whether she is good enough for you but whether you are good enough for her.' (Hugh.) 'You are very lucky to have a girl like that loving you – an incentive to endure for her sake.' (My mother.) 'We are all in love with Germaine! She has brought us all joy.' (My father.)

Joan, from her hospital bed, was more expansive:

> Germaine came in and so hopefully, so hauntingly and so wistfully gave me your letter (addressed to Bristol) and so obviously longed to read it as she hadn't had one lately. But I couldn't, I couldn't show it to her, could I, with your remarks about Respectability and Tragedienne in it? We think she is absolutely the tops but it is only too obvious you hold her heart in your hand like a pigeon's egg and that is

> a serious obstacle. Of course you will *torture* each other; of course it is magnificent and utterly right that she is respectable (what a word!). When you are older you will realise that breeding and manners matter a hell of a lot.

We would have liked a church wedding, but the only non-Catholic church in Medellín was a Baptist chapel run by American teetotallers. In the end finances dictated a civil wedding in Medellín (I promised to 'protect' Germaine and she promised to 'obey' me) and registration at the Consulate there.

I was given a bachelor send-off by Harold Norminton, Albert Dothée and others, who all gave me the benefit of their advice. One was against marriage altogether; others acknowledged it as a practical necessity but deplored the duties it brought with it; Albert regretted choosing his wife for her sexual attraction while Harold, whose wife, Lucie, was Belgian, insisted that intellect was all. Among those who were married I sensed a wistful envy and a wish that they too could start again from scratch.

After the ceremony, the Besants gave us a reception which was followed by a lunch at the Wightmans' house near the Country Club. The presents included a crystal decanter from Teresita Gonzalez de Santamaría, no doubt as a reward for wearing my jacket, and a little brass Dutch girl in clogs from Olga Posada. Antonio Mesa, with his Swedish wife, had said, 'Take my car!' and threw me the keys of his Oldsmobile with its automatic gears. I think that that impulsive, noble and unBritish gesture was the most memorable thing in the whole memorable day. Driving Germaine to the Wightman's house, we passed the Pepsi representative and his Dutch wife, whose car had slid gently into the ditch with Germaine's Bogotá friend Gerda in the back.

Marriage made life more comfortable but it also made it more predictable. I became half of an international couple with all the social obligations that implied. I was also more committed to the British Council and the chance it offered of supporting a wife – and perhaps a family. I was no longer so closely involved in Colombian life now that there was no question of marrying into it – or of joining its unrewarding bachelor circles. Germaine found in Lucie Norminton an ally against Harold's and my British chauvinism and sense of the absurd. James, being in charge, took things more seriously. But the Colombians must have thought it odd that all three British Council staff were married to foreigners.

Already I felt myself drifting away from the family at home, and less inclined to seek – or take – their advice. Most of them were together again in England, but it was to be for the last time. Joan died in March and my father, who had taken her death in his stride, remarking that it was idle to grieve as he would soon be joining her in heaven, confounded us by fulfilling his prophecy sooner than we were prepared for – and by way of Buncombe Hill on the Quantocks. Pushing his bicycle, he had stopped as usual at Mrs Giles's cottage near Cothelstone and had been refused an egg with his tea. 'If only I'd known,' she said when she heard he'd succumbed to a heart attack higher up the hill, 'the Doctor would have had his egg and welcome!'

FAMILY TIES

The date of my father's last letter, 9th April 1948, was also the fateful *nueve de abril* for Colombia. As if to echo the change in my circumstances, Colombia, unique in Latin America for not having had a revolution for fifty years, blew up.

4
The Athens of South America

GERMAINE AND I had a tiny penthouse in a downtown office block so we had a good view of events. Compared with Bogotá's eight thousand casualties, Medellín's half dozen reflected its provincial nature.

I was dozing off at about two one afternoon, when there was shouting in the street. People were always shouting, and even the sight of a few ragged people carrying red flags (the emblem of the Liberal party) with cries of '*Viva Gaitán! Viva el partido Liberal!*' failed to rouse our interest very much. The crowd moved off and the shouting faded in the distance – and then came nearer with greater force. Lorryloads of police started to arrive and post themselves at the doors of public buildings. I hastily phoned down for a supply of beer, because the cantinas are always closed during political disturbances, and didn't even count the change because a sudden surging cry came up from below.

Then we heard the reason – the Liberal leader, Jorge Eliezer Gaitán (the 'Dynamo'), had been shot dead about an hour earlier in Bogotá. His death would automatically be attributed by the Liberals to the Conservatives. The crowd swelled every minute and split into two mobs round the two Conservative newspaper offices. Meanwhile the Liberal paper rushed a special one-page sheet out with GAITAN ASASINADO! splashed down the front, but said it was probably an act of private revenge and not a political murder. Nevertheless, stones were thrown and windows broken, and it was clear that the police and the army, themselves largely Gaitanist, did not intend to spoil the fun too much. The offices of *El Colombiano* were well protected and, being largely of concrete, were abandoned, after some skirmishing, in favour of the old wood and adobe ones of *La Defensa*.

Nobody seemed to notice where the great tubs of pitch had come from that someone lit in the plaza below us. They went up with a hiss, and small boys started poking them about. A fire engine arrived, put them half out and went away again. The crowd half-heartedly started rolling the flaming tubs down the road. Every now and then they would get stuck at some shop, and flame up its front until someone poked them away again. Finally they rolled through the police cordon round the newspaper office, and stayed flaring in the road. Then the police seemed to lose interest and someone rolled the tubs against the newspaper building. Then came the tear gas bombs, and we were soon wiping our streaming eyes. The building caught fire, and the balcony came down in flames.

The radio had been silent during the afternoon, but now opened up again. On La Voz de Antioquia, a firm supporter of the government, we heard a nervous voice saying that everything was normal and everyone co-operating in preserving peace. It suggested that we might like to hear some music and put on Beethoven's Fifth Symphony. A station that had been seized by the Liberals was screaming that the hour had come for the Liberals to take over peacefully and guard their liberty by going into the streets to defend their country. Then we found the BBC news in Spanish, relayed from another local station, and shortly afterwards Radio Newsreel from London. I had to hand it to the BBC for their amazingly quick news service. They were the only people to give news objectively and we heard an eye-witness account of things in Bogotá which had not yet reached local stations.

Turmoil continued in Bogotá for many days. The textile firm Colteger had long run an advertising campaign with the slogan 'Colteger knocks at your door'; the lucky householder so visited, if equipped with a Colteger product, would receive a prize. Now the street mobs, as they smashed in shop doors, chanted '*Colteger toca a su puerta!*' while the Archbishop was quoted in the newspapers as saying '*No vengais a confesaros si dais muerte a un saqueador!*' (don't come to confession if you kill a looter). Medellín settled down sooner, but the unrest did not help attendance at the Institute. Affairs there in my case were complicated by the ill health of James Besant who was invalided home in June. Poor Colette, seven months pregnant, had a rough passage. Driving from Barranquilla to Cartagena the day before their plane to England was due precipitated things, and the next morning, after a labour of fifty-five minutes, the baby arrived. They all survived but this brought home to me for the first time what risks British Council wives were expected to run. Embassy wives may have had heavier entertainment duties but they were cushioned by bigger and non-accountable allowances and, living in bigger cities, enjoyed better medical facilities – and sometimes a Foreign Office doctor.

Harold Norminton took over as Director of the Institute. He and Lucie already had a child, and it was soon evident that Germaine would follow suit. The Besants' departure and the impending new arrival caused a postponement of my leave till Christmas, and I learned with some disappointment – as marriage had strengthened the feeling that the new chapter in my life called for fresh woods and pastures new – that after my leave I was to return to Colombia, but not to Medellín.

Bogotá itself, and the Council's presence there, had left me with mixed feelings when I had made my first visit some months earlier. The Council office and the Institute were in a creaky old building on the Avenida Séptima, and I thought the collection of London-appointed and local staff pretty creaky too – and they were quite as gossipy as Ozzie's letters had led me to expect. The longest serving among the local teachers were the choleric

'Beefy' Hardwick and Percy Winn, an amiable Lancastrian radio ham and football fan (he was to introduce the first English professional, one Higgins, to play for the Colombian team). These two were balanced by two elderly spinsters – the Anglo-Indian Miss Warde-Jones and a Margaret Rutherford lookalike, Miss Rattray. In complete contrast was a suave goatee-bearded and very black Jamaican, Howard Rochester, married to Julia, a beautiful and very white Bogotana. He had a mellifluous voice and a command of felicitous phrases with which to damn with faint praise the victims of the others' criticism. Poor Dermot Milman, for instance, heir to a baronetcy and a major in the war but not altogether happy as the Acting Director, suffered – in absentia – the brunt of their remarks.

The scale of their scandalous gossip would shock those unfamiliar with the weight of boredom that threatens teachers of English as a second or foreign language. There are those who find fulfilment in conjuring up the desired word power of their pupils and in evolving new methods of doing so (and perhaps profitably publishing them), but others become worn down by annual repetition and the frustrations of trying to express rewarding ideas in baby talk; for these the relief of a good gossip is all the more cathartic after having to be unfailingly patient and polite to pupils in and out of class. Even Council staff who do not teach have to be on their best and most tactful behaviour in the presence of foreign clients and hosts, and in private feel the need to air their franker feelings. Nevertheless, this visit to a larger office prompted the first of my generalisations about the Council which later experience confirmed: the efficiency of an office or institute varies inversely with the number of London-appointed staff in it. I have no doubt this truism applies equally to embassies. If, as used to be the case, overseas offices were run by only a few British staff (sometimes just one), but were thicker on the ground, our money would certainly be better spent.

Our arrival as a family in Bogotá was less starry-eyed than it might have been because of the marvellous leave we had had. The long voyage home with Gus, the new son and heir, was itself a refreshment. We boarded *La Reina del Pacífico* in Cristobal in 1949, and were to call at Kingston, Havana, Bermuda, the Bahamas, La Coruña, Santander and La Rochelle before landing at Liverpool. On the way from Valparaiso the ship had picked up the Peruvian Ballet Company. Like us, they were in cabin class, and while they enlivened life on deck with their exercises and liaisons, they enraged the stewards below. By our standards the plumbing was primitive – there were communal sea water baths and lavatories – but by South American standards the efficient flush water closets were something altogether new. Accustomed to drains so bad that performers were expected to dispose of used paper in special boxes rather than flush it down to block the pipes, the glamorous Peruvian dancers – in the absence of the familiar boxes – dropped their used paper on the floor. It was in vain that the stewards pinned up notices imploring them to flush the paper away, and only when they scrawled their increasingly terse message in huge letters across the mirrors was it heeded.

The other passengers were a mixture of working people, but one mystery man travelling first class stood out for his good looks and beautiful clothes. Was he, we wondered, an ambassador, a millionaire, a film star? No, he worked for the YMCA in Mexico.

Our cabin steward had been on board when Ramsay Macdonald was a passenger and died at sea. He was on watch duty when the body was laid out and had spent a restless night resisting temptation. 'He had a lovely pair of boots on, did Ramsay Mac – and just about my size. If I did a swap, I thought, no-one'd ever notice and he didn't need them where he was going. But in the end I never did nothing. After all, you never know, do you? About the other side, I mean. Supposing he was the first person I was to meet, and he said, "I've been waiting for you. I'll have me boots now, if you don't mind!" Well, I mean to say, that'd be getting off on the wrong foot, like, eh?'

At Kingston we were suddenly back in a British environment – of a sort. The local constabulary wore shorts; in Colombia they would have been arrested for indecency. Havana, approached in the evening, was a magical landfall; the castle, the fortifications and, ashore, the wide streets and tall balconied houses fulfilled the fondest imaginings of gracious Spanish colonial enterprise. It was in one of the row of harbourside cafés, as we sat drinking daiquiris, that I saw my first television set and realised that however romantic the place looked – this was in the good old, bad old Batista days – it was now the backyard of the United States. Nevertheless in the 'postings consideration form' for several years afterwards I put down Cuba as one of the countries I'd like to serve in.

Bermuda, with its little counties of Somerset and Devonshire, felt infinitely nearer home. The owners of the Hamilton drugstore where we shopped took us back to their pretty coral house for drinks, and we thought this was indeed gracious living, British colonial style. We were not there long enough to feel the absence of a hinterland.

After Havana and the cosiness of Hamilton, the austerities of Spain were a shock. The artistry of the fish markets of La Coruña and Santander and the tourist appeal of fans, figurines and leather wine bottles could not conceal evidence of great poverty stoically borne. At La Rochelle, in contrast, it was hard to believe there had been a war, let alone one five years later than in Spain; no pale faces, bare feet and threadbare uniforms there. Our English landfall was a green green Mount Edgcombe, and a busy Plymouth sparkling in the winter sun brought tears to my eyes.

In the London office Germaine and I paid our respects to A J S White, our regional supremo, who was to remain a beacon of old-fashioned courtesy until his nineties. After seeing A J, I went round various departments for briefing in education, the arts, science, films, books, visitors, courses and – ever an edgy subject – personnel. At this stage in my career these were perfunctory enough and, after letting off steam in Bristol, I – veteran of the Far East and the Far West – made my first real acquaintance with the continent of Europe.

Most of my Dutch relations were snugly ensconced in The Hague, and Holland was fast getting back into shape just as Britain seemed to be disintegrating into bureaucracy and squalor. Everything looked efficient and worked smoothly: the swift silent tramcars, the level clean cobbles, the elegant villas with freshly painted shutters, the smart shops, the neat notices, the strong stubby destrier-like horses pulling the milk floats and great barrel organs, the crowded restaurants serving delicious food, the working canals, the well-kept farms with their huge tidy barns, the sheer number of small towns like Amersfoort, Haarlem, Middelburg, Veere, any one of which would have been a major tourist attraction in Britain. Perhaps one reason was that Holland's problem – too many people in too little land – dictated that people living cheek by jowl simply must have their pleasures and comforts in order to make their close proximity bearable. Where Britain's houses were often left empty, in Holland every house had to have a pro rata number of lodgers for its rooms. Rationing and strikes were less in evidence, while a black market was tolerated, and everyone seemed to be hardworking and optimistic in spite of post-colonial problems as big as ours.

It was obvious that the Van der Wycks were bigger frogs in a less provincial pool than the Alexanders. I was summoned to pay my respects to the doyenne of the clan, the wealthy widowed Jonkvrouwe Schimelpenninck, alias Tante Jeanne. I was admitted to her overheated museum of an apartment by an ancient white-gloved butler, who served tea and later *ein borl* (an *oude ginever* gin) and later still a refill, which I always refused in order to facilitate my escape. In between I was interrogated on politics, history and especially religion.

A banker brother-in-law of Germaine's, Paul Huet, lent us his Mercedes convertible, while his wife nobly looked after Gus, and we toured not only Holland but Germany. Accustomed as I had grown to thinking of warfare in terms of colonial struggles in jungles and *kampongs*, it seemed inconceivable that civilised nations should have been led to smash up such marvellous cities; inconceivable, too, that so much had survived. In Holland the occupation was still a very live issue and the determination to climb out of it all the stronger.

Later visits with rumbustious children accentuated the drawbacks of the country: the flatness, the fact that one is rarely out of sight of houses, the lack of anywhere to let off steam, the fetish for tidiness and conformity, the keep-off-the-grass mentality. No wonder all my in-laws who could afford to – and most could – retired in due course to Switzerland, Italy and France! But on that first visit we were thoroughly spoilt.

The ties of fatherhood, with even one child, without the help of our splendid Colombian maid were already apparent, and I was happy to leave the rest of the family and return to England for a week's jaunt with Terence Charley, an old POW friend on leave from Kenya.

We both wanted to get deep into the heart of the country to recharge our batteries, so we hired a camping punt at Lechlade for £5 and went down to Eynsham and back. As we were checking the equipment I became aware of a familiar high-pitched tone beyond the weir, which grew louder as it approached, and John Betjeman appeared in a panama hat. He was intrigued with our punt, looked wistfully at it, and talked as if we were off to explore the Amazon. As we pulled away his busy voice – like Ratty's giving directions to Mole (or perhaps rather the other way round) – started to fade across the water, and then with a shout came after us;

'I say, is this your Bentley?'

'Afraid not. Ours is the Austin 10.'

'Ah, well, better really!'

After the punt it was a bit of a change to travel with the family in the *Queen Elizabeth* to New York, once more to catch the plane south – this time to Bogotá. While conditions were much better than on the old *Reina del Pacífico* the passengers came as a surprise. Even in cabin class we had a nurse and nursery, library, indoor swimming pool, gymnasium, cinema, banks, Austin Reed's and an orchestra of our own. Most of the passengers were Jewish and some dined with their hats on. Victor Kravchenko (*I Chose Freedom*) was travelling first class on his way back from his libel action in Paris. In the evenings a Jewish group danced jigs in kilts, while GI brides danced with each other, and in the bar the Liverpool Irish sang '*Nearer my God to Thee'*. One French-speaking dancer had numbers tattooed on her arm.

We found ourselves eating at the table of the ship's doctor, Bill Fosbury, a former naval surgeon on the China station. He had Somerset connections, claiming that his ancestors had been hereditary cleaners of the rhines as far back as the fourteenth century. We spent several of our five evenings in his cabin. He kept special black-edged cards for some of his patients, which ran: 'Your story has touched me deeply. I have seldom met anyone with so many troubles as yours. Please accept this as a token of my sympathy.' Also eating with us were Mrs Macpherson, editor of *The Dog World,* and Mr Royce of Boston (with a summer place at Gloucester, Mass.), the US expert in Pekinese, with six of which he was travelling; the conversation rarely rose above knee level. For one meal we also had a Russian lady travelling on a British passport, but the doctor had her and her platitudinous remarks moved to another table, and after running through six others she finished up in a corner by herself. She fell foul of Royce when she announced that she was going to the States to find out how real people lived there, the sort of people who read Emerson and John Steinbeck. Royce said it was only dollars that counted in the States.

'Ah, my friend, there is a soul there.'

'I couldn't buy my little place in Gloucester with a soul.'

'Are you sure you need that little place in Gloucester?' And she proceeded to lecture us about her family, who had been made to give up their ancestral home to the new comrades. 'And why not?' she added.

'Why not? I doubt if the comrades are better off now than they were before.'

'Oh, yes. They are! I can remember when the peasants used to sleep with their dogs!'

'Well, I often sleep with my dawgs! I hope you find your soul in the States, but I assure you you'll need dollars to buy it.'

After this break and the enjoyable voyage, Bogotá, with its broken streets and Mancunian weather, looked very sad. Nevertheless, it was not the culture shock that Medellín had been, and in any case our responses were blunted by parental concerns. I was of course besotted with what I chose to think projections of my better self in Gus and in Nicholas, who was to arrive the next year. Thoughts of leaving the Council receded.

I did go back to Medellín once, and after the cold damp sprawl of Bogotá it seemed gloriously sunny – but undeniably small. By then Harold Norminton had moved to Bogotá and been succeeded by Pat Seccombe, another ebullient and hospitable Anglo-Irishman. Though not as evangelically brainwashed as me, Harold – as well as being Church of Ireland – had been a Westminster Abbey choirboy. (When quizzed on his faith by the Rector of Mérida University in Venezuela he had declared stoutly, *'Soy Protestante*!' *'Dios mio*!' exclaimed the Rector, *'Digamos Anglicano! Suena mejor.*' ('Let's say Anglican, it sounds better.')) Pat would have needed no such equivocation; Catholicism was his hobby as well as his faith.

I was in Medellín to lecture on Shakespeare and Wordsworth (whose centenary it was) at a course for Religious, and found the Institute transformed. The only journals on display were Roman Catholic ones and Pat, to supplement them, had imported a special supply of Catholic school magazines. Over the entrance was the Holbein portrait of Sir Thomas More, patron saint of the Course, which was opened by a cathedral mass with Pat ensconced in a chancel stall. Pat's wife, Anne, conducted a choir of her Religious, singing (in faultless English) 'God bless our Pope, God bless our Pope, God bless our Pope, the great, the good!' There was an exhibition and lecture on 'Four Great Englishmen': John Henry Newman, Charles Waterton, Hilaire Belloc and G K Chesterton. There was also a pretty nun on the course, called Sister Magdalena. 'What a pity,' she said, 'that you are a Protestant!' 'What a pity,' I answered, 'that you are a nun!' She smiled and crossed herself. Anne Seccombe, expecting the first of many babies, also gave classes at the Institute – for which Pat refused to claim payment. Teaching by wives, he thought, should be a quid pro quo for a man's marriage allowance. As he had bad eyesight Anne also did all the family driving. Ten years later she was most tragically killed when driving Pat from the airport in Montevideo.

There were eight London-appointed staff in the Bogotá office and Institute and about the same in the Embassy, an equality I was never to see again. A new ambassador had just arrived from Java. My first impressions of his wife had been discouraging. Harold Norminton and I, on a visit to Bogotá, had been invited to lunch at the Residence. Arriving over-punctually we were left alone for five minutes until our hostess descended the stairs. Anxiously enquiring if we had mistaken the day, I was assured briskly that we had not. 'You were invited', she said, 'for one o'clock, not five to.' Later on the Mackereths proved a pleasant and helpful couple, Gilbert only once causing raised eyebrows – at least among former members of the ATS – by his foreword to the British Legion newsletter: 'It is a grand thing,' he wrote, 'that you, my companions who bared your breasts to the enemy and sacrificed the most valuable years of your life should unite together...' They entertained well – and circumspectly. After one cocktail party, when we had been asked to stay on for dinner, Mrs Mackereth descended the stairs with a trayful of silver ashtrays. 'Better be safe than sorry,' she said, exchanging them for the glass party ones. Geoffrey Jackson, later kidnapped by the Tupamaros in Uruguay, was Head of Chancery, while Leonard Scopes and Arthur Turner were lively and gifted actors in play readings at the Institute.

When we first arrived the Dutch Ambassador, Schuller, a dear old soul about to retire, brought out the Bols for us and rumbled away in a mixture of Dutch, French, Spanish and English. The house smelt of mould and had no flowers in it, for he lived alone with a Spanish manservant and lots of dogs. Every few minutes a puppy would come in and make a mess on the floor, which the manservant would wipe up. Schuller had been Ambassador in Portugal when a distant van der Wyck cousin of Germaine had been appointed Secretary there. In his annual report Schuller had recommended van der Wyck's retention in the service as he 'would do no harm working below ministerial rank'. When the cable announcing his successor in Bogotá arrived, he stared at it in disbelief, then gave way to paroxysms of laughter. His eyes streamed as he roared out, '*Got Verdomme!* Van der Wyck! Ha, ha, ha! *Ay, pendejo!* Van der Wyck!'

Rhyn van der Wyck proved to be most hospitable, and had both charm and wide intellectual interests. However, while his marriage to the Marquesa Pilar de Torre Ocaña (whose first marriage had been annulled in Rome) may have been a good career move in the short term, it was in the long run a disaster. At parties Pilar tended to kick off her shoes, shrug off her shawl and dance on the table, while his alcohol consumption made Rhyn's official attendances unpredictable. They did not stay long in Bogotá and some years later were reported to have been involved in a smuggling scandal.

Norman Tett, under whom I was also to serve in Spain, followed Jack Bruton and Neil Mackay as the Council Representative in Bogotá. Most likeable and considerate, he was perhaps over-considerate of London HQ, while Irène – who typed professionally at an amazing speed with two fingers – was a generous godmother to Nick.

It did not take me long to renew my acquaintance with the classroom. Returning from leave we had breakfasted stickily at Barranquilla airport (finding the lavatory in much the same state as we had left it four months before) and landed in Bogotá at 11am. At 6pm I was teaching again.

'Why are you late?'

'I – was – er – late – because – I – was – having – injections.'

'What – were – the – injections – for?'

'Clap!'

Not long after, I was invigilating at a Jesuit school. After the papers had been given out the students stood up and the nun in charge muttered a prayer. Then they all crossed themselves and the students sat down and tore into the peccadillos of Henry VIII, *'El Rey Libertino e Inmoral'*. Next to the classroom was a chapel, with a notice outside reading, 'The Master is here and calls you'. When I once gave a student a ticking off she went inside for twenty minutes, presumably to atone – or perhaps to pray for me.

One never quite knew where one was with nuns. Sometimes they would show how modern and uncensorious they were by pouring one an immense whisky after a lecture. At other times any kind of worldliness seemed to come as a nasty shock. One of the convents asked my predecessor to send them a documentary film entitled *A Lamb is Born* for their Christmas show. They were horrified to find the subject neither more nor less than was implied by its title.

With a bigger staff in Bogotá than in Medellín we could provide more supplementary student entertainments. We never managed to get any nuns onto the platform but we were not short of advisers on moral dilemmas. One of our international Brains Trust questions was, 'Which is the most successful, a love marriage or one that has been arranged?' The gentle dry British Director of the Institute, Roger Kingdon, with a fiery Mexican second wife, Martha, was non-committal. The American, a bachelor, favoured marriage for love, and the Frenchman and Colombian the arranged marriage. The Colombian said a man should never marry his lover, but should continue loving her after his marriage 'to someone convenient'; the only love that could reasonably be expected between man and wife was that for their children; in other ways they should live almost independently of each other; he should be free to see his friends alone, and she hers; she should go to church; he should do as he liked about it. The condition of marriage itself made real love impossible and as Colombia permitted no divorce an arranged marriage was the only one feasible.

Bogotá contributed to my work experience when I was moved from teaching to general cultural duties, which involved mixing with an international community – and not least with our own diplomats. My new title of Functional Officer encompassed all activities other than teaching or administration, i.e. the arts, sometimes libraries, and any general 'function' put on for either students or the general public. These varied from major 'manifestations' like the Old Vic or Royal Ballet in grander and more accessible countries to single lecturers or soloists in 'difficult' places like Colombia. There we had to make do with visitors prepared to rough it – such as Solomon touring for the Chopin centenary, or Ethel Bartlett and Rae Robertson.

Ballet had a particularly rough ride in Bogotá. The public did not take kindly to Katherine Dunham's group (which included the young unknown Harry Belafonte) because it turned out to be black, i.e. *costeño* (coastal) or 'savage', while they had expected snowy white sexless sylphides. When a local ballet school of impeccable social standing contracted David and

Angela Ellis to come out and teach for them, the project ended in tears. David had qualified as a doctor before taking up ballet and marrying Angela, the daughter of Marie Rambert and Ashley Dukes. The Ellises were lodged in their employers' house, with trams thundering past the window, and found themselves living the lives of servants and their plans for the school circumscribed by social niceties. (Remembering my tussles with Doña Teresita over her precious girls in Medellín, I could imagine the frustrations involved.) Things started well with a floodlit *pas de deux* from David and Angela at a party in the Embassy garden, but ended in a broken contract and an assisted passage home. Soon afterwards they took over the running of the Rambert company and school, based on the Mercury Theatre at Notting Hill Gate.

In a small way we used theatre as a teaching 'tool' at the Institute. Besides the one-act plays we put on for students in the Institute – and I still remember Leonard Scopes as Campbell of Kilmuir, wiping imaginary condensation off an imaginary window pane to peer into an imaginary Highland mist – I took part in full-length plays, and later directed them. A production of Rattigan's *While the Sun Shines* went down well and was 'toured' to the Shell Oil camp at Casabe. This was by no means a routine event because Shell, like their American competitors Tropical Oil, were anxious not to upset local feelings, and any manifestation that seemed to favour British over Colombian interests was treated with caution as it might, as in Mexico, encourage cries for nationalisation. Even the operatic recitals pressed upon the camp by Lifa Toone, the consort of Shell's director in Bogotá, met with resistance (a resistance which we in the Institute unfortunately had no excuse for invoking).

However, our visit was eventually approved and Harold Norminton, the French suitor in the play, and I, the English one, went down to the steamy swamps of the Magdalena. It was my first experience of an oil camp with flaring wells, donkey engines nodding like mechanical birds feeding, and earth-movers forever smoothing down oil-dressed roads. Above all it was my first experience of a camp club. The play flopped. There was polite applause at the end and the audience rushed off to do what they really wanted to do – drink in the club. It was clear that any such diversion was an unwelcome break in routine. This came as a shock. I had imagined that a big oil camp, unlike a small jungle enterprise like the cement factory on the Nare, would be a sophisticated place where people developed leisure interests and hobbies. But here the working hours, starting at five in the morning and ending at midday, seemed to have deadened any enterprise except drinking and club games. If our play had been a review about camp subjects it would no doubt have been a riot. We were there for the weekend and witnessed the drinking going on more or less continually from Saturday to Monday. It was a sobering sight. There was little social contact with Colombian staff and few wives spoke Spanish. I thought at that time that a little of Shell's profits would have been well spent on educational and recreational programmes in the field rather than on a few high-living public relations offices in Bogotá.

Some years later I seriously thought of leaving the Council to put these thoughts into practice.

In the absence of VIP lecturers from London we welcomed two of our own Council staff from other countries. One was Walter Starkie, who had held the tricky post of Madrid throughout the war. He was reputed to be the highest-paid member of the Council, because – as other Hispanists were overtly anti-Franco – he (who was more circumspect or perhaps more long-sighted) had had to be tempted away from his life fellowship of Trinity College, Dublin, to accept the job.

'I don't know,' said Mackay when the project was first mooted, 'how Dr Starkie will go down in Colombia. He's rather superficial.' But from the moment 'Don Gitano' posed in the door of his plane with his fiddle under his arm it was clear that his superficiality was going to suit us very well. He talked to everyone with a kind of confidential mischievousness and never allowed academic considerations to deprive him of name-dropping and gossip. Whether his lecture was on Wilde, 'my great friend' Shaw, Synge or Yeats, or on gypsy music, he managed to introduce an air or two on his fiddle and did not hesitate to repeat a good story from one lecture in another. After one lecture he kept going through twelve large whiskies, transporting us to the sophistications and gossip of Dublin and Madrid.

We gave a dinner party for him, with Lucy and Rafael Parga (our Junta chairman whose English and manners quite put us to shame) and the Van der Wycks. The Marquesa was soon firing on all cylinders, capping his gypsy stories with reminiscences of dancing in Lola's bogus flamenco cave at Granada and finding seven telephones concealed behind the woodwork.

Apart from the goodwill he created with the Colombians, it was a relief to see that the Council did have a senior representative who was a character in his own right. He was one of very few. At about that time Lawrence Durrell ended his inglorious career with the Council after only two months at Córdoba in Argentina, where he kept the windows shut 'to save him from breathing more of the air of the place than necessary'. Walter Starkie, on the other hand, was so pleased with the atmosphere of Madrid that he stayed there after retirement.

Our other visiting Council lecturer was Derek Traversi, and I was lucky enough to have to meet him in Cartagena, a wonderful old city on the north-west coast. The vast castle of San Felipe that proved impregnable to General Wentworth, the sea fort with its shark pit then used as a leper colony, and the old balconied houses and baroque churches later familiar in Hollywood films, breathed of colonial enterprise and decay. The museum in Cartagena displayed victory medals struck prematurely by Admiral Vernon, over-confident after his victory at Portobello. He had not counted on the General prevaricating until the troops died off with malaria. Sitting in the university hall listening to Derek's critical nit-picking in measured Spanish, and watching the sweat trickling off his chin onto his script, I could only sympathise with Wentworth's inertia and marvel at Drake's earlier successful attack.

The tropical languor of Cartagena is no doubt wearisome in big doses, but a brief descent to Fusagasuga was a marvellous antidote to the edginess of Bogotá with its drizzle and colds and headaches. Down in the town time seemed to slow down and invite confidences over *cuba libres* and *empanadas*. In this steamy savannah country it was easy to believe how far away up in the clouds and out of touch Bogotá was. Jaime Tello, a liberal journalist, told me that police chiefs were often a law unto themselves. At a town near the Magdalena one had dispossessed four *mayors* and shot some children for making a noise playing in the main square. It was incongruous to see in that very town, on my way to La Dorada, graffiti saying '*Ni un Colombiano para Korea'*. (An anxious parent in Bogotá had sought our assurance that the Embassy would not accept volunteers to fight in Korea.) Jaime had little time for either missionaries or priests. In Cucutá, he said, a priest adopted a young widow with her two daughters; for many years he lived with the mother and then with the daughters. Finally one of the daughters decided to marry someone else, so he shot her. While he was in prison one of his parishioners died and left him two hundred thousand pesos.

When Jaime's father died his brother, a priest, was asked to stay in the house and conduct the funeral. He refused, saying that he had important business to attend to in Bogotá. Later this was revealed as selling two gold statuettes, which he had bought cheaply, to the Museo de Oro. Jaime's father had had seven illegitimate children besides twelve legitimate ones and Jaime bore them no grudge and considered they deserved a share of the paternal property.

Climbing up again from Fusagasuga to the gloomy city of Bogotá was a dispiriting journey. It was no relief to go up even further in the funicular to the pilgrimage church on Montserrate, because the mountain was usually wrapped in mist. (There was also a saying that anyone going up there would come back in the end to Bogotá.) Yet away from the Bogotá plateau the weather could be clear and invigorating in much higher places. Lake Tota, for instance, above the simple Indian village of Pueblo Viejo, had an alpine climate – freezing by night, burning by day. Leaving Gus with our faithful maid, Magola, Germaine and I visited it with a couple from the Dutch embassy (we still had no car of our own). On the way we crossed the bridge of Boyacá and a monument to its battle and La Legión Británica, whose leader, James Rooke, had waved them on to victory with his severed arm but expired the day after. The hotel at the lake was like a chalet, with bunk beds, and hanging in the bar was a decalogue by the Colombian artist who ran it:

This is not a hotel, it is your house.
Here there is no clock; eat and sleep when you like.
If you are neurosthenic, don't greet us. We will continue your friends.
Lovers have preference here, because they are afflicted with fever.

We sell whisky, but we give away Alka Seltzer.
We don't wear golden buttons, nor do we have liveried servants.
We recognise no titles, either professional or noble.
We don't believe in etiquette, we prefer good taste.
We do not want women to be distant.
At this height we have lost all sense of money.

The last sentiment was not true but we had a marvellous time there. On our return we learned there had been many murders in Pueblo Viejo and that where we had been walking in the mountains above the lake was particularly dangerous.

It was obvious that Council affairs in Bogotá were going the same way as in Medellín, which was now a one-man post. The Institutes in Barranquilla, Cali and Popayan had been closed, and with devaluation at home and Council expansion elsewhere, especially in the newly independent India, Colombia was squeezed for cash. At the same time the Americans were increasing their cultural and teaching activities and our student numbers were falling. The political situation had grown increasingly volatile since the murder of Gaitán, who was said to have taken bribes indiscriminately from both Conservatives and Moscow. A Liberal MP named Jimenez Jimenez tanked up one day at the bar in the Senate and swore he'd make trouble in the chamber. Guns in the chamber were illegal, but after provoking verbal retaliation from the Conservatives Jimenez started shooting and was quickly despatched by three more sober Conservatives. As all were subject to parliamentary privilege, no-one was prosecuted, but the city had the jitters for a couple of weeks, until the arrival in state of the statue of Our Lady of Fátima calmed people down.

Our Director General (who doubled as Chairman) just missed the excitement on his official visit from London. 'He ought,' I wrote home, 'to be an artistic and efficient young Jew but is, in fact, General Sir Ronald Adam. For a simple soldierman he may be an excellent person, but he is getting on for seventy, deaf in one ear and monolingual except for execrable French. We polished up the name plates on the big front door but the rain still came through the roof and I don't think he was very impressed.'

Sir Ronald was a Socialist and it was said that what he really thought we ought to be doing, instead of teaching English to students who could afford to pay for it, was sitting down with groups of taxi drivers discussing the Beveridge Plan. Some years later the fruit of this philosophy caught up with me in Guyana in the form of Study Boxes. Stoutly constructed, these contained government forms and pamphlets on such subjects as the health service. The boxes themselves were very useful for storing gramophone records. As for the general's horror of elitism, it was to cost the Council dear in the sixties and seventies.

The Adam visit, however, and his local honorary doctorate, brought some of the impressive names on our *Junta* up from their estates on the Llanos.

With Germaine I also enjoyed at this time some unusual parties. Eduardo Santos, a former President and Liberal newspaper proprietor, sent a car to drive us for two hours down to Bizerta. It was certainly Liberty Hall, and one of his Colombian guests wore a Trinity Hall blazer and got amiably tight. Round the room were English coaching prints and pottery figures of Sam Weller, Fagin, Mr Pecksniff and Old Uncle Tom Cobley and All. In the grounds a replica of a Mexican church had been built by Doña Lorencita Villegas de Santos in memory of their only child, who had died, aged five, fifteen years before. Her rooms were kept exactly as they had been, both there and in town. 'She is not dead for us,' said Doña Lorencita, 'She keeps Eduardo and me together more than ever.' The little church was furnished with antiques.

Near our flat in Bogotá a young man ran an antique shop of such decrepit stock that not long afterwards I asked him facetiously if he was going bust yet. On the contrary, he had made a quarter of a million pesos in only a few years. For example, he had picked up two old bits of wood with flecks of gold still clinging to them, parts of an altar from a village church that was being rebuilt, for $2.50. The pair had already been sold for $400.00 – to Doña Lorencita.

Moving in *alta sociedad* circles socially made me wonder how effectively we were moving in them professionally. The Americans were obviously on the up and up in trade while we, except for Royal Dutch Shell, seemed to be fading out. Even the French ran an excellent lycée staffed by teachers within their state system, while the divisive bureaucracy apparent on my home leave between our Ministry of Education, Foreign Office and BBC bore little promise of effective co-operation overseas. And how many of our students would use the English we taught them to promote trade not with Britain but with the States? The political posturing of Britain in the fall-out from the war and the disposal of Empire seemed to leave no room for countries like Colombia, and I began to wonder what I had let Germaine in for. The Council's motto on its beautifully lettered bookplates was 'Truth Will Triumph' (long abandoned – like the BBC's 'Nation Shall Speak Peace Unto Nation', no longer appropriate for a Corporation that talks only to itself). But what was truth? If it was beauty, was our creaky old Institute with its staff of invalids and misfits and its Henry Moore prints of air-raid shelters beautiful? If beauty was truth, was the end of Empire – our moment of truth – beautiful? The truth for me was that I now had a family of my own and the beauty of that was that we were company for each other. But a growing preoccupation with the new family meant a distancing from the old and a lessening in my struggle for the soul of Colombia. I was no longer so open to vivid impressions, so receptive to confidences or so homesick for a pre-war Britain.

In Bogotá, as the end of my tour of duty approached in 1951, tentative proposals for my next posting started to filter through Norman Tett from London. Most of them sounded more like threats than promises and, after a particularly scary suggestion of Asyut in Egypt, we liked the sound of

'Director, Isfahan'. Unfortunately, before we got to Isfahan fate intervened in the pyjama-clad person of Mohammed Mossadegh, the weeping Prime Minister of Iran. The chance of a more or less independent command was missed, and I was stuck in a lecturing post in Tehran.

5
Tehran Tantrums

IN OCTOBER 1951 I flew out to Tehran, in advance of the family because of general uncertainties. The arid empty spaces of the Levant came as a shock after the jungles of Asia and South America. So did the shadows of political influence hovering over them.

When my KLM plane touched down in Sofia we were herded into a wooden hut in a corner of the deserted airfield for a glass of tea. Shifting one foot on the wooden floor I felt it land on something soft and glancing down saw a large rat looking at me reproachfully. After the Spanish colonial architecture and American apartment blocks of Colombia, Tehran itself looked at first sight like an enormous shack town running uphill to the foothills of Demavend, whose pure and perennial snow only accentuated its scruffiness. The Sir Alexander Gibb firm were slowly installing the first piped water and sewage system; meanwhile the supply was by a system of *jubes* (roadside gutters} which were opened at certain periods in the different quarters of the city, first carrying away the accumulated rubbish and then, as each house opened its sluice, delivering water. The general shortage of water (the Embassy had its own well and water carts, from which we too profited), and the hands-off attitudes of Muslims to hygiene and plumbing, contributed to a most noxious summer atmosphere, while heating depended on ungainly metal kerosene drip-stoves, whose chimneys snaked across the rooms to distant outlets.

However, first impressions are not always right, and as the searing heat gave way to autumn I began to see some justification for Harold Nicolson's enthusiastic reminiscences of pre-war embassy life there. Winter snow covered the rubbish and decay of the streets and brought a bracing dry air – so dry as to chap the lips – and the most beautiful light effects. Moreover, houses which looked nothing from the street often had lovely gardens, and indeed when I came to rent one I found that I was renting not a 'house' but a 'garden'. Persians seemed to have a knack for flower arrangement and for decoration generally, with treasured carpets hung on the wall, exquisite (if repetitive) ivory miniatures, and vases in tiled alcoves to show off their ceramic skill.

I stayed first in the morgue-like Tehran Club, where a notice in the cloakroom requested members not to remove the soap and towels. Out of this frying pan I moved into the fire of the Pension de la Bonbonnière, whose Hungarian proprietress had a French husband, said to be trying to arrange a divorce in Pondicherry. 'I haven't had no man for twelve years!' cried Madame in her more jocular moments.

It was a great relief, when the family arrived, to move eight miles up the hill to Manzel-e-Iskander, Kuchek Rezaieh, in Tajrish, just beyond the Embassy's summer compound at Gulhac, where we found the discomforts of a Spartan bungalow more than offset by a garden of cherry trees with a swimming pool (full of fish, as we found when we tried to empty it without the expertise of our landlord), and by the care and cooking of a wonderful married couple, Reza and Robobé. Thanks to Germaine's brother-in-law's investment in Shell on my behalf I was able to buy my first car, an ancient Buick which usually required a push start. The car was particularly welcome as public transport was not merely uncomfortable but often dangerous. The buses and station wagons of rival companies would race to cut each other out at the bus stops. The buses were faster, at least going downhill into town, and would try to run the station wagons off the road.

The uniformed Indian guards at the two huge British Embassy compounds were a reminder of the power politics of the former Government of India when Iran was all part of the Great Game against Russia, in which Britain exercised her power through the Government of India, who had the ships and had the men and had the money too. It was the Government of India that had nibbled away, when expedient for trade and oil exploration, at Iran's gulf ports and that could afford to pay its emissaries higher salaries than the Foreign Office could. It is not always easy to distinguish who did what for whom, but in the palmy Victorian days of the long-serving Sir John Malcolm and of James Morier, author of the light-hearted *Hadji Baba of Isfahan*, there were over fifty consulate and telegraph posts operating, most of them answerable to the Government of India. In World War II the initiative passed to the Allies, determined to neutralise the pro-Axis strong man of Iran, Reza Shah. He was forced to abdicate in favour of his weaker son, Mohammad Reza Pahlevi, and the royal hand in Iran was further weakened – or at least the pressure behind it weakened – by the independence of India soon after the war. Nehru was no lover of kings, whether they were puppets or not. In the shift of the Great Game to Europe, the field in Iran lay open to dissidents such as the Tudeh Communist Party and to the expression of national aspirations by ordinary Iranians sick of rulers backed by a foreign power. In particular the empire of the Anglo-Iranian Oil Company (BP) was targeted for nationalisation. By all accounts the uniformity and chauvinism of management in its camps were far worse than those of Shell or Standard Oil in Colombia and it was not surprising that strikes were frequent in Abadan. The nationalisation of the AIOC was clearly a matter of time and would no doubt spread to other assets, notably the far-flung halls of the British Bank. Even the influence of the Council was flatteringly suspect in some quarters and it seemed likely that Institutes at Isfahan, Shiraz, Meshed and Tabriz, if not Tehran itself, might have to close.

As it was, when I arrived the inflated establishment of HMG with its 3,000 Persian employees resembled a chicken running round in circles with its head chopped off. I was amazed at the number of people in the Embassy and never learned what they all did. They even had their own Embassy doctor. However, although they still had their weekend place in the mountains, it seemed that entertainment was not what it had been, at least not in the Nunnery, the block where the secretaries lived. 'They haven't had a party for ages,' complained Donald Whittall. 'We used to be in and out all the time. Why, I can remember the days when the lavatory seats were never down!'

In January 1952 the Ambassador, Sir Francis Shepherd, and his hostess, Mrs Campbell-Schneider, flew off to Warsaw. His prospective successor was turned down by the Iranians, who demanded someone who had no previous experience in Iran or in the British Empire. So George Middleton, as Chargé d'Affaires, presided over our eleven remaining months of horse-dealing over Abadan, with strikes, rumour, demonstrations and curfews keeping us permanently on our toes. Middleton was a tough and amusing character – tough on the tennis court too – who had started life as Consul in Paraguay. While in Whitehall it had fallen to him to sack an ambassador, and Bevin had told him how to do it: 'Write 'im a letter kissing 'im on both cheeks and tell 'im e's 'ad it.'

The British Council Representative, Dr Arthur King, was also an amusing character but he was far from tough, and was due to go on sick leave with various ailments, perhaps psychosomatic as much as physical. A Quaker with a Swedish doctorate gained during the war, King was an odd choice for Persia. He had a bushy black beard and when the locals, for centuries convinced of Britain's low cunning, saw him setting off for his university classes in a bowler hat and carrying a briefcase, they could hardly be blamed for thinking him a rabbi or a spy – and probably both. As Controller of Education at HQ in London in the phoney sixties, he was to become the Council's intellectual *éminence grise*; meanwhile he used to floor me with quotations from philosophers I'd never read and ask what I thought of them.

Arthur was a kind host, but when Germaine and I found ourselves sitting, each with a small boy on our laps, opposite the Kings, each with a dog on theirs, I was not surprised that our views on philosophy rarely converged. The dogs were the kind locally known as *jube* dogs – Alsatian mongrels with charms discernible only to their owners. Arthur and Iris worried about them continually: they left parties early to go home and feed them; they slept with them at night; at dawn Arthur got up to let them out for a pee; and when they flew home they paid £120 to fly them home too.

Arthur's conversation once took an unexpected turn. 'Have you noticed,' he asked, 'what beautiful knees Miss Palmer-Smith has?' Miss Palmer-Smith was an elderly oracle of the British colony, who had come out long ago as a governess and later turned to the teaching of English. She was a plain dumpy perky little person whose knees one would be inclined to assume adequate for their locomotor rather than aesthetic role. I wondered whether Arthur was trailing another red rag, but his closing comment did not enlighten me. 'I think it's something to do with the dimples in the back of her knees. When I see her spanking down Ferdowsi Avenue she looks like something out of Beatrix Potter – *The Tale of Miss Palmer-Smith*. I expect to see another sort of tail twitching behind her, like Pigling Bland's.'

Except in the matter of uncertain driving ability, Arthur's Assistant Representative could scarcely have been more unlike him. James Wakelin was an Arabic and Persian speaker, an expert on carpets, a teacher of science and a paterfamilias. He was even less versed in the philosophers than I was, but had made an excellent Punch and Judy theatre with which he entertained children of all nationalities. His beautiful Persian carpets had to compete with his wife's missionary décor – such as Margaret Tarrant texts on the walls and, at the front door, a plaque to flick from '*MERRY AND BRIGHT*' to '*MOULDY*'. He had met Monica when teaching at the Church Missionary Society Stewart Memorial College in Isfahan, where he had been reproved for appearing during the holidays in sandals, his pipe had been frowned upon and his taste for beer considered sinful. In a period of CMS Buchmanism the 'sharing' of sins was encouraged, and one Persian student, egged on by the other boys and in the presence of the expectant Bishop and missionaries, described his experiments with a donkey.

James also had stories about the ousted Reza Shah whose two passions were the railways and the army. When a railway hotel where an Egyptian wedding party were to stay proved to have too few beds, he had the station master hanged. When a tribesman defeated a soldier in a running race he was bidden to the royal presence to receive, as he thought, congratulations on his feat. Instead he received the royal boot in his testicles, which sent him reeling down the steps. This was a habit of the Shah when displeased, so that experienced ministers of state attended him wearing special protection. (A remedy not available to the ministers of a later dictator, Francisco Franco, who employed a more subtle tactic. To get his own way at meetings he would spin them out to a length unbearable to everyone else but immaterial to him, thanks to his colostomy.)

How many of James's stories about Reza Shah were true and how many apocryphal it would be difficult to say, for the Persians too were great tellers of stories. Here is another one as retold by James:

> One night a thief tried to climb into a house, but the window bars came to pieces as he climbed them and he fell, breaking his leg. He sued the householder for damages.
>
> 'Look here,' said the judge, 'through your neglect of the window bars this poor man has fallen and broken his leg!'

'Oh, but it wasn't my fault,' said the householder. 'It was the fault of the carpenter who made the window.' So the carpenter was sent for and the case explained to him.

'But it wasn't my fault,' said the carpenter. 'It was the fault of the builder who put in my window frame. He did it so badly that it broke away from the bricks and mortar.' So the builder was sent for.

'My fault?' said the builder. 'No. The trouble was that just as I was slapping on the mortar my attention was distracted by a beautiful girl walking along the street. It was her fault.' So they summoned the girl.

'It wasn't my fault at all,' she said. 'It was the fault of the red dress I was wearing, and the dyer was responsible for that.'

'I admit it,' said the dyer when he was tracked down and could think of no convincing excuse.

'Take this man to his own shop,' said the judge, 'and hang him from his own doorpost!'

So they took the dyer to his shop but found that the doorway was so low and the dyer so tall that they couldn't hang him as ordered. They returned to the judge and explained their predicament.

'Very well,' said the judge, 'fetch me a short man!'

I had arrived in the middle of the Council office and Institute's move to shared premises on Ferdowsi Avenue. Lower down the street were the massive mud walls of the British Embassy town compound. The combination of this move with the arrival of new staff like me and of old staff from the provinces, together with political alarms and excursions, all made for a good deal of chaos. Malcolm Welland was the Director of the Institute, an Anglo-Irishman of old-fashioned charm and occasional choler, and the Director of Studies was T J Colin Baly, a pipe-smoking bachelor whose first two initials seemed an appropriately pedantic appendage. 'I never accept invitations to lunch!' he had many occasions to say (and I wish I had had the strength of mind to follow his example). Malcolm and T J Colin Baly liked to distance themselves from the hurly-burly by retreating to Malcolm's office, where the *ferashes* would bring in bottles of beer from about eleven onwards.

It was not long before consulates were closed throughout Iran; I had arrived too late for the posting to Isfahan and Arthur King informed me that Meshed was also out. 'It's no good,' he said, 'trying to send you there now that the Consul-General has left. The Meshedis would be convinced that you were a spy.' So I found myself back in the classroom for twenty-three hours a week (8-12am and 4-7pm), and particularly noisome classrooms they were, thanks to Persian lavishness with garlic and rosewater. The intellectual level was pretty much the same as it had been in Bogotá. I don't know what Malcolm and Colin were like as teachers but they were first-rate lecturers on general subjects. Colin Baly was also a gifted raconteur. His tales of life in Egypt under Farouk were scarcely less horrific than Wakelin's of the CMS.

By the end of January it was clear that Germaine and I would never leave Tehran for the provinces and equally clear, as arguments about oil compensation waxed and waned, that we might all have to leave in a hurry at any time. To get some relief from the classroom and from rumour and gossip, I helped the Tehran Little Theatre with *The Paragon* and *I Killed the Count* and then, as a morale-booster at George Middleton's invitation, directed *The Happiest Days of Your Life* in the Gulhac embassy compound, with James and Germaine as Pond and Miss Whitchurch. But long before that we had had plenty of in-house farce to relieve the political hysteria. Files had to be destroyed or transferred to the Embassy in great secrecy. No local staff were supposed to be involved, and the door between the Council offices and the Institute were to be kept locked while this went on. When a helpful *ferash* came up the back stairs to help and started handling the files Arthur exploded, 'Oh, well, you might as well telephone the police at once and have done with it!' At that moment Malcolm, with an armful of Institute files, banged on the communicating door. Arthur stiffened with apprehension, and when it was opened cried, 'God! It's you! I thought it was the police.'

After Arthur's departure cupboard doors kept opening suddenly to reveal the Accountant, Val Thornton, gibbering, 'I'm the police!' and James would collapse into giggles.

I think we were all living on our nerves. Arthur, who had been hobbling about with a stick and complaining he had no sensation below the waist, cheered up as his sick leave approached and James prepared to take over. Meanwhile Malcolm had his moments of drama. I was walking along the passage leading to his office one day when I heard loud bangs and crashes coming from it. Hovering round the door were two frightened *ferashes* gazing at Malcolm as he thrashed around the room with his stick, swiping piles of books off his desk, hurling papers and ashtrays about, scattering files and kicking the furniture to pieces. After a bit, when he had cooled down, Malcolm explained that he had been 'unable to find something in his desk and had rather lost control'. Throughout the hubbub, Colin Baly had been sitting in the corner with his legs twined round each other, sucking at his empty pipe and quietly observing it all.

In fact Malcolm was worried about his next posting which was due shortly – as we all were about ours if everything blew up. It was hard to say whether we would miss Persia. Many Persians were charming, well-read and amusing; many were flibberty-jibbety and seemed content to rely on Armenians to keep the wheels turning. And the mullahs and street demonstrations – as in the horrible flagellating processions celebrating the death of Hussein – were thoroughly frightening. It wasn't long before a group of Tudeh Party Communists came into the Institute demanding that we take down the Shah's portrait. Old hands like Mark Stott of the British Bank had plenty of stories to illustrate the perils of disorder and justice in Iran. He told us how, on the Gulhac road, which I travelled four times a day, a Swede driving up it was overtaken by a bus. As it drew level, a man was flung out of the bus onto the bonnet of his car, and killed. It emerged that he had had no money for a ticket. The police agreed that his being thrown out by the conductor was only reasonable and his death accidental. About the same time an Iranian soldier returning from Azerbaijan discovered his wife sleeping with a lover and shot them both dead. His family clubbed together and by ruining themselves financially managed to get him off punishment on the grounds that he was only sustaining his honour.

Two years later, when Mossadegh's government came in, the new Minister of Justice set about recouping the expenses he had laid out to get the job. All legal cases that had been dismissed were reopened without the formality of court procedures. The Swede who had been driving the car that killed the man who had been thrown out of the bus was given the option of paying a gigantic fine or going to prison. To avoid either, he was smuggled out of the country as a steward on an SAS plane and as a result SAS planes were prohibited from landing in Iran for several months. At the same time the soldier from Azerbaijan was re-arrested, and as the family had no money left he was hanged in front of the British Bank – by the usual Persian method of pulling him up by the rope and leaving him hanging and kicking all day until the family were allowed to swing on his legs to break his neck.

In October, when HMG declined to pay £49 million as a preliminary to further talks about oil nationalisation, Mossadegh at last broke off diplomatic relations. (He borrowed, but never returned, a book from the Embassy library to discover how to do it.) A Pakistan Radio announcement that Guy Micklethwait, the Embassy Head of Information, and James were to be arrested as spies was followed by one from the Iranian Foreign Minister saying that 'the British Council can remain provided they do not interfere in political matters'. 'I think it would be unfair,' cabled the Foreign Secretary, Anthony Eden, 'to leave the Council in Persia as a target for Mossadegh's next circus ... and suggest they withdraw at their leisure.' Of course the students were horrified to hear we were going ('But we don't like Mossadegh. What will happen to our examinations?'), and it was heartbreaking trying to find jobs for the local staff. It was also sad to see all the stuff we had so painstakingly moved into our new Institute sealed up by a gloomy Swiss diplomat.

The Wellands had already gone on leave; Germaine and Monica Wakelin and the boys flew off to Beirut, and other staff to Cairo or London, leaving James and me to tidy up.

At the end of October Guy Micklethwait issued his last News Bulletin with an appropriate heading:

Why, Hafiz, art thou sorrowing?
Why is thy heart in absence rent?
Union may come of banishment,
And in the darkness light will spring.

The Embassy crowd had set off early one Saturday morning to drive in convoy to Baghdad, and many of their *chers collègues* accompanied them as far as Karadj to share a stirrup cup. Mossadegh sent a last Note after them which George Middleton in the old Rolls refused to accept, and the column eventually proceeded in rather a hazy state. There had, in any case, been a certain amount of jockeying for position as the Head of Chancery insisted on driving alone in the large Humber with the youngest and prettiest secretary. Back in Tehran the Swiss flag flew over the Embassy compound, where Indian and Sudanese guards crept disconsolately about looking for someone to salute.

James and I left a week later in the office Ford Pilot, after frantically clearing up by day and farewell partying by night. It was very upsetting to see odd children's toys lying about in our abandoned houses and even more upsetting to be given, just as we were setting off, a box of chocolates by Reza and, from our Armenian clerk, an enormous cake cooked by his mother.

The excitement I felt at the prospect of the drive to Beirut via Baghdad and Damascus was tempered by a lack of confidence in my co-driver. James had coped nobly with getting everybody away, clearing everything up and paying all our debts, and it was not surprising that all this activity took its toll. In the last few weeks he had smashed a wing of the car turning into his own gate, driven at speed over an excavation, and turned the car over by backing into a *jube*. However, it seemed more or less roadworthy except that the side and rear lights were stolen on our last night. During the journey he hit two petrol pumps in Persia and a rock garden in Jordan. But we started off quietly enough with a last helping hand from the local staff.

The Council driver, Nasser, came with us as far as the Iraqi border. We spent our first night full of dust at the Hotel Iran, Hamadan's best, with dim naked light bulbs, two stinking Muslim lavatories, a communal bath a mile down the road, no curtains, and fading KLM posters on the dining room walls. The waiter spoke wistfully of his days in the British Bank.

The next day we drove through more fertile country, on a lovely morning with shadows slanting down the valleys, and soon passed an amazingly clear-cut frieze carved in the time of Darius II on a rock near a deserted British army camp. At Kermanshah the English signs at petrol stations had been painted out, and we had our first puncture. Passing Kurdish mud huts and tents, flocks of sheep and goats, women dressed in red with kohl-blacked eyes and turbaned men in white woollen coats, we came after 450 miles to Qasr-i-shirin near the border. The Koran was blaring from all the radios as we walked down the main street, and two youths, one in a uniform of some sort, demanded our names and passports. James let loose a flood of Persian and asked who they were. They blustered and professed themselves satisfied with the visiting card he gave them. Next morning we descended for half an hour through moonlike wastes to the frontier, where we said goodbye to Nasser who at the last moment begged with a gleam in his eye to stay with us. The Iraqi customs were most affable. 'Have a cup of tea,' they said. 'You are among friends now.'

6
Beirut

APART FROM some old Turkish houses by the river, Baghdad was as scruffy as Tehran, but without the saving grace of a mountain backdrop. The streets were thick with new British cars and American limousines and loud with horns, but the general air of bustle and tolerance made for a pleasanter atmosphere than Tehran's. The Council office, which was separate from the Institute, had faded travel posters on flaking walls and notices pinned higgledy-piggledy under dusty pictures. It was presided over by two bachelors, Jock Jardine and Cyril Eland.

'At least,' I remarked to Cyril, 'there are open-air cafés where one can sit and watch the world go by.'

'Oh, but one can't,' said Cyril in a shocked voice. 'I mean *we* can't!'

Evidently the mantle of the British Raj, with the RAF at Habbaniyah and the Iraq Petroleum Company still British-run, lay heavily on its descendants.

We had gone to the Embassy to sort out films and found two film vans of Guy Micklethwait's from Tehran backed up against each other.

'Good heavens,' exclaimed Cyril. 'What an extraordinary way to park them! They look as if they were locked together in ecstasy.'

Jock Jardine, a frail but urbane character, was just back from a visit to Bahrain, where he had been dismayed by the cavalier treatment displayed by his hosts at the Residency towards a Mrs Wilshire, wife of the Consul-General in Baghdad. She had called unexpectedly from aboard ship to pay her compliments and was invited to dinner at eight. Everyone else arrived at nine – and drunk from another party.

'At dinner,' said Jock, 'I sat next to her, while everyone else talked round and through her, until she said, "I really think I must be going now as my boat will have been waiting for me for an hour and a half." Whereupon everyone jumped up with great politeness, bundled her out to the car and returned to go on with the party. At intervals during the next hour or two people would suddenly remember about Mrs. Wilshire and go out to see if the car had returned. But it hadn't, and eventually they forgot about it.'

Poor Mrs Wilshire! But at least she was part of the Old Firm and would have known the temptations of the cocktail circuit, and might well in her youth have given way to them. It was so much easier to tank up and gossip with one's colleagues than to talk soberly in a foreign language to people with whom one had nothing in common – not even, perhaps, the same ideas about duty-free alcohol. Jock himself was not without domestic problems. 'He keeps a shocking table,' said Cyril, 'really shocking. But he's inherited an embassy cook together with an embassy house.' He certainly seemed unfamiliar with its contents. 'Have a cigarette,' he said, offering an opulent but empty silver box, 'or perhaps in this one?', picking up an even more opulent but just as empty one. 'Have some more wine – oh, I'm terribly sorry, there isn't any.'

At dinner with Jock were James, Leonard and Mrs Pierson from the Institute, and Colin Baly who was also now working there. The Piersons, having no family, were living at the YMCA and Mrs Pierson, finding time hang heavily on her hands, adopted the habit of sitting in Leonard's office all day knitting. She made the most of opportunities to talk and tended to get herself more deeply into unretractable remarks than she intended.

Leonard, talking about a recent novel by a local resident, Desmond Stewart, said, 'Of course he's thoroughly over-sexed and works it off in his novel.' 'Oversexed?' cried his wife. 'I can't say I've noticed it.'

As a change from all such highbrow conversation James and I went out to dinner at the Select with Guy Micklethwait and two other Embassy people. Guy brought a couple of bottles of Red Hackle so we had plenty to sustain us through the Arabic singing that followed. The seats opposite us filled up with elderly poker-faced Iraqis, spinning out one bottle of beer and telling their beads as the dancers wriggled and twitched sedately through their routines. They were not of the calibre of Samia Gamal, whom I saw later in Beirut, but they were enough to get legs jiggling and send the Iraqis off home to their wives before they spent any more money. As we had no homes or wives handy we moved round the corner to Abdullah's but were only in time to see the last act of the show – an Italian roller-skating trio. The Spanish band soon packed up but suggested we should continue the party upstairs. Guy tried in vain to appropriate a roller-skating girl, and we shared four £5 bottles of champagne and a few dances with the floor girls. Andrew, one of the Embassy people, had been very much on his dignity and when James wanted to go home rather than upstairs had said, 'No, James. I'm a little past this sort of thing, but we'd better stick together to look after each other.' Now he suddenly let out a loud whoop and disappeared, and when we eventually descended we found him draped over the bonnet of Guy's locked car, with three vultures waiting patiently beside him. Guy was leaving the Foreign Service and I did not see him again. Years later at Llanvair Discoed church in Monmouthshire (where a notice in the porch forbids the playing of tipcat) I saw the squirarchical tombs of three generations of Micklethwaits. Guy's was the last – and well before he had reached his three score years and ten.

Jock Jardine also died early, soon after his retirement, but he was instrumental in pinpointing a perennial problem in the Council: the incompatibility of intellectual and administrative expertise. Unlike the Arts Council, the British Council controlled spending tightly from the centre, and accounting procedures were strictly monitored. Inevitably sharp practices, or mere incompetencies, emerged from time to time. Only the larger overseas offices had British accountants and many Representatives, including me, never attended a single financial training course, so irregularities sometimes escaped detection until an Inspector arrived from London, and the awkward question then arose of responsibility and perhaps of reparation.

Norman Tett, for instance, was the victim of one local irregularity, accepted responsibility for not having spotted it, and refunded the Council without argument. Jock, however, when caught in a similar predicament, took a different line – more or less as follows: 'Of course I admit I am technically responsible. But is it surprising? I am not an accountant; I am a cultural representative. I cannot spend all my time scrutinising accounts. If that's what you want Representatives to do you should make accountants Representatives and leave people like me to get on with education, language and the arts. And if you want me to refund money to you, that of course is not something I am qualified to argue about. You will have to thrash it out with my solicitors.' At this unheard-of threat the Council backed off, and we have Jock to thank for the beginning of a general loosening of the financial straitjacket that had governed the Council for so long.

As a penance for the excesses at Abdullah's, James and I drove out of Baghdad for an hour on mud roads to see the lonely stark arch of Ctesiphon. The day after that we set off for Amman, Damascus and Beirut. We left at 6am in a chilly dawn and bowled along an avenue of eucalyptus trees. As the red desert sun rose behind us the shadow of the car jumped from tree to tree in front. At 3 in the afternoon we were still cracking along when the radiator boiled dry. We refilled it with six bottles of water we had brought along for just such an emergency, only to see it boil dry again a few miles further on – there was a hairline crack in the radiator hose. After half an hour two Syrians came along in an IPC Chevrolet, with a gazelle sitting in the back seat. They towed us hair-raisingly at 55 mph, but the rope kept snapping so eventually I left James sitting in the Ford Pilot and shared the back seat with the gazelle for 15 miles to the IPC H4 pumping station on the Jordanian border, where I got a large can of water. I was lucky in getting a lift back to James in an empty bus returning to Baghdad. He was in a rather giggly state, having consoled himself for my absence with a bottle of rum. Back at H4 we cut the split bottom off the offending hose and reclamped it. After some fried eggs at a little Arab restaurant, we drove on to Amman, our headlights picking out an occasional gazelle or jerboa, then the odd Bedouin camp, and finally a group of what Cyril Eland called the 'Glubb Girls', in their fetching uniforms. We reached the Philadelphia Hotel, very westernised by our recent standards, about one in the morning.

Disappointingly, we received a cable here from Reg Highwood, the Representative in Lebanon, saying that James was required urgently, so we had no time to explore Jordan nor, when we got on our way again, the inviting green oasis that heralded Damascus.

The pace of life seemed to quicken as we hit the Sunday traffic at the Lebanese customs post. It was marvellously refreshing to see green mountains again, and as we came over the pass above Beirut and saw the Mediterranean glittering in the sunset below us I felt that we had indeed escaped from our arid deserts to a land flowing with milk and honey. But as we came into the outskirts of the city we saw litter lying everywhere and the streets were hideous with hoardings.

'Pff!' said James. 'Smell that? You can tell we're in the Christian quarter. They do it standing up. You remember the Bible – "even to him that pisseth against the wall"? I think I'd better take over here. The town is rather tricky and the taxi drivers are a menace.' And he banged and crashed through the congested streets, cursing and losing his way until in desperation he summoned a taxi driver to show us the way to the Hotel Biarritz.

The Biarritz was a new hotel overlooking an unfashionable beach on the airport road, and there we found Germaine and the boys. The Council Representative had called on her. 'Oh,' he said 'my name is Highwood. I am the Representative of the British Council here. The accountant will be paying you some money. Goodbye.' Fortunately Germaine had the company of the Falles, who were also marooned there. (Sam Falle, ex-Navy, was a remarkable linguist and the only non-university diplomat I knew to become an ambassador – notwithstanding early distrust from Sir Edwin Chapman-Andrews, his chief in Lebanon, until George Middleton took over, who said he disapproved of people speaking too many languages as it meant they had no time or energy for the finer points of diplomacy.)

Whole floors of the Hotel Biarritz were taken over by families from Saudi Arabia and the Gulf. The womenfolk, swathed in black from head to foot, crawled across the pavement from their Cadillacs to the hotel entrance behind their lords and masters. The manager said they performed all cooking and sanitary operations in the manner to which they were accustomed within the confines of their suites, which they left in such an unbelievable state that they had to be completely redecorated. But it was worth it for the unbelievable rent received.

Late December brought wind and rain. Long breakers came rolling in out of the mist, sweeping away the sandpits where lorries filled up to feed the concrete mixers for the apartment blocks that were eroding the fine old Turkish houses. At 3 in the morning of 22nd December the pride of the Messageries Maritimes fleet, the recently refitted *Champollion*, also came rolling in out of the mist, and when I walked along the clifftop to the office there she was, lying in the surf under the airport lighthouse; its green light had been mistaken for the white harbour light three miles further on. From the hotel, drinking our gin and tonics, we watched her breaking up amidships as the cruiser *Kenya* tried to shield her from the force of the waves. There was apparently no lifeboat in Beirut. Some of the crew swam ashore, but fourteen were drowned in the oily water. By next day everyone else had been brought ashore through the combined efforts of a Lebanese pilot boat, the *Kenya* and, some said, the Israelis, allowed in by special dispensation. The passengers brought to the Biarritz were pilgrims in the charge of a priest, some of them still in nightgowns. The oldest and groggiest pilgrim asked our chambermaid if she would be so good as to oblige him in the same way as King David in his old age had been obliged.

In Lebanon imperial rivalries were still at work. Britain and France were trying to salvage influence lost in Cairo and Jerusalem and threatened in

Algeria, while America and Russia did their best to thwart them. We were still in the Canal Zone, Aden and the Gulf and the French were in Djibouti. In spite of the wartime takeover from the Vichy French by the British 'Spears Mission', the pre-war legacy of the French mandate was still strong in Syria and Lebanon.

The French had promoted the French language in their mandated territories much more actively than the British had promoted English. Consequently French became the first language of many Lebanese, particularly the Maronite Catholics who were ill-qualified in Arabic language and literature or subjects taught in Arabic. In Palestine, however, Arabic had remained the language of instruction in some subjects, while others – particularly in the sciences – were taught in English.

The American University of Beirut (AUB) in its lovely coastal campus was amazingly liberal for a Presbyterian missionary foundation and illustrated a curious paradox. It was an Anglophone campus and for its Arabic and science syllabuses employed relatively more Palestinians than Lebanese; it also had many Arabic- and English-speaking students from outside Lebanon, some of them proceeding from the secondary school in Beirut run by the American Aramco Saudi Arabian Oil Company. For about fifty of these students the Council ran a hostel in an attempt to win friends and influence future leaders of the Middle East, as they had in Egypt before the ravages of nationalism there. As the Palestinian tragedy worsened in the bountiful but nerveless hands of the UN, this did not make for stability on the campus. Nor, when the French-run *Faculté de Médecine* bowed to necessity and sought teachers of English, did it increase our popularity; the *Faculté* declined our offers to recruit teachers and appointed anti-British Boston Fathers instead.

The Council office, library, teaching Institute and hostel shared a fine building in the Muslim quarter of Ras or upper Beirut, between Rue Sadat and the AUB. Reg Highwood, the Council representative, had given distinguished service in Victoria College, Cairo, and, if one was to believe him, had educated most of the leaders of the Middle East. In Beirut there was a London-appointed establishment of eight: Representative, Assistant Representative, Hostel Warden, Education Officer, Director of Studies, Accountant, and two Lecturers at the AUB, with James Wakelin a supernumerary science lecturer there too. The Assistant Representative elected to transfer to the Edinburgh office so that he could study for a PhD, and in January I succeeded him. At last we began to feel part of the local community. But I was also more vulnerable to Highwood's little homilies. 'Ah, Alexander!' he would cry as I slipped past the open door of his office. 'Just come in a minute. I don't know whether you've seen the paper this morning but I'd better put you in the picture about Maurice Chehab and Saeb Salam.' I don't remember him ever showing interest in anything but politics, and yet there was Beirut all round us, fizzing with French, Greek and Italian enterprise, and beyond it the most marvellous mixture imaginable of ancient remains and modern comforts: the sea was on our doorstep, skiing behind us, lovely biblical villages and amusingly vulgar resorts in the foothills, quiet palaces like Beit El Dine and Moukhtara, the still peaceful Baalbek and Château de Beaufort, and over the border Palmyra, Krak des Chevaliers, Damascus, Jerash and, in the brief spring, black irises shining on the way to Petra.

Fortunately there were other old hands more hedonistic than Highwood to help us to appreciate these delights. Attempts to found a Victoria College-style school near Beit el Dine, funded by the FO and wealthy Lebanese entrepreneurs in Africa, were aborted by events in Suez. Meanwhile the warden of our hostel was Alan Morton who was married to Ronald Storrs' step-daughter, Hyacinth. They had no children and had therefore all the more time to cultivate a wide circle of acquaintances. They were affronted when Richard Aldington's debunking biography of T E Lawrence came out for they were frequently hosts to people almost of his era. Lankester Harding, the jazz-loving archaeologist later ejected unceremoniously from Jordan with Glubb Pasha, was one, with his charming Palestinian protégé, Theo Canaan, who guided us round Jerash, only to be killed shortly afterwards in a fall there; Stuart Perowne came from Jerusalem to lecture on Herod and the Romans, Robin Fedden on Crusader castles and Steven Runciman on the Crusades. Old St John Philby arrived a couple of years later to settle on the coast north of Beirut with his Bedouin girl (young Kim Philby being at hand in the bar of the Hotel Normandie when needed). Freya Stark threatened to come several times but did not materialise. Her successor, however, in Ikhwan al-Hurriyah (the Brotherhood of Freedom) was very much there in the person of Christopher Scaife, the most courtly, colourful and civilised of our cultural missionaries.

The Brotherhood was a wartime propaganda organisation encouraging pro-Ally support in Egypt and Iraq, and Christopher, who had damaged an arm at Tobruk, leaving himself unfit for active service and only the back of his left hand index finger with which to play the base on the piano, finished the war as a Lieutenant Colonel in it. Born in 1900, he had lied about his age in the first world war and served in the ranks for eight months until rumbled. It was difficult to reconcile this physical adventurousness with the marked aestheticism that earned him a visiting Professorship of English Literature, initially subsidised by the Council, at thc AUB. Certainly this most spivvy city of Beirut seemed an incongruous one for Christopher to feel at home in. At Oxford he had been President of the Union and the OUDS and had begun a lifelong friendship with Nevill Coghill and Tyrone Guthrie. He joined the Anmer Hall company, in which his sister Gillian was the principal actress, wrote poetry and plays and exercised his skill in madrigals and folk dancing at the strength-through-joy-inclining summer schools of Rolf Gardiner in Dorset. Then in 1927 he abandoned this perhaps too hothouse atmosphere of privileged artiness for the dry winds of Africa. In a what's-become-of-Waring *coup de théâtre* he shocked his friends by accepting the post of lecturer at Cairo University and steadfastly refused their urgings to return to Merrie England. However, as Robert Graves and Bonamy Dobrée had been recent professors in Cairo, and C P Cavafy was still living hospitably in Alexandria, Egypt was by no means the intellectual desert they thought it.

By the time we arrived Christopher had installed himself at Beit Worsley, a Victorian house at Ain Anoub above the airport. It had been on a bleak hillside when the missionary Worsleys, bent on converting the Druse, had first arrived with their drunken English coachman, but it was now set in groves of pine trees. On one's first visit one was bidden to attend the graves in the garden of the two Worsleys, and, at a respectful distance, of their coachman. Inside the house were other shrines, most notably a backlit corner cupboard with a lay figure in the ball dress of Christopher's mother and some of her ornaments. He was looked after by a small 'manservant' called Slivo, who was afflicted by a villainous squint. The road to Ain Anoub corkscrewed up the mountain and it was a miracle how his old Jeep delivered Christopher safely home after convivial evenings in town.

His poetry is mellifluous rather than memorable and is not helped by what Coghill thought was 'a search for a replacement to his actual father', who had left his mother when he was four. Coghill particularly liked the elegiac *Aurelio* written in 1973 in Christopher's Virgilian retreat near Arezzo:

I shall go down that slope, westwards,
No very long time hence – perhaps when its grass is hoar
With frost; or when the starling-plumage landscape
Carries a fall of snow;
Or when the daffodils you planted
Nod underneath the olive trees, or later
When the dark and light blue irises that grow
Where I set them by the track, have broken;
... Or at grape harvest, or when they strip
The olive trees shaped by your pruning.
Whenever – I shall find a way
Up to that gap in the Chianti hills...
Wait, with our flock, Aurelio, for me,
There on the sunset side....

The Council's Director of Studies was John Gayford. For some years he had run the English Junior School in Cyprus, and when I was recuperating from hepatitis he took me over there to meet his friends, notably the archaeologist Peter McGaw and his flower-painting Albanian wife, Electra. This gave us a marvellous introduction to the island's antiquities. I was bowled over by the beauty of Cyprus, but the first Eoka bomb had gone off and the Council Representative, Maurice Cardiff, pacing the creaking floor of his old office building, said gloomily, 'They'll burn the place down sooner or later.' And they did, as I was to remember when my turn came twenty years later.

Lebanon, like Persia but unlike Colombia, had a large enough Council budget to warrant a London-appointed accountant, in this case the experienced but harassed Bob Morrish. The cause of the harassment was his handsome and socially ambitious wife, Joy. Embassy wives of titled husbands – Anne Norwich, for instance, with her abstract paintings – were pursued relentlessly. Even Anne Ponsonby, wife of an Hon., and Margit

Randall, daughter-in-law of a knight, qualified for daily visits. The Morrishes had a house near Canterbury and prominently displayed on their mantelpiece in Beirut was a long out-of-date invitation to a garden party from the Archbishop.

Not long afterwards, sworn to secrecy, I was told by the Morrishes that they were being transferred to Persia, which was opening up again. What, asked Joy, were the formalities for leaving a card on the Shah?

The running sore on the body politic of Lebanon was slow in making itself felt, at least by me. Palestine refugees were so lavishly provided for by the UN that acknowledgement of the hopelessness of their situation was, as it were, postponed with each annual budget. In an early class I gave to refugees the following essay was handed in by Maroun Akiki:

> ENGLAND
> England is a kingdom obeying a king or a queen. She is now obeying a queen named Elizabeth, daughter of George VI the last king of England. England is one of the greatest countries in the world, and she is counted the first country in the world by her politics as she has some genious politic men as: W.Churchill, A Eden, Atly and so on. England is an island. I say an island because I count Scotland and Ireland with her. England is known by her 'Cambridge' and 'Oxford', by her power, by her journalism, by her Parliament, by her agriculture, by her Clock and at last and not at least her own justice. But she didn't use them in the Palestinian Problem.

It was not Palestine but Jordan that beckoned Nevill Coghill, the first visitor I had to deal with, for he was going on to Amman where his elder brother, Patrick, the baronet, was second-in-command to Glubb Pasha. We had, rather rashly I thought, committed him to five lectures on Chaucer and Shakespeare in one week, and a letter home shows that my fears were well founded: 'In spite of excellent and free press publicity he never filled a hall and the AUB only provided audiences of forty and twenty-five. The *Ecole Supérieur* turned out over a hundred but St Joseph only sixty or so, and even the Hostel was by no means full. As usual members of the Embassy were conspicuous by their absence, and as Queen Mary had died at the beginning of the week they didn't even have the excuse of cocktail parties to keep them away. Nevill is a charming unassuming chap and spoke well though not particularly gracefully and he rather lacked fire. He nobly stumbled through two lectures in French.'

In February 1953 Reg and Shirley Highwood departed, leaving behind for their successors, the Morrays, various bottles, some half-empty and all carefully priced. Perhaps Personnel Department found Reggie's fixation on Middle Eastern affairs hard to exploit elsewhere, for they created a new post of Middle Eastern Adviser in London, of which he was the first and last incumbent. His tenure in Lebanon, however, had been long enough to cause a rupture with James Wakelin – so that he felt he could no longer support James's academic role at the AUB. A perennial problem for Council Representatives in remote places is how to preserve quiet personal relationships and at the same time reveal to their subjects, as one was supposed to do, any written criticism in annual personal reports. It was not unusual for a head of post to funk this for the sake of a quiet life, or at least to tone the report down to a meaningless degree.

What happened is a warning of the perils of gossip in incestuous organisations like the FO and the Council, where people are holed up together in lonely situations which encourage confidences. On the other hand this very gossip is the cement that makes the strain of uncomfortable postings and unnatural reticence bearable. But it is a mistake to suppose that secrets told in Timbuctoo will remain there.

James's indiscretion went something like this. In Tehran he had confided to a colleague a clerihew about Reg Highwood, composed by Alan Morton. The colleague was posted to Cairo and quoted it to someone leaving for Beirut, who told it to someone in the AUB, who told it to Highwood. This was the offending verse:

Reg and Shirley
Go to bed early.
If I were Highwood
I don't think I would.

The Highwoods' successors could scarcely have been more different. Tom Morray had the inestimable gifts of effective delegation and warm hospitality. (His recipe for the lethal gin and tonics that made his parties go with such a swing was lots and lots of fresh lemon juice.) He had been decorated for his work in wartime Iraq, and when the young King Feisal and Nuri Es Said paid a state visit to Lebanon and he introduced us to them at the Iraqi Ambassador's reception he was clearly in their good books. There was no dancing at that reception because two Iraqi escort planes had crashed on the way over, but the local girls were constantly edging up to the King and posing for photographs in their French dresses, and one very striking creature had even been flown in from Paris by her family to meet him.

Reg Highwood did in fact return to Beirut in March 1956 for a conference of all Council Representatives in the area. He accompanied our top brass from London and this was the first time I had seen them at work. Somewhat prophetically the conference coincided with an alarming earthquake. The first shock came at 10 at night while we were at a meeting on the fourth floor of the Council hostel. The whole building shook while we sat gazing at each other in dismay. After about forty seconds the shaking stopped and we returned half-heartedly to business. When, ten minutes later, it happened again we broke up in disorder, joining the students going downstairs with their blankets. With the third but lesser shock came the sound of hundreds of cars starting up to drive out of town.

Our own flat was on the ground floor, with only one other above it, so although it was a rather flimsy old Turkish-style house Germaine and I decided to stay put, especially as the children were asleep. High up in a new apartment block next to us lived Tony and Shirley Irving; Tony, an architect (and stage designer for our amateur Phoenix Players group), had chosen to live there with earthquakes in mind, assuring us of the advantages of reinforced concrete over bricks and mortar. However, in the early hours the Irvings moved in with us rather than risk a recurrence of the horrid swaying that had so unnerved their children. The next day we heard that there were a hundred and fifty casualties at the epicentre fifty miles away.

As presaged by the earthquake, all our well-laid plans at the conference to salvage what remained of British influence in the face of rampant nationalism everywhere were blown to pieces by the Suez misadventure that summer. But the Council's Director-General, Sir Paul Sinker, and Chairman, Sir David Kelly, were happily unaware of this outcome as they prepared to rendezvous in Beirut in March.

Sinker was a former Civil Service Commissioner who ran the Council on a tight rein but by remote control. He rarely acted, even by telephone, except through an intermediary, and was supported by a mafia of old Bedford School colleagues who referred to him approvingly as The Headmaster. He was no intellectual and was one of several DGs who, for someone in such a post, seemed curiously ill at ease in foreign countries. After an unusually long run as DG, Sir Paul was succeeded in 1968 by Sir John Henniker-Major from the FO. He was eased out by the mafia after four years, but not before he had broken the long hegemony of our self-perpetuating Personnel Department. Henniker-Major's new style of leadership blew like a breath of fresh air through some of our corridors. Shortly after his installation a friend of mine in a minor London post was astonished to pick up his phone and be greeted by a breezy 'Henniker here!' and a direct question that from Sinker would have been filtered through underlings. The Council has never managed to find a DG with a blend of the Sinker and Henniker qualities and a little cultural charisma to boot. With our Chairmen we have been luckier.

Sir David Kelly, ex-Ambassador to Russia, devout Roman Catholic and author of *The Hungry Sheep*, was a nice old thing with a face like a bloodhound. He was a good trencherman. At one dinner party I sat on the other side of our hostess, Salwa Es-Said, and watched him working his way through his four wine glasses – and then, as she smiled indulgently, through hers. At our meetings one of the few remarks of his I now remember was a dissident note on priorities. The fashionable Council view was to spend lavishly in newly hostile countries like Egypt and Iraq, not to mention India, and if necessary pull out of Europe and South America altogether. Sir David, however, thought that we should not forget our friends or they would forget us.

His pretty-pretty Belgian wife, Marie-Noëlle, who had acquired a brief to advise on Embassy furniture and also aspired to write on feminist subjects, was on the other hand pretty tiresome. A lecture she gave on *Women in Britain* was badly read, and full of dull facts and figures presumably collected for her by someone else. I had assembled a good audience, including Zelpha Chamoun, the President's wife, and was not pleased. I was even less pleased by her insistence on trying to visit Lady Hester Stanhope's tomb at Jezzine. This, as the epicentre of the earthquake and full of homeless and demoralised victims, was out of bounds. She did not like taking 'no' for an answer.

The purpose of the Beirut conference was largely financial. To counter the ill effects of Russian arms sales to Egypt the FO had voted us an extra £120,000, and this meeting had been convened in order to decide how to spend it. The *Daily Express,* hoping to hear proposals for sending morris dancers to Timbuctoo, had sent out a reporter to cover the event.

One of the items on the agenda concerned the siting of the regional successor to Cairo's Victoria College of Cairo. Sinker facetiously suggested converting a liner and mooring it offshore, and next day, more seriously, pointed out that if there was trouble on shore the ship could always move to a less hostile environment. 'And another thing,' said Sir David, 'there'd be no difficulty about the name being too nationalistic, like "Queen Elizabeth College". We could call it simply The Scholar Ship!'

The home and abroad dichotomy was also given its usual airing. Somebody said that people at home seemed to forget that those abroad were in fact abroad at all. They avoided coming to grips with the human problem of underpaid and over-educated staff trying to sell a declining British culture to overpaid and under-educated foreigners. I ventured to point out that a small country like Holland with a one-man legation in Lebanon seemed to do as much business as the British did, and Germany with a three-man legation did ten times as much. Even Italy, with a mere half dozen, had knocked us out of the small car market. Yet the British Embassy, with forty 'UK-based' staff, had little to show for it except oil and aeroplanes, and we in the Council had nothing to compare with the French, Americans and Germans in the way of schools, teachers or artistic manifestations. Were big institutions, full of people taking in each other's washing, as effective as a large number of small ones?

I spoke feelingly on this subject because I had recently had my first experience of an embassy 'Prayer Meeting' when standing in for Tom Morray during his home leave. 'Yesterday,' I wrote in a letter home, 'I arrived to find five well-paid and intelligent blokes sitting round smoking furiously and wrestling with one of their many reports. This one was about student societies here and the Communist element in them. We had a long discussion and smoked a lot of cigarettes; minutes were added to the report; several vague recommendations were made, such as that I should ask the Director of Education unofficially whether he had trouble with Communism among the teachers themselves, and that the most anti-Communist teachers' society should be encouraged as much as possible; and the meeting broke up. I cannot help thinking that if there were less cloak-and-dagger stuff and more subsidising of professional posts abroad everyone would be much happier and the world would stagger forward a few paces in the right direction. It's all this damned theorising that ruins things and people – advisers to advisers to advisers, and no-one actually creating anything.'

Our colleagues from London were understandably touchy on the question of staffing and bureaucracy. Jerry Earle, the combative Representative in Syria, pointed out that our staffing structure did not reflect our avowed priorities. For many years, he said, we had been told that the most important countries for Council work were the least salubrious ones such as those in the Far East or the Persian Gulf. Staff there, however, were all comparatively low grade, while influential people in the Council still managed to stay on in Europe, where we had virtually stopped operating. Out of only five Grade B posts abroad, one was in India, one in Egypt and three in Europe. Why, if underdeveloped countries were so important, were not the most highly paid and presumably important staff sent to them?

However, this was not the sort of thing our HQ staff wanted to discuss, and our attention was redirected to the launching of the good scholar ship, *Queen Elizabeth*, which in the event was never to materialise, either ashore or afloat.

In the middle of one of our meetings St John Philby called to pay his respects and was greeted in some confusion. Was he a world-famous explorer or, bureaucratically speaking, a mischief-maker who had gone native? In the end homage was paid to age but the conversation remained stilted. St John's son was ostensibly the *Observer* correspondent and did not pay his respects, but I had met him at the home of Dick and Moyra Beeston of the *Telegraph*. Kim Philby was an attractive character when sober, with an endearing stammer, the sort of accent more often heard in the Guards Club than in the streets of Beirut, and a flattering air of confidentiality, as though only you and he knew what you were talking about. He seemed an unusually establishment figure to find among journalists, but I never had an inkling that he was other than he pretended to be. The only anomaly seemed to be his bar bill at the Hotel Normandie, where he held permanent court. With his family commitments in England and little to expect from his father, I was surprised he could afford it on the salary of a foreign correspondent.

As for the correspondent of the *Daily Express*, there were no scandals to report, and his sub-editor was so busy adding some of his own to his copy that he omitted to correct his naming of our Chairman as Sir GERALD Kelly. This was, I suppose, a rare example of art triumphing over politics.

7
Upstaged

I HADN'T BEEN LONG in Lebanon when Christopher Scaife asked me to act in his production of *You Never Can Tell* at the AUB. My flirtation with the stage in Colombia and Persia had been mainly in order to entertain the foreign colony and such locals as spoke good English and liked to exercise it. In Lebanon the student audience was more sophisticated and amateur performances and dramatised play readings were serious teaching aids for the curricula of both AUB and of our own students preparing for Cambridge examinations.

Besides this, the Lebanese were anxious to attract professional companies to Beirut and expand its tourist appeal for visitors formerly drawn to Egypt. As entrepreneurs they had already established the best restaurants and nightclubs in the Middle East and would soon open a lavish casino up the coast at Joûnié. More serious drama productions could only improve the country's reputation as a major contender for international conferences. The annual Middle East Medical Symposium, for instance, took place in February and it was remarkable how many distinguished medicos found it convenient to leave the cold grey skies of Britain for a week in the sun. As for cultural manifestations, the Lebanese were adept at playing off the French and British against each other, and what started as concerts and plays in less than glamorous halls in Beirut soon spread to magical festivals at Baalbek.

I still remember vividly the first visit of the Old Vic under Michael Benthall. They performed *Anthony and Cleopatra*, an obvious favourite in that area, and, with some misgiving that turned out to be unjustified, *The Merchant of Venice*, with Robert Helpmann as a rather tactful Shylock. They were splendid performances and a great success and the company was the first of many who were a joy to look after.

We did not presume to compare performances of this kind with our own efforts, but ours did create a favourable climate for visiting performers; so much so that sooner or later the question of priorities had to be faced. How much time was it reasonable to devote to intellectual interests of one's own, as against those of the nine-to-five curriculum of the British Council? The Council has rightly been indulgent of such outside interests, partly because of the spin-off to local British influence but also because they add lustre to the reputation of the Council at large as a cultural (rather than a civil service) organisation. Besides its novelists – mostly short-contract academics like D J Enright and Francis King – the Council's permanent staff has had its songbirds (Bernard Spencer, John Press and Ronald Bottrall), its historians (Michael Grant and Roddy Cavaliero), and its philosopher (E W F Tomlin). There have also been gifted musicians and artists who have enlivened the local scene. Nevertheless it is surprising that a so-called cultural organisation has produced no really big names for posterity. Perhaps the Council should have nurtured its budding geniuses more actively; possibly the unsocial hours and quarters discouraged such men and women from joining; possibly it was our destiny to be popularisers, not specialists. But even as popularisers we tended to divide into the sheep and the goats – the ambitious sheep safely grazing their way to the top and the uncertain goats straying into fields of cultural nourishment rather than promotion.

In Beirut I moved from acting to directing, in Hong Kong and Guyana to radio, in Cyprus to dramatised play-readings; local circumstances favoured different forms.

Christopher Scaife was a perfectionist and his rehearsals for university productions were intolerably long. With play-readings or one-act plays at the Council Institute he was marvellously inventive but with the bit between his teeth at the AUB there was no holding him. I think with amateurs compromises have to be made; the director must do the best he can to preserve the spirit of the play without upsetting the cast.

One of the first Phoenix Players' productions, the contemporary London hit but now antediluvian *Chiltern Hundreds*, gave me my first lesson in unexpected audience reaction. The butler who aspires to Parliament was played by the British Consul, Donald Jackson, and, as in all West End plays of the time, he does a lot of answering the telephone. For some reason the manner in which the tail-coated Donald lifted the receiver and said 'Hello?' sent the students into paroxysms. Each time the phone rang and Donald entered right and walked across the stage to telephone left the tension mounted with each step, to burst, as he intoned 'Hello?', in an explosion of mirth. Donald, as befitted a diplomat, maintained an impeccable reserve thus, in the best comic tradition, crowning his fondest expectations.

There were other anglophone groups besides the Phoenix Players and Christopher's University company. Afif Bulos, a Palestinian lecturer in music, produced *Iolanthe* with himself as Private Willis and John Julius Norwich as Strephon. (John Julius, Second Secretary at the Embassy, who used to accompany himself on the guitar, had a voice that was pleasing but not always quite true. Lady Diana Cooper and Raymond Mortimer attended the performance and the Mortons were invited to dine with them. 'Oh, God!' said Alan, 'I hope she doesn't do the Miracle again.')

I was helped in my productions by Fred Royal, a professional actor teaching at the AUB, and by Bill Blatty, a quiet-spoken half-Lebanese American from the US Embassy. We were in accord over the nuts and bolts of production but differed in our views on theatre as essentially entertainment (for me) or heavy drama (for Bill). He and his wife and family were devout

Catholics but Bill found time to exercise the American urge for self-improvement, particularly in writing. His great moment came with the acceptance of an article by the *Saturday Evening Post*. It was heavily edited but, for the then enormous fee of $500, this was acceptable. The article described how Bill, who looked more American than Lebanese but spoke Arabic, was able to understand and report the gossip, trivial or political, that went on around him in cafés or bars. Not long afterwards, with that American adventurousness that I have always so much envied, Bill left the State Department to take a writing course and in 1970 hit the jackpot, as 'William Peter Blatty', with his film *The Exorcist*. (At about the same time John Julius, who had sensibly abandoned the Foreign Office, hit *his* jackpot with the history of the Normans in Italy.)

Bill's transition from amateur to professional status confirms my belief that the Council should have been more active in combining the two to promote drama overseas. Major manifestations like the Old Vic were all very well, but they cost the earth, were very rare and only reached the larger representations. The off-stage charm and interests of the company had no time to enrich the local scene and enliven the regime of Council staff and British residents. Meanwhile, Britain was full of competent actors who were 'resting', and overseas posts were full of people happy to put them up. Why couldn't the Council form its own overseas repertory companies to exploit local hospitality and goodwill to the maximum and so keep expenses to the minimum?

I wrote a long and earnest letter to our Arts head in London (Sir Kenneth Loch, whom I never met) and he wrote me a long and earnest reply explaining its impracticalities. I do not blame him, given the inflexibility of our accounting system in those days, and the Council's terror of the Beaverbrook press, which the Beaver was still enjoining to sniff out absurdities in Council programmes. Nowadays a peripatetic repertory system would indeed be impractical because actors are more exigent, and overseas posts are more closely linked to metropolitan culture by screen or air travel. But the idea has caught on in some of the hairier posts where small groups do now stay longer in co-operative and instructional roles.

In 1957 a young Council lecturer in the person of Donald Reeves arrived in Beirut and was put into a flat with another bachelor, Henry Carr, recently posted to the Embassy. Earnest, organ-playing and a potential ordinand, Donald was a natural for young Romanov in my production of Peter Ustinov's *Romanov and Juliet*. Christopher was the general, Germaine Mrs Romanov, and the play went well. The Chamouns attended with their escort, whose rifles clattered on the floor from time to time. Juliet was played by Bea Russell, an archetypal blonde with a cascade of fair hair, the wife of an American diplomat.

After three years in Beirut Donald left the Council for the Church – Cuddesdon, Maidstone, Southwark (as Mervyn Stockwood's chaplain) and (as vicar for twelve years) Morden, where a controversial fresco was evidence of his flair for publicity. Somewhere along the line he went to

Chicago to study urban deprivation and as part of a training course had had to spend a week on the streets with only a dollar in his pocket. From this he emerged with a new reforming zeal and a talent for making things happen. His bishop called him 'an enabler', though critics pointed out that what he enabled to happen, such as CND activity, while initially exciting was not necessarily a good thing in the end. In 1980 he became Rector of St James's, Piccadilly, and when I dropped into an evensong there I found myself in a congregation of half a dozen old ladies. Donald had filled out a bit and looked authoritative in a white cassock. He had been given a free hand, he said, to bring life back to St James's, which would otherwise be made redundant. The aged and bitter Trevor Huddleston and some church staff were living with him in the seven-bedroom rectory. I thought he was on a losing wicket, but I was wrong. He was soon headlined as 'THE TRENDIEST CHURCHMAN IN CHRISTENDOM' and the next time I saw St James's the forecourt was a flea market of tarot cards, ethnic junk, clowns' equipment and funny foods. Notice boards announced lectures by icons of the Left like Tony Benn and Bruce Kent and of the Right like Teddy Taylor, with a plethora of activities of the 'Alternative Society': 'Psychoneuroimmunology and the Language of the Bodymind', Chakra Breathing Prayer, Irish Heritage-Romancing Rebellion, Shamanic Counselling, Wiccan Traditions, Zodiac Indicators and The Findhorn Foundation. As if some of these activities raised even Donald's eyebrows (or more likely those of the bemused Bishop of London, shown on TV attending a service with barefoot women in diaphanous draperies dancing down the aisles) the programmes featured:

> A Friendly Disclaimer
> Although St James's Church, in its openness of heart and mind, includes Alternatives, the ideas in the Alternatives programme are not representative of the Church itself.

I wonder if the moneylenders in the Temple would have escaped a scourging had the Pharisees pinned up a similarly friendly disclaimer. Yet if I ask what Donald's shenanigans at St James's had to do with Christianity I should also ask what my amateur dramatics had to do with British Culture. What should Council lecturers inflict upon foreign audiences? I had nothing to do with the Gilbert and Sullivan performances in Beirut, but I lectured about them because they are uniquely British and have introduced so many people to classical music. (As a schoolboy fan of the D'Oyly Carte shows I soon found that there were other composers – Mozart, for instance, or the madrigalists – that were really 'almost as good'.) I have no idea what the Lebanese made of it, but I suppose I was giving rein to the same exhibitionism in what I thought was a good cause that Donald was to do later. Without indulging our interests, one might almost say hobbies, in this way, St James's would have remained empty and the Council classrooms, at least as far as I was concerned, unrewarding places to work in. Where, I wonder, would Donald have ended up if he'd stayed in the Council, or I if I had decided to take holy orders?

'What do you think about,' I asked Bea Russell after a rehearsal one day, 'when you have to hold that clinch with your head on Donald's shoulder? Do you think beautiful thoughts about Holy Russia? You look so soulful.'

'Do I? I'm probably counting the egg stains on Donald's jacket.'

And Donald, asked the same question by Germaine, said revealingly, 'I'm listening to other people's lines to see how much longer I've got to go on kissing that awful woman.'

Alas! Our comedy was to end in tragedy for Bea. The Russells were posted to the Gulf, where on a desert trip their jeep stalled in the middle of nowhere. Bea stayed with the jeep and was eventually rescued but Russell, who had gone off to get help, died in the desert.

And in the desert of the not-so-swinging seventies, at about the time that Donald was being inducted as Rector of St James's, Piccadilly, his old Beirut flatmate, Henry Carr, 'aged fifty-one, divorced father of two', according to the tabloids, 'was found naked and stabbed in his burning flat in Cathcart Road, Kensington'.

8
La Riviera Libanaise

BEIRUT IN THE FIFTIES was a good place in which to bring up children. The flat and garden that we found in a Turkish-type house in Ras Beirut near the office was also uncomfortably near a mosque which woke us at dawn with its amplified and cracked recording of the muezzin. The garden was nothing in comparison with our Tajrish one in Iran but was just large enough for Gus and Nick to let off steam in.

The corniche was not far away, where we could swim off the rocks, deafened by Elvis Presley singing *You Are My Destiny* and entertained by the local body builders endlessly shaving and oiling each other's bodies. At weekends we could drive down the coast in the old convertible Dodge I had bought to replace a hopelessly unreliable second-hand Standard Vanguard. (Some taxi drivers trying to compete with drivers of Mercedes diesels, bought Standard Vanguards with Perkins diesel engines; they were disastrous.) At that time the coast road, with its abandoned railway line (a ratchet railway still crept over the hills to Damascus) was as yet uncluttered as it ran down to Damur River, through the Maronite villages of the Chamoun family. Even the airport had not yet attracted the urban development and refugee camps that changed the whole landscape so drastically.

I was sitting one day in Mohammed Bey Salam's grand house overlooking it all and remarked on the beauty of the coastline.

'Yes,' said Mohamed Bey, 'we used to be able to walk straight down to the sea from this house, and where the airport lies there were fine thick pine woods. The airport is a great nuisance. It makes an awful noise all day and half the night.'

'Who owned the land that the airport is built on?'

'I did.'

At Damur we could choose whether to swim in the sea or in the river which ran down from Beit Ed Dine and the Druse hill country where HMG had bought land for Queen Elizabeth College. Some people thought we should have subsidised the existing Quaker school in the Beirut foothills at Brumana instead. As befitted a Quaker foundation, it was (then) the essence of peace and tranquillity. I once arranged a lecture there by the musician and composer, John Gardner. It was to begin at 6.30 and the headmaster had suggested we arrive at 5.30 to 'meet the staff over tea'. One is always tense before a lecture, particularly one like John's which was to include his own illustrations on the piano, and a cup of tea to break the ice and settle the butterflies had sounded like a good idea. What had not occurred to me was the significance of these particular Quakers coming from Yorkshire. When we arrived, instead of sitting quietly on an airy verandah sipping tea in the cool of the evening, we were ushered into a dining room and seated at a table groaning with food. The entire staff was there and the hubbub served to thicken an atmosphere steaming with honest sweat and savoury smells. Dish after dish was borne in from the kitchen – bread and butter, fruit cake, biscuits and fruit were followed by potatoes, vegetables, roast beef and ... Yorkshire pudding. Poor John literally turned green and had to excuse himself.

He had composed attractive carols and motets and was gestating his opera *'The Moon and Sixpence'*, but also had up his sleeve an irreverent piece on the wreck of the *Titanic*, with the rollicking refrain, 'It was sad, it was sad, it was sad when that great ship went down!' The piece reminded me of a contemporary pianist, Joe Cooper, whom he knew and who had been at school with me. During my next leave Joe asked me if he could branch out from his Prom concertos into tours for the Council, and I put his proposal to our musical adviser, Avril Wood, daughter of Sir Henry. 'Oh dear!' she said, 'I'm afraid not! Too many wrong notes!' Joe, who had delighted us with his party pieces (for example, *Three Blind Mice* in the manner of Bach, Wagner, Stravinsky, or Hutch), had not made it into the classical big time. Yet it was eventually those party pieces that got him into the even bigger time of 'Face the Music' on television.

To John Gardner another source of embarrassment beside the Brumana tea arose from a delegation of local jazz composers who sought his aid in publishing their works in London. 'How can I help them?' he whispered. 'Don't they realise that Wardour Street is Jewish from end to end?'

Further up in the mountains was another spectacular place for children, which a quirk of Foreign Office indulgence made available to us. To give respite from the sticky summer smog diplomatic families and Council families had their expenses paid to 'estivate'. They could either move to summer homes in the nearer hills from which the wage earner would commute down to his Beirut office, or they could take shorter holidays in higher hills, which is what we did at the Victoria Hotel in Ain Zahalta, run by the Anglican bachelor Majoum brothers. The climate was hot and dry by day and cold enough in the cavernous bedrooms at night for two blankets. Donkey tracks led up past some cedars and over the lonely, bare passes of the Jebel Barouk to the Bekaa, and one really felt on top of the ancient world there. The children loved the place, with its bumpy grass tennis court and an irrigation tank they could swim in – not to mention a nearby rubbish tip haunted by hyenas. In the hall were engravings of Queen Victoria, Edward VII and Alexandra, and the bookshelves groaned under religious works of the nineties, one of them presented by a Mrs Alexander (no relation). It was a select hotel – no tric-trac, no radio, no newspapers; just wealthy Egyptians chattering in cane chairs on the terrace, with cicadas scraping away among the pines.

One night we didn't get to bed until 2.30, after attending a Comédie Française production of a voguish piece of whimsy, *La Guerre de Troie n'aura pas Lieu,* in the Temple of Bacchus at Baalbek. On the way we had supper at Zahlé, where a stream flowing through a gorge had been enclosed by a dozen or so enormous cafés in a kaleidoscope of lights. It was a remarkable contrast to the sophisticated simplicity of Baalbek where even the bats flickering in and out of the footlights added to the authenticity of the scene. The floodlighting was magical, with the vast Jupiter pillars glowing softly above us away on the right, and the brightly lit Temple of Bacchus brought back to wondrous life.

Our children learned to swim at the British Club in St George's Bay where the swimming was presided over by the ancient walrus-moustached Hassan, who had taught countless children to swim by tying gourds round their waists.

St George's Bay, with the St George's Hotel, was a haven of old-fashioned if slightly seedy quiet. Coming down the taxi-choked hill from Ras Beirut one found in the palm trees and memorials of the Place des Canons a reminder of pre-war French elegance. Away on the right was the even more elegant Quartier Sursok with its Turkish houses. (In the grandest of these Desmond Cochrane, descendant of the dashing and contentious Thomas, had slung his hammock with the Sursok family and was Irish Vice-Consul.) On the bay of St George itself was the faded elegance of the old Grand Bassoul Hotel where Gertrude Bell had stayed and the always deserted Australian Bar of the Polish 'Anzac Harry' with his 'Tea As Mother Made It'.

There was still plenty of unspoilt coast on the Tripoli road running northwards. Where it crossed the Nar el Kelb (Dog River) rocks bore graffiti of two world wars and others as far back as Rameses II and the kings of Assyria. Beyond Joûnié the road crossed the Nahr Ibrahim, and nearby was a Roman aqueduct repaired by the Arabs and renamed Qanatir Zébeidé (the Arches of Zenobia). From here a path ran up the valley to the river's source at Afqa, where it issues from the Cave of Adonis. Time and again in Lebanon, to scratch the surface was to uncover classical and mythical sites. Yet the land, at least in the towns, was also a spiv's paradise where people spoke many languages, were ever ready to do you a service, were ever outgoing, friendly and egalitarian in a 'you-scratch-my-back-I'll-scratch-yours' way. Perhaps the ancients were similarly sensitive to the main chance, and the Romans did no more than facilitate the enterprise of the Phoenicians.

A few kilometres further on, Byblos was still biblical in feel, with its donkeys and winnowing grounds, and a living calendar in stone from Alexander to the Crusader church of St John the Baptist. Eventually the road climbed to the HQ of the Maronite Patriarch and the frivolities of the ski centre on the sunlit slopes beneath the few remaining but still famous Cedars. Primitive as it was, the centre was a favourite of Beirut society, not least because it was tacitly accepted that whatever went on there would not be bandied about in Beirut or Tripoli. However, this discretion didn't always seem to apply the other way round. When I danced with Zelpha Chamoun she chattered away uninhibitedly about Camille saying this, and Camille doing that, and about the domestic habits of *le tout Beirut* and the financial affairs of wheeler-dealers who were mere names in the headlines to me.

The social round in Beirut was increased by the size of the British Embassy and its adjuncts: the British Middle East Office, which had inherited area responsibilities from Cairo, and MECAS, the Middle East Centre for Arabic Studies up the hill at Shemlan. Our first Head of Chancery was John Barnes, son of the 'controversial' Bishop of Birmingham. Other members of the staff included Eddie Gathorne-Hardy, who was busy collecting *double entendres* from impeccable sources like Jane Austen of the 'Fanny loved balls' kind; Ian Scott, one of three remarkable brothers educated at Queen's Royal College, Trinidad, and his wife, Drusilla, a daughter of Lord Lindsay of Oxford; while Bob Porter's wife, Thea, sister of the Middle East correspondent and London gallery owner Patrick Seale, was to become a top London dress designer.

We owed a lot to embassy staff for helping in plays and play-readings and for relaxation after being on our best official behaviour with 'clients'. They opened windows onto the political worlds beyond our classrooms and lecture halls, and introduced us to 'The Game', i.e. dumb crambo. (Who could have guessed that forty years later the BBC would be spending tax payers' money on a succession of nonentities playing it on camera?)

Embassy friends were also useful in having better cars than ours and being more venturesome in them than we could be. On one occasion I abandoned the family and my old Dodge convertible, which was fine for holding its own with Beirut taxis but risky on long journeys, to drive with friends to Jerusalem and Petra. (This was before the tourists got at them.) We slept in army tents and ate bully beef and tinned plum and apple jam that seemed to have 'walked' from Aqaba. In the High Place there was nobody but us to greet the dawn. Yet just as unforgettable was an incident in the cave where Diana Kirkbride was living while she did some archaeological work. We were sitting with an American visitor whose business I forget, while she displayed some of her precious finds – among them a number of flints. As she discoursed on their provenance he took one up and proceeded to clean his nails with it. She was too well bred to protest, but I have seldom seen more horror in a woman's eyes.

I had switched from learning Persian to Arabic when I reached Lebanon, but learning difficult languages is a full-time job and I soon took the softer option of improving my schoolboy French. As an official local language, the cost of French lessons was refundable by the Council. My teacher was a Bordelaise, Françoise Dahan, wife of a humble member of the Embassy. When she went on leave she passed me on to another Bordelaise married to a man in Shell. Perhaps it was because she was leaving that Françoise was so forthcoming about her likes and dislikes. One of her likes was a nice-looking but prim and proper young student at Shemlan named Anthony Acland. Had she known he would eventually head the FO she might have liked him even more. As it was, I was astounded to hear, after leaving Lebanon, that she and

Sir George Middleton were to be seen wheeling their baby about the streets of Kensington. It was the flighty Françoise who was Lady Middleton when George retired as Ambassador to the United Arab Republics, no longer the forthright, horse-riding, bridge-playing Tina. I found it rather endearing that a tough and worldly character like George could be ruled by the same human frailties as the rest of us.

The social round of one country does not always suit those used to that of another. My brother Noel ('Robin' to the family and still in the Chinese Protectorate branch of the Malayan Civil Service) paid us a visit on his way home on leave and never quite got used to our politics, our time scale or our drinking habits. In Lebanon he was thrilled to see so many creeds represented and it was difficult to get him past any Maronite, Greek Orthodox or Greek Catholic church, or to drive him past a priest without giving him a lift. Yet the diversity of faiths, which Noel found so intriguing and which had at first come to me as a pleasant change from the monolithic Shiite fundamentalism of Iran, appeared more conducive to mutual suspicion than tolerance.

Just as the diversity of churches went to Noel's head, so did the diversity of drinks. After the leisurely downing of long *stengahs* in Malaya, the rapid succession of spirits and wines at Tom Morray's table caught him unprepared. Tom, who had taught at Raffles College before the war, was eager to talk about Malaya, and his patience was sorely tried by Noel's unstoppable monologue.

'Yes, I opened a British Council exhibition on Westminster Abbey in Kuala Lumpur. Half of it hadn't turned up and there were only eight people in the audience. "Why don't they come?" asked the Council chap, Brady. "It was announced on the wireless two weeks ago!" Next day there was a photo of me in the paper and a headline "ONLY 8 PEOPLE AT THE BRITISH COUNCIL". A week later the exhibition moved on to Penang and the newspapers headlined "ONLY 7 MORE PEOPLE THAN AT KL AT THE BRITISH COUNCIL". The same thing happened all over Malaya. But Templar is pro-Council. He says "I know Winston's allergic to the British Council but I think it's a bloody good thing".'

I don't know what Noel would have made of his fellow, though older, Old Cliftonian who arrived a year later. I A Richards was one of our more interesting, and idiosyncratic, visitors because his book, *Practical Criticism*, had provided an endless source of argument for me and my fellow FEPOWs when we were guests of the Japanese in Thailand. He was to bring his wife who, to my alarm, was described in *20th-century Authors* as 'also a writer'. In the glossy landscape of Beirut she and the gnomelike Richards made a quaint couple with their rucksacks and hiking boots. But whereas I A was a stimulating talker on and off stage, Dorothy, with her old-fashioned bangs over the ears, was not, though she liked to have her say. Only liberality with drinks could remove her as a serious contender for attention.

I A was at that time in Harvard, teaching – as he put it – Americans to read by the means of TV 'before they become totally illiterate'. His lectures on 'Reading a Poem' and 'What is Man?' were cunningly delivered and illustrated by the kind of diagrams with which he claims in his books to make the abstruse simple. He would start off his lectures by inveigling his audience into deep waters unawares. 'Now I'm not going to say anything important for a moment, while you get used to my voice. I'll just say what I'm doing here and how I came to be here and what I hope to cover in my lectures. Or perhaps I should start by saying what I shall *not* cover in my lectures, because the words philosophy and linguistics sometimes put people off. They are rather like poetry in this. And like poetry they are really very simple, if you are not afraid of them. For example you may have seen some of those mannered poems – George Herbert used to do some – written so as to imitate certain shapes, a diamond perhaps, or a cross, like this ....' And he would draw some shapes on the blackboard. 'Some people think this is a very frivolous way of approaching a kind of sacred ritual, but I find shapes and diagrams useful anchors on which to float even the most sophisticated theories. For example, I could represent Einstein's Theorem like this ...' and he would change colour for a few lines and dots, 'and of course you see at once what I am driving at. But I am no Einstein and what I am going to talk about is not so much facts and theories as the language in which we express them. So if this circle is the world, say, and we divide it into the proportions of literate and illiterate people ... like this, and then do the same for it 2000, 12,000 and 50,000 years ago ... and, if things go on as they are going now, in 100 years' time ... it would look like this....' And before we knew where we were we would be well into the deep end and, as far as I was concerned, pretty much out of my depth. Not that it mattered. I A was entertaining and if his message was ephemeral so, in due course, would be those of successors like Chomsky.

The Richards left us for Turkey and I received a thank you letter from Dorothy in Istanbul. It enclosed a 5 piastre piece neatly embedded in a bit of cardboard. 'The bitch!' exclaimed Tom Morray who had been exasperated by the chores she had saddled us with; he had come into my office one morning shaking with rage and carrying a pair of old shoes she had asked him to get mended for her. Excellent with the more worldly of our visitors such as high-flying consultants, Tom was never at his best with intellectuals; he was horrified to hear that the scruffy Ivor Richards earned $20,000 a year at Harvard.

The Richards's visit was child's play compared with two others, from which an attack of infectious hepatitis insulated me. Both visitors were notorious for the space they occupied in Council files. The first, Dorothy Neville-Rolfe, came from a small village near Bristol where her father, a ship's captain, had a charming cottage with a scroll painted on it, reading 'TOMORROW'S TANGLE TO THE WINDS RESIGN'. She had been at school with my sister Margery who described her as 'very ladylike, if it is possible for someone slightly masculine to be ladylike'. Perhaps it was having to lie on her back with spinal caries for a year that had made her career-minded, for after teaching at Westonbirt she became principal of Ashridge College, a finishing-cum-business school for young ladies. She liked to combine holidays with touting for overseas students and collecting fees for British Council lectures.

James Wakelin, by now our man in Lahore, had had to look after Miss Neville-Rolfe in the hot season when all the VIPs she had expected to meet were up in the hills. James had only just arrived at post ahead of his family and knew no-one. He suffered endless tête-à-tête meals with her and paid her for three lectures to audiences of 13, 15 and 20. Unable to put her up himself and unauthorised to pay for her accommodation as she was not an officially sponsored visitor, he had to use her fees to pay her hotel bill. When she left she said that she considered it part of her duty to report on Council staff overseas when she got back home. (Our man in India sent us his own 'Private and Confidential' report, beginning: 'Miss Rolfe is a pain in the neck ...' and going on to describe the dullness of her lectures and her overbearing demands, but he added a note of warning that although her lectures were not officially sponsored by the Council she was allegedly a friend of the new DG.)

It was Easter, in Lebanon not a propitious time for audiences in a country that celebrates two Easters, the Maronite and the Greek Orthodox. We already had a mixed bag of visitors lined up: Eiluned Lewis, the rural poetess, Sir George Thomson, physicist and son of J J Thomson, a Dr Sturley of BBC Engineering, Watkin Shaw of Tenbury Wells College, also L Dudley Stamp, the prolific author of school geography books and one of the first businesslike academics to come to my attention. (He had a Cockney-like pride in his methods. During the war he had been employed by the government, driven by a government-paid chauffeur – his wife – in a government car that he had had commandeered from himself. With his American royalties he had formed himself into a limited liability company and he had property in Canada, whither his son had emigrated.)

We had already declined a lecture from one Bristolian on the not very alluring subject of *The Life of a J P* and now did so again. Undaunted, Miss Neville-Rolfe replied, enclosing a long list of lecture titles 'just in case' and saying that she had told the wealthy father of a Moslem Lebanese girl we had sent to her that she was coming to Beirut and he had replied 'offering me the earth. Could you find out if I may take this to include free accommodation for me?' Greatly shocked that formal expressions of politeness should be taken so literally, Tom rang up her putative host who, after a pause, expressed great delight at the prospect of seeing Miss Rolfe and said he would at once reserve a room for her at the St Georges Hotel. The sea-girt St Georges was enough to melt a heart of stone, so it may or may not have been a coincidence that it was not long after this that Tom got his OBE.

Our second importunate visitor was at least a more glamorous one, for he was titled and well-off and looked like a Greek god. I had known Sir Eugen Millington-Drake by hearsay in Colombia. I heard of him again from Malaya, where Noel had been at a dinner with him and seen him fall asleep at the table. Millington-Drake's apogee had been reached in wartime Uruguay, where he was Minister when the *Graf Spee* was sunk. Thereafter he represented the Council in Argentina and, after retirement, chose to be a kind of cultural Flying Englishman, storm-tossed on the winds of missionary enthusiasm and fated to land only where he could lecture on 'The Olympic

Games' or recite 'Gems from English Poetry'. His private means and personal contacts made the world his oyster, and remote indeed were the Council offices that did not sooner or later receive a packet of his prospective talks.

Undaunted by our inability to fit him into our own lecture programme, he asked us to put him on elsewhere, 'if you would be kind enough to arrange it', and we managed to send him to the *Alliance Française* for 'Gems in French and English Poetry' and to the strictly sedentary Brumana High School for 'The British Tradition of Sport'. He was staying with the Irish Consul, Sir Desmond Cochrane, and Linda Sursok, and our friends Edward and Sue Southby were asked to dine with them. At 10pm Sir Eugen dropped off, remaining asleep till 11.30. As the guests started to leave he came to and prevailed on a group to go to the Caves du Roy, where he danced spiritedly till 3 in the morning.

Edward, who had been in the Foreign Office in the war, described Sir Eugen's departure from Montevideo. He had arranged for a special band to play him out of the harbour, with floodlights focussed on him as he waved goodbye from the ship's deck. Hearing at the last moment that he'd have to stay on a few weeks longer he went through the whole performance, slipping quietly ashore again as the ship steamed out of the harbour. When he finally left he did so incognito.

There were two sequels to his visit. A week later Brumana High School declined our offer of a lecture from an official Council visitor, while Sir Eugen wrote a letter of thanks saying there was obviously such a rich field for activity in Lebanon that he hoped to return the following year for a longer stay. 'And may I say,' he concluded in his letter to Tom, 'what a tight ship you run there and how well I thought you looked the part?' Sixteen years later, on succeeding George de Saumarez in Caracas, I inherited the Millington-Drake file which ran to pages of confident proposals and requests on the one hand and ever firmer excuses from two successive ambassadors on the other.

Sir Eugen never got to Caracas so I never heard his 'Gems of English Poetry'. However, they are described by Maurice Cardiff in his book of reminiscences, *Friends Abroad.* It was Laurence Durrell who, during his brief and unhappy Council posting to Cordoba in Argentina, having seen Sir Eugen in action, recommended him to Maurice in Cyprus in 1954. 'From first line to last,' writes Maurice, 'the recital with its vocal inflexions and the gestures, which accompanied them, held his audience, schoolboys and all, silent and amazed. "I shot an arrow into the air ..." As he drew one hand away from the other, you could hear the bowstring twang ...' And in 1971 it was Maurice, by then our man in Paris, who witnessed and most poignantly described the one and only occasion when Sir Eugen's lecture was pre-empted by a prior and inescapable engagement. It is, incidentally, a strange reflection on mortality, and a reversal of the *'ars longa vita brevis'* tag, that Maurice Cardiff, author and distinguished career Officer, will be remembered not for this but as a minor character in the pages of a best-selling novel, *Captain Corelli's Mandolin* by Louis de Bernières.

9
Family Frailties

OF ALL MY COUNCIL POSTS Beirut was my favourite; it was so beautiful and so much was going on there. Our children were at the age when parents and children are most inspiring to each other, and the British colony was a hospitable one, spanning several generations. There were old hands like the Jollys and the Southbys, the Goslings of the Ottoman Bank (with their country dancing parties), and Norman Nairne (whose buses had pioneered the desert route to Baghdad); there were the pilots of Middle East Airlines and Air Liban; there were the staff of the AUB, Shell and the Iraq Petroleum Company (IPC); there were dozens of journalists; there were mystery men and women who would appear at cocktail parties and establish high profiles, only to vanish a few weeks later; there were the UNWRA staff, busy sweeping the Palestinian Problem under their expensive carpet; and there were frequent courtesy visits from the Royal Navy.

However, events began to take a more serious turn as the stresses of Suez heightened the tensions of daily life. The odd bomb was exploded, one under the car of a politician, blowing off his legs. In 1955 the Dutch wife of a student at the AUB sleepwalked out of a window, and the French wife of a cabaret proprietor was murdered. When the old caretaker at the Belgian Legation was beaten to death one night, her small grandson recognised her assailant as the Belgian First Secretary. He had been in the Free Belgian air force during the war, and had married his Birmingham landlord's daughter. Since then he had had treatment in mental hospitals. His wife had taken their two children home for a holiday, leaving him to amuse himself in the cabarets, and on that particular night he had been seen by the caretaker taking cash out of the safe. The police arrested him but allowed him as a diplomat to stay in his own flat where, two days later, he cut his wrists.

We too were at last hit by tragedy, though of a less lurid kind. We had been remarkably free of misadventures, considering how long we had been knocking about in comparatively primitive places. The Wakelins, for instance, lost three of their children: one very young from a tonsillectomy that went wrong in Bahrain, one from drowning in the Irish Sea, and one from a fall in Penang. Our third child, Clare, a lively three and a half year old decided one morning that there was no reason why she shouldn't run round the corner to the grocer on her own to ask for some chocolate. She and her two elder brothers, being fair, were grossly spoilt by the local tradesmen who often gave them sweets on our shopping expeditions. As she crossed the road she was hit by a taxi. She spent weeks unconscious in hospital with a fractured skull, fortunately attended by a Canadian neurologist from the AUB. Gradually, very gradually, she recovered her senses – except the hearing in one ear – and her strength, but it was a time of dreadful anxiety, particularly for Germaine who practically lived by her bedside.

Once she was out of danger Germaine's diplomatic friend, Kees Vroon, provided us with the most perfect form of convalescence imaginable: he lent us his house on Ibiza, Ses Brufador, at Cala Gracio. San Antonio was then a small fishing village and the coast a paradise known only to diplomats like Kees who had served in Spain – and to some of Franco's ministers who, like Kees, had built themselves houses there.

We flew first to Barcelona to catch the Ibiza ferry. The Director of the British Institute in Barcelona was a Yorkshireman who disapproved of bull fighting and of me 'using him as a tourist agent', but having registered his disapproval he was very helpful. He drove us up to the funicular for Tibidabo, which entranced us as much for its exotic view and absurd church as for its distorting mirrors and funfair and haunted castle. I was fascinated by the city, then magnificently dowdy and, compared with spivvy Beirut, steeped in an austere grace and courtesy.

The Institute was in an old mansion on the Diagonal, and as I watched the hundreds of students pouring into its classes I thought, 'This is the place for me!' From then on I put Barcelona at the top of my preferences when I filled in my annual Posting Consideration Form, and the Council eventually paid attention and sent me there.

The old tub of a ferry that took us to Ibiza was as Spartan as the rest of Spain at that time, and we were all seasick before we docked at sunrise. But the sight of Ibiza town climbing up to its citadel in the morning sun, our breakfast of fresh rolls and coffee on the quayside, and the nine-mile traffic-free coast road to San Antonio sent spirits soaring. The house was on the rocks, and the pools and *calas* (coves) were an endless enchantment to the children. This and the peace and quiet worked wonders for Germaine and for Clare, whose hair was growing again and who had almost learned to swim by the time we left for England.

In England, most unwillingly, we left eight-year-old Gus with my brother Hugh to attend the local village school before going on to Clifton College. He came out to join us again in the summer, but we felt like murderers when we saw him off at the end of the holidays, so subdued in his grey school uniform, after getting used once again to the easy-going life of Beirut. Already the days were drawing to a close when we could bask in the hero-worship of our children; even as Ian, our fourth child, was welcomed we were abandoning his elder brother to the care of strangers.

In other ways Lebanon was becoming less friendly, and Syria and Iraq very unfriendly indeed, with the shadow of Nasser hanging heavily over all three. Youths flung stones; curfews were frequent; bombs were common and one was thrown at the Council building an hour after a lecture. As rioting increased more journalists arrived, and the incongruity of danger and the pleasure of cabarets, and sun, sea and snow became more and more surreal. One evening at the *Bains Militaires* as we sat with the Beestons and Douglas Stewart of the BBC drying off in the sunset, with Elvis Presley coming over the loudspeakers and children playing happily round us, Douglas said, 'Oh, that reminds me, the news should be coming over about now', and switched on his radio. As he leant back sipping his drink his voice, hoarse with excitement, came over the air describing a deathless ride in a taxi across some borderline between warring factions and signing off with the usual hopeful promise of worse to come. Meanwhile Zelpha Chamoun flew to England hoping to stop her younger son, Dani, who was supposed to be studying engineering at Loughborough, from marrying an Australian five years his senior whose first husband had been the son of Victor Sylvester – not a name to conjure with in an Arab environment – and George Middleton was knighted and went to church for the first time for seven months.

I suppose, in view of what happened to Lebanon later, our cultural pretensions were equally surreal. No doubt, also, the political disintegration around us contributed to the disintegrating personal relations between Germaine and me. It will sound extraordinary that after ten years, and with four adored children and many interests in common, this should have happened. Some say that the danger of physical attraction can be averted by tolerance from the innocent party, but I wonder if this is true. It is the strength of the attraction that determines everything, distorting and magnifying feelings and events and clouding everyone's judgement. Germaine was not inclined to toleration and nor was this the first time hers had been tested.

One danger of a job overseas is that towards the end of each tour of duty life seems to quicken and relationships that are about to end suddenly assume a new dimension. Sir Robert Ker Porter, if we are to believe his Caracas diary, after suffering fifteen years of blameless exile from his family in Moscow, and on the eve of his retirement, fell in love with the child wife of a Scots doctor in La Guaira. Sir Robert had to endure a hard slog on horseback over the precipitous old colonial road to the coast in order to pay stifled court to 'the fair Peruvian'. My temptations in Beirut were nearer at hand. I had at my service the telephone, my first new car, nearby beaches and not too distant ski slopes. Above all I had amateur dramatics where for a few heady weeks the director is like a pasha with his harem. And it was in a production of *Blithe Spirit* that Germaine's and my incompatibility was brought home to me most forcibly. She made a superb Madame Arcati. It was a shock. Could I really hope to be a happy Monsieur Arcati?

Overseas life for Council wives was in those days infinitely worse than it is now. They could rarely pursue careers of their own, let alone be the Council breadwinner, and if there was unhappiness they had little relief from it. When I reflect what frightful partners some of my colleagues or their wives put up with, I am all the more ashamed of the short time I allowed for trying to make a go of things. But once the mere idea of separation enters the mind of an unhappy couple there is little chance of turning back. And where there are loved and trusting children involved, the horror of it is too painful for words. Even now, with my family long launched, I can hardly bear to recall my feelings of deception.

In spite of interests in common, Germaine and I had been growing farther apart. The children, whom we both loved and who should have cemented us together, had supplanted me in her attention, and my attention – in that city of wandering eyes – had wandered.

Things came to a head after one of my productions. The after-show party had loosened what I suppose were the classic forked tongues of every dissimulating couple. 'If you're not going to behave yourself,' said Germaine, in her Madame Arcati voice, 'I'm going to marry Peter.'

That took the wind out of my sails. Marry Peter! What a blow to my self-esteem! So much for my eagle directorial eye! Then first thoughts of self-pity and indignation gave way to a wilder one: could this bolt from the blue be a heaven-sent way out of our miseries? To have abandoned four children without a father would have been unthinkable. To leave them with a stepfather whom I knew and liked would be awful but not impossible.

Peter Wilson was a bachelor in the Iraq Petroleum Company. He was a year or two younger than me and had been stage manager in my plays. I had had no idea that he and Germaine were on anything but friendly terms and I was, I confess, intrigued that a woman so down to earth could play two such incompatible roles simultaneously and with such success. But now we had to consider seriously the question of the children. Over the next few months ways and means were discussed, and I suppose in retrospect it was Germaine's drive and determination that carried things through. Peter, it appeared, was prepared to look after all four children and pay for the education of the two youngest, and there was to be no question of denying access to them or fighting for their affections. If Germaine and I were both abroad, Gus and Nick, who would soon join his brother at boarding school, could stay with my brother Hugh or my mother in the holidays.

Two imponderables, however, remained. The first was my own future. I had been unfaithful and deeply in love with someone who was not so much in love with me. Now that remarriage was a practical possibility we both knew that it would not work. I assumed that I would eventually remarry, because I could not see myself as a quirky bachelor for ever and thought a second marriage would provide a more popular alternative home for the children than a bachelor establishment. But I had no second Mrs Alexander in mind.

The other imponderable was how my future whereabouts would affect the family. My next posting was announced in 1958: I was to go to Hong Kong to set up a new office as 'Regional Director, Kowloon, on temporary promotion to Grade E'.

The post itself sounded satisfactory, implying more autonomy than being an Assistant Representative in a capital city, but the adjective 'temporary' started a long-running sense of grievance. I had been sitting at the top of Grade F for five years, with no annual increment, and was therefore due promotion – if I was ever to have it. 'Temporary' promotion applied only to service in a particular post, so one could, as I was to do twice, get to the top of the grade but still be 'temporary'. One could then be posted to a job carrying a lower grade and revert to that grade. This option was never used on me, but the system created anxiety and ill-will. As for Kowloon, I was pleased to be going back to the Far East, though a bit puzzled about where the Council fitted in to the colonial scene. As I was to find out, it didn't – at least not in its then form.

To the Alexanders divorce had always been unthinkable. When I did eventually announce our impending break-up, my mother's long and horrified letters were echoed by shorter pithier ones from the rest of the family.

'It is beyond me,' my mother wrote, 'to understand how the parents of four nice children could think for one moment of leaving them to others in this hard world... Most couples have to put up with tiresomenesses in each other but endure them for the sake of the sweetnesses.'

My siblings did not in essence disagree with their eldest bachelor brother, Bim, writing from his igloo tent near Applecross: 'Ten years plus four children should be regarded as a point of no return in a marriage; and a woman with a family should endure pretty well anything short of being beaten to death.' But who can resist the hammer blows of unhappiness and when did their victims follow advice? At any rate it was two very unhappy people who, with three of their unsuspecting children, finally left Beirut.

Our departure coincided with the arrival of the American Marines. They stormed ashore on the beach from which we had watched the *Champollion* break up five years before. The sea was a good deal calmer and the Marines must have felt a little foolish having to jump over the girls in bikinis lying on the sand. Germaine left by air with Clare and Ian while I took Nick, then six, with the car (I had at last been able to buy a new one – a Hillman convertible) by ferry to La Spezia and across Europe to join them in Holland. Nick posed on Juliet's tomb in Verona, was sick as we crossed the Dolomites, and spent most of our time on the road fizzing and banging beside me in a private game of cops and robbers. In Salzburg I dragged him round one fabulous church after another, until we entered one by a small northern door.

'Good heavens!' I exclaimed, 'this really is the best of the lot! Have you ever seen anything like it?'

'Yes, Daddy. This was the first church we looked at. Only we came in by that big door over there.'

We found the rest of the family, apart from Gus, staying at Wassenaar in the Hague with Germaine's sister and banker brother-in-law. We had not yet told them of our uncertainties, but Paul, after a day or two, made a perceptive remark. 'What's happened to you, Stephen? Since you were last here you've grown up.'

In Bristol we rented a house in Clifton. In September Nick and Clare went to local prep schools, and in October, leaving Germaine and the children behind, I sailed for Hong Kong, telling the Council that the family would join me later when I had opened the new office and found accommodation for them. I still half believed that this would happen. A month's voyage and facing a new job alone on my side, or second thoughts on Germaine's or Peter's, might yet bring about a family reunion. But it was soon evident that Germaine knew her own mind more than I mine. She pressed me by post to go through with the divorce, and I, with the new life in Hong Kong distancing me from the doubts and inhibitions of the old, agreed.

As it turned out, we were so much happier apart that I think the children in the long run must have benefited too. I felt dreadfully homesick for them, but after marrying Germaine Peter Wilson more than fulfilled his promises. By the time my first home leave came along two years later we were able to establish an inter-family routine free of bitterness, and this was soon blessed by the birth of Andrew Wilson.

10
At Sea in Kowloon

AFTER TWO YEARS in Hong Kong I was in no mood to return. My divorce came through while I was there and the finality of it renewed the feelings of deprivation and guilt at betraying the children's trust. The two elder ones were at school in England, spending holidays with my relations; the two younger ones were living with Germaine and Peter in oil camps in Iraq and later Qatar. In addition to this, I had found the nebulous role of the Council in Hong Kong deeply dissatisfying. That was especially disappointing after the build-up of a month in a first-class cabin – so far had the gap between Council and FCO service conditions now narrowed – aboard the P&O *Chusan*, which carried me to my new post.

There was still a markedly imperial and slightly stodgy air about the passengers compared with those I'd met on the American runs, but the really awkward squad in our grand quarters were the uneducated girls, mostly from the north, going out to marry or to join Indian students. I sat next to a witless Australian, married to a Malay she had met at Sydney University who was now a diplomat, and wondered how much of a help he found her in steering him through stuffy diplomatic parties.

There were also two groups who played a kind of sexual Tom Tiddler's Ground with each other all the way to Ceylon. They were young tea planters and tea planters' daughters returning from school or university, and they lived largely in a state of suspended animation, for the *Chusan* had bags of space, excellent sports facilities and a good library, but these and the formal evening entertainment – we dressed for dinner – were not conducive to white-hot burning passions. Baulked in their campaigns, the planters would be seen sharing umbrage together over drinks, while round the corner the girls sat alone, looking self-conscious.

Their ill temper was somewhat justified: the girls would happily accept the drinks they paid for and then go dancing with the ship's officers and not come back. From time to time there would be a rapprochement and they would all sit together again. But the men would talk to each other across the girls and vice versa, and it seemed to be tacitly understood that no single chap would talk for long to a single girl in the absence of the rest of the gang.

In sharp contrast to the giggly, tongue-tied and gregarious English girls was the dark and demure Denise Loos, a Berger girl (of Dutch settler descent) aged eighteen returning from being presented at court (for which her parents had paid £500 – exclusive of travel and accommodation). When Denise was in the swimming pool it was remarkable how many men decided to have a swim too. What Denise lacked in conversation she made up in poise, for she succeeded in keeping half the men in the ship at a friendly arm's length through the run to Colombo – though the young planters gave her a wide berth. Evidently she was too composed, too beautiful or too dark for their peace of mind.

In sailing east I was sailing back into wartime memories – and in some places to family contacts, though many of these had by now left their colonial jobs, or at least lost their colonial status. In Aden a colourful figure in a matelot's striped jersey came aboard and played jazz on the ship's piano. He was, I learned, one of the most widely known entertainers from Cairo to Beirut, and incidentally Representative of the British Council in Aden – Onslow Tuckley.

Bombay and Colombo had had ten years in which to lose their colonial gloss, but Penang, a year after *Merdeka*, showed no signs of losing its shine. The nearest I had been to Penang was Kuala Lumpur, which I had clanked through in a Japanese cattle truck in 1941. Now I found it both beautiful and lively, but James Mandy, our man there, explained the uncertainties of social life in the limbo between a colonial and independent state.

'It's a pity,' he said, drawing on one of his innumerable cigarettes, 'that the Penang swimming club is exclusively a "white" one. The Chinese girls are so much prettier than the English ones. As it is, one can only sit in the club surrounded by lumping great European women, knowing that the Chinese girls walking past so alluringly on the public beach can't get any nearer than the barrier.'

Whether this barrier was real or imagined I am not quite sure. Perhaps James was one of those perennial bachelors who need a barrier to sit behind in comfort. At any rate he eventually retired to Spain. My unmarried sister, who met him there, thought he 'had beautiful eyes' but both he and his brother, Sean, who also lived there, retained their bachelor status.

Singapore, like Penang, was on the crest of a wave – clean, prosperous and not yet submerged in skyscrapers. While there I was curious to renew acquaintance with one of its old colonials. Bobbie Green was a partner in the law firm of Braddell Brothers and had been a prisoner-of-war with me. When his wife left on one of the last ships before the fall of Singapore, she had taken one of their dachshund puppies with her, and he had kept the other. He carried Ludwig into captivity with him and up to the Burma-Siam railway, feeding him with scraps on the marches and concealing him in his haversack during searches by the *Kempitai*. The little creature grew adept at keeping quiet and became a symbol to us all of the civilised life we had left behind. To Bobbie he became even more precious with the news after eighteen months that his wife's ship had been sunk and she had not survived.

'I married again,' said Bobbie when we met, 'and oddly enough I married another Margaret.'

'What happened to Ludwig?'

'Ah, Ludwig! Ludwig died.'

He drove me out to his bright and cheerful house where I met the bright and cheerful Margaret and – gallumphing among the cannas – two bright and cheerful Dalmatians. Bobbie had done well in the years before *Merdeka* but was uncertain of Singapore's future in the Malayan Federation and had taken the precaution of selling his house and renting another. Whichever way things went Ludwig was to have no part in them. He had come with us to Ban Pong, Tamarkham, Kinsaiyok, Takanun, Tamuang, Kanchanaburi, Nacom Nyok, Bangkok and Rangoon. Now he was a diminutive and diminishing memory in a way of life to whose loss some of us had not yet resigned ourselves.

On the *Chusan*, however, among the ragtag and bobtail of Empire one passenger epitomised the brave new world of liberty with youth at the helm. On the first evening aboard, I found her sitting by herself in the bar. A dark-eyed girl, she was in chatty mood. Katharine Dove was an Oxford graduate aged twenty-seven and late of the Panorama team under Richard Dimbleby. It was an exciting but stressful job and a knee injury had precipitated a state of depression and indecision. Should she soldier on or seek a change? Her boyfriend of two years' standing – if such a term is appropriate for such a sober personality – was the producer, Charles Wheeler, and when he was posted to India she thought the idea of seeing Nehru's country freed from the shackles of colonial rule an attractive one – or at least a change from endless booze-ups in the 'Glue Pot' or the Windsor Castle. So she had married Charles two months before and was now on her way to join him in Delhi.

But 'between the idea and the reality, between the motion and the act, falls the Shadow' – or in her case two shadows. The first was that of the Grote Professor of the Philosophy of Mind and Logic at University College, London, and the second – only two days after the wedding – that of the deputy editor of the *New Statesman*. As the date of sailing approached she had begun to regret her Indian commitment, and the more so as the consolation afforded by Freddy Ayer failed to extinguish the kindling flame of John Freeman.

As the mail came aboard at Gibraltar, Port Said and Aden she flung aside the thick envelopes from New Delhi to devour the cables from London. 'Has anyone got a bloody Bible?' she cried when baulked by the verse references to the 'Song of Solomon' with which John Freeman had chosen to express his passion in the warmest (and most economical) terms. She had the habit, now fashionable with female columnists but not then usual outside BBC and theatrical circles, of using four-letter words and this led the more lecherous members of the crew to assume she was giving them the 'old green light'. It was amusing to guess the exact moment she would choose in which to rake them with her stern-chasers and sink them without trace.

I did wonder if the Freeman technique as evidenced in his *Face to Face* programmes augured well for future domestic relations. As for Charles Wheeler, I watched him escort his new wife down the gangplank at Bombay with a sadness not unmixed with *Schadenfreude* since my own marriage had only recently foundered. I heard afterwards that they did 'try to make a go of things' but circumstances were against them as Freeman and Wheeler played a game of professional musical chairs between Delhi and Washington. In neither the Freeman nor the Wheeler entry in *Who's Who* does Katharine receive as much as a mention – a ghostly omission I find difficult to reconcile with my memory of the flesh and blood passenger who so briskly saw off 'Chiefie' in the *Chusan*.

In 1958 Hong Kong was booming as though there was never going to be a transfer of power. 'What's the job?' asked Charles Hill, Minister of Information (and ex-Radio Doctor, promoter of prunes as the 'black coated workers'), on his official visit. I found this difficult to define, beyond acting as a kind of bridge for local residents to educational opportunities in Britain which for one reason or another might not fit into the routine of Hong Kong government exchanges, and in general to familiarise local Chinese with metropolitan practices that would succeed colonial ones. But even to make our presence felt was not easy when there were forty thousand civil servants in Hong Kong, and many of these expatriates spoke Cantonese or Mandarin. Our funds were tiny and the three London-appointed staff spoke no Chinese. (As with Arabic, I soon found that Cantonese without full-time study was beyond me.) We did our best to encourage the dynamic population of this regional powerhouse to talk sense as well as money, but we had not then been charged with the teaching of English, which later made Hong Kong the jewel in our post-colonial crown. Meanwhile, it was hard to take cultural strategies seriously when mainland Chinese, 'voting with their feet', were facing hell and high water daily to swell the grim resettlement camps of their promised land.

I had been sent out to set up a regional office and library in Kowloon, and there seemed to me a fundamental flaw in the establishment of such a scheme. There was already an office in Victoria on Hong Kong Island, and between the two ran the most efficient form of public transport I have ever seen – the Star Ferry. This exemplary study in perpetual motion – a moving necklace of boats across the harbour, which barely touched the landing stages as hundreds of passengers leapt on and off – reduced the distance between the two offices to a mere two miles as the crow flies.

Nevertheless, I went busily ahead establishing an office and library in Nathan Road in first-floor premises already selected for me above a nightclub and next to U FAT LADIES TAILOR. And I established myself and an imperturbable black cheongsamed cook-general in a flat on the thirteenth floor in Mody Road in Kowloon. At that time it had a fine view of the harbour and of Jardine Mathieson's gun ('In Hong Kong they strike a gong and fire off a noonday gun'), but a typhoon soon afterwards blew in the window and waterlogged the carpets. The Hong Kong climate is deceptive; books become mildewed, houses are marooned for days in dank mists, droughts follow floods and cause water-rationing, and there are a lot of coughs and colds about.

AT SEA IN KOWLOON

Hong Kong Island was already like a human ant heap, with the skyscrapers of the Hong Kong and Shanghai Bank and the Bank of China leapfrogging each other in reaching for the Peak. I have never known a place so pullulating with people in its twin capitals of Victoria on Hong Kong Island and Kowloon opposite – and so devoid of them in the bleak surrounding hills. I soon began to feel myself transmogrifying into just another of the millions of ants scurrying busily about. I got used to the ceaseless crowds and noise, with double-decker buses whizzing down the major roads, and the side roads just as noisy with rickshaw coolies honking and beggars spitting and people slamming down their mahjong pieces; children pouring in and out of makeshift schools, many of them working three shifts on rooftops far into the night; funeral processions slow-marching past, scattering funeral money and exploding crackers, and accompanied by bands playing *Abide with Me* atrociously out of tune. I grew accustomed to the marvellous Chinese and Indian food and to Chinese wine with lizards embalmed in it; and to chic chemists shops divided between Western and Chinese medicine; and to Westernised pony-tailed Chinese teenagers in jeans poking about among fish fins, dried gall bladders, antlers, tiger-livers, flying foxes, powdered testicles, eyeballs, bits of cat, philtres and embryos of this and that.

It was essential to escape now and then from this urban claustrophobia by walking in the New Territory hills or on a then remote island like Lantau, where one could stay in a Buddhist monastery and listen smugly to devotees banging a gong throughout the night. Or from Victoria one could take the 'Peak tram' which rose steeply through the prosperous flats and houses of the 'Mid-level' to the peace and quiet of Governor's Walk. From there it was difficult to imagine the impending transfer of power as one gazed down at the harbour with its multitude of ships like water beetles, junks like windblown leaves and, in the more distant coves, mothballed freighters like the immobilised victims of giant spiders. The Ghurka troops contributed to the misleading atmosphere of permanence.

One night an old hand took me to the 'street of brothel boats' in the typhoon shelter at Yaumati on Kowloon side. We paddled slowly down lines of sampans, luxuriously cushioned and brightly lit, each with a girl sitting under a capacious awning. This would be lowered when needed, and some had already been so – leaving the sampans lying silent and dark like some hunchback amphibious beast. It was quiet and very sinister, like a last obscene temptation while 'crossing alone the nighted ferry with the one coin for fee'.

I soon began to discover that 'squeeze' lurked behind the clean faces of government departments and private enterprises like the Happy Valley race course. Charming Chinese Inspectors of Education saw to it that schools ordered books from firms they owned; bribes secured places in favoured schools, or planning permission by the PWD for a block of flats that would subsequently be altered (the skyscrapers which looked so impressive from a distance were often claustrophobic inside). A bus conductor's job would cost him HK$500. A Chinese (but not a Briton) taking a driving test would be instructed to back into a space and told 'It lacks three feet', which is ambiguous in Cantonese and can mean 'It lacks HK$300' (i.e. HK$100 for the inspector and HK$200 for the instructor) if you want to pass.

A mile or two inland from the harbour, at Kow Loon Tong, was Christchurch, presided over by Tim and Mary Rose Beaumont. A year later they returned to England and Tim turned his attention to religious publishing and Liberal politics, ending as a life peer and busy committee man. I wonder what they made of their unquestioning and pragmatic congregations. At a scholarship interview I asked a student what religion he professed, and he said, 'What you like.' I said, 'What shall I put down here? Church of England?' 'Yes,' he said, 'if you like.'

As far as cultural co-operation was concerned, the Anglican and Nonconformist churches showed up very badly compared with the Jesuits of St Joseph School. There seemed to be a Jesuit expert involved in every branch of the arts, and none more actively than the warm-hearted Father Sheridan in music and drama. The Chinese were not easy to stir into any activity which called for self-expression, and when I lectured at Hong Kong University for Edmund Blunden, who was – if it isn't putting it the wrong way round – the Christopher Scaife of the place, it was like lecturing to a busily scribbling audience of blotting paper. I got absolutely no reaction and was told that the pressure for places and ambition for self-improvement was such that no-one cared to risk putting a foot wrong or being thought too clever by half for asking questions.

Meanwhile, the Star Ferry made my post an absurdity. The Island was where the cultural action was, and anybody in Kowloon or the New Territories who wanted any of it was quite happy to go there for it. Though it must be said that they might have been surprised by the Council office in Gloucester Building when they found it. It was so cramped that the Representative, John Jenkins, and Assistant Representative, Janet Tomblin, who had precious little in common except their age (about fifty) were constrained to share a common office.

John was a kind, shy man, a chain-smoking teetotaller, and music was his great, indeed his only, cultural interest. He played the organ at the cathedral and wanted to train a Chinese choir to sing church music but was thwarted by the Bishop, Ronald Hall, who was a Sinologist and prickly about the Chinese. The local taipans called him the Red Bishop, and I think he may have had the kind of proprietorial feeling towards his 'native' flock that pioneering clerics like Trevor Huddleston too often acquire. It is the 'don't-feed-my-sheep-I'm-the-shepherd' syndrome. So he was hostile to John's idea because it would mean the Chinese singing English, rather than Chinese, music and having to learn English to sing it in. Seldom can there have been such a division of minds over the role of the British Council.

John had a ward, an Anglo-Burmese boy of eighteen, with whom he lived in the house he had inherited in Repulse Bay. But it was too big for him and was a long way from the office and the cathedral. When Janet was transferred, not long after my arrival, he and Randolph moved into her convenient flat halfway up the Peak, sharing its only bedroom. Randolph, who was studying at night school, was also given a job at the Council.

One day John greeted me with a long face, saying that Randolph had gone down with mumps. 'And you know, Stephen, mumps can have an unfortunate effect on a boy of eighteen.' However, his fears were proved groundless when our Chinese assistant librarian announced that she was carrying Randolph's child. A shotgun wedding was arranged and the bride moved into John's flat and into John's bedroom, where a screen was rigged up to separate the nuptial couch from the Representational bed.

This arrangement hardly suited John's successor, who could scarcely have been more different. A down-to-earth character, who had worked in China for the Quakers in the war and spoke Chinese, Tod Lawry had married a girl in Council headquarters. But before that his life had not been without incident, as I discovered when, soon after his arrival, I took him out for a drink with the *Daily Telegraph* correspondent, also an old Peking hand. They were soon swapping reminiscences and the name of an American girl cropped up.

'I was engaged to her,' said Tod, 'for ten days!'

Thus encouraged, the *Telegraph* man regaled us with the story of her brainwashing by the Communist regime:

'She was thrown into gaol with a lot of criminals. And her hands were chained behind her. So when she went to the communal lavatory she had to ask the other prisoners to help her. And they were all male. And she was always such a fastidious girl!'

Tod was very silent.

In view of the unclear role of the Council and the overlapping and sometimes competing activities of the two offices and libraries I found myself, especially after Janet Tomblin's transfer, drawn more and more into fringe activities such as the Theatre Guild productions and cultural programmes for Radio Hong Kong. Besides bringing Council visitors, ships that passed in the night carried legendary figures – Somerset Maugham, Tennessee Williams and Frederick March. Margot Fonteyn and Michael Soames were pleasant and unaffected (though, having seen Panama from Colombia, I was surprised to hear of the Fonteyn connection with it). Eileen Joyce was more exigent, with her dresser and changes of costume in mid-concert and her obsession with publicity. Other talented but less known Australians made a longer lasting contribution to Hong Kong life, staying long enough on their way to Britain to finance their onward journeys by playing in dance bands, painting, designing or running restaurants.

One day the *South China Morning Post* announced the arrival of Orson Welles to make a film about a stateless man travelling to and fro on the Hong Kong-Macao boat with neither port letting him ashore. Word got round that Welles held court at the Marco Polo bar in the evenings, and local thespians hurried over to hang upon the great man's words. But as the evening wore on so did the words, with the great man averse to anyone else getting a word in. Soon he had the Marco Polo to himself again.

Our longest-staying official Council visitor was E Arnot Robertson, who was best known not so much for her popular novel, *Four Frightened People*, as for having been sacked from her London film critic's job at the behest of MGM, who demanded only favourable reviews from her editor. She spent six weeks in Hong Kong with her husband, Sir Henry Turner, looking for copy for a novel about the rooftop squatters of Hong Kong, *The Stranger on my Roof,* and the Council sponsored her for lectures on literature and women's emancipation, which she gave very well.

Arnot was determined to see as much as she could, not only of the Island but also of the New Territories, but although Sir Henry was small and nippy on his feet, Arnot, very much the dominating partner, was of a larger conical build and soon found herself in trouble with ascents to monasteries. Fortunately there were palanquins available for elderly persons, and our little procession must have sounded quaint as we toiled breathlessly upwards, with Arnot, swaying on the shoulders of wiry little porters, holding forth on the landscape, Buddhism, Hampstead, MGM, 'Hen's' obsession with messing about in boats, Chinese cooking (an army wife had told her 'Oh, we never eat Chinese food; it's so dirty!'), and a grey mullet 'farm' she had seen, consisting of an artificial lake with a privy conveniently overhanging it and a plaque beside it commemorating its opening by the Duke of Edinburgh.

On one of our walks we encountered the Governor, Sir Robert Black, striding along, and about 20 yards behind him a flunkey carrying his haversack. (I was reminded of the eccentric Sir Tatton Sykes, who began his walks wearing seven coats, discarding them one by one as he warmed up, for collection by a following footman.) Lady Black was public spirited but horribly nervous; once, sitting next to her when she was presenting prizes, I was alarmed to feel the platform beginning to shake.

The Duncansons and I took the Turners to Macao for a weekend at the old Bellavista Hotel, so quiet compared with the clatter of Hong Kong, and backing onto an even quieter convent. Macao was a mixture of modern sleaze, in its casinos and brothels, and ageless dignity, in the buildings and roads surviving from the great days of Portuguese power. The churches recalled the enterprise of Mateo Ricci, the Camoens monument the international fame of this now claustrophobic little city. In the crumbling Protestant cemetery were elegant monuments to the artist Chinnery and to one of the Churchills. A cluster of eighteenth-century official buildings included a little red plush theatre, to which on a later occasion we took the appropriate Theatre Guild production of *The Strong are Lonely*. Above it all was the toy castle, looking down on the free-standing facade of the ruined church of Sao Paulo. For us it was all a delightful change from the materialism of Hong Kong, but for the locals relations with China were a constant source of anxiety. Out in the Pearl River we could see Chinese gunboats playing cat and mouse with the Portuguese launches, and we were told that at the land gate Chinese border guards enjoyed relieving themselves over the black Angolan sentries snoozing below.

The Turners were a pleasant couple to look after, and Sir Henry seemed quite happy to be chivvied about by Arnot. We were sorry to see them go but glad that our local colour was duly reflected in the novel. Then, while 'messing about' in the boat they kept on the Thames, Henry fell into the water, got tangled up in some ropes and drowned. As for Arnot, 'she for a little tried to live without him, liked it not, and died'.

Dennis Duncanson, our guide, philosopher and friend whom I had enlisted as dragoman during their visit, suffered a longer drawn out tragedy. He was highly qualified academically and spoke difficult languages, including Amharic, which he had learned when in Intelligence in Abyssinia, and was at this time working for the Hong Kong Information Department. He moved after two years to the BBC Overseas Service and a year later to the University of Kent as Reader in Southeast Asian Studies. He had, however, made a wretchedly unhappy marriage, and when he asked Elizabeth for a divorce she said that if he went ahead she would make his life a misery as long as he lived. He did not go ahead. She made their Bayswater mews house charming, attended his learned society lectures in London, and when he retired they travelled together in Europe and took Swan's tours further afield. Then Elizabeth really did make Dennis's life a misery – with Alzheimer's disease – and his death soon followed hers.

While I was in Hong Kong I did not appreciate the depth of the Duncansons' unhappiness, though I did wonder at the aimlessness of Elizabeth's existence. Nevertheless, the clinical atmosphere of their home life, not to mention the awesome stoicism with which it was preserved later, was a reproach to my own domestic volatility. My professional role in Hong Kong seemed no less volatile and when I flew home on leave I was determined not to return.

11
Swinging London

I FOUND ENGLAND in the early sixties still in a state of post-Suez hysteria and the London streets a disturbing mixture of tat and razzmatazz. At the Council a 'fast stream' of people of my vintage and of later recruits was emerging, and it became clear that I was not in it. Personnel Department declined to confirm my promotion to Grade E, and I declined returning to my anomalous Kowloon post, and thus began the cat and mouse game over temporary and permanent promotion that was later outlawed but which dogged the rest of my career. Such things happen in organisations that are not sure whether to behave like a civil service, a business enterprise, an academic institution or a branch of the arts.

At that time the headquarters building in Davies Street had a basement canteen, and on the top floor a small restaurant and bar where one could take guests, drop in to see who was holding court there on their home leave, or go to make one's number with the top brass over drinks. I found Arthur King there, now elevated from Pakistan to the home post of Controller of Education Division, and told him my predicament. There was a job going, he said, in his Division, and that was where I ended up – and in my one and only home posting. It was not an exciting job but it did show me some of the ins and outs of headquarters policy and – which was what weighed most heavily with me – it allowed me to see the children. It also allowed me to see something of England, which, apart from five months immediately after the war, I had only seen in a few short leaves over the previous twenty years.

I became a PG with a Mrs Fitzroy in Carrington House near Shepherd Market while I hunted for a flat. Mrs Fitzroy was a widow and evidently accustomed to better days; she had bread for my breakfast delivered by Harrods. An American girl called Marion was a fellow guest. She was in publishing and was being pursued by Kenneth Tynan. One day he had arranged to meet her outside the Curzon cinema, and she found him there being interrogated by a couple of policemen. 'Marion, darling,' he cried, 'tell them about our date. They won't believe I'm not soliciting.' The area was at that time a busy one for lonely hearts.

It was odd to walk to work from Shepherd Market through the elegance of Berkeley Square and Davies Street and down to earth again in the dusty offices of the Council. I was determined to rent a flat within walking distance and eventually found one near Regent's Park. It was a tiny mansion flat at the Great Portland Street end of Devonshire Street, and it proved an unwise choice for three reasons: 'Doctorland' is very dead at night; Regent's Park is a very dull park to walk in; and I was soon moved away from HQ in Davies Street to outlying offices, first in Albion House in New Oxford Street and then in State House, High Holborn. These areas, however, did have advantages over the prim surroundings of Davies Street. Albion House, long since redeveloped, was an ornate curlicued rabbit warren of passages, ironwork and creaking lifts, distinguished for having at one time housed Dr Crippen. It was also an excellent base for exploring Bloomsbury and Covent Garden. State House was even more rewarding as it was near the Law Courts and the City, and I munched my way through many happy lunchtime concerts in City churches. The City – between great gaps of bomb damage as yet unfilled – was still surprisingly Dickensian, with its markets and chophouses and culs-de-sac. At weekends I would go to the end of one tube line and walk to the end of another. Or for 1/8d I could get to Syon House, cross the Isleworth ferry and walk to Kew Gardens station. In Devonshire Street I was within reach of Handel operas at St Pancras Town Hall, but the Marylebone area, apart from Regent's Park Theatre and the Wigmore Hall, was disappointing.

There were then half a dozen Council offices on or just off Oxford and New Oxford Streets, and in going from one to the other I acquired a wealth of topographical, architectural and circumstantial information about London. (Perhaps the most surprising was the interior of Carpenter's church of St Mary Magdalene in Munster Square and the story behind the Greek Street mansion of Richard Beckford and later of Gladstone's fallen women, with its chapel of St Barnabas, a miniature of a church near Nîmes.) An article I wrote in the staff magazine about these observations caught the eye of Sir Paul Sinker, particularly my mentioning that one entrance manhole to the sewer complex based on Tyburn Brook lay immediately outside our Davies Street HQ. So I was invited to tea on the '5th Floor'. Would I, asked the DG in what I thought an uncharacteristically adventurous mood, like to go down this manhole with him if he fixed things with the District Engineer, and walk down to the outfall at the Thames? I would. So, kitted out in municipal overalls and watched by curious staff, we vanished together down the hole in the pavement and started wading. Nervous memories of illustrations to Edgar Allan Poe's tale of *The Pit and the Pendulum* proved groundless; the rats kept their distance, the air was unusually fresh for London, and it was with a belch of satisfaction rather than a note of menace that trapdoors opened to discharge their contents as we passed. The interplay of major and minor sewers, and the air of a busily preoccupied god of the underground moving in a mysterious way opened a new world to us, and one in which it was clear that our guides were happy to work. So much so that as we bade them farewell on emerging into the noise and dust of Grosvenor Street – beyond it the sewage was pumped out to boats on the Essex marshes for dumping in the North Sea – we envied them their secret watery kingdom.

The work in my part of Education Division was of two kinds: general educational information and specific efforts to encourage and control the teaching of English as a second or foreign language (TEFL). The general work included answering enquiries from overseas, recommending lecturers, validating degrees, preparing teaching aids and editing *Higher Education*, an annual guide to courses in Britain which is published in conjunction with the University Central Council for Admissions (UCCA).

TEFL work involved setting up with universities and training colleges diploma courses for teachers and inspecting and certifying schools of English for foreigners. The validation of degrees was perhaps the first occasion when my doubts about the achievements and motivation of the Ministry of Education were confirmed. (I had already been puzzled at the playtime atmosphere of Gus's village school. Now I was puzzled by the end products working round me – the new English graduates in the office. A mention of some character from literature or a quotation of a line of poetry drew only blank looks.) The validation of degrees introduced me to the underworld of bogus degrees, where con men advertised degrees by correspondence, or PhDs for one down payment to 'universities' operating from caravans or box numbers and headed by self-styled doctors, knights or patriarchs, and at least one prince. Year after year the same practitioners were exposed in the popular press, but the Ministry of Education pleaded the legal impossibility of doing anything about them.

Now, thirty-five years later, with further education colleges calling themselves universities and offering doctorates in tourism, film appreciation and food science, there is less scope for the 'Bishop Boltwoods' of the past to trawl for fees. But as the years have passed it has become obvious that the policy of not rocking the boat, which I first met in the Ministry of Education, is common throughout the Civil Service. The Council's laborious response to ministerial inertia was to abandon efforts to close down bogus institutions, and to list instead those it recommended and implore potential clients to use only those.

In the sixties the Council was trying to redefine its role in a post-imperial world. Egalitarianism required that classes of English should no longer be confined to the élite – those who could pay for them – but facilitated for everyone. That meant that instead of supplying teachers and actually running classes the Council ought to supply teacher-trainers and leave overseas governments to run the classes with indigenous teachers. In some ex-colonies, as British teachers in subjects other than English had also left, it was clear that subsidised teacher-trainers in, for example, maths, science and vocational education would be required as well, and thus a new world of Overseas Development and Technical Co-operation was born. In this new world, too, there were shiny new teaching tools to be exploited – teaching machines and language laboratories and, above all, radio and television. The Council, always anxious to dispel the public image that had stuck so obstinately to it, of being an airy-fairy, country dancing sort of outfit, found in this new 'development money' an opportunity for extending and rationalising its role. It was the birth pangs of this new role that moved me out of Davies Street and Albion House to State House for the next three years, and that brought into the Council a new fast stream – the 'specialist'; these specialists, initially teachers of English and science, later included other disciplines and, notably and most controversially, those connected with 'management'.

After the extremes in office hours and climate of life abroad, a 9-to-5 routine in a coldish climate tends to lack variety. So any chance to escape from the office was welcome, even if only for a dry-as-dust committee meeting or an indeterminate conference whose practised bureaucrats made sure nothing inconvenient would result from it. A stifling earnestness seemed to seep down from the 5th floor in Davies Street, creep along Oxford Street and thicken the fug in State House as we designed teaching aids for Mogadishu, which had no written language, or concocted 'Study Boxes' of Community Development for British Guiana, whose communities were developing a mutual distrust of unstoppable momentum.

We became very serious and earnest ourselves in our efforts to attune ourselves to Civil Service working practices. One of us was perhaps only copying them when he came to grief. He was a recent 'specialist' recruit, taken on to advise on audiovisual matters and, being an ex-actor, had brought a refreshing worldliness to our cloistered corridors. One day, however, a tactless call from a supplier revealed that in recommending their make of teaching machine he had accepted a kickback. The next day he vanished.

There had been a few scandals in the Council, mostly concerned with Iron Curtain countries – a defection here, an attempt to smuggle a girl across the border there – but this was the only one I had so far witnessed myself. (I did just miss an earlier one in Holland, when Germaine and I called on our office in Amsterdam. The urbane Representative had good social connections and lived in a château at a peppercorn rent. He greatly shocked me, when I mentioned possible future postings, by saying airily, 'Oh, I only joined the Council on condition I came to Holland. I'm not interested in going anywhere else.' And nor did he, for not long afterwards he was unwise enough to insert in the newspaper an announcement to the effect that if the handsome young soldier observed at such and such a gentlemen's hairdresser at such and such a time on such and such a date would ring such and such a number he would learn something to his advantage. This caught the eye of the local police, who were not as broadminded then as they are now, and that was the end of that.)

Now that our actor was 'resting' again, there was only one colleague whose personality stood out from the grey pattern the rest of us adopted once imprisoned in our London cells. This was Michael Glover. To remind his visitors of his priorities he decorated his walls with old military prints. One posting in Europe had been enough for Michael, and when filling in the annual 'Postings Consideration Form', which many of us agonised over, he filled the section under 'Overseas countries preferred' with the expletive 'UGH!'. Michael was one of the nicest and most guileless people I have known, and was quite unfazed by authority. Perhaps this was because his great hobby was military history – albeit, like his prints, somewhat idealised; he was a dedicated Territorial. He couldn't understand my ambivalent attitude to military service. Camaraderie, yes; discipline, yes; discomfort, yes; I accepted all this in wartime, when a traditionally bolshie eye for bullshit helped the fighting man to keep his feet (literally and metaphorically) on the ground. But I had never thought of testing my bullshit threshold in peacetime conditions. For Michael, however, the highlights of the year were his Territorial exercises and camps, and he was puzzled by my declining his invitations to join him. Certainly his hobby was unusual in a Left-leaning pacific organisation like the Council. I was, however, very happy to join him in exploring Hampstead, where he lived, and particularly the Holly Bush on Hampstead Hill.

Perhaps one reason why Michael could maintain his lordly attitude to the Council, even in the London office, was that he was chosen to pioneer its work in television and was often therefore not in the office but hobnobbing with the BBC. So, to a less extent, was I, and it was often a relief to escape from the constrictions of State House to the ampler halls of Langham Place. The canteen alone was Lucullan by our standards. I had a marginal role in producing a series – *Educational Recordings* – of dramatisations of set books used by schools overseas. The actors were required to articulate more clearly and speak more slowly than usual, while preserving the spirit of the words, and they did that very well. Chinua Achebe's *Things Fall Apart* was the first title, and my introduction to the newly fashionable Commonwealth writing. The staff of the Educational Service of the BBC were an efficient, civilised and pleasant lot and it is impossible to reconcile their broadcasting standards with those of today. I also used to go to the BBC in the evenings to record talks of my own for Radio Hong Kong, which had asked me to continue them. I found plenty to talk about in the palmy days of satire, with shows like *At the Drop of a Hat*, *Beyond the Fringe,* and delightful evenings at the Establishment Club.

However, neither Michael's nor my relations with the BBC were destined to last long, for I was posted abroad again and Michael was one of the few to risk leaving the Council for the uncertain life of an author. In his case it was a consummation of his love affair with the army, for he was to devote himself to writing military history.

The BBC was not my only avenue of escape from the office. There were also educational conferences, some of them offering an overnight change of scene at places like the Administrative Staff College at Henley. One organisation which specialised in training in industry was very keen on conferences, and at one of them I met an old friend. He had left the army, he said, when he found his chances of reaching the rank of general poor. He was already an old hand at exploiting conferences to maximum advantage – by establishing in the shortest time a reputation for enterprise and gravitas. It is remarkable how quickly such a reputation can spread, over a series of conferences, so that when the chance of a handy career move comes along it is remembered in high places. Hardly had we settled down in that first reunion and begun to shuffle our papers when Monty rose to his feet.

'Mr Chairman, I'm sorry to interrupt proceedings – er – FLASH, Admiralty, Bath, Civilian Dockyard Training. Before we get down to business may I suggest that we have a window open so that we do not engender too much – er – HOT AIR?' (At other conferences he would, as appropriate, propose that the windows be closed, so that we could hear 'the – er – WORDS OF WISDOM FROM THE PLATFORM.')

The Chairman, glad to have the ice broken and his authority appealed to, would glance at his attendance sheet.

'Oh, thank you, Mr – er – COLONEL Mortimer Flash, isn't it? Thank you for bringing the matter up. Would you see to it over there, please?'

Then, in the afternoon, when everyone was half asleep and the speaker had run out of steam and nobody showed any sign of keeping things going by asking questions, the Chairman would remember Monty's name.

'Colonel Flash? Perhaps you'd care to give us the Admiralty view?'

'Thank you, Mr Chairman. I don't claim to be speaking for their Lordships now, but one of the speakers' remarks reminded me of a story which I'm sure many of you know. But it does illustrate the importance of communication between management and factory floor. There was once a Yorkshireman who was so unfortunate as to lose his wife. He commissioned a local mason to carve a memorial stone, and the lettering on it was to include the phrase "LORD, SHE WAS THINE". When the stone was delivered he was shocked to see that the final E was missing so that the inscription read "LORD, SHE WAS THIN". So he complained to the mason. "That's terrible!" he said. "You've left out the E." "That's all right," said the mason, "I can soon put it in. It's not as if it were in the middle of a word." In due course the altered stone was returned. But there had been poor communication between management and shop floor. The E had certainly been inserted but the inscription now read "E LORD, SHE WAS THIN".'

Monty's fruity voice would get every ounce out of the story and he would be blessed for waking everyone up and getting them interested in proceedings again. The reason why his voice was so fruity and carried such conviction was, as Monty liked to relate, the strong admixture of Welsh blood with the enterprise inherited from his Polish-Jewish great grandfather Fleisch, who had been coachman to George the Fourth. The voice that swayed many a conference and had us singing rounds together in the evenings was kept in good trim in the Bath Operatic Society, and it was not long before it carried further afield as Monty joined the ranks of international experts in conferences abroad.

Other old friends I saw more of while working in London were the Ellises, long recovered from their traumatic venture in Bogotá. David was now managing the Ballet Rambert and Angela was running the school. David had recently taken the Ballet Rambert to Russia. It was his first visit and he had been impressed on the one hand by the preferential treatment enjoyed by ballet companies but on the other by how much harder the dancers worked.

He had also felt upstaged by his opposite number's views on the British economy. 'Why on earth,' he was asked, 'do you pay your workers so much? No wonder you are plagued with strikes and go-slows. We in Russia do not make that mistake.' David had qualified in medicine before taking up ballet, and when the Ballet Rambert later went mod and dropped its corps de ballet he returned to research in microbiology.

He was also knowledgeable about vintage cars and was responsible for a memorable day in the service of culture. I had been to see Arnold Wesker's plays *The Kitchen* and *Chips with Everything* and had not warmed to his pacifist class-warrior message or accepted his assumption that a sow's ear is better than a silk purse. But the noble-savage myth was rife in the land and officialdom smiled on efforts to 'bring art to the people' – especially the people unlucky enough to live in the provinces. 'Art' in this sense was comprehensive enough to include a national dance competition – not ballet or ballroom dancing in today's sense, or anything elitest like that, but the ordinary *people's* Saturday night hop kind of dancing. Regional heats were to be held in the main cities, and the winning couples would compete in London finals. Arnold Wesker was involved and David had been asked to judge the heat in Ansell's Brewery canteen in Birmingham. He pressed me to go along to give him moral support.

It was a grey and threatening evening as we set off for Birmingham.

'I know what the trouble will be,' said David. 'This isn't the first of these things I've had to judge. The difficulty is not to choose the best dancers but to get anybody to dance at all. The girls all sit together for safety at one end of the room and the men hang round the bar at the other, trying to get their courage up.'

I particularly remember that day for three things: it was my first trip up the newly opened M1; the rain started to come down as we reached the outskirts of London and never stopped; and, as we tried to find our way to Ansells through the sodden back streets of industrial Birmingham a man we asked directions from shouted after us, 'He's gone in, you know!'

'Who's gone in?'

'Kennedy. He's gone into Cuba!'

By then I was in no state to absorb more shocks, for our drive had been horrific. David was at that time running a pre-war open Lagonda, and as we cowered under the vestigial hood, with rain blowing in through the windows, the windscreen wipers stopped working and from then on had to be manually operated. Ansell's canteen seemed a haven of peace, and nobody knew anything about Kennedy or Cuba. In fact there were very few people there at all, apart from the band of '23 Trombones', or some such name, who were setting up their microphones, and the patron himself, Arnold Wesker – a mild figure to be such an angry champion of the people. Gradually the hall began to fill up but, as David had predicted, the sexes stayed well apart long after the twenty-three trombones had begun to play. At last one or two couples took the floor.

'We don't want to hang about all night,' said David. 'We'll have to wait a bit until the floor doesn't look quite so empty. A dozen couples will do. Then I'll dive in and pick out the first who aren't actually hideous and tripping over each other.' This he soon managed to do. Unfortunately it turned out that the couple were not locals but had come up from London for the party. But that was Birmingham's bad luck and yet another example of how – Wesker or no Wesker – the provinces always lost out to the metropolis in the end. But the trip was not entirely wasted for David was persuaded to switch his Lagonda for a less lethal Lotus.

Both in London and elsewhere I was, as I had hoped, able to see my children frequently, which helped to heal the wounds of my divorce. I hoped that it did for the children too. Gus and Nick stayed with me from time to time; there was one nasty moment when Gus nipped into a tube train just as the doors closed, leaving me marooned on the platform. Fortunately he had the nous to get out at the next station, where I eventually joined him.

In 1962 Clare came to England as a boarder, and I was very glad to be within reach. She and Ian had been at day schools in Doha, where Peter Wilson now worked for the Qatar Petroleum Company. St Christopher's in Burnham-on-Sea was particularly good for children whose parents were abroad, and though it was off the beaten track I used to enjoy the drive; there was all the more time for my excitement to mount. I took the road over Bleadon Hill and always stopped to look at the view. It could be positively Arthurian, with the light shining from the gleaming Parrett estuary across the wetlands, and I imagined Princess Clare waiting for rescue from her academic imprisonment. Would she be as delighted to see me as I to see her? What would her first words be?

A few years later they were not very happy. I was summoned one Sunday by the house mistress of her secondary school to deal with a serious misadventure. Clare, by then head of her dormitory, lacked either the wish or the will to be a spoilsport in a scheme cooked up by one of the sillier of the girls. This was to smuggle in her brother – via the fire escape – to spend a night in the sick room free of charge. The brother got tight, turned up so late that everyone had gone to sleep, and went round the dorm flashing his cigarette lighter to find his sister. He found instead the unfortunate Clare, and both found themselves confronted by the house mistress. Now I in my turn was confronted by her and by her headmistress. The wayward girl, who – I was told pointedly – came from a broken home, would certainly have to be expelled and, since Clare had failed in her duty, they saw no option but to expel her too. I explained why I thought this was not a good idea (mainly because Germaine was abroad and I soon would be), and eventually they were good enough to agree with me. As I listened to the hushed tones of these two spinster teachers I heard with astonishment that they had done that one thing that, to avoid the headlines, they ought not to have done – they had rung the police. Any teacher who risked making her school a hostage to fortune like this hardly inspired a parent's confidence.

Confidence, however, sometimes comes second to convenience in matters of education. It was convenient to have all the children in one town, especially when they had relations there, and first Ian and then Andrew Wilson followed Gus and Nick to Clifton. At least for me this made life more enjoyable, and the Sabbath strictness that Gus had to suffer from his grandmother gave way to the genial hospitality of their Uncle Robin (Noel), retired from Malaya to his paternal roof.

It was about this time that I began seriously to question my competence as a parent. I had driven Nick to visit his Uncle Bim in the beguiling but domestically dotty schoolhouse he had bought at Cwm Ystwyth, near Devil's Bridge, and we were descending the mountain road from Nant-y-Moch reservoir to Talybont when I stopped to take a photograph. Somehow or other we both managed to slam the doors and lock them – it was easy to do in those days – with the keys still in the ignition. Talybont is not the liveliest of places but I managed to borrow a wire coat hanger, scrabble the window down enough to admit it, and actually 'fish' up the door lock inside. I thought at the time that I had learnt my lesson.

After I'd been in London for a couple of years the Council at last made my 'temporary' E grading permanent, and in 1964 I was offered the Grade D post of Representative, British Guiana. Needless to say this was to be yet again 'on temporary promotion'. 'BG', as old hands called it, was one of the more obscure of the countries that the Council has long since abandoned – Fiji, Sarawak, Mauritius, Somaliland, Aden and, also, in the West Indies, Jamaica and Trinidad – and it was only a two-man post. Still, it would be my first independent command, and it was imperative that I should go abroad again soon because Council assistance with boarding school fees would lapse after five years' service in Britain. I was intrigued with BG's position as an English-speaking enclave of mainland Latin America, bordered as it was by Venezuela in the north, Brazil in the east and Dutch Guiana (Surinam) in the south. But I was daunted by a total silence about its tourist attractions, when the islands of the Caribbean were becoming so well-known for theirs. (Paddy Leigh Fermor, in *The Traveller's Tree* and *The Violins of Saint Jacques* had shown that their glamour could tempt even devotees of the Isles of Greece.) Books about the country were suspiciously few. The Victorian world described by Charles Waterton was fascinating but hardly relevant. I could scarcely claim travel allowances for riding crocodiles, overnight expenses for slinging a hammock up the Essequibo River, or medical refunds for sticking my toe out of the mosquito net to tempt rabies-bearing vampire bats. Evelyn Waugh was nearer the mark with his combative description of the infrastructure in the thirties, but *90 Days* and its sequel *A Handful of Dust* scarcely painted a field ripe either for professional advancement or personal hedonism. Still, 'better to reign in hell than serve in heaven'; a Representative was a Representative.

It was not always obvious, however, what a Representative in these post-colonial posts was supposed to do (BG was to become fully independent, as Guyana, in 1966). Since the country was – apart from the tribes of the hinterland – English-speaking, our work was apparently to be of the adult education and community development kind. The Council had until then been only marginally concerned with industrial development there, which was largely dependent on Booker Brothers with their sugar plantations, the Canadian Bauxite town up the Demerara River, and agricultural schemes of the Commonwealth Development Corporation. Everyone I spoke to agreed that, taxing as British Guiana was physically, and in parts still as savage as Waugh had found it, the people were a hospitable, attractive and highly literate lot. None guessed what vipers were being nursed in Britannia's bosom, with the future decay of Guyana under its first president Lyndon Forbes Burnham and his successors, and the export to London of such pioneers of the race relations industry as Rudi Narayan, Bernie Grant and Herman Ousely.

It was strange, after four years in England, to be facing once more the bitter-sweet reaction to 'going abroad'. On the one hand it meant leaving children and friends, and no longer having time to do things at leisure; I would be back to a life where time dragged while abroad but rushed past on home leave, with half my plans remaining unfulfilled. On the other hand there was the excitement of going to a new place and the satisfaction of being a big frog again – even if the pool was small. British Guiana, if one disregarded the jungle and the savannahs, did indeed seem to be very small. It was a 'land of six peoples' – Amerindian, British, Negro, East Indian, Portuguese and Chinese (in that order chronologically) – but all six together amounted to little more than half a million, most of them working in sugar and rum, in bauxite, or in rice farming. The productive coastal land, below sea level and dependent on a dyke system built by the Dutch for its drainage, was very hot, and the muddy shoreline was uninviting for sailing or swimming. Roads were few and communication between the coast and the Amerindian highlands – unless one braved the old river routes used by Evelyn Waugh – was by ancient Dakota or amphibian Grumman aircraft.

However, a glance at the map and at the history books was intriguing. Until the defeat of Napoleon there had been a free-for-all among the British, French and Dutch enclaves up and down the coast, with the Dutch dominant, particularly under the long and energetic governorship of Laurens Storm van's Gravesande. Even when the British finally asserted their rights over what is now Guyana, and Longchamps and Stabroek expanded into Georgetown, other names remained to commemorate the languages of the early pioneers. In many cases these places had become little more than names because inland settlers, especially the Dutch, had abandoned their mixed riverine plantations for the rich drained land of the coastal strip. But no-one could read those names, tucked away in a map rich in geological features but almost devoid of towns, without a quickening of interest: Kijk-over-al, Vreed-en-Hoop, Werk-en-Rust; La Bonne Intention, Rossignol, Lusignan; Sir Walter Raleigh's Cataract, Monkey Jump, Kitty.

These names, however, did not sound as romantic to the woman I was then interested in as they did to me. She had a job and children at school in

England. And she was perhaps not over-impressed that I had not suggested marriage before, and thought that I did so now more for reasons of convenience than of love. My uncertainties, as over my first marriage, were no doubt all too obvious. At any rate she understandably declined to follow her Walter Raleigh over his cataract and on to El Dorado. I set off alone in the French liner *Flandres.*

As far as Port of Spain I wallowed in luxury. There were trips ashore in the French Antilles, recently glamorised by Paddy Leigh Fermor. Guadeloupe and Martinique were indeed almost threateningly beautiful and the neat French villages built round a formal square, *mairie* and church hardly prepared me for the ramshackle settlements of the British West Indies. The crew of the *Flandres* were distinctly offhand; I shared a cabin with a morose Frenchman who was even more put off by them than I was. The ship, he said, seemed to be run for their benefit rather than ours. His gloom may have been the result of being thwarted in his approaches to two French teachers returning to Cayenne. While ready enough to accept drinks in the bar, they retired alone each night to their first class double cabins thoughtfully allotted by the Purser. 'Teachers,' said my companion darkly, 'are not entitled to have the first class cabin. And why do you think each one is given the double cabin? It is not for you and me!'

The food on board was superb, diners taking it in turns to have flaming *crêpes suzette* served with a flourish at their tables. Sitting at mine was a pleasant but rather gloomy doctor. He had worked for six years at a Reynolds Metal mining camp deep in the *Handful of Dust* hinterland of British Guiana and his marriage had, perhaps understandably, broken down. During leaves he had fallen in love with Tobago, where he indulged his passion for skuba diving, and had eventually decided to leave the mine and live there permanently, putting up his plate in the main square of Scarborough and trusting to private practice to keep him going. He had bought the caravan used by Princess Margaret on her honeymoon to live in while he built his first home. However, this first house had been blown down in a hurricane two years before, and he was now engaged on a second and more substantial one. A couple of years later I went to the Trinidad Carnival and flew over for a few days in Tobago, certainly a most beautiful island if on the somnolent side. It was difficult to credit its miserable history of alternating occupation by the Spanish, Dutch and French and even by the Duke of Courland (from Latvia and a friend of Charles I). Little remains of all that apart from three old forts and a Georgian town hall in Scarborough. Near it I found the surgery with its plate: 'John Draper, MA Cantab., MRCS, LRCP' and inside, beside the framed diplomas, a notice: 'Please do not ask me for Leave Certificates; I only give these to people who are really sick, so you will be wasting my time and your own.' A receptionist, named Angela to judge by the label on her well-filled white uniform, said that John was at home with a cold, so I took myself to the Robinson Crusoe for a drink. The hotel was decorated with stills from a film made there in the twenties and the bar had a timeless air and a clientèle who seemed to have all the time in the world to spare. One of them was a distinguished-looking American, Major Timmerman (retired), who spent six weeks every year on the island. He introduced me to another guest as 'Father Alexander' and next day on the beach was waggish again.

'Come along with me for a minute, I've got something to show you.'

'What is it?' I asked, thinking of octopuses or mangrove oysters or glass-bottomed boats.

He took me out to the ends of a little jetty.

'There it is! Let me introduce you to my cousins.'

Lying in the sun were two girls in bikinis and, presenting me as 'Dr Larkin of Ulster', Timmerman made off. The girls were in fact the Misses Norah Cleary and Felicity Connolly of Dublin, hostesses of Aer Lingus enjoying a discount holiday. Dublin men, they explained, lived with their mothers until their forties and never went out with other women if they could help it. I promised to meet them for dinner but when I got back to the hotel found John Draper waiting for me, with an invitation to dine at his house. I explained the air hostess situation, so we all set off together, calling at the surgery on the way to pick up Angela.

The house was five miles from Scarborough in a spectacular position, perched on a windy height with wooded cliffs running down to a beach where white horses rolled into the coconut palms. It was a Robinson Crusoe creation but on a grand scale, with wood on concrete on stone, and windows and verandahs everywhere, and painted round the main room above the shutters in large letters the line 'ROLL ON, THOU DEEP AND DARK BLUE OCEAN ROLL'.

It emerged that Angela lived in the house as well as John, and by the time I left I could see the convenience of a lifestyle as practical and romantic as this one of my modern Crusoe and his Girl Friday. Why shouldn't I abandon the austerities of an independent Guyana and move to the kinder shores of a Windward island too small to encourage developers or racial tensions? Perhaps I should open a school of English with an obliging local registrar in Pointe à Pitre?

For a year John and Angela watched from their eyrie the deep and dark blue ocean roll. Then one day John went diving with a Canadian friend. Their usual boat boy was away, so they went with a stand-in. They dived and were not seen again. The boy, who had lost the marker buoy and drifted away, did nothing until it was too late to do anything.

Georgetown harbour in Guyana is shallow and little visited except by bauxite boats. "Guiana," wrote Sir Walter Raleigh, "is a country that hath yet her maidenhead, never sacked, burnt nor wrought. The face of the earth hath not been torn, nor the virtue and salt of the soil spent by manurance, the graves have not been opened for gold, the mines not broken with sledges." Unfortunately this is no longer true and the decrepit harbour is evidence of the country's ineffective struggle to make the most of nature's bounty. The salt of the soil has been spent and the mines broken with sledges, but to what compensatory effect? In order to catch leave boats home, I had to fly to more populous harbours. St Lucia was one, where I picked up the Grimaldi-Siosa Line *Caribia*. Of 1926 vintage, she had been the old *Vulcania* and presented a sad contrast to the *Flandres*; although the crew were much jollier there were barely thirty-five passengers in each of the first and second class and only the third class had a full quota of immigrants. Sometimes as I paced the empty decks, passed the three swimming pools, the lounge, verandah bar, Bavarian Room, Chinese Parlour, Writing Room, Card Room or Gymnasium I felt as if I'd strayed onto the set of *Outward Bound* or boarded the *Mary Celeste*. Between Madeira, Lisbon, Vigo, Le Havre and Southampton I had the library to myself. I soon abandoned a novel by Edna O'Brien, *August is a Wicked Month*, a blow-by-blow account of her heroine contracting venereal disease from a waiter on the Riviera, but I think of it still when I see a glamorous photograph of the author. In Lisbon I bought a newspaper which reported a law case in which a school friend of mine was counsel for the prosecution. The cross-examination suggested that Edna O'Brien might usefully have studied it to bring light relief to her leaden plots:

> Miss Smith: 'Miss Jones invited me to tea to make the proposition. He didn't want ordinary sex; he wanted whipping. I was disgusted.'
> Desmond Vowden: 'Why didn't you just walk out?'
> Miss Smith: 'I didn't want to offend my hostess. Besides I hadn't finished my tea.'

On my last trip home from Guyana in 1968 I was a minor adjunct to a cargo of bananas. But the *Geestbay* was as smart as paint: Dutch-built and British and West Indian-owned, she carried sixteen passengers in great comfort. There was a small swimming pool and we ate magnificently with the officers – and had to contribute to their evening variety shows. I flew to Bridgetown to embark and for the first week we loaded bananas from St Vincent, St Lucia, Grenada and Dominica, giving passengers a day or two ashore in each island. It was an amazing sight to watch the chains of brightly dressed women bearing on their heads huge bunches of bananas in an endless crocodile for hour after hour. At one port they had already been replaced with a mechanical loader and there was soon to be resistance to further mechanisation. I was sorry to think that such a colourful and communal parade was doomed to give way to the march of progress. After Dominica we went straight across to our anything but lush landfall at Barry in South Wales. The idea that Raleigh had of Guiana can scarcely have proved more misleading than that of a first-time visitor to England when faced with a Barry landfall. I was told of a previous trip of the *Geestbay* which had been dogged by misfortune, with only two lady passengers who, by the time they approached Barry, had long ceased to be on speaking terms. As luck would have it – bad weather, strikes, bank-holidays, or all of these – the ship could not land them and they had had to suffer each other's unalleviated company for another week. As for me, I had no complaints whatever of the ship or the company, but the contrast of a cold, wet Barry with our last port of call was so abrupt that I felt I had left the Caribbean for ever. But I was wrong.

12
British Guiana – Land of Six Peoples

'EH, EH, I'M SORRY FOR YOU,' said a Trinidadian fellow passenger cheerfully as we went ashore at Port of Spain on my first journey to British Guiana, 'flying on to Georgetown so! Is hot, man, and nothing but mud in your eye!'

From the air, a couple of hundred miles out, British Guiana looked extraordinarily sober in comparison. So did the sea, which had turned brown from the effluents of the Orinoco to the north, and the great rivers of Essequibo, Demerara, Berbice and Courantyne within its own shaky borders. The coast near Georgetown, unlike the cliffs and forests and beaches of Trinidad, was as flat as a pancake and as orderly as a chess board, with sugar plantations laid out as with a ruler and neatly criss-crossed by canals. The impression of sobriety, however, was quickly dispelled on landing at the spartan airport in a kind of no-man's-land of scrub. The twenty-mile road to Georgetown along the bank of the Demerara, only recently metalled, was already breaking up. It was lined with wooden shacks on stilts and ramshackle smallholdings, while white prayer flags and mosques distinguished the East Indian villages. ('East Indian' was the term used to distinguish descendants of indentured labourers from India, now in control of the rice industry, from indigenous Amerindians of the interior.) African villages were scruffier but less prim and better served by rum shops. The rum itself soon became all-pervasive as the road passed through Diamond Plantation where the factory treatment of molasses emitted the stifling rotten-egg smell of sulphurated hydrogen.

Georgetown was signalled by the quaint turret of the Dutch-style Stabroek Market, and Dutch influence was at once obvious, both in the white wooden houses, most of them with their open 'bottom houses' filled in with shops or living rooms, and the grid plan of the streets, based on the plantation land on which they had been built. In some cases – notably in Main Street – the original canals had been filled in to form beautiful avenues. In contrast, the town centre boasted ornate Victorian Gothic buildings – such as the Law Courts – and towering over them all the 1892 cathedral designed by Blomfield, said to be the largest wooden building in the world, its white walls topped by a shimmering aluminium roof. Alan Knight, the celibate Archbishop of the West Indies, and the Dean were still British, and well-run

Anglican services both there and in smaller parish churches were on the 'high' side, in contrast to those of the many nonconformist sects. Oddly enough, I never met the Archbishop socially (I think few people outside the church did) but he rang me up once to ask if the Council could help a protégé of his with his education in England. 'By all means,' I said. 'When can he come and see me?' 'Well, that's rather difficult. He's on his way to the airport now.'

I put up at the old wooden Park Hotel on Main Street, run with a rod of iron by Mrs Gonzalves (pronounced in two syllables). It was not as smart as the concrete Tower Hotel further down the road but it had more character. (The Tower, however, had a swimming pool, where I met one evening an elderly journalist called Wilson practising his casts with a fishing rod. He lived in Cuba and had no time for Ernest Hemingway, who had insulted him in a bar and then declined to come outside.) A regular diner at the Park was 'Tiger' Long, a retired DC who apparently spent most of his time at the Georgetown Club. He always wore white and sat by himself. We were the only two *buccra* (white) men there but, like Alexander Kinglake's two travellers passing each other in the desert, we never spoke. I have always regretted this because the more I saw of British Guiana the more inconceivable it seemed that any non-Guyanese, unless he had family interests or was a 'white hunter' (like, as will appear, Tiny McTurk), should want to spend his retirement there.

Soon after my arrival I was invited to watch the Buffs 'Beating the Retreat' – for not quite the last time – for the Queen's Birthday, an elegant performance evidently enjoyed by the locals. As soon as it was over and the Governor had driven off in his official car – an ancient Austin Princess – hoards of little black boys came whooping and capering and somersaulting onto the grass under the floodlights.

Eighteen months later the British army left the new Guyana and her problems (such as Jonestown and the People's Temple) to the Guyana Defence Force to sort out. They also left some broken hearts behind them, as I noted in a letter home:

> Derek Horsford's lot, the King's, who haven't seen action since Korea and were disappointed not to get any at Kuwait, are moving out shortly. Derek is dying to go to Borneo. The Paras are already out and perhaps licking their wounds. A silly little Bookers wife threatened suicide when the Colonel explained why he couldn't marry her. "Of course he was dying to do so but it wouldn't be fair to his wife, who really *was* dying – of leukaemia." Unfortunately for her peace of mind she learned from an unsympathetic fellow officer that the Colonel's wife was that very week playing hockey for Hertfordshire. The Colonel's second-in-command, a good Catholic with nine children, would have been just the man to keep the Colonel on the straight and narrow had he not been heavily involved with the wife of the Foreign Office Adviser to the Governor. Fortunately the Adviser is not unduly

> worried because he is infatuated with the wife of my Assistant. My Assistant is the object of the affections of the Norwegian wife of an Afro-Guyanese barrister but is himself more interested in an East Indian girl that I take out from time to time. So I suppose I should really do the decent thing, get off the ladder and leave them to it.

The Council office and library was an absolute slum in Robb and Hincks Street. It was on the edge of the characterless commercial centre, which had been rebuilt in concrete after a fire in 1945. It was extremely hot, there was no air-conditioning, and papers tended to blow about if the fans were run fast enough to make any difference to the temperature. At the corner of the street an old black man, said to have once been a teacher, used to perform his daily ritual. Every morning Mr Johnson wheeled up a wooden box filled with old newspapers, sat on it, took his clothes off, searched them for (presumably) fleas, and tore the newspapers up into tiny shreds which he scattered on the pavement. A street sweeper solemnly cleaned them up in the evening when Mr Johnson had gone home.

I soon found, wandering about at night, that Georgetown was no Beirut or Hong Kong. Steel bands, especially in the distance, have great charm (to hear them approaching at dawn in the Trinidad carnival is magical). But when they thunder out amplified from one rum shop after another it is a different matter. Apart from one Chinese restaurant, I never found anywhere where it was not a penance to eat. Exasperated one evening with the Guyanese indifference to temperature, I asked why, if the meat and sweet potato were served hot, the obviously tinned 'mixed veg' had been slopped onto the plate stone cold. 'Is only garnish, man,' I was told, 'not for eating.' Still, in all my four years of walking about I was never jumped. As the political and racial situation worsened there was a lot of 'choke'n'rob', particularly on visitors, but I seem to have been thought not worth bothering about – though my house was robbed three times.

It was a relief to get out of the Park Hotel into a flat, though the flat itself was a mixed blessing. My first Assistant Representative, Ivor Watts, was going home on leave and I was to keep his flat warm until his return. 'Warm' was the word! 'I will not,' said Ivor, for he was nothing if not dogmatic, 'I will not live in a combustible wooden house!' So he had taken a flat in a row of little concrete boxes that cooked up all day and retained the heat far into the night. He had his reasons. Racial tensions were prompting dreadful acts of arson that were easily effected in the bottom house of wooden buildings; the entire family of Abrahams, the Permanent Secretary at the Ministry of Agriculture, had been burned to death not long before my arrival – except for one girl who was out late at the Theatre Guild.

I shared Ivor's hot little box with Hamish Wilson, an expert on stage design, who was out on a long visit to advise the local thespians. As we tossed and turned under our mosquito nets our sleeplessness was exacerbated by the barking of hundreds of dogs, and Hamish would leap from his bed from time to time and scream through the windows, 'Oh, shut up! Will you SHUT UP!'

I eventually moved into a wooden house on Church Street, a green double avenue leading out to the botanical gardens (where huge manatees browsed inertly in the pool, looking very unlike the mermaids for whom early seamen were said to have mistaken them). There was a verandah overlooking the garden in the back, and it was delightful to sit there, watching the hummingbirds and having a sundowner, as the evening breeze sprang up and brought relief for two or three hours.

On one side lived Mary Gadd, sister of 'Tiny' McTurk of whom I was to see more in the interior, and on the other was a small and unassuming mosque. Unlike my neighbouring mosque in Beirut, it did not ruin my slumbers with an amplified muezzin. However, it was curious to gaze down through the slats of my bathroom when relieving myself in the morning, across the garden and straight onto the backs of the faithful as they bowed towards the East – which in this case was me. (I felt similarly discountenanced some years later at the magnificent *parador* in the former monastery of San Felipe in Leon. The beautiful monastery chapel was still in use and from the upstairs bar one found oneself, as one sipped one's gin and tonic, gazing down as though in the gallery of a theatre at the communicants celebrating in the chapel below.)

I was soon able to move the Council office into an airy wooden house in Carmichael Street beside a park made from plantation land. (It was intriguing to hear some of this far-flung land linked with names familiar at home for different reasons. William Gladstone's brother, for instance, had been one of the most vociferously anti-abolitionist plantation owners, while a Quintin Hogg had made over his estates to the schools and sports fields on the edge of town.)

Unfortunately, the greenery and the canal waterways were not as nice as they looked. The grass harboured *bêtes rouges* which burrowed into the skin causing itching in sweaty places (the cure was suffocation, for which nail varnish was effective) and the water was part of the lifecycle of the parasitic worms carried by mosquitoes that caused filariasis. It was painful to see many country people – particularly women – with the enormously swollen legs it caused.

It was a great advantage of my house that the 'bottom house' had not been filled in and was large enough for film shows. Films in the open air, and yet under cover, with drinks while the reels are changed, are particularly enjoyable in the tropics, and the very incongruity of the scenes on screen and the place of their showing adds to the drama. The aggressively non-Caribbean extravagances and affectations of the Royal Ballet's *Sleeping Beauty* kept the locals coming again and again – and were, after all, echoed in the amazing Carnival fantasies of Trinidad.

For showing educational films we had two long-wheelbase Land Rovers with petrol generators (until one of them was inserted neatly into a malarial drain in a drunken moment by the junior driver-projectionist). The senior driver, the admirable Robert Bollers, introduced me to schools and plantations on the coast road (then still the only road) up to Charity in the north, and down 60 miles to New Amsterdam and beyond it to Springlands on the Dutch Guiana border. The drives were bone-shaking for the road surface of burnt earth disintegrated each rainy season. Between the rivers ran the oldest railway in South America, founded in 1848, but it was slow and uncertain (and anyway we needed the generators for film shows), so we rarely patronised it.

We had another office and library at New Amsterdam, on the far side of the Berbice River and reached by a decrepit ferry from the Rossignol railhead. I used to stay at the very grand Colony House, immaculately run by a housekeeper addressed by all as 'Mistress'; occasionally there was an immaculate lawyer staying there too. (There were said to be four hundred lawyers in the country, with only four dentists including the Prime Minister, Cheddi Jagan, which was part of the country's problem.) New Amsterdam, with its charming old Lutheran church, was greener and more picturesque than Georgetown, and the coastline was more attractive. It was hard to associate its faded prettiness with the savage Berbice slave rebellion of 1763 on one of the Dutch plantations there.

I shall always remember a night in New Amsterdam during the wet season, when a plague of enormous flying beetles made going outside or anywhere near a light a misery. Four of us sat inside an enormous mosquito net, suitably furnished with refreshments (not, needless to say, in the resthouse) and played poker by torchlight.

In the wet season the road to Rossignol was depressing in the extreme. There was often brackish water as far as the eye could see, with the houses on their stilts sticking forlornly out of it, and the bottom houses – if they were not submerged – giving sanctuary to pigs and sheep. Nearer Georgetown, places like Uitvlugt, Le Ressouvenir, Bachelor's Adventure and Maiden's Despair enjoyed better sea defences from their proximity to a sugar estate.

The road to the north, with a wider crossing over the Essequibo, was called the Cinderella Coast because many of its estates had reverted to subsistence farming. Bartica, 30 miles up the Essequibo, still had the raffish air of an old gold town, and the fact that the Dutch built their first fort, Kyk-over-al, hereabouts added to the air of romantic decay. There was a pleasant beach at Suddie, where I used to enjoy a swim after the rather nerve-wracking film shows at the Reformatory School. (The sea near Georgetown, kept at bay by the old Dutch *stellings* (wharves), *kokers* (sluice gates) and *polders* (dams), was useless for swimming or sailing because it was not only thick with mud but endlessly shallow.)

The Essequibo was the hunting ground not only of the Arawak and Wapishana Indians but also of Charles Waterton; modern travel writers still follow in his footsteps along its length from the southern border with Brazil. It is a moot point whose tales should be taken with the biggest pinch of salt. Gerald Durrell, in *Three Singles to Adventure,* describes a swim he had in a lake near Adventure, a little ferry port at the mouth of the Essequibo; afterwards the locals are amazed at his daring: didn't he know that the lake was swarming with pirai – the local variety of pirana – and that he must be the only man to have swum in it without losing precious parts of his anatomy? The lake is delightful and I used to swim regularly in it. Nicholas Guppy, in his book about the 'blind white fish' of the Rupununi, describes returning from a trip and being welcomed by 'Tiny' McTurk who, as Guppy emerges from the door of the plane, raises his arms as a salute to his achievement. 'But it wasn't like that at all,' said Tiny. 'I raised my arms to catch him because he was shaking like a leaf and looked ready to fall at any moment.'

Tiny, so called because of his great height and strength even in his seventies, was head of a dynasty that lived and worked among the Amerindians. He and his wife lived surrounded by animals in an open-sided ranch house at Karanambo that was more like a tent than a building but yet had Georgian furniture and silver in it. His daughter, Diana, was a PRO for Booker Brothers and later took over the farm and bred otters there. His sister was the object of interest to Sir Charles Woolley, one of the former governors invited to celebrate the independence of 'Guyana' in 1966. I was asked to put him up and when he learned that Mary Gadd was my neighbour he was eager that I should arrange a meeting. She, however, was equally eager that I should not, and I gathered that in his days as Governor he had been known locally as 'Champagne Charlie'. ('And, oh dear!' said one of my secretaries when she saw him again, 'hasn't he gone off!') Instead of Mary Gadd he had to entertain a group of artists and dancers brought in by our Theatre Guild people, including Rex Nettleford who ran the Jamaican Ballet, and the Trinidadian-Chinese king of the Carnival Bands who drank an immense amount of rum.

The Governor in my time was Sir Richard Luyt, pronounced 'Late' and thus the inspiration of the *Guiana Chronicle* headline 'BETTER LUYT THAN NEVER'. He had been proposed when Colonial Secretary in Northern Rhodesia and Cheddi Jagan, as Prime Minister, had demurred at his South African background. Kenneth Kaunda, however, had said, 'Take him, he's a good man' and a good man he proved to be. Government House was a handsome clapboard building on Main Street and very much in the public eye. That didn't worry Luyt who was a walk-about sort of chap and liked to take his constitutional along the sea wall. This was a popular place of rendezvous, as celebrated in a calypso.

Take me, take me!
I am feeling lonely.
Take me down to the old sea wall -
But don't let my mother know!

Luyt was often to be seen knocking up a cricket ball with the beach boys on the mud. He had been a sergeant in the Abyssinian war, commissioned for gallantry in the field, and had had little sympathy with Wingate's messianic ways and his reluctance to share glory with anyone else. 'I realise,' Wingate had said, 'that I am God's instrument and will of course carry out my task. But I wish He had given me better material to carry it out with!' Luyt described one night when the big breakthrough from Kenya was expected and he sat up with Wingate listening to wireless reports. As each success was reported, Wingate banged his fist into his palm, crying, 'Damn! Damn! Damn!'

The independence celebrations in 1966 were organised by a retired Colonel who had plenty of practice of doing the same for larger colonies, remained admirably cool through all the excitement, and succeeded in presenting what everyone agreed was a thoroughly enjoyable national 'jump-up'. Thereafter we tried to get used to calling the country 'Guyana' and dropping its affectionate diminutive of BG.

After independence a huge new presidential complex was built out near the Botanical Gardens. The old Government House became the British High Commissioner's residence and a new air-conditioned block of offices housed a surprising number of dark-suited staff. Their houses were large and guarded by night watchmen, and I was curious to see how all these people could be gainfully employed when most of the work that Luyt had done as Governor with a man and a boy had been passed over to the new government. My first 'prayer meeting' did little to enlighten me. A lot of characters with important-sounding portfolios – Information, Commerce, Development – sat round discussing what they could busy themselves with. 'I thought we might do a survey on prospects for developing the rice industry further inland,' said one. 'Isn't that the responsibility of the Colonial Development Corporation?' said another. 'They are a bit cagey since the failure of their coffee scheme,' said a third. 'What about timber in the Bartica Triangle? Is that something we can usefully help them with?' 'I shouldn't think we can help anyone with anything until we've done something about the appalling roads.' 'And sea defences.' 'And air transport.' 'And trade unions.' 'And ... shall we have coffee?'

Sooner or later they had to face the fact that although, since 1941, British Guiana had had more financial help per capita than any other dependency, scheme after scheme had failed, remaining little fleas on the backs of the few big flea corporations – Booker Brothers (sugar and general foods), Alcan (at Mackenzie, 60 miles up the Demerara River) and Union Carbide (at the remote Matthews' Ridge on the Barima River). Rice, the second crop of the country, remained largely in private Indian hands.

But of course there was now another outlet for diplomatic energies and that was taking in the washing from other new embassies – especially from Venezuela (who disputed her frontier with Guyana and may or may not have been fermenting cessation from the settlers in the interior) and from the United States (who had missionaries equipped with the only non-commercial planes in the interior, and were interested in the communist leanings of local parties, at that time more overt in Cheddi Jagan's East Indian People's

Progressive Party than in Burnham's breakaway African People's National Congress).

The PPP/PNC division had occurred in 1953, the year when a new constitution was introduced to facilitate a general election and the introduction of home rule. The PPP was victorious and – inspired by Jagan's American wife, Janet – declared a Marxist war with such enthusiasm, against commercial interests in general and the sugar industry in particular, that riots and arson and strikes resulted, the British army was brought in to restore order, and the constitution was suspended. By the time I arrived it was racial difference that most distinguished the two main, 'East Indian' and 'African', parties, with a third 'United Party' of Portuguese, Chinese and Creoles – headed by Peter D'Aguiar of 'D'Aguiar's Rum' – which was very much smaller but retained some influence in industry and education. Burnham and his PNC were eventually deemed amenable to democratic persuasion and, with support from the British, American and Canadian governments, were ushered into power in 1966.

Jagan, apart from his politics, was a man of considerable charm, but Burnham was a more sombre character with a sardonic humour. His law scholarship in England had left him with bitter feelings of discrimination, and perhaps this encouraged a tendency to grandiloquent display in his early days of power. He used to ride, immaculately dressed, past my house on his white horse of an evening and raise his whip in gracious acknowledgment of my salutation. Afro-Caribbeans are said to consider manhood ill-served by birth control and ill-proved by the birth of daughters, and Burnham was disappointed in two marriages without male issue. In the years of his later 'co-operative republic' he can have had few friends, but he started his premiership with plenty of goodwill – though the goodwill was unfortunately not mutual between him and the first British High Commissioner, who departed after a year. I was sorry about this for he and his wife had been helpful over Council affairs. He was not, however, the only one to suffer after the transfer of power.

Former ministers in the PPP government did not take kindly to rule by the PNC, and several were arrested and exiled to detention up the Mazaruni River near Bartica. There they were visited by the former government vet, Ptolemy Read, a great gorilla of a man and now the new minister in charge of prisons, charged with the welfare not of animals in their cages but of members of the opposition in theirs. The former Minister of Education was particularly vociferous in his complaints, haranguing Ptolemy as he went round the prison with the refrain, 'Man, you ugly! When you gonna let us out?' Ptolemy ignored him until he was leaving, but when once more the cry came, 'You ugly, man! When you gonna let us out?' he turned and bared his teeth in a crocodile smile. 'When I's pretty,' he said.

Creole English has the bounce and fizz of Irish English but with even more dimensions, not surprisingly since in Guyana the legacies of Amerindian languages, Yoruba, Dutch, French, Portuguese, Cantonese and Hindi are all represented in it. No wonder the new wave of Caribbean academics, not to mention their American and English colleagues, have been lured by the fascination of describing it.

In 1963 the new University of Guyana had got off to a rocky start under the wing of the University of Essex. I reported the event in a letter home of October 1964: 'Sir Christopher Cox is arriving today to see whether the University of Guyana deserves financial support. It started prematurely a year ago with a lot of leftist lecturers under Lancelot Hogben (*Science for the Citizen*, *Mathematics for the Million*) ... The university is really a night school operating in a secondary school building and taking people with five 'O' levels. But it is INDEPENDENT, and that of course is all that matters. I am relieved that it is independent of the British Council.'

Inevitably, the Canadian Vice Chancellor, Alan Earp, was to find himself more and more resented as a foreigner, starved of funds and subject to the general corruption as the country disintegrated under Burnham. Even in my time prognostications were not good, for UG seemed in danger of perpetuating the weakness of its feeder schools – a bias towards the arts which turned out literate and amusing people bored by, and untrained for, the kind of work needed to develop the country. Yet there were impressive schools in Georgetown – like Queens College and the Jesuit St Stanislas for boys, and Bishop's High School and St Mary's Ursuline Convent School for girls. The Mother Superior of the convent, which numbered the daughter of the notorious Michael X among its pupils, endeared herself to me by producing, after one of my lectures, a full bottle of whisky for my refreshment. The principal of St Stanislas, Father Hopkinson, urged me to bring out from England on a lecture tour a bright young Campion Hall lecturer and poet named Peter Levi. (I wish I had done so. In 1999 Levi, who had jumped over the wall in 1977 to marry Cyril Connolly's widow Deirdre and become sometime Professor of Poetry at Oxford and somewhat over-exposed in print, referred in the *Spectator* to this period as the time 'when I left school and started a long impersonation of a Jesuit priest').

Even the poorer schools were rightly a source of pride to staff and parents, with strict discipline and careful attention to dress. I accompanied a visiting lecturer from Leicester University and a local teacher-trainer on a trip up the Cinderella coast. The visitor had taught only in Nigeria and compared everything he saw to his African experience. The teacher-trainer was bewailing the absence of jobs in a country unsettled by independence. 'Guyana is such a poor undeveloped country,' he said, 'and anyway what is there to develop. We have no natural resources which are exploitable.'

We were passing through a small ramshackle village just as its two schools were discharging their pupils, and the dirt road was flooded with well-scrubbed brightly-clothed pupils, changing the scene like flowers in a forest clearing.

'There are your resources,' said the visitor, 'these children.'

'But what will become of them? There's nothing for them to do.'

That indeed was the problem, both on the coast and with Amerindian children in the interior. The birth rate had risen with the eradication of

Bogotá: Harold Norminton and friends

Ozzie Pope and Gus

Tehran: the house in Kuchek Rezaieh

James Wakelin and Nasser: 'Can I come with you?'

Beirut: the *Champollion* goes down

A scholar-ship comes up: Lady Kelly, Fouad Ammoun, Kit Morray, Maroun Arab, Mme Moreno, Sir David Kelly

Anglo-French rivalry at Baalbek: Jean-Louis Barrault, David Dodimead, Michael Benthall, Robert Helpmann, Madeleine Renault, Barbara Jefford

The Order of the Cedars: Zelpha and Camille Chamoun, and Robert Helpmann

The Old Vic: SCA, George Middleton, Germaine, Barbara Jefford

The young Phoenix Players in *Romanov and Juliet*:
(clockwise) SCA (director), Tony Irving (set), Ruth Watkins, Bob Chase, Bea Russell, Donald Reeves, Tim Williams, Christopher Scaife, Germaine, Pamela Moore, Don Marquardt, Robbie Arab, Peter Wilson (SM)

St Vincent from the *Geestbay*: 'Tally me banana!'

Georgetown: a brighter future?

1969: Old Spain watches and waits

No tourists in Toledo yet

Plenty in Catalonia: sardanas in Montblanc

Clare in Colonia Tovar, Caracas

malaria and TB, just as the backlash to colonial status was immobilising the economy. 'Development' was a vogue word as the Empire broke up, but what exactly was to be developed and how the locals were going to be persuaded to co-operate in it was never clarified. Schemes by the Commonwealth Development Corporation had rarely prospered in British Guiana and some of their representatives were far from impressive. I also took against my first emissary from Oxfam; I had not then appreciated its resources or its political agenda. 'A horrible bearded representative of Oxfam,' I wrote home, 'who is normally resident in Basutoland, is in town offering Guiana money for some agricultural schemes; good schemes, I think, in themselves, though hardly what the Charity Commission might think justified tax exemption nor in line with Oxfam photos of starving babies. He also, like the lecturer from Leicester, assumes that what's good for Africa is good for the Caribbean.'

All these educational advisers and development experts were viewed with a jaundiced eye by the major employers struggling against local lethargy and militant trades unions. Cane cutting is not a pleasant occupation, but Bookers were enlightened employers and the demand for jobs far outstripped the supply. The estates had their own way of life, even to race meetings with the magnificent mules that used to pull the cane barges along the canals. It was much the same with bauxite mining. But all this went west after nationalisation in the bad Burnham years. The Chinese and Portuguese fled the country (mostly to Canada), roads disintegrated, ferries sank, and the importing of 'luxuries' like wheat flour was banned so that Guyanese returned from abroad with suitcases full of bread. And in the end Bookers had to be invited back by franchising the sugar industry to them.

But this was in the future. In the meantime the Voluntary Service Overseas organisation had recently started up, and for some years the Council acted as its overseas arm. One of the first volunteers in British Guiana had been a school leaver named Colin Henfrey who had upset his sponsors, Bookers, by writing an idealistic and critical book called *The Gentle People* about the treatment of Amerindians. Elsewhere it had proved unwise to send out untrained seventeen-year-olds to remote places with little supervision. So a reconstituted VSO eventually limited recruitment to graduate volunteers. In my last two years I had twenty-five of them to look after, and they greatly increased the interest of my work. Their presence also encouraged me to have Gus to stay with me in his gap year between school and university. He came out on a bauxite boat and taught at a school in East Rhuimveldt, one of the poorer suburbs, and with the help of one of the ubiquitous mopeds that thronged the narrow Georgetown roads was soon independent of me for transport and entertainment. In fact the local environment was then infinitely less dangerous than the druggy scene beginning to envelop England, and I greatly enjoyed having him with me.

Most VSOs, too, were teaching, some in parts of the country I would otherwise not have visited. About a third were first-rate, a third useful, and a third useless or worse. I had no real authority over volunteers, could only refer crises to VSO headquarters in London, and couldn't help but wonder what the future held for some of the 'flower girls' I met at the airport with their guitars on their backs. I had a visit from the police about one of them; was I aware that she was living with a notorious burglar? There was a very real temptation for VSOs to succumb to the charms of British-passport hunters. The locals were in many ways more mature than these young British graduates. Certainly they were more pragmatic about the institution of marriage, and there was a great difference between the easy-going life of the Caribbean and the stresses of black ghettos in Britain. It was during a home leave that I first heard Enoch Powell's warning on mass immigration, and when I dropped a Guyanese friend at his relative's house in darkest Clapham I was depressed by how grey and chilly the scene appeared compared with the colourful warmth the residents had left behind.

'Is there racial prejudice in Britain?' asked Robert Bollers mischievously at one of my talks to British Council scholars, expecting me to deny it in the usual weasel words.

'Of course there is. Just as there is here and in every country in the world. It's a fact of life. But it's like any other sort of prejudice. It is manageable with tolerance and common sense. With legislation it gets worse.' Bollers laughed.

It was as overseer of the VSOs that I met the Queen during her tour of the West Indies just before Guyanese independence in 1966; Prince Philip, who came with her, was patron of the VSO organisation. Georgetown had had a facelift for the occasion; shacks and rubbish heaps disappeared, choked canals were cleared, hedges were trimmed, and the buildings on the royal route had had the sides facing the road repainted. Esso advertising hoardings, which had been hopefully erected to catch the royal eye, were demolished, and PPP slogans – 'BRITISH GET OUT', 'RELEASE DETAINEES NOW' – were whitewashed away. Flags and bunting appeared everywhere, including some 'GR' decorations too good to waste, and floodlighting and coloured lights gave the chief buildings with their Victorian turrets and fancy white woodwork a fairyland appearance. About a hundred choke'n'rob boys and known bad eggs were wheeled into custody, and for a couple of weeks we could walk the streets and leave our houses untenanted in safety.

I attended the Investiture at Government House so that I could present eighteen of my Volunteers in the ten-minute interval between that and the Governor's garden party, while the Governor dashed upstairs to get out of his 40 lb uniform. In the ballroom the British Army band played softly, while some twenty-five local worthies, with their wives bursting out of frilly dresses and topped by amazing hats, waited expectantly. The English wife of Sir Lionel Luckhoo, High Commissioner in London, had had the courage to appear in a sari.

At last the national anthem heralded the royal entrance, and in came the Queen, on that hot airless day, looking very unsunburnt and dressed more for Budleigh Salterton than British Guiana, but with her famous smile and dignity intact. As each recipient of an honour bowed or curtsied in front of her, she had to say a little something before the farewell handshake. This meant that before our turn came she had already had to think of twenty-five little somethings and must have been feeling the strain.

After the Investiture we adjourned to a private room. The plan had been that, after my introduction, drinks would be handed round and the Queen with Prince Philip would circulate informally among the Volunteers. However, she chose to stand with the Prince while each Volunteer was formally presented. I had thought up a leading remark to make as I introduced each Volunteer, but it was never followed up, and after a tedious and repetitive question and answer session the presentation was over, and the Queen took a soft drink and switched off. Prince Philip, however, made a beeline for the girls and chatted away uninhibitedly.

I don't know what the Queen thought of the private lives of her local prime ministers. Burnham's wife had departed for Trinidad a fortnight before the Queen's visit because of his philandering, ignoring his orders to return; and in Trinidad Eric Williams was being sued for alimony.

It was either Clairmont Tait or Ricky Smith of the Guyana *Graphic* who, when I expressed surprise that the paper syndicated Andy Capp cartoons as they were not merely British but regional British and showed men in such a bad light, said 'Oh, we Guyanese identify with Andy Capp. He has all our national characteristics. Ask our wives.'

13
Land of Hope and Glory

PTOLEMY REID'S use of Creole to enliven more formal 'received' English was universal. Transference from 'village' English, incomprehensible to strangers, to a more sophisticated Creole occurred in most schools at six or seven and with further schooling became more metropolitan. But the language of early school leavers remained picturesque in both African and East Indian communities. In 1955 Michael Swan was commissioned by the Colonial Office to write *British Guiana: the Land of Six Peoples*. (He later wrote a more personal and gossipy sequel.) Inevitably, the book is filled with facts and figures, but Swan catches the feel of the place and the flavour of the language as soon as he drives in from the airport. 'The car slowed down to negotiate a pothole and a young African in a spotless white shirt cried to his girl, "Gal, me say wi'out fada pravacation, me and you is for d'pictures dis rainy night".'

Later, at Port Mourant beyond New Amsterdam, he interviews Cheddi Jagan's father, a former 'driver' or foreman of a sugar plantation labour gang, taking a 'snap' in the Rock Diamond rum parlour. Jagan Senior exercises his irony on the then Governor (Savage). 'Me has known five governors, and this governor him best of lot. This governor very nice man. Before him came us had no money in BG, and him come and get forty-four million dorras for we. Him very nice man. But till this day us down here in Courantyne no see one cent. Him very nice man, me say. Before him come us in BG no see British sojer, no see kilts, now British sojer here pointing gun at me, and so I say this governor him very nice man. Him think of me when him take away Constitution, think to do good for me and my son Cheddi him oh so bad for Colony. Oh, yes, I say, this governor him very nice man.'

The Creole of African rather than East Indian origin is even more idiosyncratic, and the cultural review *Kyk-Over-Al*, published in Georgetown by Ian MacDonald, features articles by academics like Ian Robertson and Jeanette Allsop who are beginning to turn over the linguistic compost heap of Creole English with its vocabulary derived from so many languages. The Dutch, besides many marine words and place names like Beterverwagting and Goed Fortuin, bequeathed *baas* (master) and *mauger* (thin) and *scrawly* (sickly). There are Amerindian loan words for creatures (*agouti, baridi, gueriman*), fruit (*awara, papaya, sapodilla*) and food (*casareep, mauby* – a bitter bark making a refreshing drink). Portuguese words introduced by immigrants of 1830 include *bacalao, ole-yard* (evil eye), *cob* (brown-skinned, from *cobre*) and *santantone* (an African-Portuguese). The French have left comparatively few loan words – the hated *bête rouge, crapaud* and *chiffonier* – but, like the Dutch, many plantation names – L'Heureuse, Beau Voisin, Le Désir.

Other loan words may have come from West African languages such as Yoruba, and the way words are put together echo African constructions. Dhanis Jaganauth gives examples of the vernacular that are only comprehensible to the stranger when transcribed. Here is an interview with a rice farmer:

> Nowadeez ting difren. Evribade yuuz chrakta. De gon plou wid chrakta, kyer-iin pade wid chrakta, an de yuuz aal mashiin an so aan tu du di work. Den wen di rais groo-op, wel, de go yuuz kombain, dem fansi kombain. We no das get dem ting de lang ago.'('Nowadays things are different. Everybody uses a tractor. They are going to plough by tractor, carry in the padi by tractor and they use machinery and so on to do the work. Then when the rice grows up, well they will use combines. Those fancy combines. We don't usually have those kinds of things long ago.')

Kean Gibson describes the Kwe-Kwe (stamping) marriage ceremonies of Kikongo origin, that were particularly popular between 1900 and 1950. When the groom arrives at the bride's home there is still reference to Queen Victoria in the chorus:

> *All a we a one family*
> *Open the door let the man come in*
> *Cousin lay down pon cousin belly*
> *Queen Victoria family a royal family.*

Thereafter the advice given by her elders to the bride is long, dctailcd and scarcely Victorian in tone. A bride, they say, earns her living by providing a service:

> *A me living*
> *Auntie Minnie a wa da da*
> *Thing so black and shine*
> *With that curly hair*
> *How he middle red*
> *How he de pon me?*

A more sinister legacy from the Ashanti kingdom is the local version of voodoo, Obeah. At its worst it involves human sacrifice, and the last such case occurred in New Amsterdam in 1950 when – as Michael Swan relates – a woman of forty-six 'learned that when the Dutch settlers built the town they buried gold money in these gardens for safety. She believed a fortune lay buried in her backyard and that if she could get in touch with the spirits of the Dutchmen they could tell her where to dig'. An Obeah 'bishop' and his 'reputed wife' instructed the woman and her brother in a gruesome ritual involving the murder of an East Indian girl of six. Three of the conspirators were hanged and there has been no similar crime since then; but there is still enough talk about Obeah to suggest some people's interest in it is more than academic.

The gulf between Obeah, Kwe-Kwe (and indeed the fervour of East Indian celebrations like Pagwar, when everyone wears old clothes expecting to be doused with pink water) and the kind of urbanities espoused by the British Council was wide. I chaired earnest brains trusts on the radio and was active in the programmes of the Theatre Guild. While Gus was with me I directed Giles Cooper's *Everything in the Garden* and he was excellent as the unfortunate son. In more ambitious plays, however, particularly Shakespeare or plays with verse in them, there is a dilemma to which I see no solution. What do you do about stress and intonation? The whole charm of Creole English lies in its sing-song intonation; it is this which gives it its special wit. Because the stress often falls so differently from 'received English', to the English ear a Creole rendering of verse can change the whole meaning. Do you, as it were, simultaneously translate the Creole 'mannerisms' into your own metropolitan ones? Or do you think yourself into a Creole skin and try to feel the lines as the actors do? At the Theatre Guild I did the latter but cannot say that I ever really felt that the actors and I were at one. I was nevertheless happy to treat the production as a new and exotic interpretation of the play, like *Hamlet* in Japanese or the manic interpretations of the ageing Peter Brooke.

This dilemma was to dog the theatre in Britain as immigrant communities increased. Do physical differences that 'interfere' with the plot matter? Is a Chinese Giselle or black Carmen at a disadvantage? In singing and dancing probably not, though I personally find the make-believe of ballet and opera a tender plant easily damaged by the interference of geographical incongruities. But speaking lines is a different matter, as has been long recognised in the United States where blacks have developed their own shows or played black characters in other plays. Perhaps because the very exclusion that encouraged excellence in diversity in America was frowned upon and legislated against in Britain, immigrant drama of this kind has not emerged. Britain's multicultural policies imply two incompatibles – that ethnic differences should be respected and catered for (in schools, religion, food, marriage customs) and that they should be so totally dismissed as to become invisible (in certain jobs, including acting). Thus subsidised companies, notably the Royal Shakespeare Company, make a point of including black actors and actresses in every cast, however incongruously (e.g. a black Cavalier colonel), so much so that their plays have been credited with an extra act, the Race Relations Act. Inevitably this has meant that black actors have had to imitate white ones, so losing their regional accents and allowing their own dramatic potential to be, as it were, bred out of the system.

The production of *Hamlet* I saw in Georgetown displayed a fine variety of diction and none more metropolitan than that of the King, by a thickset Englishman. Bill Carr was a lecturer in English Literature at the University of Guyana. Thrown out of Jamaica after six years for agitation against the Bustamente government and for drunken violence, he came to UG in 1966 and at once established his credentials as a martyr for Britain's past sins and stern foe to any post-colonial development infringing the ideals of copybook socialism. After eight months his tormented family were repatriated and he settled down to playing the role of an anarchist Mr Chips to UG and parade mascot and Aunt Sally to both political parties. Initially Jaganite, he was to marry a follower of Burnham – and die after a torrid public and domestic life aged sixty-two. In *My Father's House*, his son Matthew records that at ten he had been happier under Fr Hopkinson at St Stanislas than at any of his schools – one of them a special school – in England. The irony of this sad story – which would have been a not unfamiliar nightmare for the British Council had Bill Carr been recruited by them – is that in Guyana he was tolerated, exploited, and even revered, largely for his exposition of Shakespeare. Which of us two, I wonder, would Shakespeare himself have been more interested in – the cultural tearaway or the cultural bureaucrat?

It was a far cry from the birth pains of UG to the Amerindian country of the interior and I rarely had an official reason to visit either. UG kept its distance and there were few occasions that justified a flight on the Grumman amphibian to the Rupununi cattle country of the 'White Highlands', or to Lethem, the little administrative capital. Mission and government schools borrowed films but did not need me to show them. The phrase 'White Highlands' is not entirely appropriate but does more or less describe that rugged country, its climate and the principal residents, apart from its indigenous Amerindians. I was taken by friends on noble fishing trips up the Essequibo into their country, sleeping in hammocks and catching the biggest fish I've ever seen – though many were savaged by the fearsome *pirai* before we could land them – and I just began to get a faint idea of the challenge and excitements and time scale of living so close to a not all that friendly nature, and of its pleasures, too, provided one avoided the *maribunta* and *kabouri* fly seasons – or getting caught in an Amerindian booze-up. I particularly remember one night in a hammock slung beneath an Amerindian hut whose privy was a plank on the edge of a precipice. Balance was preserved by holding on to an upright post, while far below, paddling about offshore, crocodiles circled hopefully.

I did think it courteous to hold the hand of my visiting lecturer from Leicester on his tour of Amerindian schools. The little button-eyed children shocked him by chanting happily by rote instead of being shown the child-centred way to knowledge. They were said to do well until puberty and then drift off into ancestral bypaths. Manari Ranch, where we stayed, was efficiently run by one of the ubiquitous multicoloured Melville family. Their Scottish ancestor, prospecting for gold at the turn of the century, caught fever and was left for dead by his men, but was nursed back to health by Indians with whom he explored the Rupununi. He had ten children by two wives and has many descendants on both sides of the Brazilian border.

In the visitors' book at Manari was the signature a couple of years old, in a neat housemasterly hand, of Evelyn Waugh, and under it 'Margaret Waugh' and 'Giles Fitzherbert'. It is a pity that the articles Waugh wrote for the *Daily Mail* about his first visit to the country since the pre-war '90 Days' journey that led to *A Handful of Dust* were never published.

The whole devil-may-care atmosphere of these ranches, and I suppose of the gold and mineral mines dotted about the interior, was quite different from the neurotic preoccupations of the African and East Indian dominated coastline. One can well imagine Conan Doyle choosing its timeless routines as a background for *The Lost World.* Academic fashions in Britain seemed remote indeed, viewed from the Rupununi. So did penal fashions viewed from the coastal strip. Choke'n'rob, burglary, petrol bombing, arson, premature burning of the canefields; with so many lawyers in the country crime was necessarily rampant. Frank Farally, a psychiatrist at UG, was burgled so often that he carried his case of instruments with him wherever he went.

To advise on the problem the Council sent out a convivial old-fashioned socialist named Howard Jones, lecturer in criminology at Keele University. His lectures were well attended, especially by women, and it was the women who gave his advanced views on remedial education a rough ride: they wanted criminals put away for life, lashed or hanged. I accompanied Howard on a tour of prisons, which were not nearly as forbidding as British ones. For one thing they were more *al fresco*, often in wooden buildings which look less implacable than stone or concrete ones and, for another, life outside prison is so much more uncomfortable than in Britain that to be deprived of it is not such a hardship.

I also took him for a drink with the Venezuelan ambassador and his Chilean wife. They were unhappy because they loved London and the British but were expected to lay the foundations for the annexation of a third of Guyana. The long-standing border dispute had remained dormant during the pains of independence – except as a useful distraction at critical moments in Caracas – but soon surfaced as the responsibility for national security passed from the British army to the Guyanese defence force. Venezuela had already printed maps showing the northern part of the country as 'disputed territory'. Part of her softening-up process had been to send a troupe of ballet dancers, and I was surprised to see with what condescension the dancers treated their ambassador.

Venezuela, since her own economy began to wobble, has not pressed her claim to a third of Guyana but had she invested heavily there might have solved the communications problem and tapped new resources. France and Holland have managed to leave Cayenne and Surinam more prosperous than Guyana; why is that?

Michael Swan quotes Jock Campbell, chairman of Bookers, saying in a 1954 lecture that 'Africans and Indians both tend to live and to labour under a sense of grievance ... which can be played upon and exploited by unscrupulous politicians and must be eradicated before the peoples of British Guiana can reach selfhood', and, in a letter to the *New Statesmen,* that 'the wonder is not that life in British Guiana is not Utopian but that life and production can exist there at all'. Swan, comparing Cheddi Jagan's social charm and urbanity with his irrational paranoia on the subject of nationalisation, concludes: 'Although he is prepared to wait for the inevitable communisation of South America before implementing his Marxian theories in their extreme form, I had the impression that he was willing to do almost anything, even if it entailed economic chaos and misery, in order to satisfy his strangely compulsive hatred of King Sugar.'

Swan's book came out in 1957 and it is difficult to fault him, at least when reading between his lines: primitive communications, ruinously expensive sea defences, vast geographic extremes; how could these be dealt with when ideology and racism split the country and drove out its most highly qualified and energetic citizens? Colonial place names in Guyana are being changed and the old wooden houses are giving way to concrete blocks, but such half-hearted modernisation appears to have brought neither prosperity nor happiness. Today, it is as though Swan's own life was blighted by the hopelessness of it all. Living in the peace and beauty of Italy, he was nevertheless involved in the suicide of two women before himself committing suicide.

The journeys that most stick in my memory are those to the least developed areas, particularly up the Cinderella Coast between the Essequibo and Pomeroon rivers, in the years before its notoriety. Once-prosperous plantations had long been split into subsistence plots, and the decline of riverine mining towns like Bartica had affected their supply villages as well. To the artist's eye a natural profusion and melancholy decay appeared picturesque and the remoteness from officialdom an added attraction. But children growing up there would hardly appreciate those qualities and the remoteness would prove a sinister attraction to Jim Jones.

I wrote a blow-by-blow account of one of my excursions for the staff journal of the British Council. For me it is still an accurate reflection of that famously friendly, fascinatingly old-fashioned, challengingly uncomfortable, exasperatingly casual and irresistibly endearing country of six peoples. It makes a fitting end to this chapter:

> We fill up the Land Rover with personal and cultural impedimenta, the smallest item being a bottle of liquid called 'Shoo', the heaviest a generator for the film projector. I suppose one day someone will get down to an O and M survey of Council film vehicles and come up with a plan of neat Dunlopillo pads, spring mountings and roof racks, but every projectionist I have ever known has had his private routine of bits of string, old cans and wooden boxes that boast their own assembly code and supply a special orchestration of squeaks, bangs, and crashes as the Council cavalcade clatters to the attack.
>
> On this occasion our advance receives an early check; at the ferry over the Demerara River, only 600 yards from the office, the

gate clangs shut as we reach it; the ferry is full. This is awkward, for the next ferry will miss the connection over the Essequibo River, but just as we are beginning to give up hope a pontoon comes over for us; we drive delicately onto the unrailed platform and are nudged carelessly across. Today the Demerara has changed its appearance from Bisto to lentil soup; the water is thick with those small amoeboid jellyfish that are causing such alarm on many of the James Bond beaches in the Caribbean this season.

Over the other side, at Vreed en Hoop, we get going at last on the eighteen-mile road to the Essequibo. Thundering down the tarmac, we overtake the venerable engine, *Sir Wilfred*, puffing down the oldest railtrack in South America; plantation names flash past – for the original estates were narrow strips running up from the shore, and villages today will have their school named after one, the police station after another, the church after another and perhaps a post office after a fourth: Versailles, Blankenburg, Anna Catherina and Leonora. At Uitvlugt, a large Bookers estate, the tarmac ceases. This is a trouble spot in more senses than one, with African houses on the left and Indian on the right. Thereafter the road is said to be very good for the liver. As we descend a crater at Met en Meerzorg, the generator becomes airborne and we meet it coming up the other side with a sickening crash. At De Kinderen we heel over to take to the *padi* for a bit and the film screen escapes from the Bollers patent forget-me-knot, swings viciously across the back of the seat and deposits in my lap the can of *The Moving Spirit*. We must be averaging a good five miles an hour through Greenwich Park. 'Budget and Control,' writes the Regional Officer, 'are concerned because your Land Rovers are not doing the statutory minimum mileage to justify their retention. Is there any way – apart from rushing madly about the country in all directions – to remedy this?' (My solution: to drive out to the airport on the only twenty-mile stretch of metalled road, tie the steering wheel, and let the vehicle go round in circles on the old runway.)

At Parika we drive onto the car-ferry *MV Malali*, built by Sprostons. Squire Sproston jumped from a window when his firm went bust in 1905, but his name lives on in this subsidiary of the mighty Alcan. The boat presents a lively scene: husky black crew bawling witticisms, Indian women dripping with gold bangles, in bright yellow or blue dresses that always look freshly laundered, little black girls in starchy pink with bunches of hair gathered into small ribbon-tied pigtails, their fathers in striped shirts, tight trousers and tip-forward narrow-brimmed hats, ascetic-looking Indian farmers with voices like corncrakes, schoolmasters in ties, stocky inscrutable Amerindians, Portuguese civil servants looking purposeful in pith helmets, and Chinese concessionaires taking care to look much less prosperous than they are. And while tractors, sheep, cattle, bananas and endless crates of soft drinks come on board, and the permanent beggars start their rounds, all these people wind themselves up for a jolly good uninterrupted gossip, with plenty of time to indulge the ebb and flow of the wit and drama of Creole English.

The Essequibo doesn't look so big here because the far bank is in fact a cluster of islands, through which we must thread our way. But it takes three or more hours to do this, depending on the tide, and by the time we reach the wharf at Adventure the river feels very big indeed. For twenty miles out to sea the water is as brown as the Severn at Aust and much less salty. Up river, some hundreds of miles beyond the rapids, Squire Waterton rode his crocodile and, more credibly, Tony Last read Dickens for ever and ever to Mr Todd. And just here, as the Guyanese like to point out, you could drop Barbados into Old Man Essequibo and he wouldn't feel the difference. The sun has set in a sullen pink, suffused with the smoke of forest fires, long before we dock, so I am saved another interview with the manager of this ramshackle little landing stage, who is anxious to attend a Council course on port management at Liverpool.

It is now only a few miles to Suddie, the administrative centre of Essequibo County, where we can expect the traditional resthouse welcome. It is no fault of Mistress Reid that the ferries arrive after 8 pm and leave at 5 in the morning. She has only one girl to help her and their working hours are 7am to 7pm. However, we have taken the precaution of asking her to leave something out for us and sure enough, after letting ourselves in, we find a note directing us to our rooms and our suppers wrapped carefully in a napkin. It was evidently a delicious hot meal – an hour and a half ago: rice, potato, breadfruit, plantain and stewed steak with plenty of gravy. And, if we cannot ourselves do justice to it, it has not been wasted for the ants have already done it.

But it's not for the cuisine that we enjoy Suddie Resthouse, but for its position on the beach. A sea breeze blows through it, and though the beach is poor by Caribbean standards it is sandy and a pleasant change from the bottle-strewn mud flats of Demerara County. It is also comparatively deserted, for the Cinderella coast went into a coma about sixty years ago when transport shifted to the deeper harbour of the Demerara River. Along it the rotting wooden jetties still mark the outlets of once prosperous estates. John Stedman tells us that in 1760 these waters were alive with shipping 'like the wherries on the Thames, often accompanied with bands of music ... the adjacent woods adorned with the most luxurious verdure, the air perfumed with the utmost fragrance, and the whole scene gilded by the rays of an unclouded sun'. The more practical Governor, Storm van Gravesande, noted that 'applicants for land are arriving daily; various materials for mills have already been landed, more are expected and there is every appearance of rapid progress'.

In the morning, resisting an invitation from the DC to go labba-hunting, I begin my rounds. Again the romantic roll call of evocative names – there are almost more names on the map now than buildings on the road: Johanna Cecelia, Perseverance, Bremen, Hoff van Aurich, Aberdeen, La Belle Alliance, Hampton Court, Paradise, The Jib, Bounty Hall, La Resource, Opposite, and – just short of the Pomeroon River – the Somerset and Berks Canal! I call on a VSO teacher who has declined an official invitation from Georgetown because he says it would prevent his preaching at a village church; I suggest that for once he might render unto Caesar but he gets That Look in his eye and, as his headmaster is pleased with him, I decide to leave well alone. I talk and show some Nuffield Foundation films at Anna Regina Teachers' In-service course; everything goes smoothly; on to the local Borstal where some 400 lads are lowering the flag at sunset. In the preliminary talk, I decide, for the last time, to tell that funny story about the drunk and the shooting Gallery … He gets three bull's-eyes – bang, bang, bang! (roars of excitement). The attendant, thinking it a pity to waste his prize vase upon a drunk, searches round and offers him a tortoise instead; he goes off happy. (Puzzlement; good heavens, have they ever seen a tortoise? I plunge on.) An hour later the drunk comes back (laughter) and takes a rifle again (guffaws) and fires – bang, bang, bang! (shrieks of excitement) – and gets three bull's-eyes again (howls of merriment, explosions of mirth). 'Eh man!' thinks the attendant, 'Dis man in' as drunk as I t'ought... I better give he de praper prize dis time.' So he hands over the china vase (laughter). 'Eh, eh! says the drunk, 'Wha' is dis? Yer ras t'ink I is a fool nuh? Why ah can' get a meat pie jus' like las' time?' (Heavy, impenetrable, expectant silence.)

I move quickly on to the films. The hit of the show is a Canadian film, *Neighbours*, showing in cartoon style a fight brewing up about nothing. The stages of the fight cause a sensation: the audience hits the roof and the masters look deprecating; at the end the graveyard scene brings a sudden eerie stillness. After this *The Beavers Break Through* seems pretty tame but disaster strikes as I speak through the mike and the jack comes apart – irreparably. I have to shout from the front of the hall, and by the time we pack up my voice has fallen as flat as my poor little joke.

Next day I join up with three speakers from the Adult Education Association to run two seminars. This system was started seven years ago by my predecessor, John Gale, when Study Boxes were young, and his ghost marches steadily with us. At the first seminar Something Has Gone Wrong, for no one turns up except three unemployed youths looking for jobs; we hang about in vain for a couple of hours while the town crier is searched for, and eventually go off to start up the other seminar. At Danielstown it is a different story. Mrs Barker is very welcoming ('Have you heard from Mr Gale?') and has assembled a good audience. The Chairman of the Village Council, Mr Jackson, introduces us ('... very honoured ... the British Council... Mr John Gale ... without more ado ... today's speaker, Mr – er – Mr – er – the Representative of the British Council, Mr – er – oh, yes, Mr

Alexander!') The Community Centre is open at the sides but I keep my end up well, until ominous drops patter on the corrugated iron roof. My voice rises; the drops multiply; I shriek; they thunder. I give up, and we sit looking at each other for five minutes, until the roar suddenly subsides. By that time what I was going to say seems somehow less important, but I say it and we return to our other Seminar, where by now an audience of ten adults and four toddlers has assembled.

Afterwards we call on Mr Roach, a patriarchal retired goldminer who runs a guesthouse at Henrietta. His room has enormous rocking chairs, coat stands, mirrors, antimacassars, love seats and an ornate piano; at the head of the stairs hangs a magnificent engraving of the Old Queen herself. We are offered Russian Bear rum with ice-cream soda; the rum is superb; conversation flows: 'And where is John Gale now? Ah, John Gale ...!'

On the way back we have a puncture. In the moonlight an alligator slides across the road and splashes into the trench. A ruined tin coffee store looks like an ivy-mantled tower. The mosquitoes note that I have left the 'Shoo' behind. At the resthouse Mistress Reid has defeated the ants with a Dutch-inspired canal system, but someone has let in the cat ...

Up at 4 the next morning, we try to pretend that dawn over the river makes it worth it as we cross to the Island of Wakenaam. These islands are mangrove swamps, dyked by the Dutch and built up by river silt. For all its austerity there's a fine independent air about Wakenaam ('John Gale? Who's he?'). After a film-show at Maria's Pleasure (with Julian Bream's *East and West Encounter* replacing a newsreel of the Independence Talks in London, for this is Indian country), I am accosted by the local wild man, wearing only an old rice sack. 'Ha! Reverend!' says he, 'You're not American are you? Good, good! English? Ah, Shakespeare! "Tell me not" – no – "Let me not" – yes – "Let me not to the marriage of true minds admit impediment". I've studied you see. Where? In Canada. What? Engineering. Yes, you know Captain Keith of the helicopter? Ah, yes, we drink all day when he comes; and the Vidal Commander too. Mr John Gale? No, never. Ah, yes, but London, I know it all – Southwark, the Globe Theatre. And the 400 Club. Yes, Reverend, don't go, Reverend ... just a little ... you know: the cup that cheers but not in – um – bru-ha-ha. Not a Reverend? British Coun-ah CONSUL, British Consul! Yes, yes, good. Reverend, give me a passport. We're subjects of the Queen, ho, ho! Don't go, don't go! Eh, Reverend ...'

But Bollers has tied his last knot tight, wrapped his last bit of cloth round, wedged his last bit of corrugated paper down, and we're off to the resthouse, leaving the plaintive cries behind, for a quick sleep before another dawn flitting. We normally like a beer or two before turning in, but with the wild man of Stratford waiting for us at the only rum shop in Sans Souci we'll call it a day. Guyanese resthouses are rather like Irish hotels: they've all got something but none has got everything. This one is a bleak hot hut in the middle of barking dogs, braying donkeys and shouts of activity at the wharf; but there is delicate toast and guava jelly and the cook-up is excellent. In the visitors book a previous guest has noted testily that Mistress Russell has still not gained her well-earned substantive promotion from Acting Caretaker. Mistress Russell is rather attractive but it is not for this reason that I endorse the comment so feelingly.

And so home to Georgetown, with its extravagantly broad, 14 ft motorways, its sheer four-storey skyscrapers, its immense town hall, gigantic cathedral, and myriads of dazzling coruscating 40 watt lights; swing into the baronial gateway of the Representative's noble mansion, up the backstairs to the kitchen door; now for a shower and a long, cold ... the house is very quiet; it has a sullen, shifty look. Why has Sophie left the door of the fridge open? And of the drinks cupboard too? Where's all that food – and those clothes? Camera? And mattress gone too! Oh ho! 'Well, thank you, just a little rum, or whisky will do.' The police are sympathetic. Yes, they say, it has all the signs of our old friends Leslie da Silva, Lillie Hamlet and Neville Small, released after the royal visit and returning to their happy hunting grounds. Once they know the way in, why look elsewhere? And with such Shakespearean names it seems churlish to complain. In a way, I should feel flattered. Am I not now one of the gang?

So ended my excursion. I had come to like the people and enjoy the human scale of the country. When I left Georgetown in 1968 Burnham was still boxing clever and the disasters ahead were not yet obvious, but the problems had changed little in the twelve years since Swan had observed them. I was sorry when the British Council four years later closed its centres in Guyana and the West Indies. The Guyana *Daily Graphic*, a subsidiary of the *Daily Mirror* and not, needless to say, of the *Daily Express*, deplored the closure: 'The British Council,' it said, 'has always sent the finest type of public servant to represent it and they will be much missed.' Hmm!

14
Barcelona la Rica

Hostal Plaza
Plaza de las Catedrales
Zaragoza

1st September 1968

I AM SITTING in the dining room with half a bottle of Aragón *Clarete* inside me, also mushroom soup, fish cakes, fried *merluza* and a large bunch of grapes ('What would you like for *postre?* Melon?' 'Fresh or tinned?' 'In syrup.' 'No, thank you!' 'Flan, then?' 'Hmm!' 'Of course you can have grapes.' 'Ah!') There are twenty other diners – two Germans, six Catalans, twelve Spaniards. All the women except one are large and plain. All the men except four are short and podgy. In one corner is an enormous blue, grey and gold Madonna, in the other is an even bigger bas-relief of the Sermon on the Mount. The ceiling mouldings are freshly painted in grey, yellow, orange and mauve. In the ceiling are two yellow fluorescent lights and one 'daylight' one. On the tops of pillars are posies of plastic flowers. In the lounge through an archway the television is blasting away. There are toothpicks on the table. Besides the two cathedrals and Moorish remains here, there are some fine old mediaeval princes' houses and the Jewish baths.

We sailed into Bilbao in the darkness and everything was pretty chilly until midday when the sun blazed out, but a bitter wind blew across the vast open spaces between Vitoria and Zaragoza. The vineyards are beginning to turn colour and the trees are like England's three weeks ago. But what adds to the autumnal beauty here are the red earth colours of the hilltop villages and the stark hill erosion picked out in the slanting sun. There was snow in the Pyrenees foothills. The Pilar cathedral here gives the impression of being considerably larger than St Paul's, and the old Seo cathedral is especially interesting for its mosque layout. In El Pilar there were two masses going on at different ends, one choral and one not. I heard the organ played properly for the first time in Spain. There is a hole in the wainscoting where the faithful kneel and poke their heads through to

> kiss the actual pillar on which the Virgin descended. There was a long queue waiting to do so. I didn't pause long in Lérida because I wanted to see two places just beyond – Bellpuig, where there's a marvellous 16th century tomb of a Viceroy of Sicily, and Cervera, an old village with a fine hilltop church and a huge decaying university built in the 18th century by Philip V to replace Barcelona University but later abandoned.
>
> I had a cold shave this morning, as there was only an electric geyser in the bath. When I let the water out of the basin it filled up the bidet.

This letter typifies my mixed feelings about Spain. After my four years hard in Guyana the Council rewarded me with the posting of my choice – Barcelona. It could not have been a greater contrast. To be able to drive to post across Europe was a new and wonderful experience. I had been to the Far East, the Middle East and the Far West but never, except very briefly, to Europe. Its history and riches poured over me as from a cornucopia. There was also plenty to irritate and be deplored – shoddy workmanship and materials, vulgarity, noise, a lingering long depression – but in Barcelona, with immigrant labour flooding in from Andalucia, there was a heady air of optimism, enterprise and push.

Yet this city, by far the finest I have ever worked in, has left me with least to say about it. This is partly because life there is no longer strange and romantic as it was in the days, say, of Richard Ford's vivid *Handbook for Travellers in Spain.* (He talks somewhere of the black eyes of its women 'going through you like a bullet', and seldom passes up an opportunity to recall the exploits of the Great Duke.) So descriptions of my forays in northern Spain, and further south, would risk smacking of a tourist guide.

Also, much that might have seemed strange to me was familiar from my Colombian years – bullfights, clericalism, a peasant economy – while, contrariwise, my colonial Spanish was all too familiar to my brisk Catalan hosts; words like *plata* for money, courtesies like *tenga la bondad*, softeners like *haga me el favor,* diminutives like *chiciticitico,* raised indulgent smiles. No doubt as a small frog in a very big pool I missed a great deal that was going on in it.

The Council had long been ambivalent about Spain, happy to collect vast revenues from English classes but reluctant to spend them on prestige events that might imply approval of the Franco regime. Major manifestations were therefore rare, unless the Spaniards could be cajoled into paying for them.

Spain was in the last years of Franco, and Barcelona was poised between the austerities and repression of the Franco years and the fizz and bounce of free enterprise. The British Institute in Barcelona was in a large rented mansion on what was officially the Avenida del Generalísimo Franco but called *El Diagonal.* The Catalan language was forbidden in schools but fast returning outside them. Franco himself had encouraged the tourist boom in the teeth of ecclesiastic disapproval and there was a general relaxation of government censorship – though we still had to drive up to Perpignan to see films censored by the Church. The city was run down but had installed an efficient underground system, leading for instance from the Plaza de Catalonia up to my flat on the slopes of Tibidabo to the north of the city. Many people were still doing two jobs to make ends meet, but prosperity was obviously just around the corner. Just when British youth was at its long-haired tattiest, the Spanish were dressing spotlessly. Yet there was still a vogue for things British, and aficionados in tweed caps, hacking jackets and breeches were to be seen spanking up and down the Paseo de Gracia on their 500cc Nortons, as was a famous restaurateur with his glittering horse and trap.

Unglamorous as the right-wing Nationalists under General Franco were, in the civil war I had tended to side with them over the 'romantic but wrong' Republican government forces (heavily supported by the International Brigade). Surely the Church could not have deserved the hideous violence unleashed against her? I had felt that nothing was worse than disorder; even repression must in the end carry the seeds of its own destruction. The chaotic twenties and thirties had torn Spain to pieces, and I felt few foreign intellectuals knew any more of her background than they knew of her language. The Roy Campbells and Peter Kemps rang more true to me than the John Cornfords and Stephen Spenders, with George Orwell letting the cat out of the bag in between.

Barcelona was poised between the pleasantly old-fashioned and the enterprising new. The *fin-de-siècle* harbour and Barceloneta fish restaurants led up through the marvellous Gothic quarter and frenchified grid 'new' town to modern blocks that were already sought after for being above smog level. Little factories still made things and little shops sold them, while grim high-rise buildings crept out along the shorelines to house workers in factories like the SEAT car works. A desultory tinkering was going on in Gaudì's mercifully unfinished Templo Expiatorio de la Sagrada Familia, but more happily his Parque Güell and charming crypt at the Colonia Güell were being restored, even as more practical moneymakers such as motor racing circuits and a funfair said to belong to Frank Sinatra were being extended on Montjuich.

My thirties flat on Tibidabo, where the little tram ground up the hill to the funicular railway, was delightful. Although threatened by development, the slopes were still half wild and half gobbled up by institutions: a large convent nearby emptied its rubbish and farm refuse into a ditch that was a great favourite of rats; just below me was the Art Nouveau Rotunda Hotel, a favourite of the film star Robert Taylor. (Another star, George Sanders, chose the gloomy surroundings of a beach hotel in Castelldefels just down the coast in which to silence his splendid voice.)

I was thoroughly spoilt by the motherly Lola, who came from far away Soria: she did everything from scrubbing the floor to cooking and serving meals to VIPs, helped out at Institute receptions, and was gratefully inherited by my successor. When I left, instead of me giving her a farewell present, she gave me one. It was a magical spot to live in, looking down over the sea-girt city, the metro at my door and at my back wild hills running north-west to Hostalrich and the mountains of Montseny, or north up the Congest valley to mill towns with decaying factories and noble Romanesque churches, as at Vich, or Visigothic chapels, as at Tarrasa and San Miguel del Fay. Beyond me, a rough track led over the hills seven miles or so to San Cugat del Vallés. Dotted about in isolation were towered mansions and follies dating from the turn of the 19th century, their gardens now 'bare ruined choirs', their shutters closed. I could, if cavalier with the car, avoid the weekend rat run by driving in lonely splendour along these deserted tracks from deep country to my very door.

To the west, beyond the sour runnels of the Llobregat River lay honey-coloured monasteries like Santas Creus, the tumbled hills of San Sadurni de Noya and Santa Coloma de Queralt, with their brews of *cava*, and the little town of Villafranca del Panadés with its Moor's head hanging in the church; it also had the gleaming refineries of Miguel Torres, whose family despatched a case of wine to me each Christmas. Along the coast to the west was the Art Nouveau promenade of Sitges and further on the dramatic cathedral of Tarragona. (Sitges was not then a favourite of the gay community but beginning to fill up with stodgy German tourists. I watched an altercation between one such determined to wash his car in the street and a Guardia Civil equally determined that he should not break the local law by doing so.) To the east lay old fishing villages like Arénys de Mar, the convenient bustle of the Costa Brava, the vast aisleless nave of Gerona cathedral, and my hedonistic favourite resort of Cadaqués.

I have followed here the old spelling of names of places and public buildings used in my maps of 1968; later ones adopted Catalan nomenclature.

I don't know any city that combines the old and the new, the practical and fanciful, as strikingly as Barcelona; the Gothic buildings near the cathedral – even then beautifully floodlit – and the relentless spread of metro-fed suburbia; the plethora of museums and the colour fountain and fantasies of Montjuich. The most sober endeavour is rarely without a trapping of frivolity: the cathedral has its geese, the Gothic quarter its Ramblas. There is something about a seaport that seems to close up the centuries, and it is easy to visualise the Catalans as masters of the Kingdom of Sicily or Catalonia as a Republic, proclaimed as recently as 1931. As I drove my car up through the well-kept tunnels of the fortress of Montjuich I owed the convenience to the sparky little Lord Peterborough, who had so unexpectedly stormed the fortress as long before as 1705. After my departure the whole coastline was remodelled for the Olympic Games, but the city seems able to retain indefinitely – in role and appearance – both her commercial and her intellectual flair.

It must be admitted, however, that the Catalans – industrious, innovative and self-confident as they are – have little time to waste on old-fashioned courtesies familiar further south. Southerners in their turn think the patience and dedication of the Catalan national dance, the *sardana*, might be better spent on dances as exciting to outsiders as to the dancers. The same sense of exclusiveness applies more seriously to the Catalan language. Always a catalyst of local loyalties, it was often banned by Madrid, only to re-emerge after Franco's death stronger than ever. Since then – and notwithstanding the growth of immigration and tourism – it has become almost universally compulsory, and notably so in schools. This follows the pattern in Wales and Ireland, but it remains to be seen what babies in the long run will have been thrown out with the bath water. *Butifarra*, after all, is a welcome alternative to *paella* but may be an unwelcome substitute for it. Those who have never learned a minority language tend to resent this secret weapon of those who have and to deplore positive discrimination in its promotion, but to even the most impartial observer Catalan as a language of national culture must seem to lack the euphony and scope of the two great languages from which it derives. It would be sad if its hegemony were only achieved at their expense.

The state of Barcelona's revival by 1968 may be judged by the value of the mansion on the Diagonal rented by the Council for its Institute. A local bank was so determined to get hold of it that it offered my predecessor, in exchange for our lease, the price of purpose-built freehold accommodation on two floors in a new apartment building going up only a couple of blocks away. It was an offer we could not refuse, and I arrived just before the move into the new premises.

First, however, I had to go to court. I had inherited an unhappy case involving the dismissal of a long-serving porter. In those days the Council was very careful of taxpayers' money and insisted on legal niceties being observed; these invariably ended, after great trouble and unpleasantness, in having to pay out more than if we had settled out of court. I was treated with great courtesy by the court, but in truth all my sympathies were with our old employee, and I was not sorry when he was vindicated in his claim.

The new building, complete with language laboratories, classrooms and a splendid library, was not without teething troubles – lasting indeed till at least 1983, when I called in and found buckets of water all over the place, catching leaks from the upper floors. Our own architect, Busquets (who was not responsible for the building itself), was an engaging character who had fought in the Blue Division against Russia in World War II. We later mortally offended him by adopting the more flexible internal arrangements in the building suggested by the up-and-coming firm of Martorell, Bohigas y Mackay. Busquets took me to dine with the Abbot of Montserrat, a far from saintly-looking figure, who was said to be a doughty dueller with Franco over the rights of the Church and of Catalonia. Certainly he interrogated me shrewdly about the extent to which the Council could help him – a necessarily brief interrogation – before we went in to lunch and to listen to the reading of the day (a life of Loyola). Thanks to its tourist development it is only from a distance that the sight of the monastery continues to inspire an elemental awe.

It was with the architect, David Mackay, that I experienced my only trouble with the security forces. The traffic police, especially the jack-booted and breeched motorcycle police lurking in predatory pairs, were much feared; but they needed to be to restrain the exuberance of Spanish driving. Walter Oakeshott was writing a book about the stained glass artists at Winchester, and he wished to see the fenestration – even if long ruined – of the convent at Sigena. It was a remote spot and David came with us as guide. Within a few miles of the site we stopped for a picnic lunch. Hardly had we taken the first bite when two *guardias* appeared.

'Good day!'

'And a very good day to you!'

Pause.

'What are you doing here?'

'We are having lunch.'

'Why?'

'Because we are hungry.'

'I mean why did you come here to have lunch?'

'Because we are about to look over the convent.'

'Where have you come from?'

'Barcelona.'

'Show me your papers.'

'They are in the boot of the car, and, as you see, we have food spread all over our knees. Perhaps you wouldn't mind waiting until we have finished eating?'

They disappeared – and came back twenty minutes later with a lieutenant.

'Good day!'

'Good day, Captain!' I had had time to reflect that we were not far from the Burgos trials country.

'What are you doing here?'

'We have come from Barcelona to look over the convent, which I hear is very interesting.'

'Show me your papers.'

'With much pleasure. I shall get them from the boot of the car.'

'Who is this?'

'Dr Walter Oakeshott.'

'Where are his papers?'

'He has none, because he is a tourist.'

'What does he do?'

'He is a professor at the University of Oxford.'

'What does he teach?'

'Er ... classical languages.'

'What's he doing here?'

'Look, Captain, you see that large notice saying that the Ministry of Public Works is carrying out a phased programme of restoration on the convent? Well, don't you want people to come and look at it?'

'Nobody ever comes here.'

'And they won't unless they get a warmer welcome.'

'Why didn't you show your papers when my men asked you to?'

'Because we were hungry and thirsty and tired after a long drive and had just settled down to our lunch. So when I was suddenly interrupted I was put into a very bad humour.'

'Ah well! We haven't had our lunch yet either, so we were in a bad humour too. I'm sorry you have been disturbed. Enjoy your convent! And you too, Professor.'

The Barcelona Institute, like other European centres with competent long-serving locally-engaged staff, more or less ran itself. The profits from our English classes far outweighed expenses and still left room for competitors – the Americans, International House, the Jesuits and many smaller operators. The demand for adult English classes was insatiable and spoke poorly for the teaching in schools. Schools were indeed still spartan, with few frills and few sports facilities, but they were disciplined. The exceptions were the Opus Dei schools, and their elitist University of Navarra, which like the French *grandes écoles* supplied the government and the commercial world with financial and professional high fliers. I visited the local Opus Dei secondary school and found a remarkably well-equipped but very un-Spanish place with very much the air of, say, Downside – the iron fist beneath the velvet glove, masters in tweed jackets and caps, extraordinarily polite boys, and the feeling that argument was not a common practice. The Council's policy, as expressed by Jack Bruton, good socialist as he was and now our representative in Madrid, was not to touch them with a barge pole. By the end of the century the subject-led discipline of the Spanish state schools was to follow the British child-centred system, just when we were abandoning it in despair. In my time students from the London Institute of Education and the Spanish Faculty of Bristol University enlivened the scene for six weeks each year doing their teaching practice, and we arranged many exchanges at a higher level. When John Kendrew, Nobel prize winner in chemistry, lectured at the luxurious Barcelona Medical Club on microbiology, I suspect his diagrams were as much Greek to his distinguished audience as they were to me. But I reflected uncomfortably on the gap in attainment between us: with only a couple of years' difference in age we had been at the same school and the same Cambridge college.

With hundreds of academics jetting round the world on tight schedules, it is only to be expected that there will occasionally be embarrassments of one kind or another. I was lucky in this respect, and my only experience of it was with a visiting expert on autism who was in the middle of a nervous and alcoholic-fed breakdown. He was a nice man and had endearingly brought me a university ashtray but, in spite of filling him with black coffee before springing him on his sleek and courteous audience, I have never sweated so much at a lecture – or, rather, at a series of slides with uncertain comments trailing after them. My guest was due to repeat his lecture in Madrid and I wondered whether to cancel arrangements or hope that he would recover his composure. I gave him the benefit of the doubt but the hope unfortunately proved misplaced and from Madrid he was invalided home.

Visitors from the arts world caused no such crises, though there were many of them for Barcelona was very much on the cultural circuit. The city council begged for the ageing Laurence Olivier. They had an almost mystical faith in the British theatre as a beacon of traditional values and freedom from censorship, just when it was in fact heading straight down the kitchen sink. The marvellous *Palacio de la Música Catalana* with its Rhine maidens (if that's what they are) projecting from the proscenium arch and plaster horses galloping out of the ceiling, was the scene of many visits. Artur Rubinstein's Chopin recitals were still great favourites when he was well into his eighties and hitting a few wrong notes. Yehudi Menuhin was a particularly charming visitor, but even Homer nods. He started to bring in the Bath Assembly Orchestra for a non-existent repeat at the end of a Mozart symphony only to find them staring at him in silent amusement. The guitarist, Julian Bream, was also an engaging guest, though his particular genius was rather a case of carrying coals to Newcastle and did not fill the Palau (as it was popularly referred to).

The Palau was not the setting – how could it be? – for works by the local avant-garde composers who were following in the footsteps of Roberto Gerhard and Montsalvatge. They were nice people with nice manners but, for me, made no music at all. In a cheerless modern hall I sat wincing as Jane Manning hurled her splendid voice in scoops and clicks and screams round the walls, while the instrumentalists did their best to imitate the sounds of scrap merchants, washing machines or mosquitoes. (Thirty years later I saw Jane Manning at the Victoria Rooms in Bristol acknowledging the orchestra's tribute, Stravinsky's jokey version of 'Happy Birthday to You'. She was there with her husband, Anthony Payne, for his reconstruction of Elgar's Third Symphony.)

A not very happy visitor to the grand old Liceo opera house was the up-and-coming Peter Glossop in Verdi's *Macbeth*, stuffing himself with vitamin pills to stave off a cold and particularly anxious to do so because he was at odds with Grace Bumbry as Lady Macbeth. 'She's always trying to upstage me, but I won't let her get away with it, the bitch!' He must have lost his battles in the end for he soon dropped out of the operatic scene. The Liceo chorus and staging were old-fashioned in the extreme, but its soloists were topnotch, including, of course, Catalonia's own diva, Montserrat Caballé. My charismatic neighbours, the Villavecchias, who awed me by keeping a harp in their drawing room, had a red plush box at the Liceo, with a room behind it for the pink Freixenet. 'We're told she's in good voice tonight,' they said happily as we settled down to hear Montserrat in *Manon*. Hearing was fine but seeing was more of a challenge, and when Manon was unwise enough to sit on her little tenor's lap entirely engulfing him a titter went round the house.

The Villavecchias were useful guests when I needed help in entertaining people like the Ambassador, Sir John Russell, and his operatic wife; it was during their visit that news came of Allende's election victory in Chile. The Villavecchias thought it was a marvellous thing that – unlike Cuba – Chile had achieved a democratically elected communist government for virtually the first time in Latin America. They saw splendid reforms ahead. The Russells were no less pleased, for when did the Foreign Office ever let right and wrong and human nature interfere with the pleasures of pontificating on the fascination of the great game? Remembering Colombia, I did not share their optimism, but I little guessed to what shameful absurdities in Whitehall that Chilean affair would lead thirty years later.

As for Sir John's views on Gibraltar, I did not appreciate their complexity until they were aired thirty years later in a report on declassified documents by the Sunday Telegraph. 'Had the Great Armada succeeded,' he had written, 'we should today much dislike seeing a Spanish garrison on Land's End or Portland Bill.' The Foreign Office had gone so far as to consider a compromise plan of handing over the territory to the Catholic Order of Malta, also known as the Sovereign Military Hospitaller Order of St John of Jerusalem of Rhodes and of Malta. 'The Order,' wrote Sir John, 'would allow the citizens to be British or Spanish as they wished. We would take a long lease or whatever we need. And there might be a provision for eventual reversion to Spain.' One Foreign Office official, comments the newspaper, was less impressed. In a note attached to Sir John's original letter, he wrote: 'I don't know if Sir J R has ever seen the Order collectively assembled. I have. I would rather entrust Gibraltar to the Young Liberals!'

The Liceo was also host to Beryl Grey's ballet company but, expecting more traditional fare, its audiences found *Witch Boy* strong meat. Anton Dolin had come along for the ride but it was John Gilpin, then in his fifties, who danced as memorably as ever in the role he had made famous. After such youthful exuberance the news of his death soon afterwards came as a particular shock.

At that time I was, of course, seeing Spain at her best; evidence of her amazing history was still intact, her courtesies, *grandeurs* and wildness, and her superstitions, savagery and stoicisms, were still apparent. Village churches were full and woodland paths still trodden; in town squares young people danced *coplas* on Saturday nights and Sunday afternoons; the rich were romantically inclined to spend their money on restoring crag-perching castles and living in them, rather than on bigger and better yachts; monasteries and convents were not yet starved of religious to run them; dim *fondas* were crowded with men in dark suits playing dominoes – men of all ages, too, chattering away to each other oblivious of the generation gap (places where Richard Ford would still feel at home and arouse only mild curiosity); and townspeople preserved an affection for their roots, returning to the old village property with its church and its *fonda* and its *coplas* whenever they could, planting fruit trees or vines and packing the family off there for the long hot summer while father stayed in town to go through the motions of working. At the same time, the comforts of tourism were to hand and were bringing prosperity and confidence to the whole country. There were still small manufacturers and craftsmen at work, still age-old agricultural habits in evidence, and only a few miles inland from the mod cons of the Costa Brava were mediaeval places like Besalú, Cantallops, La Póbla and Pontons. I was fortunate in having as guides Christopher Witty, of a third generation British shipping family, and his ebullient wife, Gudi, who did not easily take no for an answer from obstructive locals.

It was a treat, too, after being in distant posts, to be able to have all four of the family out for holidays, and to drive across Europe with them. Dick and Moyra Beeston, friends from Beirut days, holidaying in the still unspoilt Dordogne helped us to explore it and opened our eyes to the enviably logical pleasures of French living.

The attractions of Spain had already been spotted by other friends from long ago in Beirut. Edward and Sue Southby had retired to Alhaurín de Torre in the Costa del Sol, and were to be followed by Farid and Prue Hanania of the AUB (though to my mystification they settled for an apartment block in the middle of a golf course); but my affection for Cadaqués on the Costa Brava was due to Roderick and Karen Roch. They had established a fine little empire on the road to Cabo Creus, with tower houses commissioned from a local builder, a berth for Roddy's catamaran, and a stable for Karen's old white horse. Karen did not get on with her neighbour, Salvador Dali, whom she accused of lusting after not only her but her horse. For months he implored her to sell him the horse, which was past riding age and not over-popular in the neighbourhood as it wandered about nibbling at people's gardens, and she adamantly refused. Eventually he found one elsewhere, which he stuffed and exhibited at a party on the top floor of the Ritz Hotel in Madrid. 'There!' cried Karen, 'I knew that horrible man had some perversion up his sleeve!'

Dali was not the only one to try Karen's patience. I behaved very badly when I was staying there with Gus. It was his first visit to Spain. He had arrived with his hair tucked tactfully under his cap and fresh – or fairly fresh – from the obligatory hippy trail. After reading architecture at Peterhouse he had been on a three-month trip to Istanbul, Van, Iran, Quetta, Afghanistan and Kathmandu, returning with the regulation £1 sheepskin waistcoat. (Being imperfectly cured, this became in due course impossible to live with and was put out of its misery by Germaine.) Karen had invited neighbours for drinks that evening but, first, I took Gus to see the ruins of S Pedro de Roda. I soon realised that it was going to take longer than I had remembered to climb up to the monastery itself. Should we turn back to get to the drinks party in time, or carry on and risk being late – because Gus would never have another chance to see the place? Well, for parents – and perhaps above all for divorced parents – the children always come first, especially when there's an opportunity to 'add to their education'. We arrived back as the last guests were leaving. Gus did his best to expiate my crime by doing a drawing for Karen, starting in the middle and working his way outwards. I think she was mollified, because she welcomed Nick, Clare and Ian when they came out with school friends, and she enjoyed dining out on the story of my iniquity for months to come.

With Nick I had tried to repeat in Barcelona the experience I had had with Gus in Guyana. When I first went to Spain Nick was in his gap year; he came out with me and stayed for eight months, attending a Spanish course at the university. But, unlike Gus in Guyana, he couldn't get a teaching job because of his lack of experience together – here – with the language barrier; there were no VSO teachers for company, and he could not rely on me for contacts because I hadn't yet made many myself. Although Barcelona had so much more to offer than Georgetown, I had not realised how important to the young an English-speaking environment is. I am afraid that – voracious reader though he was – he read more books from the Institute library than he really wanted to, and he enjoyed his later visits with his siblings more than his first solitary one with me.

It was during a visit to Cadaqués with Clare (in her turn attending a Spanish language summer course) that the car key horror struck again. I opened the boot and rested the keys on the floor while I took out a suitcase. Clare drew my attention to the moon and reminded me that at that very moment a man was landing on it. Then she obligingly slammed the lid shut – with the keys inside. In those days there was no remote control for the boot, so I had to take the train 80 miles to Barcelona to get my spare keys. Never again, I swore, would I be caught like that!

Mrs X, who had judiciously declined to accompany me to Guyana, was also tempted by Spain and wrote from an overseas job proposing a stopover on her way home. She arrived for an enjoyable week, but this time it was I who left matters unresolved. Six months later a colleague who had met her in Barcelona asked me for her address. I gave it to him, and a few months later they were married – and lived happily ever after.

It was a wrench to leave Spain after only three years, though my next posting – Venezuela – had the virtue of being a Representation of my own. But I was also left, when the time came, in my usual state of domestic dither. Should I take with me to the free-wheeling fastnesses of South America another lady whose company I had come to value in Barcelona, or wait to see if Venezuela would reveal 'that not impossible she' that even divorced men imagine awaits only discovery? Madame Y applied her Gallic logic to the prospect of a probably impossible me in an unfamiliar and ever-changing environment and stayed put. We remained friends but probably would not have done so had we married; our domestic commitments and national interests were too divided. This was to be increasingly the case, with ever more improbable friendships, stimulating or restful enough in a brief foreign setting, being absurdly contemplated for a permanent partnership. No doubt the unsettling nature of overseas service encourages hasty and unwise proposals. The Council was admirably tolerant of marital failings and I have no reason to believe my own were detrimental to any but perhaps two of my postings.

I was sorry to leave this one after only three years (to make way, I was told, for a colleague whose wife required European medical care): there was much of the country I had yet to explore; I would miss its proximity to family and friends; and I was curious to witness the transfer of power when Franco went. In any transfer of power the first consideration would be to avoid rocking the boat in a further sea of ideological conflict, though, needless to say, this was not the view of the British media, hungry for an apocolyptic fall-out from Franco's rule to feed their headlines. Anxious to do his bit, a Mr Roebuck, MP, in the First Report from the Expenditure Committee, was recorded as asking the Council spokesman, 'Do you send *Tribune* to Spain?' I forget what the official reply to this question was, but mine was this:

In the streets of Torremolinos
The British strum the guitar,
While gypsies swig their Watney's down
In the Galloping Major bar.

Al-fresco chilled gazpacho
Suits the British when it's warm;
But Valencians like their wimpies hot
At El Pub in Benidorm.

It's not wine-drinking British
Who most appreciate the charms
Of the barmaid's pants and breeches
At the Sitges Yorkshire Arms.

Flamenco nights at Tossa
Put Blackpool lads in a sweat
While the Catalans all call 'Bingo!'
In The Castle at Lloret.

For the go-go girls in Barbarella
They drive from Gerona in a queue;
But the British take the boat trip for
The bulls at San Feliú.

In the Cadaqués sardanas
The British are the biggest troupe;
Dalí and the other Cadaqueños
Dig the Bread-and-Butter Group.

So when you're woken, Mr. Roebuck,
From guilty siestas by the sea
Never send to know for whom the bell tolls;
It tolls, my dear, for tea.

15
Caraqueños

THE PAIN OF LEAVING Barcelona in 1971 for Venezuela was lessened by a rainstorm that blanketed out the whole city. As I squelched through the docks, carrying my luggage because the porters were sheltering elsewhere, I consoled myself with thoughts of green forests, immense waterfalls and another angle on El Dorado. The bad weather continued and the good ship *Rossini* rolled horribly. Cascades of china smashed in the dining saloon and in my bunk, wearing a thick pullover because the air-conditioning was over-enthusiastic, I rolled from side to side wondering if I too had been over-enthusiastic about travelling in ships. Things had quietened down by the time we reached Tenerife. Lying at anchor looking spick and span was HMS *Blake*, but her crew were returning after a night out as we left at 2am, and spoilt the effect by beseeching us to 'roll them over in the clover, roll them over, lay them down and do it again'.

Soon afterwards the weather improved, the swimming pool was filled and things livened up in the evening. Commandante Elio Bolzano was very much at ease socially, and I marvelled at his technique on the dance floor. He drew the prettier women one by one onto the floor and, after a couple of turns, passed them on to the shyest-looking men, then worked his way through the older and plainer ones till everyone was dancing. What British captain would have the flair to do that? But, alas, two days out of La Guaira the gallant commander was smitten by a stroke and, though he reappeared in the dining saloon and bar, determined to make light of it, his left arm was paralysed and I noticed the ship's doctor eyeing him with a mixture of tenderness and exasperation.

Disembarking in the warm air and uninhibited chaos of the port at La Guaira I felt again the lift of spirits that a landfall in the New World always gives. Even if the port itself is squalid one senses, in the south, the fecundity of the interior and, in the north, the huge achievements of free enterprise. There is a free-for-all atmosphere in both government and commerce and, although this often goes with a free-for-all attitude to corruption, it came as a pleasant change from the creeping bureaucracy in Britain and the centrist controls not wholly relaxed in Spain. The loud voices, juke boxes, Coca-Cola signs, shirt-sleeved crowds, taxi drivers with their left arms hanging out of enormous American cars, glaring sun, bright blue sea and crumbling streets all reminded me of the promise and disappointments of Colombia. As well they might, for Venezuela, Ecuador and Colombia, including the isthmus of Panama, emerged from the 1820 wars of independence as the federated state of Grancolombia; only later did they split acrimoniously and the United States pinch Panama. Now, after ten years of misspent oil revenues under Perez Jimenez, the second of two megalomaniac dictators, Venezuela was again a democracy, but she was held in low esteem by her neighbours for aping North American ways.

The advantages of Venezuela's exploitation by the USA became apparent as soon as I left the tropical heat of La Guaira by a motorway that climbed smoothly for 15 miles through tunnels and up a thousand metres to the perennial spring climate of Caracas. Its disadvantages were equally obvious as soon as I emerged onto the traffic-blocked streets of the city, which were not then relieved by a metro system and were being steadily imprisoned by apartment blocks leapfrogging each other in height. Caracas lies in a long basin divided from the sea by the steep mountain of El Avila, along whose foot ran at that time the only city bypass. Just below the bypass was 'El Country', a golf course and country club which included grand houses and embassies and served as a lung for the rest of the city. Two follies on a grand scale commemorated the years of dictatorship: to the south, like a vast empty tortoise shell, sat the unfinished Helicoid; and running up the slopes of El Avila was the Teleférico, a funicular leading to the Humboldt Hotel, a skyscraper just below the summit, with a further line of cable cars running – or, as was the case by the time I arrived, no longer running – up to La Silla (the Saddle). What the planners had ignored was the depressing effect of the mists that so often shrouded this summit (just as it did that of Montserrat in Bogotá).

Not long before my arrival, members of the Royal Ballet had been accommodated as a special treat in the Humboldt hotel and found themselves imprisoned at night, like so many ghosts of Hamlet's father, when what they wanted were the bright lights and restaurants of the city. The hotel soon fell into disuse, after an abortive period as a catering school, and the main cable car was often out of order, sometimes for months at a time. Nevertheless, cable car or not, El Avila remained a godsend: a stiff climb on foot took one rapidly up to its silent gullies and deserted farms, providing a wonderful escape from the noise of Caracas and avoiding the weekend queues that dogged attempts to get out of the city by car.

In 1971 evidence of a recent earthquake was not at first obvious, for the shocks seemed to have been very selective. Gradually, however, I noticed apartment blocks half collapsed here and there, and the word went round, as I started house-hunting, that the bottom had dropped out of the rents of high-rise buildings. However, when I found that a millionaire's penthouse on the 32nd floor of the Caromay Building in Plaza Altamira, with an enormous terrace and a kidney-shaped swimming pool, was now within my price range, I let my fantasies take over and moved in. My daughter Clare, when she came to stay, called it my 'James Bond' flat. It certainly made an unusually worldly background for earnest Council parties and also banished once and for all Clare's notion, which had lingered ever since being told as a child that I 'worked for the Council', that I was remarkably well-paid for a dustman. For her, the flat now seemed a very fitting background as she had, it seemed almost imperceptibly, turned from a schoolgirl into a young woman – and even had a driving licence; I actually invited her to drive the car – the supreme test, even on a remote jungle road, of a man's affection. In the Caromay I never felt particularly anxious about lightning striking twice but I did wonder how I'd get out – except by helicopter – in case of fire. Several times when the lift was out of order I wondered if I'd ever get in; I had to walk upstairs and once met a cat on the 15th floor, descending composedly.

Returning to South America also meant a return to the *Cultura*, the English-teaching Instituto Cultural Venezolano-Británico, and its board, or Junta Directiva, of the local great and good. I was both Council Representative and Institute Director, and my Assistant Representative doubled as the Institute Director of Studies. The Instituto was in a rented villa in the suburb of Las Mercedes, but the Board were on the point of buying new premises.

The long-serving chairman of the Junta spoke little English and was more interested in the status than the culture of his post, but their Administrative Officer was none other than Mac, the Bill MacLaughlin who had welcomed me to Barranquilla 25 years earlier. Now locally employed and locally married, he had purchased a plot and was building a house for his retirement in the Colonia Tovar. This picturesque but somewhat claustrophobic enclosure of inbred descendants of South German indentured labourers, established in the woods about 30 miles from Caracas, had recently after years of isolation and decay been developed as a tourist resort by an entrepreneur from Germany. An elderly Rumanian lady was in charge of student affairs at the Institute and the secretary I acquired was Spanish, as was the cheerful driver and handyman who lived with his family behind the classrooms and library. This heavy European presence was typical of Caracas, where almost every enterprise depended on immigrants for its success – building on Italians, business on Germans and Spaniards, farming on Portuguese, petrochemicals on North Americans and Britons. In the tolerant climate that existed these communities were able to exercise their abilities to the full and had turned Caracas into the Los Angeles of South America. Unfortunately, I had arrived just in time to find this give-and-take optimism rebounding on my head.

But first I had to cope with the British secretary I had inherited from my predecessor. My hand was forced when a row erupted between her and the Assistant Representative who was clearly efficient at his job and to all appearances a sober family man. As soon as I gave her notice she broke into a torrent of accusations: he was sleeping with one of the teachers; he was a sexual maniac; she had observed him masturbating in the office when he thought nobody was looking. I took these fantasies with a pinch of salt but it made me look at future office staff with a new eye, and I was to find that it was not only locally engaged staff who caused crises.

Meanwhile the move to new premises brought major trouble. The lease on the old ones was due to expire and a new one would cost 40% more, and that without the former parking area. The Junta had decided to raise a bank loan to buy either a space in an unbuilt block of flats in the centre of town or a £55,000 villa on the edge of the Country Club. I favoured the latter, to allow for future expansion, immediate occupancy, and simultaneous building in the garden of two classrooms and a language laboratory. The Junta declared they could fix planning permission in this highly residential area so the only serious disadvantage was its lack of public transport. The move went ahead and we soon found, as we opened classes and started building, that there were other serious disadvantages – the neighbours. They very reasonably objected to this new traffic and to having their drives blocked by students' cars. I was summoned to the Municipal Engineer's office to swear that I would stop all building, otherwise our whole operation would be closed down. The Junta arranged a judicious 'settlement' with several subsequent inspectors and the Italian builder forged ahead ('Signor Alessandri, you no pay attention. You finish quick. Police no do nothing. You stop now and you no finish never!'). Both the City Engineer and the Planning Director privately promised to turn a blind eye to our activities if only we could get the neighbours' injunction removed.

Eventually things settled down into the state of manageable illegality not unusual in those parts but after so many crises I was particularly anxious that my assistant, who had been posted elsewhere in the middle of them, should at least be succeeded by someone equally reliable. But I was not optimistic when I read the CV of the successor. X was one of the new English Language Teaching (ELT) brigade, who were being recruited in bulk – as it were – and given a year's diploma course in the Teaching of English as a Foreign Language (TEFL). They were then despatched abroad to effect an expansion in both direct teaching and ELT advisory work, made possible by an increase in funding through the Overseas Development Ministry. In the effort to meet targets quickly, emphasis in selection was inevitably laid on academic qualifications rather than overseas experience or personal qualities, and there had been some embarrassing recruits not only from Britain and the Commonwealth but from vocal supporters of a united Ireland.

X seemed to lack the experience I had hoped for. From school teaching in England he had gone to South America under local contract and married there. Thence the Council had recruited him and, after a brief posting in Europe, he was sent on a year's TEFL diploma course. There had been some hitch over completion of his thesis but here he was at last and, notwithstanding the disquiet I voiced, I must take him or leave him. He was to arrive 'unaccompanied' as his wife was to clear up their affairs and follow later with their little boy. There was nothing unreasonable about this, but with a further flicker of disquiet I remembered my own journey 'unaccompanied' to Hong Kong.

X himself, when he arrived, was clearly determined to dispel any cause for disquiet but he seemed to have a curious idea of priorities. He very soon informed me with satisfaction that he had made his number with the local Rotarians and proposed to speak at one of their lunches. As I had already done this, I was surprised that he had taken time away from class work to duplicate our public relations message and perhaps confuse its recipients. My feelings about Rotary – and even more about the curiously garbed Lions Club members whom I had met in Guyana – were ambivalent. Any avenue of publicity for the Council was welcome, and doubly so if it was the way to meet local businessmen whose interest and support was vital to us. But all too often the interest and support expressed at Rotary meetings was nominal and, though their charitable work was of major significance, the very mobile nature of the organisation demands that its activities are ritual but fleeting. So I have welcomed invitations to speak at Rotary but have avoided regular commitment to heavy lunches and to time-consuming formalities of dubious worth.

X, however, clearly thought Rotary a serious part of Council work and struck out happily in American circles. At the same time he started to confide in me about his own family: his wife, it appeared, was the daughter of a general who had never approved of the marriage, and she had not enjoyed life in the cold north of England looking after the child while he was having a convivial time with fellow students. Did I know, too, that voodoo still flourished in the country from which she came? Then X began to suffer ill health and at 4 o'clock one morning he rang me and poured out his sorrows. His wife had sent their boy back to her parents and now, with the proceeds of the car sale, had followed him; he couldn't sleep; he was worried about his mother, who was a charlady and was missing him; he was feeling awful and knew why: now that those people who were making him ill had got his son, they wanted him to die. Did I know what he meant? He meant voodoo ...

A week or so later X said he must fly out to talk things over with his wife. I rang up Personnel Department in London to say I strongly disapproved of him going on leave so soon after taking up his post, that he appeared to be heading for a nervous breakdown and that if he were to go he might very well not come back, and I asked if I could say that the exigencies of the service precluded leaving Venezuela at this stage of the Institute's development? No, they said, I could not. He had over a week's leave due to him and I could not refuse him leave, especially if requested on compassionate grounds.

And so one morning, a few days later, off flew X; and that evening his wife rang me from Caracas airport to ask where he was because he had said he would meet her there. She had indeed, she said after I had settled her in a hotel, been unhappy on the outskirts of their university town; there had been nothing to see when she looked out of the window but cows. 'Cows!' she cried, 'something that only peasants look at in my country.'

It all ended in tears and X was repatriated to England after attempting to kidnap his son. While packing up the things in his flat I found on the window sill a small primitive doll ... with pins stuck into it.

To console me for X's defection, London sent out an Ulster farmer's daughter of thirty, who was intelligent and reliable but unable to drive and quite extraordinarily buttoned up. 'She doesn't say much, does she?' said Emmanuel Hurwitz when I took them both out for a Sunday drive. Manny was the lead player of the Aeolian Quartet which had given two sparsely attended recitals. I had been dreading their tour because I knew quartets were not popular with Venezuelans, but it was fixed up between London and the notoriously inefficient local Arts Council. The Quartet had played to audiences of eighty in a theatre seating eleven hundred, and the British colony was conspicuous by its absence. The players were pretty shattered at their reception, hence my country drive and a buffet supper for twenty-three in my magnificent flat. The Ambassador, by this time the hospitable and supportive Alexander Mayall, also gave a lunch for them.

Pushing unknown soloists or small groups of instrumentalists, who were expected by the Council to play British music, at audiences not particularly interested in music was a perennial problem in many countries. German and French colleagues had a natural advantage in national repertoires, and there also seemed to be an endless supply of first-rate soloists available for minimal fees from Iron Curtain countries like Czechoslovakia and Poland. Whipping up audiences for British soloists was often a thankless task, except in the most primitive places where any distraction was welcomed. A tour of this kind was undoubtedly very wearing for the players, and I suppose only the hope of something better emerging kept them doing the Council rounds year after year.

It is dispiriting to be unable to get good audiences for pleasant people, but equally dispiriting to find that people who do attract good audiences are not necessarily pleasant. Emlyn Williams, whose Dickens act was certainly effective, was not himself unpleasant but seemed curiously ill at ease – possibly made so by his entourage. It was a relief to welcome Bob Cohan's London Contemporary Dance Theatre Group, who were excellent ambassadors, both on and off stage. The sixteen dancers and ten backstage staff filled the theatre for three nights, as well as giving morning workshops. (One of the youngest was Siobhan Davies who, twenty years later, would be running her own company dancing her own ballets.) The dancers included an Argentine, three Americans, a Canadian, a German, an Israeli, a Jamaican and a Jugoslav. They had had a gruelling time, flying from town to town and settling into theatre after theatre, getting tummy troubles, pulling muscles, and even losing an appendix – the wardrobe mistress's. They arrived from Colombia looking like creatures out of Belsen and it was amazing to see how they bounced back to form next day. They were popular offstage, too, and my buffet supper in the flat went on till 2 in the morning. The Ambassador gave a relaxed 'swimming lunch' for them and, seeing some of the dancers giving each other massage, had one himself from the Canadian. Thereupon an amply proportioned secretary asked for one from the Jamaican; on the last night she disappeared with him and turned up at 6.30 in the morning to see him off, looking effectively relaxed.

The amateur theatre scene in Caracas scarcely impinged on Council work. There was an efficient and long-established Anglo-American group, but I had neither time to join it actively nor funds to assist it financially. The Venezuelan amateur productions were mostly musicals and strongly imitative of US shows. I was invited to a preview of Oscar Martinez's lavish musical, *Marco*, a kind of *Jesus Christ Superstar* treatment of the travels of Marco Polo. The time announced was 8.45, so I got there at 9.45 and only had twenty minutes to wait before curtain-up. Half the microphones didn't work, so some of the characters opened and shut their mouths noiselessly while others blasted us out of our seats. Pictures flashed on a backstage screen off and on, and not always when expected, and bits of ornate scenery crashed up and down from the flies, sometimes decapitating our view of the characters. I left at about midnight, when we were still with Kubla Khan and his (inaudible) daughter.

Curiously enough, apart from the London Contemporary Dance Theatre, the 'manifestation' of British achievement that most successfully penetrated the cultural hide of the Caraqueños was due not to me but to the Americans. The Metropolitan Museum of Modern Art sent out a display of paintings by Francis Bacon, which created a sensation in the National Art Gallery in Caracas. On the assumption that any publicity is better than none, I basked in the reflected glory of his screaming popes while not presuming to lecture upon their cause and effect.

It may sound less than complimentary to the Venezuelans, but Caracas is something of a melting pot and Caraqueños have a mercenary attitude to the arts. They lack, for instance, the charm and cultural pretensions of Colombians, and their student population, spoilt by misapplication of oil revenues, was often on strike or busy vandalising their premises. On one occasion I was asked to the national day at the Belgian Embassy because the Ambassador had a drug problem with a son of nineteen whom he wished to send to England. There was a group of similarly unhappy, privileged youths whose parents lived in the expensive Country Club area. North American habits were deeply engrained; Venezuelans were gadget mad, and drugs were simply a particularly dangerous and therefore fascinating gadget. There were less dangerous ones. I had my first experience of cordless phones when an applicant for a Council scholarship was paged in the middle of our interview, and I was left to twiddle my thumbs while he talked to a girlfriend. Notwithstanding his cockiness, I supported his application, but at the last moment he turned down his award for one in the US. (It was not always easy to evaluate Venezuelan candidates. The next applicant was a black primary school teacher from the Gulf of Paria whose first language was Creolese English.) It is not perhaps surprising that Henri Charrière, 'Papillon', was so much at home in the shifting population of Venezuela, and set up his sleazy café, Mi Vaca y Yo, in the hills above Caracas. (I never knew how much of his book to believe since he got British Guiana police uniforms wrong – 'spotless white' instead of the actual grey and blue of colonial territories like BG and Hong Kong.) Nevertheless, there were of course many highly civilised Caraqueños – one of whom, Dr Kerdel Vegas, was a valuable friend of the Council and later Ambassador in London – and in the provinces there were pleasant people full of the traditional warmth of South America and free from the brashness of the capital.

As I had in Guyana, I visited provincial towns on VSO business, though with less happy results. I think this was not so much because the Venezuelan environment was less receptive to VSO activity as that the activity itself had grown less altruistic and – like the universities that fed it – more politicised and self-seeking. The hands-off policy of VSO, which was eventually changed by the appointment of its own field officers, seemed to me less effective than the group activity of the Peace Corps. In an exasperated letter home I described my disappointment:

> The views of my new assistant, who is herself an ex-VSO and accompanied me on this 800 mile trip to the Andes (remaining as silent as ever, except when I filled her up with gin), were even more depressed than mine. I did not envy the charming Anglophile Dean of Humanities in Mérida where the students – and VSOs – are blissfully unaware of the disastrous effects of their activism in the name of democracy. He was from Galicia and had some splendid modern Spanish paintings. He also had 3000 gramophone records, on which he had spent £40 a month steadily for the previous fifteen years. They included, although he spoke no English, many speeches of Winston Churchill and Laurence Olivier.

It is a pity the Mérida work was so disappointing because the old colonial city itself was attractive and the drive to it, over a 16,000ft pass through 'Indian territory', was spectacular. The journey was a great contrast to a reconnaissance trip I made to Barquisimeto with an administrator from VSO HQ. Douglas Whiting, its Director, had recently married an ex-VSO, and I wondered whether he was not doing his bit to relieve my solitude in the same way when Ms S arrived, for she was bewitchingly beautiful. By an odd coincidence I knew her uncle as the landlord of a pleasant fishing pub in Wales. She had a weakness for adventure but whether she was as efficient as she was beautiful seemed doubtful, for she said she had found herself disengaged after overturning her fiancé's VW on one of Africa's dirt roads. We certainly found ourselves in a ludicrous situation which faced us in Barquisimeto. Hotel after hotel had just one double room free, and the hotel owners couldn't understand why I didn't take it; nor could Ms S. 'I don't mind,' she said helpfully, 'if you don't.' I have seldom faced such a test. But however unwise my attachments have been, I have tried not to mix business with pleasure and, as the fantasy of a night of unorthodox voluntary service overseas flashed before me, so too did the professional and domestic consequences of an entanglement with this lovely girl of less than half my age, and eventually a kind or unkind fate revealed a particularly scruffy hotel which had two rooms vacant. Neither did we, in the end, agree on our official recommendations to HQ, which is not surprising for most aid organisations are anxious to build up their empires at any price, while those on the ground cannot fail to see practical shortcomings. We did, however, keep in touch, and on my next leave were to meet for a drink with Ms S's current interest. Arriving at the address I found the two of them in the street, trying to open the front door with the assistance of a policeman. It was a chilly evening and, sensing that my presence would only be an added complication in a night of mishaps, I withdrew from the scene. Had fate decreed that Ms S, as well as being beautiful, should be accident prone? If so, to what mischievous end?

Another dispiriting journey was a flight to Bogotá for a regional conference on aid and cultural relations. It was, of course, raining when I arrived. The Sábana looked familiar enough from the plane – green, green, green – but was dotted with irrigation tanks which I did not remember from before. Nor did I recognise the drive in – or, rather, under – the Parque de la Independencia surrounded as it was with rather fine new buildings, including the Tequendama Hotel. But there was still that familiar acrid smell of the imperfect combustion of petrol at high altitudes, the beggars with twisted limbs and people with sad, flat Chibcha features, and everywhere an air of depression and failure. However, the people were infinitely more courteous than the Caraqueños. I remembered how sick I used to get of their routine courtesies, but now it was a pleasure to hear good Spanish spoken again.

Little by little familiar buildings reasserted themselves, including the old British Institute on Carrera Septima, now some kind of school. On three corners of a crossroads in the centre of town stood the fine new language institutes of the United States, France and Germany. The Colombo-British Institute, conspicuous by its absence, had fizzled out eight years earlier, and the remaining Council office and library were now tucked away in an office block two floors below the Embassy. The Challen piano sat forlornly in the entrance as the last relic, with one of the secretaries and the driver, of former Institute activities; the locked lavatory was in the public passage outside and, of the two WCs, only one had a seat; and the fairly new office Ford Zephyr was in such a shocking state that we were quite nervous when driven to the only party given for us in six days by Council staff. Yet their annual budget (with a cost of living half that in Venezuela) was £50,000, double mine (or to put it in perspective, one twentieth that of India). 'The Council,' I was told, 'gave no priority to work in Venezuela.' The staff in Bogotá did not seem to be on familiar terms with Embassy staff or with any of the old teachers, and I failed to locate Ozzie Pope, who was said to be teaching at the English School. However the Ambassador in Colombia, Tom Rogers, who had been Consul in my time, entertained us lavishly and Arthur Turner, who had helped me with my dramatised play readings, ran the conference with his accustomed aplomb. Monserrat was its same old self, covered in mist, but I heard that some Americans ascending it recently in a jeep had been relieved of their belongings.

The chatty taxi driver who took me back to the airport said he had thought of joining some of his mates in Venezuela. However, he didn't believe it was quite as civilised as Colombia. Meanwhile he was learning English at the American Centre. We conversed in Spanish.

In Venezuela, in contrast to Council parsimony, the FO had a large presence. Both the Ambassadors during my time there, and their staff, were helpful and friendly. Hobson had been in the news while Ambassador in Peking for the rough time he had had at the hands of the Red Guards. In Caracas he ran a very tight ship: 'prayer meetings' were conducted with precision and his staff were kept very much on their toes. Once, leaving the Embassy at lunchtime, I found the corridor looking like a scene from a gangster film. Office doors were ajar, with black-coated secretaries lurking nervously in the shadows.

'Has he gone yet?' one of them hissed at me as I passed.

'Who?'

'H E.'

They were itching to get out for lunch but none dared leave before the boss. Hobson was very energetic in spite of having to walk with a stick because of an arthritic hip. From Caracas he was posted to Rio, and while on leave had a hip replacement done. Tragically after only a few months at post he died of a stroke.

Sir Alexander and Lady Mayall were a more easy-going pair but perhaps even more active in furthering the interests of the Council. I'm afraid I shocked them once by declining an invitation to meet the Prince of Wales. My alternative engagement was to fly for the day to Los Roques, a little group of offshore islands delightfully untouched by the Caracas blight. How could I think for a moment of exchanging this for a stiff cocktail party with a teenage boy as guest of honour? But I suppose I was defying a royal command.

Los Roques were not the only islands I visited. Margarita was much larger and already beginning to feel the effect of tourism. More unusual, and in a somewhat melancholy way infinitely more romantic, was the Bahamas island of Hopetown, off Abaco. Once again my visit was thanks to the Beestons, then in Washington, who had rented a holiday house there from a neighbour and invited me to join them. I flew up to Miami to catch a connection to Nassau, and a long wait in the airport gave me time to marvel at the grotesque figures and weird dress of people passing through. After this the neat Georgian architecture of Nassau and the slender build of its black inhabitants came as a welcome contrast. However, on closer acquaintance I found them a nervy lot compared to the laid-back Guyanese or Trinidadians. Abaco and its smaller islands are almost entirely white, both in seasonal and permanent residents. The latter are descended from Royalists escaping the aftermath of the American War of Independence, and their wooden clapboard colonial houses looked quite unchanged from that period. Yet

Hopetown was also a kind of Venice, with modern houses dotted about on islets served by radio rather than telephone. If one wanted to go ashore to dine one radioed the restaurant and went over by boat. The peace and the pace of life there after Caracas were therapeutic, but to live there permanently must be very odd. Very odd, too, were some of the people who did so, and it was obvious that inbreeding, as with the 'Redlegs' of Barbados and the Germans of Colonia Tovar, had taken its toll.

Caracas is not well placed for golden beaches. The coast on both sides of La Guaira is rocky and only intermittently receptive to rough swimming. Caraqueños were beginning to build beach houses at Coro, nearly 300 miles west of Caracas and halfway to the oil wells of Lake Maracaibo. One of my friends had been astute enough to buy a pleasant village house at Tucacas, nearer Caracas and on a then unspoilt beach, but the developers were already beginning to move in, and driving back into Caracas was a terrible price to pay for a weekend's tranquillity. This tranquillity, however, was only comparative. In Latin America, even in villages like Tucacas, noise is the ultimate and unsleeping enemy, as I recorded in a letter: 'The *cantina* in front blared away until 1am, mosquitoes came and went, a next door cock started crowing at 4am, some Texan divers on the other side got up noisily at 5am, a radio started up at 6 and the children began creating at 6.30.' The same kind of disturbances were to be expected in the coastal places to the east of Caracas, like Puerto La Cruz and Cumaná.

To the south lay Indian country and the spectacular Angel Falls, but unless time was no object these could only be reached by air. It was round the delta of the Orinoco and Caroni rivers that the main government-sponsored development was going on, based on the new town of Ciudad Guayana, some 500 miles from Caracas. From the days of the dictators the government had inherited big ideas about this area, and also the land south-east of it – including about a third of the former British Guiana. This land, down the coast as far as the Essequibo (and including Bartica) and then south to the Brazilian border, was shown striped in Venezuelan maps and labelled ZONA EN RECLAMACIÓN. I was intrigued by this ancient claim and curious to see country so close to Trinidad and Guyana and was lucky in having a neighbour who enabled me to do so in style.

John and Elsa Mortimer lived on the ground floor of my skyscraper. Elsa was Argentine and doing Diploma English at the Institute while John, an engineer, had the franchise for a large part of South America for Metallock, a process by which broken machinery could be 'knitted' together. It took John all over the country and to remote places that would not figure in the more delicate requirements of the British Council. Work permitting, I would sometimes go along with him for the ride and to relieve his solitude on the long journeys. It so happened that he had business in the Guayana country when my school-leaving youngest son, Ian, and his friend Peter Evans were staying with me, and John proposed that we should all go with him in his luxurious air-conditioned Chrysler, no mean consideration, for we would be back in the damp heat of the Cinderella Coast. The trip was a fascinating mixture of the old and new: the old Spanish colonial relics, and the state-of-the-art Ciudad Guayana at the junction of the Orinoco and Caroni rivers. Many of the villages en route were pretty primitive and the only considerable town, Ciudad Bolivar, which is 60 miles up the Orinoco from Ciudad Guayana, is nothing to write home about. I forget which of these places it was that had a pretentious hotel that was fast disintegrating, notwithstanding the management's efforts to preserve the proprieties. Over the swimming pool was a notice in Spanish: GUESTS ARE RESPECTFULLY INFORMED THAT THIS SWIMMING POOL CONTAINS A DETECTOR OF URINE.

I don't know what Ciudad Guayana is like now, but it had then only just, as it were, got off the ground and was very new indeed. Its construction was proving problematic: different zones were being built simultaneously, leaving gaps in between to be filled later; meanwhile, however, the gaps were filling up with squatters. It was interesting to compare the promise of developing squalor with an earlier description of the view from La Llovizna:

> When we ran to the tops of the first hills of the plain adjoining the river, we beheld that wonderful breach of waters that ran down Caroni, and might from that mountain see the river, how it ran in three parts above 20 miles off, and there appeared some ten or twelve overfalls in sight, every one as high above the other as a church tower, which fell with that fury that the rebound of waters made it seem as if it had all been covered over with a great shower of rain; and in some places we took it at the first for a smoke that had risen over some great town. I never saw a more beautiful country, nor more lively prospects ... and every stone that we stooped to take up promised either gold or silver by its complexion.

Thus wrote poor Sir Walter Raleigh in his *Relations of his First Voyage to Guyana*. The passage is quoted in a book published in 1809, called *A Voyage to the Demarary* by Henry Bolingbroke. Bolingbroke had unorthodox views on British strategy for the early stages of the War of Independence, when Spanish control still remained in the balance. They read strangely today:

> If, instead of employing the celebrated enthusiast of liberty, General Miranda, to agitate the Caraccas, his knowledge of the country and his intelligence among the people had been called in merely to direct the conquests of the western bank of the Orinoco, by a regular army whose presence and whose principles would have excited no apprehension of a servile war, and of a general insurrection of the working negroes, that strip of country might lately have been added to and consolidated with our possessions in Guyana ... A conquest of the province of New Cumana is the only fundamental remedy. This fine district up to Ciudad Real [now Ciudad Bolivar] might surely have

> been attained without any greater expenditure of life and effort than was lately lent to General Miranda ... The assertion of independence is a far greater hazard to run than a ready submission to a British army ... The worst that can happen after a British conquest is to be ceded back to the parent country, when war ceases in Europe, after tasting the profits of a freer trade, and forming some acquaintances in an heretical garrison ... with Irish merchants of the Spanish colonists' own faith to conduct their intercourse and to amalgamate with their population.

In sharp contrast to all the developmental activity round Ciudad Guayana, the Castillos de Guayana 20 miles down-river bear an extraordinarily strong and silent witness to early Spanish enterprise, as does a ruined but handsome colonial church standing in green isolation and used only by the marvellous birds of the jungle and river. The castles evidently caught the eye of a film producer because a few years later they were the scene of a World War II film called *Kelly's War*. It was the usual one-man miracle hokum with Peter O'Toole and Philippe Noiret but it did give a good idea of this ghostly and romantic site.

John Mortimer was also a companion on walks nearer home, on El Avila where there were colonial remains among the trees. As there had been banditry and arson on the mountain one had to get a permit to walk on parts of it and this helped to preserve its solitude. However, on the precipitous slopes of its Caracas side the solitude could be oppressive, especially when, as at El Infiernito, one came across a melancholy ruined farm. On the sea side the descent was more gradual and the country more open, with Portuguese fruit farms that were very much going concerns. The old colonial road to La Guaira, still cobbled in parts, ran over the western end of the range. Being only negotiable by jeep, and having long been superseded by the Carretera Caracas-La Guaira, and subsequently by the Autopista lower down the valley, it remained remarkably deserted. It climbed up through almost the only remaining undeveloped suburb, La Pastora, where single-storey patio houses lined the narrow streets, and not far away El Libertador lay in state in a chapel patrolled by dress-uniformed soldiers; so the colonial atmosphere was still quite strong. The twisting Carretera was itself now deserted, except by the owners of the villas and farms on its shady but not very hospitable slopes. On the edge of Caracas it ran slap through the middle of the city tip, where trucks were discharging their loads and hundreds of vultures waited impatiently to examine them.

The average Caraqueño rarely climbed El Avila (too steep), pursued the colonial road (too archaic), or penetrated the Carretera and its shameful tip (best ignored), but to me these offered the quickest escape from the car-crazed city, together with exhilarating views of its past. For me, too, the colonial road had an especially poignant interest, for it was over this that Sir Robert Ker Porter used to ride, first to escape the ennui of Caracas by dining with the officers of HM's ships that had put in at La Guaira, and later to pay surreptitious court to 'the fair Limeña'. Different as were our circumstances, I could not but feel a strong affinity with him at moments in his highly charged journal.

16
Adiós

KER PORTER IMPINGED on my life three times, apart from his posting to and description of Caracas. In Persia his book of travels and sketches made between 1817 and 1820 are still standard works of reference. In Bristol his doctor brother, and later his two novelist sisters, settled in an elegant Georgian square in what is now the problem area of St Paul's. ('Monday, 9 August 1841. Visited the Great Iron Steamer. A one thousand horse power engine is to act on the new invented system ... called the Archimedean screw ... I have my doubts as to the thing answering in its present *infant state.*') In the monument to Tipu Sultan in Shrirangapattana I saw a mutilated copy of his mural of the siege, which had won him fame as an artist in 1800 at the age of twenty-three.

The original, exhibited at the Lyceum to paying customers, was destroyed by fire, but not before it had brought him an invitation from Tsar Alexander I in 1805 to go to St Petersburg. ('*All, all, all* cannot balance the value of the condescending friendship the revered and ever venerated Alexander bestowed upon me.') In Moscow he met a Russian princess and, with her Tsar's blessing, married her six years later. In the interval of shifting alliances in the Napoleonic wars he accompanied Sir John Moore's peninsular campaign and published his own letters from Russia, Spain, Portugal and Sweden. He also collected knighthoods from Sweden in 1806, Württemberg in 1807, the Prince Regent in 1813, and Futeh Ali Shah of Persia in 1820.

Having moved with an aplomb rare in an artist up through the courts of Europe and the Levant, he was appointed British Consul for Venezuela (then part of Grancolombia) in 1825, becoming Chargé d'Affaires in the detached Republic of Venezuela ten years later. Thereafter his interest in art – as also in his family – appears desultory. He remained *en poste* for fifteen years – in what must have been one of the most back-of-beyond '*postes*' in the service – with only one home leave of a year. Why did he do it?

'Left La Guayra at 2 pm,' he writes after fourteen years, 'and after a pretty *fairish* agreeable ride reached Caracas at 6. Very glad even to find myself once more in a city I am sighing to leave for ever – but so it is and such is the restless character of human nature ... My pen, my horse and my few books occupy me from 6 in the morning until half past nine at night ... and thus wears away the day in the great wheel of the year cog by cog.'

On his leave in 1829 he is much fêted by the Aberdeen ministry but his leave is cut short by events in Venezuela, with Paez plotting a republic without Bolivar, and he bewails not having time to see his daughter (though he had had nearly a year to do it in). 'I trust this terrible sacrifice may prove in the end advantageous to my hopes for the St Petersburg appointment. I put my *faith in Ministers* – and hope not to be deceived.'

It is 1841 before he sees England again. Made much of by Palmerston and presented to the Queen ('she is indeed very short'), he drops hints that he is still anxious to serve his country, but is left to return to Russia – for the first time for sixteen years – in a private capacity. Perhaps it was only the hope of getting the St Petersburg job that drove him to Caracas in the first place.

There seems never to have been any suggestion that his wife and daughter should go there too. They had stayed in Russia during the twelve years – many spent on his travels and writing them up in England – between his marriage and departure for Caracas. When, only a year after his arrival in Caracas, his young wife died from typhus, she elicits a formal epitaph: 'Few can feel who are not thus sadly situated what those feelings are of a husband being bereaved of an affectionate and adored object. My Princess was all virtue, benevolence, and possessed a heart few could boast of. My heart is sadly torn by this unexpected blow ... The packet boat reached La Guayra at 3 o'clock this day, having left Barbados 5 days ago. Thermometer at 7,72, at 4,74 Rain in the morning.'

Though sociable and even gallant to the ladies, the widower Ker Porter gives no hint that he ever strays beyond the proprieties, or approves of those who do. 'Mr Ackers's lady is exceedingly pretty and interesting for one of these countries and only 16. Mr Ackers is 62 – and I think now a few days past keeping so young a *chère amie*, but he is a thorough West Indian – never was married, and has, and has had, crowds of natural children of every shade from black to white.'

Ker Porter was himself something of a philanthropist – for instance in creating a British burial ground – but was not easily misled by the motivation of others. 'Campbell, the Irish baker, died last night (a drunkard) ... Being a Catholic, of which I was not aware, he had nothing to do with our cemeterial ceremonies. He deceived me getting married as a Protestant, as also did his wife – both being Catholics. But then it was *cheaper*.' He was even more critical of the accounting methods of the educational reformer, '*the benevolent and philanthropic Mr Joseph Lankester*', at his failing colony of 250 'Scotch weavers and mechanics – a worthless drunken set' at Topo. (Today all that remains of it is a name on the map – near the top of the La Guaira motorway – 'La Quebrada del Inglès' – The Englishman's ravine). The Topo colonists are not the only objects of his disapproval. Certainly for such a widely travelled man he seems over-censorious of those more easy-going than himself, deploring, at a play, the 'barbarous and *ungentlemanlike* custom of smoking during the performance', and deprecating the Caraqueños' mania for gambling. 'Billiards, gambling and cockfights are very prominent features in the daily occupations of most of the ministers and rulers. Mariño, the Minister of War, who lives in a dirty house, regularly signs the State Papers on the billiard table, during his game.'

The Diary, edited by Walter Dupouy in Caracas in 1966, is 1,200 double-column pages long, and most of it is concerned with the ebb and flow of local politics. However, to the casual reader it is the changing social and domestic details that acquire particular interest with age. The savage habits of the War of Independence, still evident in Ker Porter's early days (the last loyal troops only left South America in 1826), have by the end of them become – at least on the surface – almost prudish. We hear no more of scenes like those at the charismatic Bolivar's banquets, when his *chère amie* would relieve herself in the corner of the room. Bolivar's successor, the illiterate General Páez, whose reputation for running captured Spanish officers through and lying on the ground foaming at the mouth when crossed at first repels Ker Porter, becomes in the end 'that grand old soldier' with whom he picnics, and to whom he looks for moral support on sticky occasions such as a visit to the Archbishop. 'We took our seats near him, and Páez seemed to measure his time of halt for we were no sooner down than up and bidding adieu. He attended the general and all to the top of the staircase, when each kissed his hand, or rather a huge Amathyst ring he wore; I escaped behind some who had done the thing and descended to take the arm of Páez, whom I accompanied to his mansion.'

It comes as a surprise when the 64-year-old diarist, after fifteen years of an increasingly equable acceptance of his circumstances, a formal ease with his hosts and a gentlemanly comportment towards most of his compatriots – and on the very eve of his departure – falls head over heels in love with a young Peruvian girl married to an Englishman. Some months after their meeting in La Guaira she calls on him on her way from church. 'She looked most lovely! And bright in eye, and sweet expression of countenance as ever Cleopatra did! ... Mr Harrison has a treasure of an *esposa* – but he does not know her value, or how to preserve her love for him. It is fortunate for my friend that my principles of honour and rectitude are not like those of ...!'

From then onwards Sir Robert's farewell parties are interspersed with his pursuit of Maria Luisa. 'At one rode out to pass a few hours with my Limanian favourite ... Made a sketch of my dear and lovely friend ... Dined with Mrs H. The hours passed delightfully – and every passing one seems to augment the ardent esteem she has now for so many months entertained for me. *This close of my residence in Venezuela* will for ever be unfadingly impressed on my heart – and has inoculated it with a feeling of sorrow and regret not because I depart from the shores, but because I leave *one behind me worthy* of a better, aye! far better fate.'

In England, though wined and dined for six months, Sir Robert receives no offer of further employment and sets out with his sister Jane for St Petersburg, where he meets his daughter, now married to a Russian army officer. Here, for eight months, he engages in the social round as busily as though he's never been away, but misses the climate of Caracas and suffers from colds and headaches. Returning one day from a visit to court, he falls from the running board of his coach and dies the next morning.

I found Ker Porter's diary particularly fascinating because I so often felt as he did. I shared his feelings of solitude (my family, too, was far away, though Clare and Ian did come out for brief holidays) and of tedium ('the great wheel of the year cog by cog'). Like him I was there to show the flag, though my resources, unlike his, were declining. The frigates that called at La Guaira and brought him riding eagerly over the 'old Spanish' road to dine on board arrived frequently; I only drove down the motorway once for a naval reception. The animosity towards him of the Topo colonists, blaming him for their failure, was not very different to the Junta's towards me. He, too, liked to escape the committee meetings and social obligations of Caracas by travelling to the interior or, nearer home, climbing La Silla (when he was sixty and without the benefit of the *teleférico)*. I shared with him the mixed feelings of affection and exasperation towards the host country but above all the feeling of detachment that all diplomats or short-term contract workers overseas inevitably have. No wonder that after such a long unrelieved tour of duty poor Sir Robert became infatuated with 'the fair Limeña'. Yet I, with far less excuse, led an equally inept life as far as romance was concerned and, as usual, left Venezuela still detached domestically.

I also left it unhappily, but for professional rather than personal reasons. After three years of legal and staffing problems the Institute, with 850 students, was at last promising a sound future and I was beginning to extend both my and the Council's interests in the marvellously diverse country outside the Americanised capital. One morning I was at home with a heavy migraine (another trait which I shared at that period with Sir Robert) when I got a call from the office. The Ambassador had telephoned and wanted to speak to me. I drove to the Embassy with no breakfast but Veganin tablets, and Mayall showed me a cable announcing that the Council had to save half a million pounds as part of a general cut in public expenditure and were withdrawing their representation in Venezuela. They would make a small subsidy to the Institute to hire its own Director locally. Later I heard from the Embassy, not from the Council, that we were withdrawing also from Uruguay, Guyana and Belize, and were not opening as planned in Zaire. Eventually the Council cabled and I learnt that the Institute would be given '£3,000 per annum for two years – and nothing else'. Later I learned that the language laboratory promised to Venezuela would be diverted to Peru, but the Council did relent enough to allow me to give our station wagon to the Institute.

I need not describe the reaction of the Junta to my news. A reformist group of us had tried to amend its constitution to limit the length of service of members, but had failed, and the same old core remained to push their particular vested interests. I think they believed that because we had failed to effect our reforms I personally had arranged for the Council withdrawal. At any rate I was shunned socially from then on and only one nice Venezuelan member invited me to a farewell lunch. I also had the shaming experience of announcing our departure to my colleagues from the French, German and American Institutes at our regular working lunch, and receiving their tactful sympathy in reply.

A British member of the Junta offered to supplement the Council grant with £5,000, and the job of Director was offered to my Assistant. She decided not to risk it (and was wrongly suspected of being influenced by me), and the Junta eventually appointed a local freelance British teacher. But the independent Institute did not flourish.

Instead of being able to pass on my James Bond flat furniture to a successor, I had to sell it, and the owners of the flat, now that earthquake fever had subsided, refused to transfer the lease to the Embassy, who were anxious to rent it for two 'visiting firemen'. I could not help reflecting that as far as our enormous Embassy and tiny Council were concerned, the British policy of national representatives seemed to be 'to him that hath shall be given and from him that hath not shall be taken away even that that he hath'. What particularly irked me was that, while the only Office and Institute in what was then a vibrant and debt-free country was being closed down, the Council was opening a further provincial centre at Recife in debt-ridden Brazil.

At my debriefing in London I expressed my dismay at this spoiling of the ship for a ha'porth of tar. I said, 'You'll have to go back into Venezuela sooner or later, and it will cost you infinitely more in the end.' Only nine months later, an Office was reopened there, because 'new opportunities had arisen', and it did indeed cost the Council a very great deal. Rumours reached me of expensive mistakes and nervous breakdowns all round before things settled down. I don't know how many *Culturas* still exist, and my Venezuelan experience was not to be the last to make me wary of committees. The idea of delegation, of exploiting local contacts and of avoiding expensive commitments is beguiling, but a Council figurehead who is in nominal charge for only three or four years is in no position to compete with an entrenched Junta of local residents when scandals occur. There is no substitute for authority, and to Directors and Juntas, as to governments and people, Ker Porter's assertion applies – that 'no bad government can do half the mischief that is occasioned by civil contention'.

The success of Council-run Institutes in Spain was due to the fact that local staff were efficient and the Council was in direct control of them – and of class revenue. (Oddly enough, in Barcelona the American Institute suffered from the very Junta trouble that the Council had avoided there.) Certainly my experience of working with small national committees only increases my distrust of large international ones like the UN or the European Union.

I might have felt less aggrieved had I known that at about that time Spain, traditionally the most welcoming and profitable country to the Council, was also suffering illogical cuts. The victim was the British School in Madrid, which, since the aborting of the 'Queen Elizabeth College' project in a troubled Lebanon, remained the only secondary school overseas entirely run by the Council. Its development plan, involving a move from cramped premises in the centre of town to the outskirts, had been costed, architectural designs approved, future profitability assured and funding provided. Finally the plan was submitted to the Board in London for their customary rubber-stamping. But politics intruded. Would not the wrong impression be created if funds were voted for a school overseas – and a fee-paying school at that – when at this time they were being denied to state schools at home? It would; and that was the end of our feeble challenge to the chain of French *lycées* and German colleges all round the world.

Whether the Council felt guilty about my treatment in Venezuela and thought I deserved a cosy nearer-to-home posting I don't know, but before I left Caracas I learned that my next post was to be Cyprus – certainly a comfortable one, if only a sideways career move. It was another two-man post, but mercifully with no Anglo-Cypriot Junta to deal with.

17
Cyprus War-War

WHILE I WAS on leave in the summer of 1974 prospects in Cyprus suddenly grew less cosy domestically but more interesting professionally. She had prospered since independence, not only from her intensive agriculture and nascent tourist industry but also as a haven for those concerned with the troubles in Lebanon and Israel, but she had not escaped troubles of her own. The struggle by Greek Cypriots for *enosis* (union with Greece) and consequent pressure on the Turkish Cypriot minority came to a head when the Sampson faction drove out Archbishop Makarios and declared *enosis* with Greece under 'the Colonels'. For good measure one of the lads shot dead the American Ambassador in Nicosia. With the northern port of Kyrenia only hours away by boat from Turkey, it is not surprising that a Turkish invasion (or Peace Operation, depending on your point of view) followed. Britain, with bases in the south (vast but not wholly undeserving of their Butlins-in-the-Med tag), was a guarantor of the communal status quo. She might have been expected to intervene – at least before Turkey's capture of Varosha, Cyprus's main beach resort adjoining Famagusta. America, however, with her bases on Turkey's USSR border (and spy planes in the Cyprus bases too), could scarcely support British action against Turkey, and 200,000 Greek Cypriots did not wait for it, but fled southwards; so did many Turkish Cypriots, seeking refuge in the British bases. Some British High Commission and Council staff had sat out the fighting in one of the bases and by the time the 'Green Line' was established between the two communities the High Commissioner's and Council Representative's residences found themselves on the Turkish side of Nicosia while the Office remained – just – on the Greek side.

As the airport was on the Green Line and out of action, I had to fly to Athens and take the boat to Cyprus. In Athens I was hospitably entertained by two colleagues – Ian Fraser, who was worried about his Women's Lib librarian printing her official cards 'Ms Jones', and Derrick Aspinall, whom I had known in Port of Spain. Athens was still comparatively free from traffic and pollution, but restaurants and hotels in the Piraeus were bombarded with the noise of aircraft. I was impressed, when queuing at the airport to retrieve my baggage which had come by another plane, to be pushed forward to the head of the queue by neighbours saying *'Einai Xenos'* ('he is a foreigner'). Could there be any stronger reminder of classical sophistication? I was equally impressed with the strength of tradition at the Anglican church of St Paul's where the service was kept on track by the most efficient one-man choir I have ever heard – a Friar Tuck-like figure in a white cassock with a stentorian baritone voice. He was, I was told, a lay reader named Winterbourne and the local representative for Metal Box. Athens, notwithstanding the Colonels, still seemed a gentle and old-fashioned place, with well-behaved little families in the parks and elderly English and American gentlemen sitting about in restaurants with young friends. I was quite sorry to leave it and board the *Adonis* for the 36-hour crossing to Limassol.

Landing after dark I was met by George Pitsillides, the Administrative Assistant, with a taxi and a pass for the curfew, and we drove through eerily silent villages and several check points to Nicosia, where I was comfortably housed and nobly fed by the Assistant Representative, Ralph Isaacs, and his wife Ruth. Morning light brought scenes of desolation, though the burnt-out cars and frozen building sites were not really as dispiriting as the charmless new development that had gone up since my visit from Beirut twenty years before. A Greek Cypriot tank was parked by the Municipal Theatre opposite our office and UN armoured vehicles clattered by on their way to the Ledra Palace crossing on the Green Line. The old walled town had not changed much. The *hamam* was full of refugees and the neo-Byzantine Archbishopric had been badly shot up in the Sampson coup; it was easy to see how Makarios could escape through the maze of little streets behind it. The brothels were still functioning in a half-hearted way; one of them had adopted the topical title of 'The Blue Beret' (as worn by United Nation troops) but 'The English Barmaid' and 'Red Hakol' (for Hackle) retained names designed to attract British troops. There were anti-Kissinger slogans on the walls and one printed notice read:

WHITE HOUSE
<u>DRIVE-IN MENU</u>
NAPALM SOUP
BARBEQUE
WITH
BLOODY HENRY SAUCE
<u>DESSERT</u>
TURKISH DELIGHT

Going through the barrier at the Ledra Palace with Alec Ibbot of the High Commission (last seen at MECAS in the Lebanon) I met for the first time the two indomitable 'Majors', Phyllis Heyman and Betty Hunter-Cowan, an ex-Service couple known as the Cave Women because their house off the Kyrenia road had a cave in it (and was now marooned in a camp of Finnish UN troops). Turkish Nicosia was much quieter and shabbier than the Greek side of the town. From the war-damaged roof of the Saray Hotel we surveyed the Khan and mosques and descended to Richard Coeur de Lion's ruined church next to Santa Sophia (Selemiya Mosque) and the Lusignan tombs at the back of St Nicholas of the English (Bedestan). In St Catherine's (Haidar Pasha Mosque) the floor was covered with desiccated bats; they were attracted by neighbouring date palms and were smoked out from time to time. As Laurence Durrell wrote, the walled city could have been another Carcassonne if it had been restored with sensitivity. As it was, it looked like a deserted film set.

As a contrast to the damage in Nicosia Ralph Isaacs took me to see the British Director of the Forestry School in the Troodos mountains and the sixteen miles of burned forest that surrounded him. The Greek coup supporters, who were said to have caused 2,000 deaths and far more damage than the Turks in Nicosia, started the fires to smoke out supporters of Makarios.

The Isaacs also took me for a drive nearer home down a rough wooded track near Makheras Monastery. After a while we came upon a group engaged in the illegal but traditional activity of liming birds. Ralph stopped the car with an angry jerk to inspect their bag – about a dozen of what looked like nightingales – and the limed stick to which their feet had been glued. But among the smaller birds was a magnificent kestrel whose legs they had just finished pinioning. Greatly shocked, Rafe managed to buy it for ten shillings (Cyprus still had 'chelines') – or 1,000 mils – and it was put beside me in the back seat. We drove on, with the creature nearly decapitating me with its flapping wings, and pulled up when we were out of sight of the group. It took us some time to get the bird out and untie its legs, and as it took off over the trees one of its captors came round the corner on his motor bike. He looked at us in amazement and as he went past gestured his incomprehension. I was reminded of the scene in Bunuel's film *Viridiana* – or perhaps it was *Un Chien Andaluz* – where the do-gooding girl, disapproving of a peasant driving his cart with his dog tied by a lead to the back axle, buys it from him. As he drives off, another cart comes from the opposite direction with another dog padding along behind it, tied to the axle by a lead....

After a few days I moved from the Isaacs' house to the rather bleak Kennedy Hotel, near the Office and on the edge of the walled city. So desperate were hotels for custom that I paid only £2.50 a night for half board. The other guests were a dozen UN staff and an old army man, Captain Leach, who had been evacuated from the more attractive Acropole Hotel, now unnervingly close to the Green Line. UN staff, cocooned as they are in the financial and constitutional featherbedding of their trade, live a detached and uncommitted life of their own and are rarely good company for outsiders. I had plenty of time, therefore, in that nervous breathing space between hostilities and the resumption of 'normal' commercial activity – irrepressible on the Greek side, stagnant on the Turkish – to observe the foibles of 'old hands' like Captain Leach and the tolerance and skill of the Cypriots in dealing with them.

I still see him sitting on the other side of the dining room, a tall figure shrouded in a spare tablecloth to catch the drips and grape-pips of his breakfast.

'WAITAH!' he shouts. (Everyone else calls the head waiter Costa, but not Captain Leach.) 'Waitah!' he calls again impatiently. 'Bring me my toast!' Costa is in the kitchen getting other breakfasts, but Captain Leach does not believe in waiting, although he will have to spend the rest of the day – perhaps all his days – waiting for the next meal ... for the BBC news ... for Sunday ... and the Sunday after. The other guests eye him silently. I never hear them greet him and suspect that they gave up the practice before my arrival. There is an Irishman who does say 'Good morning!' sometimes, and it is he who goes to the kitchen and says 'Costa, Cap'n Leach wants you.'

Underneath the Captain's tablecloth are an invariable grubby check sports jacket and khaki drill trousers, and on the table is the elderly bush hat which he will clap on his bald head when he rises from the table. He has long well-shaped hands and a 'chiselled' face that must have been handsome once. Sitting down – and shouting – he could be anything between sixty and eighty, but on his two sticks he shuffles along with the dedicated hypochondria of the lonely senile.

'WAITAH!' he shouts again. 'Give me my sticks, please!' As he always sits at the same table next to the wall he could well lean the sticks against the wall or put them on the floor within reach, but then he would not be able to shout for them.

'Thank you! Now, tell the maid that I should like to see her when she comes.'

'Pardon, sir?'

'The maid.'

'Yes, sir. The maid....'

'When she comes I want to see her.'

'Alright, sir. I'll tell her.'

'Now I want to go downstairs.'

'OK, sir. This way. Turn around. Now straight ahead ... to the right ... right again ... left.' And Costa shouts to his messenger boy downstairs to come up and take over. 'To the right!' Tap, tap, tap! 'To the left!' Tap, tap, tap! For Captain Leach is blind. But blind people are proudly self-sufficient, are they not, with their other senses heightened? After breakfast and lunch Captain Leach shuffles up and down the pavement outside the hotel, with a tooth pick clenched between his teeth as part of his strange ritual, resting every lap or two in the chair put beside the hotel entrance for him. Otherwise I never see him, but I *hear* him at six in the morning, when he taps about his bedroom and clears his throat and ostentatiously coughs. Although he is three floors below, the sounds come up through the bathroom ventilator.

I therefore resent Captain Leach. I resent him at 6am and at breakfast. Above all I resent his blindness for making me feel guilty at not saying, 'Good morning, Captain Leach. How are you today?' or even 'Can I buy you a drink before you have your siesta? Let me help you over to the bar. Now, tell me the story of your life.' But we all avoid him.

I could put such unworthy thoughts away in the more convivial circles of the High Commission. The High Commissioner, Stephen Olver, was on leave, but on his return was – with his librarian wife, Maria, from Gubbio –

consistently supportive. The acting head of mission was Derek Day, who later distinguished himself in Africa, and there seemed a surprisingly large number of functionaries for an island that for all its strategic importance was so modest in size. But that was an impression common to most of my postings. A sense of overkill prevailed at the diplomatic parties here, with no locals present – Britain was so unpopular that they were tactfully not invited, or, if invited, tactfully omitted to turn up. We were unpopular with Greek Cypriots for not having intervened in the fighting, and with Turkish Cypriots for not 'repatriating' to the Turkish north of the island those who had sought sanctuary in British bases in the south. The Turkish Director General of Education was very hot about this when I made my first call upon him.

I soon discovered that the featherbedding in High Commission circles – not to mention the bases – was echoed in our own establishment. We rented a handsome purpose-built library and offices on three floors, whose owners lived in a flat above it, in a prime position next to the Archaeological Museum and opposite the theatre and zoo. It was also handy for the Ledra Palace crossing into the Turkish north, for our budget was split pro rata between Greek and Turkish interests as far as teachers in schools and other aid projects in educational development were concerned. The Council building could perhaps be criticised for looking more like a superior car showroom than a cultural institute, and as one for whom libraries are sacrosanct I was pained to see the main entrance and staircase going slap into, and climbing up through, this one. We were soon to learn that for the less library-minded this architectural innovation could be very convenient.

I was able to get an excellent flat within easy walking distance of the Office, which, thanks to the general commercial depression, cost less than half my James Bond flat in Caracas. But I could not help comparing all this grandeur in a small island of 700,000 people with our parsimony in the wide open spaces of Venezuela with nearly 20 million. Yet, where strategy is concerned, it is remarkable how irrelevant the purse strings become at the first whiff of grapeshot. Certainly Cyprus, for all the tragedy of lost lives and homes, has benefited financially from the no-peace-no-war status quo that has continued now for so long. A settlement between north and south, with money no longer flowing from British, American and UN aid, would be a mixed blessing, certainly for the south. The format and contents of the Greek Cypriot Government Information Newsletter have remained unchanged over the years, and if examples from 1980 and 2003 were put side by side and the dates removed it would be difficult to tell which was which. With Turkey wanting to join Europe and Greek Cypriots wanting to keep her out until they get their land back they have both continued to cry not very convincingly all the way to the bank.

In 1974, however, they were crying in earnest. Tourism had stopped dead, and hotels in Limassol and Larnaka were offering cut-price accommodation, of which we took guilty advantage. Paphos and Ayia Napa were then delightfully remote, and the wild Akamas peninsula and green rocky windmill country beyond Cabo Griego made marvellous avenues of escape. Skiing in the Troodos mountains was still largely run by the British army, cost very little and was even easier to reach than in the Lebanon, where I had last enjoyed it. So for us outsiders the ill wind had blown a privileged experience of the many beauties and archaeological sites of this lovely island. No wonder it had so intoxicated the Lusignans – to whom Richard Coeur de Lion had flogged it – that they had built their fairytale castles with one hand, hunted with two hundred pairs of hounds with the other and inspired their jealous queens and mistresses to bite off each others' noses!

Travelling on both sides of the Green Line, however, had its drawbacks. In the south there were still strong feelings for *enosis*. The boat which had landed Grivas to start the fighting was enshrined in a cove beyond Paphos – the Dighenis Landing Place – and in the pretty village of Omodhos the church and monastery that preserved the bonds of Christ's hands preserved also a display of horrors attributed to the British in their battle with EOKA extremists; I felt far from welcome as I walked up the main street. It was distressing to see the ruined mosques and Turkish quarters of predominantly Greek villages like Lefkara, many of which had suffered persecution long before the Turkish landing. In the north, which apart from the Troodos area had the best of the scenery, it was equally sad to see ruined Greek Orthodox churches, but their spoliation occurred after the battle and more for reasons of neglect and looting than racial bigotry. In the north, however, the Turkish army was more menacing than in the south and the general air of uncertainty and depression was stronger. For farmers used to growing grapes and evacuated to lemon plantations adjustment was difficult – and the south did its best to make it more so by spoiling their export markets. The north, especially round Kyrenia, had also been the preferred area of retirement for 'Ancient Britons', many of them from the services, who now found themselves marooned in the edgier and least convenient part of the island. They were allowed over to the Greek side for shopping but had to get passes and were limited in the length of stay. Unkind critics said that all this excitement gave them a new lease of life and something to talk about besides bridge, but many of them lost their houses or – like the Cave Women – found themselves so isolated that eventually they had to move closer to town.

We did not do any direct teaching at the Council but the reason, apart from 'strategic' flag-waving, that our premises were so large was that our hard-working and efficient local staff ran a huge exercise for London University and similar external examination bodies. Some Greek Cypriot students found the balance delicate between expressing robust disapproval of the lack of British support against Turkey and preserving their examination prospects intact.

In the library I found two very contrasting books. One contained the reminiscences as Governor's lady of Hugh Foot's wife, stressing their popularity and implying that all Cyprus's problems could have been solved once and for all if only everyone had thought and behaved as they had. The other, amazingly prescient considering it was written in 1901, was *A Winter Pilgrimage* by H Rider Haggard. I quote:

> We went for a ride to the military camp, about 3 miles from Limassol. Perhaps those empty huts will be filled again one day ... The Turks, who generally live in villages by themselves, are going downhill rapidly, both in numbers and in wealth, being poor, lazy, fatalistic and quite unfitted to cope with their cleverer Christian compatriots. In many instances, however, they are respected and respectable members of the community, brave in person and upright in conduct. Few of them can afford more than one wife and as a rule their families are small. The richer and more successful class of Cypriotes [sic] have a habit of adopting Greek names, but in fact very few of them are Greeks except for so much of Mycenian blood as may remain in their veins. Still some of them intrigue against the British Government and affect a patriotic desire for Union with Greece, that even the disillusionment of the Turkish war has not quenched.
>
> That not very attractive banner, the Greek flag, is everywhere. The villages of the remote hills and plains care little about banners, but if they see continually that of Greece displayed on every church tower and high place and never, or rarely, that of Great Britain that rules them, they may, not unnaturally, draw their own conclusions ... Eastern peoples do not understand our system of laissez-faire where the symbols of authority are concerned, and are apt to argue that we are afraid to show the colours which we do not fly.

Rider Haggard would have been pleased to see the show of strength to which his 'empty huts' had advanced, but puzzled to explain his government's reluctance to exploit it. Having failed to take the initiative at the beginning of hostilities it was difficult to see how Britain could take it effectively now, and in January 1975 the British Council was at the sharp end of local feelings just as much as the High Commission.

Makarios had returned to the island in December, to resume his amoeba-like reaction to events and in the first case to the question of federation. Failing a settlement, impatience on both sides escalated, and the last straw for the Greek Cypriots was the evacuation of the Turkish Cypriot refugees from their camps in the British bases, thus depriving the Greeks of their bargaining counter for the return of their own refugees in the north. The Turkish refugees had been pressurised by one of their Turkish-Cypriot MPs to pretend things were bad in the camps and to resist any attempt to improve them, for instance by organising classes for the children. Anxious to forestall a serious 'incident', the British shipped them all to the north (leaving behind mountains of TV sets with their hire purchase dues unpaid).

Greek schools were closed to allow students to demonstrate, and at one of our film shows some English and American wives of Greek Cypriots harangued the audience to support a meeting of 'British Residents for Justice'. The next day two nervous youths asked if we had a Union Jack they could tear up. More seriously, the news arrived of the death of a student named Demetriou at one of the bases; he had been run over during a demonstration and the Greeks now had their martyr. Makarios sanctioned a meeting of protest, and a demonstration convened near the British Consulate, preferred to the High Commission itself which was in a discouraging no-man's land on the Green Line.

We had expected some warning if the demonstration moved on from the Consulate, and had anyway taken precautions – the women on the staff had been told not to come in, while the more sensitive files, *objets d'art* and the office car had been moved out. But things moved more quickly than we expected. When I rang the High Commission for news the telephonist was not much help. 'The British what? Council? What's your telephone number?' Then the Consul broke in to say, 'I've just got out of the Consulate; they've been in and thrown all our files out of the window. It was very nasty. I should get out quickly if I were you!' Even as I hung up I heard a tumult down the road; there must have been three groups operating – one at the Consulate, one at the American Embassy and one now upon us. As we went out of the side entrance the crowd smashed the main doors of plate glass. The police chief loud-hailed them, saying this was Cypriot property and that people were living in flats over the library, but he was greeted with shouts of 'Traitor police! Demetriou!' The cordon of police in front of the building only had batons and no riot equipment and the attack was in the classic mould – sweet young schoolgirls in front to nonplus them and throw the first stones, young huskies behind to throw bigger ones and smash in the doors, and experienced veterans of EOKA and AKEL (the Communist Party) to tell them what to do when they were inside. 'Quick in – smash everything – quick out' seemed to be the order, and the new open-plan library and staircase were made for the purpose. On all three floors bookshelves were tipped over, furniture was thrown through the windows, a piano was upended and filing cabinets tipped over – but fortunately not emptied; in my own sanctum my desk was smashed and my bottle of whisky thrown at the portrait of the Queen. But the film store and central heating in the basement were undamaged, and one set of offices where entries for GCE and other examinations were kept was carefully left untouched. One of the rioters threw petrol at a library cupboard but this was presumably not in the plan because if it had been they would have made a proper job of it. As it was, the police rallied as the rioters left and soon put the fire out. The whole thing was over in about twenty minutes, but it left a shambles of broken glass and furniture that cost £3,500 to replace. By 10pm we had got all the windows covered by plastic sheets in wooden frames, just as an appreciative audience emerged from the National Theatre. A few days later I attended a meeting of the Board of the English School – an excellent, largely Cypriot English-medium secondary school (which enjoyed a £10,000 yearly subsidy from us) – but none of the Cypriots mentioned the attack.

After a breathing space – for the next day was a Sunday – the demonstrators turned their attention to the USIS library. Makarios decreed the closure of government offices for an hour at 11am.

Schools were supposed to be open and children off the streets, but in fact all were out and in full spate by 10am. From my flat I watched a crowd converging on the library. The police chief told me later that they asked only to paint the walls with slogans for Demetriou's death, but stones were thrown and the police, distrusting their motives, kept them at bay for an hour or so with riot shields, fire hoses, tear gas and finally a volley in the air from the National Guard. Just at the critical moment His Beatitude appeared, with the Greek Ambassador, and was escorted with chanting – *'Makarios sto Moscou!'* – to the Greek Embassy, while slogans were painted on the library walls – *'Bibliotikee I Demetriou 16/1/75'* and 'BRITISH AND AMERICAN MURDERERS OUT'. As the Greek Embassy was also visible from my flat, the BBC kept telephoning me for a progress report.

In the middle of all this my doorbell rang. As some of the demonstrators were in the street outside washing the tear gas out of their eyes, I opened the door with circumspection. Standing in the porch was the Reverend Basil Pitt, whom I had last seen in 1945 in Rangoon where he was army chaplain and I was on my way out of the Siam Railway camps. Now Anglican chaplain in Kyrenia and in the early stages of Parkinson's Disease, he had come in to Nicosia to do his usual Monday shopping and get petrol, blissfully unaware of untoward political developments. Hearing I was there, he had dropped in for a sherry. (In the next few months he was to do a good deal of dropping in until, sadly and much against his wishes – he had hoped for the Paphos incumbency – he was invalided home with an MBE. Till then, when waiting to lunch with me, he proved a very mixed blessing to our patient Armenian librarian, whom he engaged in old-fashioned and irreverend flirtation.)

As for Makarios, I was told that the reason he appeared as the calming angel of the trouble he had instigated was that the American Ambassador rang him and said that if he didn't call off his crowds he wouldn't get another cent of American aid. I did not myself meet Makarios until Easter, at the Greek National Day party. He certainly had presence – but I wondered how much of it was due to his beard. It was touching to see old moustachioed veterans in First World War uniforms kneeling and kissing his hands. I'm afraid I did not rush to follow their example and Makarios slid me one of his knowing looks.

My excitement over the attack on the American library did not end with the anticlimax of Basil Pitt's visit. Every time the phone rang that day I had lifted it anxiously and I nearly jumped out of my skin when it shrilled its warning at 3am the next morning. Had the Council gone up in flames? No, it was John Gibbs, my youngest son's teacher of Spanish, who was 'terribly drunk and of course didn't want to steal his thunder but really did think it would be rather a good idea to ring and tell me the news that Ian had been accepted at Wadham and when I came home – when *was* I coming home? – he'd buy me a jolly good dinner to celebrate. Cheers!'

As soon as wider travel in the north was allowed, I went to see an old family friend, Paul Wilkinson, marooned in the Greek village of Lapithos nine miles west of Kyrenia. He had been a colleague of my eldest brother in the Colonial Medical Service. Paul was very much a loner, but at the same time he had a wide circle of acquaintances, not all of them estimable characters. He had recently been visited by Tom Driberg, who had written a piece in the *New Statesman* about conditions in the north, and in the palmy days before the invasion he had dined in Famagusta with my old acquaintance from Beirut, Eddie Gathorne-Hardy, whose slim volume of literary *doubles entendres* had come out in 1966. ('What he had heard was the tear of the ripping tool as it ploughed its way along the sticky parting' – *The Woodlanders*; 'She gave a little scream and a jerk, and so relieved herself' – *The Duke's Children*.) Eddie had transfixed the patrons of the restaurant, as he passed over a bread roll, by shouting, 'I don't need to say "Excuse fingers". This is the hand that has touched Marlene Dietrich and tossed off the Duke of Kent!' Paul lived apart from his wife, and his son, Anthony, worked in Brazil. ('I had an Anglo-Irish youth accentuated by ill health. My wife and I between us inherited gout, asthma, epilepsy and migraine. I was left alone as a child to choose my own reading in the house and my two most formative influences were on the one hand Ezekiel and the prophets and on the other John Keats.') He was dauntingly well read and spoke several languages, including Icelandic and Cantonese. He had moved to Cyprus because he wanted to 'use his Greek' after a spell in Taormina. (Watching him write a letter there, Caitlin Thomas had shouted, exasperatedly but percipiently, 'Why are you always so bloody dainty?') He had a disconcerting habit of sinking his voice to a whisper as he approached his punch lines, and he enjoyed embarrassing people, especially officials of any kind, by both the loudness and the softness of his delivery. He claimed in this habit an affinity with George V, whose sentences, starting loudly, led with three repetitions to a dying fall – 'I THINK SO, I THINK SO, I think so' (as on hearing that an equerry had been caught in the bushes in a state of undress. 'Did you say *hanging* out, or *sticking* out?' 'Er, hanging out, sir.' '*Hanging* out, eh? THAT'S BAD, THAT'S BAD, that's bad....').

I don't think Paul would have told this story to Stephen Olver when Olver called on him with a visiting Under Secretary, even if there had been time. It had been a trying day, with *The Times* publishing a letter by Lena Jeger, who had been out for the 'Women's Walk Home' Greek Cypriot demonstration, claiming that the High Commission was doing nothing for British subjects.

'We mustn't stay long,' said Olver, looking at his watch.

'Oh,' said Paul. 'Well, if you haven't time to sit down, do you mind if I do?'

Thereafter he referred to Olver as the Plastic Gnome and was reluctant to use the services of the High Commission to alleviate his problems. Not the least of these was his isolation, with only two other British residents in the village, with neither of whom he was friendly. One, Brierley, he never mentioned; the other, separated from the Russian owner of an estate in Java and now teaching painting to a young ex-army officer (for whom my gossip of the skiing at Troodos brought wistful memories), was referred to as 'the floozy'.

Paul appears in Han Suyin's novel *A Many Splendoured Thing* (about her affair with Ian Morrison) as her boss at the Queen Mary Hospital in Hong Kong. He had enjoyed his time there but, as a constant thorn in the flesh of Colonial Office bureaucrats, he had been sent at one period to cool off in St Helena. He found it much to his taste. Among the treasures in his eclectic library was Martineau's memoirs of conversations with Napoleon on St Helena. On the flyleaf the Governor, Sir Hudson Lowe, had written 'This volume was lent to Mr William Hazlitt; the annotations are his'. Hazlitt's underlinings were frequent, with such marginal comments as 'Very true' and 'Stuff!'.

I had seen Paul briefly in December by courtesy of the Cave Women ('He *will* speak Greek to the Turks, he will *not* have his car repaired, he will *not* have a regular maid and he refuses to come into Nicosia') but I had not seen his house. Now, in February, I had to get a Turkish pass to go in convoy to Kyrenia and there have it signed by the Area Commander to proceed to Lapithos. (There had been a scare one night when the Turks were said to be threatening the rest of Nicosia airport. The High Commission staff silently folded their tents and melted away to the Dekhalia base and it was only when one of them later spoke out of turn – 'Oh, I thought you were in on that!' – that I knew they had gone at all.) The Commander at Kyrenia was not in his office and I was told I could either wait for his return or risk going on without his signature. We had passed many military convoys and columns of troops and the town was very dead, with a few miserable-looking men hanging about at deserted street corners. My two companions, an Anglo-Israeli estate agent and a mysterious Dutchman who had lost his house near the Green Line ('My business used to be buying and selling') decided they 'didn't like the look of things' and went no further. I drove on past more troops digging trenches, past empty and damaged houses, a car pound of wrecked vehicles, signposts with the Greek names painted out, statues of Atatürk on whitewashed plinths, and stillborn beach developments with fading hoardings of dolphins, bathing belles and Churchill smoking his cigar. Nobody stopped me at either of the check points on the way. 'It's easy to find me,' Paul had said, 'and if you can't, ask at the police station.' The young policeman thought it might be 'up there' and directed me to 'Mr Brierley's house' to ask further. The only two shops still functioning couldn't help, and then I saw what must be 'Mr Brierley's house' because of the Union Jack painted on the door. I rang the antique camel bell several times but nothing happened. At the coffee shop opposite the owner said, 'That *is* Dr Wilkinson's house' and came back with me to ring again, bang on the door and shout 'Dr Wilkinson!' After a pause there were some growls from within and Paul opened the door, looking disturbed and ferocious.

'Yes?' he said angrily and then, with studied politeness, 'Good morning!'

'Hullo, Paul.'

'You want to see me?'

'That was the idea, yes.'

'Oh.' Silence. 'Then perhaps you had better come in.'

The café proprietor gave me a knowing look as he was dismissed, and I entered a courtyard with orange trees, a fish pond, draped fishing nets, a biblical plough and winnowing board against one wall, a millstone in a corner and ancient pots and broken columns standing about with careful casualness among trailing creepers.

'Would you mind telling me who you are?' said Paul, seeing that I was not going to help him out and beginning to feel that he was being rumbled.

'Stephen Alexander.'

'My dear Stephen, come into the sitting room; it's warmer here.'

Well, it wasn't *much* warmer, with only a small electric fire to relieve the chill of a delightful split-level vaulted room with two enormous fireplaces in it.

'I'll just show you the house quickly and then we'll have a drink. You'll stay to lunch, of course; I haven't cooked enough meat for two but I can do you an omelette.'

Pinned over the cooker in the kitchen was the first of many notices dotted about the house: 'PLEASE LEAVE THIS KITCHEN AS YOU WOULD LIKE HIM TO FIND IT'. Others were in Latin, Greek or Italian, reminding guests of Dantesque aphorisms on love, death and the more enjoyable sins. The house was a monument to Paul's eclectic taste: silks and scrolls from Pekin, lithographs of Anglo-Irish worthies, antique local shelving painted with angels, magazine reproductions of Tiepolo nymphs pinned onto beams, framed maps of St Helena and Iceland, paintings of the house by guests, bits of masonry with classical Greek inscriptions, West African trays and embroidery, a Chinese medical lady lay figure in ivory, tapestries, the citation of Sir Robert Biddulph's GCB when Governor at the turn of the century (given to Paul by a successor, Sir Harry Luke, because his middle name was Biddulph), and a long-handled spade from Lebanon.

'Only two countries in the world have long-handled spades and clotted cream,' said Paul. 'Lebanon and Cornwall. It's the Phoenician influence.'

When I quoted this remark to our mutual friend Martyn Skinner he capped it with a quotation from Wordsworth:

Spade! with which Wilkinson hath tilled his lands ...
Who shall inherit thee when death hath laid
Low in the darksome cell thine own dear lord?
That man will have a trophy, humble Spade,
A trophy nobler rather than a conqueror's sword.

There were books everywhere, a lifetime of past and future browsing, and they had been kindly treated by the climate. 'No rats,' said Paul, 'no damp.' There were Dante folios, vellumed illuminated editions in original bindings and one with leather ties intact, Beardsley, a huge Chinese dictionary, Fred Burnaby's travels in Asia Minor, works in French, Spanish, Italian, Latin, Greek and Norse, and a fine spread of Eng. Lit. Everything I picked up had something interesting about it, either in subject or, like the book about St Helena, in origin.

'I loved St Helena,' said Paul, flicking over faded photos in an album. One showed a tough red-bearded figure in his East India Company house and park, with two black children: 'This is what we used to call fairyland and, do you know, when I first saw them I couldn't make out what they were doing. What they were doing was raising their skirts to curtsy to me.' Another showed Philip Gosse, whose *History of Piracy* was inscribed 'To Paul – the most savage and dearest pirate of them all'.

I must admit that the unremittingly intellectual delicacy everywhere was a little daunting. There were no whodunnits, for example, and Paul said he hadn't been to a cinema for thirty years. He showed no interest in *The Times* I had brought but there were several newly unwrapped *Times Literary Supplements* on the sofa. 'I have a radio which some Greeks left with me, but I never listen to it.' And the house itself was demanding in its perfection.

'Of course they don't make these red tiles any more. I have to try and find them from old buildings. And string seats they don't do any more either; I have to tie them up as best I can when they wear out.'

Although he had come here for the Greek environment he was not without sympathy for the Turkish reaction to their 'endless persecution' and blamed the Greeks for their headlong evacuation, rather than staying to try and look after their property and make things more difficult for the Turks. He said the Turks had never meant to occupy Famagusta. They halted outside it and sent in for the Mayor to parley, but he and everyone else had left several days before so they had no option but to move in.

'Of course, all this happened before in '63,' said Paul, 'but it was the other way round then. A British sergeant knocked at the door and said "You've got two hours to get out with a couple of suitcases!" I took him into the drawing room and just pointed at the bookshelves. "Hum!" he said, "I see what you mean!" "I'm staying," I said, and it was the same thing this time. I'd rather die with all this intact than leave the books behind to be used as bog paper. I lived for ten days on grapes, and rice heated in a tobacco tin over methylated spirits. Philipides next door, a Cypriot British subject, said, "My Queen is good enough for me!" and flew off to London, asking me to keep an eye on his house. He wrote to me the other day and asked about the house, saying he thought he'd be coming out soon. I wrote back and said, "Your house is still there. I used the tap in your garden when my own water was cut off. Through one broken window I could see your dentist's chair, but there was no sign of any other furniture through the gaping doors." Look at this.' And he passed me a letter he had just written to the Police Superintendent at Kyrenia. 'Dear Superintendent, You may be interested to learn that last Sunday as I was sitting at lunch I heard noises in my hall and on going out found two men there. They were drunk. One had a gun and said he was a soldier, tho' if he was he must have been wearing a particularly scruffy mufti. They demanded a bottle of vodka and a bottle of brandy and said they would kill me if I did not give it to them ...'

He showed me his bullet-riddled garage.

'Where were you when this happened?'

'Sitting on the balcony, I suppose. I never noticed it with the row that was going on everywhere.'

He took me outside to see the neighbouring houses, all looted, with doors and windows gaping. A few evidently new Turkish villagers were wandering aimlessly about, to whom he made no sign.

'Mine would be like this if I'd gone,' he said. 'Bog paper!'

I'm afraid Exercise Bog Paper proceeded apace from then onwards. Paul was burgled many times – once while he had slipped out for only twenty minutes to go to the post office – and when his books started to follow his Tang vases he could stand it no more. His son came over to help him decide on the disposal of his treasures, and by May, having first thought of 'returning to Taormina and committing suicide', he had decided to drive home to his sister in England, dawdling in Italy on the way.

About this time it so happened that I was in the north on business with Ivor Kemp, our Area Librarian from Rome, and a pleasant Turkish Cypriot librarian, and I thought it might be salutary to see if a visit to Paul and a mutual interest in books might help to heal wounds, and that even if it did not a firsthand report of the sorry state of public order in places like Lapithos would be no bad thing in official Turkish Cypriot circles. I left the others in the car outside '1 Atlantis Drive' while I saw how the land lay. I hammered on the side door. Behind the faded paper Union Jack pinned to the wooden panels all was silence. I hammered on the door again and shouted, 'Paul!' I was just thinking of going away, my duty done, when there was a faint shout within.

'Ugh?'

'It's Stephen here; open up those pearly gates!'

Paul appeared in a singlet and old khaki trousers. There were packing cases about and the pictures had begun to come off the walls. The latest robbery had not been a systematic one by experts or bibliophiles but another quick spree by house furnishers and yobbos out for cigarettes, electric kettles and small but alas valuable carpets.

'Look, Paul, I can't stay because I've got some people outside.'

'Bring them in.'

'One of them is a Turk.'

'What's he like? Is he a nice chap?'

'Yes, he's a very nice chap. What d'you think?'

He grimaced noncommittally.

'Well, if you don't feel too strongly about it, I'll bring them both in. The other is the Council Librarian from Rome.'

'From Rome, is he?' said Paul, perking up, but as soon as we were settled and Paul had brought in the china tea in its muffled Chinese pot I knew I had made a mistake. The expletives and heavy sarcasms about the Turks – savages, imbecile so-called officers of the law, conscienceless thieves – came bursting out to relieve the bottled up bile of lonely reflection.

'Are you a Turk, my dear sir? Then will you tell me when you are going to make this glorious free republic of yours fit to live in by a civilised resident?'

Fortunately his guest had beautiful manners, was genuinely shocked (as I had hoped he would be) and did not explode in retaliation. But I had not expected him to be so heavily tried and laid an apologetic hand upon his knee.

As always, when the bitterness had flowed for a time, Paul began to relax. He was leaving the place for ever in two weeks, he said, and asked if he could stay with me for a few days. Then he chatted about Hardy, whom he had been rereading (perhaps to cancel a lesser with a greater misery) and about the new *Young Hardy* by Gittings which he had just finished and which he gave me to take away.

A fortnight later Paul dodged into my office looking as though he expected the walls to close in on him at any moment, and whenever anyone opened the door he looked up with a glare that frightened them off again. While he was staying with me we listened to recordings of Cavafy, which he left with me when he went, together with two volumes of the poems. A friendly Turkish policeman had moved into his house, which still had the less valuable books and furniture in it, while bits and pieces were stored on the Greek side until Anthony should decide on its future. Eventually a letter arrived from Paul in Haifa:

> At Limassol horror became piled on horror... every one of the suitcases and bags torn out of the car; we had not realised that every book is a bomb *in posse* and when put on a ship in Near Eastern waters naturally becomes one *in esse* ... I am reading the Odyssey, a book I love, and saying to myself every five minutes Stephen will be reading this book with care and pleasure after another six months of Miss Plant! Love to Lougeia – admirable girl – George Pitsillides and yourself. And *listen* to Cavafy!

On a separate sheet he had scribbled lines from *The Tempest*:

> *... now 'tis true,*
> *I must be here confined by you,*
> *Or sent to Naples. My project fails*
> *Which was to please. Now I want*
> *Spirits to enforce, art to enchant;*
> *And my ending is despair.*

Two weeks later a letter came from the Albergo Senato, Piazza della Rotonda, Rome. He had written to the Cave Women complaining of topless girls on Italian beaches but to me he was less censorious:

> You can't imagine how lovely it is to be away from Cyprus and out of sight and smell of Turkish troops. To find oneself again among people who are pleasant and polite is so staggering that it takes some days to get used to. One crowning mercy is that Signora Cacciatore who looks after the Keats house positively encourages me to use the library, so I tend to spend the mornings there after a brisk 6-to-8am walk ... Despite heat and 'religious' scum (L'Anno Santo) the city is still adorable....

The next letter was from Reggio di Calabria:

> ... Old Bova speaks a form of Arcadian and has affinities with Cypriot ... Rohlfs, aet.83, discovered that the Doric words for mouse-shit survives in Bova and only in Bova ... A Bovan chum is letting me have a stone-floored room. 1 bulb, 1 tap and I can shit. Rather fun ... I can't write letters now as you can see from this. My life? *Mi prendi in giro!* I have only watched shadows, listened to echoes, pursued dreams ... If you are ever in Lapithos see if the house still stands ... I always stayed through the summer for the sake of the garden and the trees. Bath water, you know....

The last letter, enclosing a map-tracing of La Magna Grecia, was in Italian, except for a Latin quotation from Cicerone and the final sentence '... As for Aspromonte you might find somewhere *Jousting in Aspromonte and Montalban*. I've been jousting there since I was a boy ... Give my love to Betty and Phyllis and to anyone you think might like it or want it.'

In one of her journals Frances Partridge describes staying with the Heygates in Kyrenia in the palmy days before the invasion and being taken to visit Paul as one of the local characters. She catches his quirkiness very well but adds in a footnote that 'he was later murdered by the Greeks'. When I wrote to correct her alarmist (and unlikely) claim with the all too prosaic truth, she replied – in her late nineties – with a charming and faultlessly written note of acknowledgment. In fact it was only in January 1976 that Phyllis Heyman – with Betty Hunter-Cowan by then in the Military Hospital – told me that Paul too was in hospital, in Yeovil, with cancer of the bladder. A fortnight later she had 'a letter to say goodbye, just that' from him, adding only that he was not going to go through a series of operations. In June he died.

The Miss Plant Paul referred to was my Anglo-Cypriot teacher of Greek. After several failures of the oral I managed to pass the Civil Service intermediate level exam. Lougeia was my cook-maid, who came in by bus three times a week from the family farm 30 miles away near the Green Line. One day she arrived in tears with her father. Out early one morning to see to the potatoes he had mistaken two British soldiers on patrol for Turks and shot one of them dead. Could I intercede with the British Army authorities? I did, and perhaps my intervention helped in his exoneration.

Several Council colleagues had been seduced, like Paul, by the beauty of Cyprus and bought property in the north that was wrecked by the invasion. My predecessor, James Took, who wrote an excellent little book on the birds of Cyprus, had wisely bought land near Paphos, but *his* predecessor was not so lucky. I had heard of him as a forerunner of mine in Barcelona and as a contemporary of my brother Noel in Malaya, but I was surprised when he was ushered into my office as the *Reverend* Robert Brady.

'You must be Noel's brother,' he said. 'I liked Noel. He gave a talk on Martyn Skinner's *Letters to Malaya* to some of my people. I wrote a play about Templar once; at least I had him in mind ... When I first came to Cyprus I thought "I'll never stand this place, it's so provincial". I used to go out by myself to the villages and I felt awful - all those arid plains and miserable little forests, compared with green jungles and huge rivers. But by the time I left I felt I simply had to have a bit of it; so I put all my savings into buying the house at Myrtou and now the Turks have got it. At least, I don't know what's happened to it. I'm going to try and see it tomorrow, if they let me through.

'Yes, when I was here I was working for a BD with Wolsey Hall. And I got it and had a year at Ridley Hall. And they offered me Alexandria. Oh, there are very few British there now, about a hundred I suppose. I like to think my ecumenical work is worthwhile. I put on plays in the church, you know. I write them myself and with the profits we buy wheelchairs for the disabled.

'My wife? No, she's not Berger, she's a Singhalese. I used to know her family in Ceylon, but when I met her she was working as a librarian in Hull. No, I'd never been married before, but when I retired I thought I needed a wife. She doesn't feel very at home in Alexandria. I like it better than Cairo though. You still feel that it's a Christian place. It's a great scandal that they're pulling down Cairo cathedral, one of the few good buildings there. Of course, Gamal Abdul Nasser said the bridge had to go through there out of *spite*. It could easily have gone elsewhere. And we could have fought for it, because in Egypt no-one can pull down any religious building of any faith. But the British have never fought; we thought it would be diplomatic to acquiesce. And, you know, we even had a *prayer* "for the bridge builders". I must say I thought that was carrying Christian resignation a bit far.

'I went for a walk from the hotel this morning to the Catholic church by the Paphos Gate. I'd forgotten the border had changed since my time. The young Greek guard said, "Hey, you can't go through there!" and then the young Turk on the other side of the barrier shouted, "Yes, you can. Come on over!" Oh, these nice young people! What they suffer for their elders! Well, you're very important now. Everyone knows the British Council. We're the most important people here in this crisis. We're the only people who can do something. We've let everything go, but people still think we're clever.'

After his departure from Cyprus Brady's car had sat under the Office for three years because nobody would buy it. He was also remembered for being attentive to his female teachers, and for a lecture he gave on 'Nothing'. After speaking extempore for an hour or so he invited the audience to join him for refreshments. As the lecture had had no beginning, he said, so it had no end, and they might as well turn the lights out now and all go home with him in comfort before it went on any longer.

18
Cyprus Jaw-Jaw

IT MAY SEEM extraordinary that the British were soon buying retirement homes in Cyprus again – at least in the south where the economy was picking up and tourism reviving. I myself looked at village houses near Paphos, and so did my new walking companion, John Cambridge, Derek Day's successor as Deputy High Commissioner. The redoubtable Dr Gertraud Stoep Word bought a house at Orga, a former Greek village on the coast beyond Lapithos. Gertraud, however, spoke Turkish as well as Greek and was used to living dangerously as her Goethe Institute was right on the Green Line, in the former manager's house of the Ledra Palace Hotel. For a long time no Greek Cypriot would go near it, so I gave her moral support by attending her lectures and concerts. Consequently I once found myself, to my embarrassment, seated next to the guest of honour at a dinner for the diminutive son of Thomas Mann. He was an academic in the States and seemed to have no interests apart from lecturing and talking about his father. As I had never managed to get through a book by Thomas Mann I fear I did my profession little credit.

The American Embassy had a weekend house on the beach near Kyrenia, and the Ambassador and his wife, Bill and Ginger Crawford, were particularly glad to use it because only in northern Cyprus could Bill dispense with his bodyguard. They were a spirited if not always pacific couple, and attended Council events more often than their British colleagues did. One of the walks they organised on Mount Kornos was particularly spectacular. Gertraud was in the party and so was John Cambridge, who had only recently arrived and was quite a change from his much married predecessors.

'Hey, John,' said Ginger, 'I guess from the way you speak you must come from a pretty aristocratic family. Wasn't there a guy called the Duke of Cambridge? Are you any relation to him?'

'No, my dear. My paternal grandfather was a porter on Swindon station. Then he was put in charge of parts of the line and made rather a good thing out of growing things beside the track and selling them. Such a good thing, in fact, that he was sacked. So he went out to work for the Indian Railways. He did well there too, and my father did even better. When people ask me patronisingly if I "sail" I flatten them by saying, "My father built *Lively*

In the steps of Ker Porter: the old colonial road, Caracas

Quinta Coromoto: the cause of all the trouble

Tuscany, where ignorance was bliss: Celia Turvey, SCA, John Cambridge

Indian summer at Balakrishna, Madras

Dreams from Gemini Studios, Madras

Information technology on the way

Penny Aspden lends a hand

The Buckingham Canal: gathering winter fuel

Shantivanam saint, sinner or sanyasi: Bede Griffiths with SCA and Venugopal

Bishop Heber in St George's Cathedral, Madras

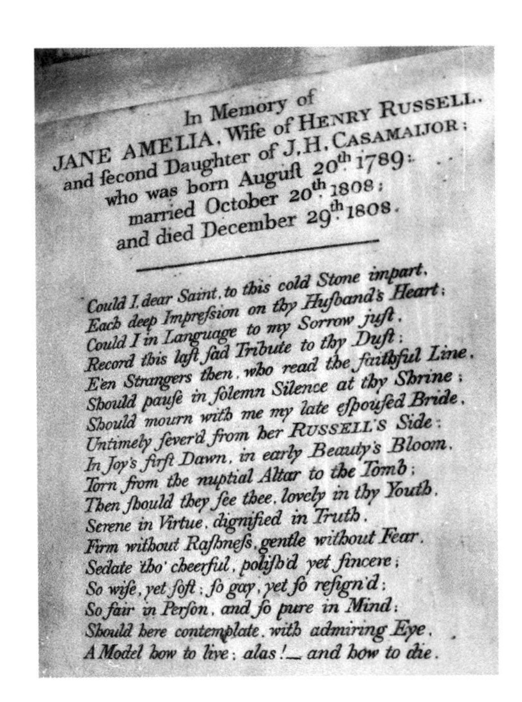

Another 'dear Saint' in St Mary's, Fort St George

James Achilles Fitzpatrick's Hyderabad Residency

David Horsburgh at Neel Bagh, Andra Pradesh

Farewell to India - perennially photogenic, perennially poor

Europe beckons

John Cambridge and Ruth in Rabat

Lady", which he did – or at least his workmen did – in the Indian Railways dockyard in Bombay. He only sold her to Alec Rose when he got too old to look after her himself.'

It was a beautiful day and the view from the summit of Mount Kornos to the melting snows of the Troodos in the west and the Taurus mountains in the east was breathtaking. Spring burgeoned around us and we should all have been as happy as birds but the Crawford teenage daughter, Sarah, was over for a visit and saw to it that her parents were kept on the hop. Ginger's customarily dry humour soon had an acid edge to it and Bill's bonhomie was more oppressive than usual. It had been a stiff climb and everyone was more than ready for a rest and lunch. While they argued about the best place for the picnic there came piercing screams from Sarah, so piercing that it was obvious they were due to hysteria rather than pain. Both parents bounded off, but by the time I arrived Sarah's shriek had subsided into snivels and everyone was making bright conversation and looking the other way.

Unfortunately walks in the north part of the island could be dispiriting for other reasons. One Sunday I went walking with John and another bachelor in the High Commission, Michael Pawley, in the hills above Ayios Ambrosius and past the ruined Antiphonitis monastery. The church was a beautiful building with many frescoes, some of them old and interesting. The big painted crucifix and bits of the iconostasis were lying on the floor. We pondered on the recent scandal of Christie's trying to auction antiquities looted from northern Cyprus. Could they really have been as ignorant of affairs in Cyprus as they claimed? If they were, they only had to ask Vasos Karaghourgis in his museum next to the Council to put them right.

When we got back to the car there were four of the inevitable police waiting beside it.

'Good afternoon, gentlemen. Are you waiting for us?'

'Ah, no sir! Good afternoon. We think you are having trouble with your car.'

'No, thank you. The car is quite alright, as you see.'

'Yes. It was here a very long time.'

'How did you know it was here a very long time?'

'There is a military post on the mountain and it saw the car.'

'I see. And where do you come from?'

'From Apecteta. As you say, Ayios Ambrosius ... Er, have you any form of identity on you, sir? When I get back to the station I shall be asked who you were.'

'That's very kind of you,' said John sunnily. 'But you needn't have worried. Can I call on you next time I go to Ayios Ambrosius?' And with the smile on his face and much hand-waving as we drove away, he snarled 'It's a bit thick that I, a diplomat in a so-called friendly Commonwealth country can't go for a walk without being interrogated as though I were in a Communist police state!'

However, things weren't always sunny and bright in the south either. We went off for the weekend once to the then wonderfully wild country beyond

Cabo Griego. It was early October, still hot in the mornings with the sea warm enough to snorkel in and the nights cool enough to make two blankets necessary. What we had forgotten was that this season had a special and baleful significance, especially in that area. My favourite spot was on the edge of an old quarry where John could pitch his tent in the open ground while I slung my hammock from eucalyptus trees. After a swim we sat on the bluff with a bottle of Sodap, watching the sun go down and the lights come up in the lighthouse. We retired snugly to bed and hammock under a bright moon and slept soundly ... until dawn, when I half awoke to peculiar cries. I thought at first they were a shepherd's, but there were too many for that and there was a lot of stone-throwing to back them up. Then I thought that the shooting season must have started and the 'hunters' were out, as it was a Sunday. But there were no shots. Soon stones and clods of earth came whistling past the hammock, and a couple of boys broke through the bushes nearby.

'Kaliméerasas!' I said, popping my head out of the hammock and causing them to jump. *'Ti kánoun me ólo áphto to thórubo?'* (What's all that noise about?)

'Kinigoúmai ta poulákia!' (We are hunting little birds.)

I dozed off again but was awoken by an angry shout in my very ear. I looked up to see a rough-looking character shaking with fury, who asked me if that was my friend over there in the tent. If so, he said, my friend had been rude to him. I found John going through the motions of making a cup of tea, flushed with anger and watched with a mixture of hostility and curiosity by several locals. Strung between the bushes around us were nets and I realised we had woken up in the epicentre of the *benfica* campaign, when everyone turns out to net and lime migrating birds and pickle them in jars for sale in the village square.

'Where do you come from?' I asked the angry man.

'Paralimni. This is my land, my land, d'you hear? And he behaves like that on my land!'

I suggested we left, but John insisted he would not be done out of his tea. So, although it was choking him, he completed the ritual while the onlookers grew more and more impatient. At last we packed everything up, but even this was no mean ritual, for when John went camping he did so in style, his object being to make himself as comfortable as possible as close to nature as possible. The parts of nature he liked to get really close to and on which he was an expert were the flowers – and the birds. So we packed up the flowers-of-the-Mediterranean book and the bird-spotting book, and the tent, and HMG's Diplomatic Service Bag which he used as a door mat, and the chairs and the table and the saucepan, kettle and frying pan, and the water containers and ice box and bottles and pillows and blankets and toilet rolls and the OBEV and the half-empty tins crawling with ants, and departed in the car ... and a cloud of umbrage all round.

Nowhere have I seen nature more beautiful than in Cyprus – not in England or Spain, or South America or the Far East, which are conceived on too large a scale for beauty. Nor can any of them compete for variety of climate, landscape and flowers, and all within the confines of an island a hundred miles long and fifty miles wide. And much of the beauty is due not to nature but to Greek Cypriot husbandry – the olive groves, the cypress trees, the terraces, the way the villages are folded into the landscape, the frescoed churches, the rock-hewn monasteries and, miles away from anywhere, the hundreds of tiny chapels stumbled across on a walk, sometimes ruined but more often faithfully preserved for celebrations of saints days.

It was frustrating being able to see through my window the five-fingered Pentedactylos hills beckoning me from only eight miles across the Green Line and not being able to go there without getting a permit. But there were pleasant wooded walks on the Greek side near Nicosia, and it was surprising how few people used them. I fear that I interrupted an idyll one Sunday when, climbing up through a pinewood well off the beaten track, I came across a Lawrencian couple on the summit, both scions of Cypriot society, she less formally dressed than at a ministerial party the night before and he in breeches with a shotgun beside him. Evidently their spouses were less keen than they were on strenuous exercise.

For extended expeditions the Paphos area was the best. Development had only just begun before being halted by the invasion. There was no airport or motorway serving the town, and life there was still village-like and informal, so much so that Terry Frost ran a popular semi-alfresco summer painting school in the St Paul's Pillar area for several years.

We three bachelors tended to drift together for company in our weekend walking – John Cambridge, Michael Pawley and me. We liked to think we made an impressive trio; we were certainly impressively different.

One reason why John was a keen walker was that he fought a perennial battle with his Friar Tuck figure. Another was his sensitivity to landscape and his expert knowledge of flora and fauna. He was an intellectual but an unassuming one, and a voracious reader, with up to five books piled round him on the breakfast table; he was interested in art and was a talented pianist. He was also a talented performer at my dramatised play-readings, an asset to any party, and an informed and inventive cook. An Arabist with a first class brain, and ten years younger than me, he was obviously destined for higher things. He was, however, not much given to crashing about on tennis courts, like George Middleton or Derek Day, and was certainly not the most adept person with machinery.

Michael was twenty years my junior and was clearly not on a fast track to promotion in the FO. Abysmal in personal letters, he was nevertheless generally 'good on paper', and in a gossipy *Private Eye* kind of way well informed and shrewd about international affairs. He was also refreshingly guileless, gregarious and good-natured, if socially inept. Prone to physical ailments, he had a bad digestion and would panic at inconvenient moments, demanding food – any food – immediately and wolfing it down without waiting for anyone else; and he would pour wine for himself before attending even to his hostess. Yet at home he did no cooking, keeping no food in his flat except Weetabix, on which he practically lived, relying on restaurants for meals. In his two years in Nicosia he never gave a single party and was reproved by the FCO inspector – my old Caracas Head of Chancery, Eustace Gibbs – for not having done his proper share of entertainment.

Unlike John, whose charm was irresistible but interest purely social, Michael's appetite for female company was as undisciplined as it was for food. He was obsessed with a great big mountainous sports girl at the High Commission, who treated him like dirt because she was interested in somebody else, and he was relieved when she left because 'as long as she was there he could never stick to his resolve not to see her again'. After ricocheting round the other girls in the office like a wounded bumble bee, he settled for a divorcee outside it – but edged away when she showed permanent designs upon him. It was ever thus: uncommitted he was lonely; committed he was frightened. A few years later he was sheltering in the doorway of Selfridges when the motherly Danish wife of a Danish doctor joined him. Michael, his usual ricochet impeded by the weather, made the most of his umbrella, and – to cut a long story short – she bore him a daughter. In the easy-going Danish way the child was absorbed into the family. Michael was thrilled and used to go over to see his daughter, until it was made clear that his presence was no longer welcome. So, in the sad way in which so many of his enterprises ended, he drifted back into unrelieved bachelordom.

Behold us, then, three of HM's musketeers sallying forth to adventure in the Akámas peninsular. As we bowled along in the sunshine from Limassol to Paphos, the theatre and golden pillars of Curium ought to have prompted between us a display of apt classical tags relevant to current world affairs. But as we passed Petra tou Romiou, the Rock of Aphrodite, I could only quote Captain Charles Frankland RN, whose journal of 1827 I had with me: 'God only knows how this island ever attained its celebrity for beauty; for to judge of it from the specimens we saw one would have said it was the last place which Venus would have chosen in which to fix her favourite residence ... The male part of the population is handsome and robust; and perhaps the laughing and wanton goddess had an eye to this circumstance.'

Next day, as we walked along the peninsula to the Fontana Amorosa and up to the ruined farm and pine grove, with its mysterious atmosphere and fertility symbols tied to the branches, our talk was finally of serious matters: what was the latest ploy of Denktash, the stolid Turkish leader in the north?

Stephen: 'The French paper this morning comments on an article by Denktash's son in the Turkish paper, saying, "Now is the hour for the Turkish-Cypriot leaders to declare independence".'

John: 'Good heavens! Are they going to do it at last?'

Michael: 'Maybe they will. They'll be just in time for Bairam and can celebrate on Monday as free men.'

John: 'Very possibly. The thing is that I have been summoned as Acting High Commissioner by Denktash *père* to a meeting at ten on Monday.'

Michael: 'That's it! They won't give anyone time to do anything about it before Bairam begins.'

John: 'Actually I wasn't summoned. The Secretary said "Mr Denktash 'invites' you to come at ten". The question is, has anyone else been 'invited'? Perhaps we ought to go back and ring up the Americans and see if they've been summoned.'

Michael: 'Oh, hell! What difference does it make? Suppose we telexed London? They'd only tell us to dissuade Denktash, which we'd try to do anyway.'

John: 'And it won't make a blind bit of difference. If they're declaring UDI they'll declare it, whatever anyone else says. So we may as well forget it and enjoy ourselves while we can.'

Stephen: 'The Greek paper also says that ten Belgian film makers have arrived in the Turkish quarter; one of them is a friend of Denktash and is staying with him.'

Michael: 'That's it! They've got them in to film the declaration of independence.'

John: 'Oh, God! I've just remembered! I left five pairs of trousers to be let out round the waist at the Turkish tailors. The moment UDI is declared the Greeks will close the borders. How can I survive without any trousers?'

As for the Greek Cypriots, when we returned to our hotel in Polis we had an example of their unquenchable enterprise and optimism. A service mum was there with two children who were being choosy about what to have.

'I want prawns.'

'Don't be silly, dear. You can't have prawns for breakfast.'

'Why not? We had them in Hong Kong.'

'Well, this is Cyprus, and you can't have them here.'

'Wait one minute!' said the waiter. 'I think there are some in the kitchen. I will see,' and he bustled out.

'Here you are,' he said returning proudly, 'plenty prawns!' And he put on the table a large bowl of prunes.

John needn't have worried about his trousers (because of its weaker currency it was cheaper to have things like suits and shoes made in the Turkish quarter). But we none of us imagined that the sort of shadow-boxing across the border that Denktash was doing would go on for twenty years, and that the ageing men who had started it would still be at the head of affairs, ducking and weaving in their dotage. Meanwhile, people began to get used to an anomalous but semi-permanent situation. Satellite towns for refugees were built largely with US money (said to be 74 million dollars since 1974) and the bases still employed 5,000 civilians, many of them Turks who were bussed from Nicosia through the Greek sector only to hang about unemployed on arrival. The bases themselves still supported three yacht clubs, a broadcasting station and a comprehensive school completed two years previously for 1,500 children – just after all but 400 children had been withdrawn).

In August 1977 'Black Mak' (Makarios) – ever a heavy smoker – died of a second heart attack. He had elected to be buried at Ký́kko Monastery. 'I see,' said one of my Turkish guests, 'that he wants to be as high up as possible, as usual.' 'Yes,' added the Director of Education, 'I'm surprised he didn't choose Mount Olympus!'

In the South, students were not slow to avail themselves of the aid money that was floating about. Those were the days of Judith Hart's munificence at the Overseas Development Ministry, though it seemed at times in the unholy trinity of the ODM, the Ministry of Education and the Home Office that one governing hand did not know what the other was doing. Students with the right passports found they could pay for holidays in Britain with the dole they could collect there, and when a scheme was introduced to help some of the 500 who were studying there and whose families had lost property in Cyprus, with their fees and subsistence, claimants were not always as deserving as they alleged. Many were there to avoid military service rather than to study, and when one father, an ex-police chief, complained that his daughter had not got a grant while all her fellow students had, I discovered that her address was Pont Street in Knightsbridge, that she was flying back to Cyprus for the Easter celebrations, and that she had visited the London Office 'dripping with jewellery'. This might have been explained by the fact that she was actually studying jewellery at an art college, but a reference to the Cyprus cultural attaché brought the brisk reply that her father didn't need the money.

Cyprus was the place where I first became aware of the strong leftward current flowing through Whitehall (and Lambeth, too; it was in St Paul's Church in Nicosia that the suicidal prescription of the ASB was trickled between my hesitant lips). In my first two years our local excitements had obscured events elsewhere, but now it was becoming clear that cultural propaganda was giving way to 'Aid' and 'Development'. This was where the big money was to be spent, and its administration required 'managers' rather than – oh, horror! – intellectuals.

My link with these new administrators was Peter Collister, a former teacher in Tanganyika and HMI in England, who came out to assess the projects we had recommended for Aid funds. In a memoir he wrote after his retirement he gives some personal impressions of his visit:

> I was thankful to exchange my reluctant part in the dismantling of a sound national education system in the name of social and political engineering, in which as one of Her Majesty's Inspectors I had to collaborate, for the altogether more pragmatic and less dogmatic task of advising the Ministry of Overseas Development on the nature and scope of British aid to education in developing countries....
>
> The British Council, who lived in the country, had cultivated good relations and liked to be liked, were nearly always over-optimistic, and one of my tasks was to look with a more jaundiced eye at the proposals put to us ... Stephen, the caustic British Council man,

whom I grew to like, introduced me to the splendours of a Greek *mezé*, eaten in the open outside a *taverna*, and to the medieval layout of old Nicosia.

Although sympathetic to everything Greek I found it hard to understand the attitude to the Turks, refusing to concede that they were in any way at fault as a result of years of their superior economic and political clout and Turkish poverty for centuries. They all seemed to be comparatively well-heeled and were bitter at the loss of what refugees in most countries would have called luxuries.

I always found Peter's recommendations (we were to meet again in a later posting) eminently sensible, but he and I were both working in a system that was becoming increasingly fragmented. To the bodies involved in overseas information work – the FO, the Council, the BBC, BIS (British Information Services), BTA (British Travel Association) – was now added this new and increasingly fashionable Ministry, which funded us to administer, but not to approve, some of its overseas schemes. To the outsider it must have been both confusing and frustrating and it was not surprising that the remit of one government committee was to examine the system and recommend improvements. The result was the Berrill Report which recommended abolishing the British Council, except for a small rump in London, and transferring its work to the FO and ODM. As I only had three years service to go before mandatory retirement at sixty, the implementation of this report – and it never was implemented – was of largely academic interest. But it was not very encouraging to read that an ethos established over forty years had been so totally dismissed.

It was therefore particularly cheering to have a letter from the Chairman of the British Council, Lord Ballantrae, to say he and his wife were coming out 'to pat us on the back'. After his visit to Caracas three years before, he had written a note of thanks concluding 'that last pleasant hour or two in your flat was possibly the most useful feature of my visit. I reckon that one of my functions is to act as a sort of "rubbing post" or, to mix my metaphors, to act as somebody with whom Representatives can "let down their hair".' I had long admired the books he had written as Bernard Fergusson on the Chindit campaigns, but he had his detractors. John Masters in his memoirs ridicules the monocle and cigarette holder and portrays him as anti-American and a snob, while Dick Beeston, on the receiving end of his mission to muzzle Sharq al Adna, the Arabic-language broadcasting station in Cyprus, in the unhappy days before Suez, calls him in his memoirs, *Looking for Trouble*, gung-ho and short-tempered. I found him a warm and attractive character with an intriguing mixture of ebullience and sensitivity, an ability to get on with anybody and an endearing love of poetry (and he could even quote my old school song by Newbolt); in fact he was very much the sort of person to let down one's hair with. He was also a tireless worker for the Council and infused it with some much-needed swagger.

Other memorable visitors were David Parkhouse and Eileen Croxford with their Music Group of London and, under the wing of the Goethe Institute but a British subject, Kurt Schumacher with his second wife. It seemed particularly perverse of providence that two such lively people as David and Schumacher should die so soon afterwards. While I was in Barcelona I had met the crime writer P D James (Phyllis White), whose daughter was teaching there. She had worked in the NHS and was now Principal in the Criminal Policy Department of the Home Office (while managing to look after her children and her sick husband). With the political upsets in Cyprus complicating problems of crime and deprivation, some lawyers and magistrates had asked me to bring out someone to talk about practices in Britain, and it occurred to me that the future Baroness James was well placed to do so, and, wearing her other hat, could also lecture on women novelists and crime writers. The London Office at that time had never heard of her but, after making enquiries, agreed to send her out. She was indeed equally effective under both hats.

Flushed with the success of Phyllis's lecture tour, I proposed a similarly two-hatted visit from Auberon Waugh – indeed a three-hatted one, if we include a return visit to the bases where he had shot himself with a machine gun during his National Service in the EOKA period. He could, I thought, talk about his father, but my primary interest was his gift for irony and humour in his own columns. The solemnity of the Cyprus newspapers was dreadfully boring, and I thought a little of Waugh's sense of the incongruous might enliven their papers and also help journalists to widen their own views. (I don't think I ever saw the faintest suggestion in a Greek Cypriot paper that Turkish Cypriots had been treated badly, or in the Turkish Cypriot papers that the invasion had had an element of 'overkill'; nor in either that politicians should ever be treated with anything but respect and trust and their words printed virtually without comment.) But the good ladies in Head Office clearly thought Waugh father and son dangerous characters; they offered me instead someone from the other end of the political spectrum, Tom Bairstow, deputy editor of the *New Statesman*. Perhaps it was because he had been busying himself on scurrilous articles about 'Phil the Greek' that they thought he would be popular with Greek Cypriots. I did not put their supposition to the test.

In January 1976 a letter arrived from Sir John Llewellyn, the DG, congratulating me on thirty years' service with the British Council. I received it with mixed feelings. Here was I, steaming busily through the complexities of a divided Cyprus, only to be reminded that in three years I was to be beached, whether I liked it or not. In one's fifties one feels still in the prime of life – walking, skiing, swimming, even working – and perhaps the more so if unmarried and unconstrained by domesticities. I firmly believe that in an ideal world one should change one's job at fifty to something more enjoyable and less taxing, and remain in it for the rest of one's active life. I was visited not long after this by Paul Gotch, my colleague in the Lebanon, who came over to see the archaeological sites on the eve of his retirement. A much travelled, well read and most lively soul, he was positively incensed at being thrown on the scrap heap at sixty, and all his worldly wisdom with him. Fortunately he was able to transfer his cultural baggage to a lecturer's cabin on many Swan's Tours before finally going out to grass, but an alarming number of our colleagues died soon after retirement, many of them, I suspect, from illnesses induced by boredom.

My own retirement date provided for one more shortish posting, and I pushed for one which would bring with it the satisfaction, and higher pension rate, of promotion. I had been floating on the ceiling of Grade D for so many years that if promoted to Grade C (equivalent to Counsellor grade in the FO) I would enter it well up the scale. On my home leave I did the rounds of Regional Controller, Personnel Department and Controller of Recruitment, ending with the routine DG interview. Llewellyn, an ex-Colonial Vice Chancellor, had a matey way with him. 'We owe it to you,' he said, promising me a move on promotion for my last two years of service and inviting my preferences among Turkey, Sri Lanka, South Africa and Bombay. For cultural, political, historical and geographical interest Turkey had it every time. I had marvelled at Istanbul (before pollution engulfed it). I had liked the Turkish Cypriots. Even xenophobic outbursts like the Armenian massacres could, at a pinch, be interpreted as all part of 'the rich tapestry' of the empire of the Sublime Porte; and this 'rich tapestry' would be within easy reach of my family. Cyprus, once the war clouds dispersed into a distant fog, had been very hospitable to both old and young members. All had been able to profit from the special flights and hotel rates with which the Greek Cypriots were wooing tourists (in the north recovery was slower).

As the international airport at Nicosia remained closed to civilian traffic, a new one was built at Larnaka, and the first to use it was Clare. I used to look forward to these family arrivals with terrific excitement and to their departures with a kind of bitter sweetness; the children were being torn away from me to fend for themselves again just when I was growing accustomed to their company; on the other hand their company did get more exhausting the older they grew, and sinking back into bachelor ways and an office routine undisturbed by family considerations had its appeal. For Clare, as the only girl in the family, I felt particularly on my mettle, and when I took her back to Larnaka for her return journey the air was heavy with unspoken grief and spoken trivialities. After watching her disappear into the departure lounge I would drive to a little beach on the other side of the airport and, lying on my back in the sea, watch her plane climbing above me and carrying her far far away ... to the Froebel Institute at Roehampton.

With the boys I did not feel so much on my best behaviour. Where Clare was no doubt still keeping me hopefully on a pedestal, the boys were of an age to be more critical. Gus was now working with architects in London and beginning to wear his hair a bit shorter. I introduced him to the pleasures of sleeping in a hammock, without interruptions from 'hunters', but what most impressed him was arriving late at night at the Axiothea Hotel in Paphos long after supper time, and the owner producing a marvellous Greek salad –

without turning a hair. Nick had followed psychology and sociology at Birmingham with librarianship at Manchester and, having seen his appalling sociology textbooks, I couldn't blame him. Ian was reading languages at Oxford. I managed to get them some respite from my company helping with and living at a dig at Kalavassos. It was hot work and I have not noticed any marked interest in Neolithic sites in either of them since.

With Clare, on the way to Kyrenia, I paid a call on the Cave Women; she thought their way of life a wonderful example of good companionship. On our way to Paphos we spent the night in hammocks on the military beach at Happy Valley; such was the lull in hostilities by then that it was deserted and no-one challenged us. We spent more austere nights, with John Cambridge and Ian, at the old wooden mist-shrouded Jubilee Hotel at Troodos, where the smoking log fires failed to dry the damp sheets.

My parson brother Hugh also came out with my artist sister Margie. He was reminded of his teaching days in Jerusalem in 1922, and he gave me an object lesson (a habit to which he was inclined) in Middle Eastern hospitality. We were picnicking in a remote spot when an old shepherdess greeted us. Even as I was summoning up my Greek for a condescending cross-examination Hugh, instinctively, broke off half the pie he was eating and offered it to her; and she, instinctively, accepted it. I arranged for Hugh and Margie to stay in a village in the Troodos foothills, where Margie could do some sketching. She was also able to carry away with her as a souvenir an *objet d'art* of her hostess which had taken her fancy – an embroidered cover for a toilet roll.

At the end of the year my posting was confirmed. The *Record of Living Conditions* warned me that 'regular snow can be expected in Ankara from December to March', and that 'winter smog is debilitating and lowering to the morale and newcomers tend to have initial intestinal troubles and colds and sore throats – and sometimes insomnia too'; also that 'the electricity supply fluctuates and fresh milk is usually out of stock', that 'Turkish drivers are completely unpredictable', and that 'the Representative, as Cultural Attaché, should bring a tail coat and orders in case he has to accompany an ambassador when presenting his credentials'. Well, I could take all that with a pinch of salt. I was to go the following autumn, and I set about learning Turkish (which I found exceedingly difficult after Greek) on the other side of the Green Line.

Of course, I knew that Turkey had, and always had had, its ups and downs. In his travel diary, published by the Hakluyt Society, Robert Bargrave, who spent five Cromwellian years in Izmir and Constantinople, summarises both the ups and the downs at the ceremonial launching of new ships 'built by some Fleming Renegades, and so faire in shape ... that some of them scarce could swimm out of Port, particularly theyr Admirall; which being to be lanchd in glory, they omitted to putt into her sufficient ballast, but mounted her Gunns, & run them all out to celebrat the Triumph: besides all her Deck was covred with Men, & hangd all Over with Banners: & thus her upperwork overweighing her lower, & all her Port holes open; when the

Trumpetts, Drumms and brass instruments began theyr Clangor, the Gunns theyr roaring, & the People theyr shout, the ship very orderly sinkes right doune, transforming the Turkes Triumph into the Devills Feast: who loving to fish in troubled waters, received here a plenty full Draught, & had abundance of Musique into the bargaine.'

Bargrave is more impressed at a 'Publique Appearance of the Grand Signor, so glorious as amazd my Memorie so that I can recollect only that before him and after him marched in regiments so many hundred Janizaris, so many hundred Bustangees, so many hundred Archers, so many Capigees, hundreds of Hitchoglans, of Eunuchs, & of Mutes ... severall troups of Churbagees ... on noble Arabian horses; yet neerer to him rides the Grand Vizier, the Janizary Aga, Caputan Bassa & all the great Beighs, Bassas and Primats ... on each side of him rid his two Grand Favourites ... dressed in habits of extreme wonder; & thus he marches stately on, with admirable Silence, unless the people sometimes interrupt it with theyr soft murmeres of prayers for him; who pay him so much reverence, as if somewhat were in his countenance more than humane which they dare not behold.'

I knew I could not expect such charisma from Bulent Eçevit, in his neat lounge suit, but I trusted also – and notwithstanding the hotly disputed horrors then recently depicted in the film *Midnight Express* – to be spared such sights of torture as Bargrave 'had confident Information of'.

> ... For very hainous Offender; with an Iron Engine they contract the man's body above his hipps, to the slenderness of his Chine bone with the litle Flesh & Skinn about it, forcing his bowells upwards, till his body and head be ready to burst insunder: being drawen into this narrow compass, they divide his upper part from his lower: & with the same motion slide his body on a flaming Brass or Iron Frame, which as they pretend seers up all Conveyences of the Vitalls, so that the body still remaines alive; & thus they are to stand (like Roman Statues) untill they sterve to Death.

Historical alarms and excursions of this kind, however, failed to alert me to the dangers awaiting me in the more humdrum surroundings of the British Council. In the Ankara office the can of worms I opened was to prove overwhelming.

19
Carpeted in Turkey

'BARBARIC!' I EXCLAIMED, wringing the egg from my fingers. 'When it's so easy to be civilised in such matters, why are Turkish hotels so barbaric?'

I was staying in one of the more upmarket hotels in Izmir, while visiting a teacher training course with two of my colleagues. Although food in restaurants was often delicious – especially the vegetables and peerless yoghurt – hotel meals could be fearsome, with television blaring out pop music or panning round the audience at some political meeting. At breakfast we had been served eggs in their shells piled on a big dish, but there were no implements to eat them with. On the first morning they had been rock-hard; on the second they were raw. I am not alone in my complaints. Twelve years later, in her guidebook to Eastern Turkey, Diana Darke could still write 'when [the hotels] are started – new and clean and rather expensive, with the latest available devices – the owner sets out his chair in the shade of his doorstep, places his magenta-stockinged feet comfortably out of his shoes onto an opposite chair, reads his paper, and expects his clients to carry on with all remaining details.' In my time the hotels were cheap enough, but one had to expect austerities; in some it was assumed that guests would share rooms and I once paid a derisory sum for a room to myself with twelve beds in it.

I was happy to put up with inconveniences for the sake of seeing the endless chain of ancient cities along the Aegean coast. Perhaps it is because I was alone there that Priene, overlooking the plain – once the estuary – of the Meander, seemed to me the most perfect of them all. I sat in the Mayor's seat in the theatre, prayed unmolested in the Temple of Demeter, relieved myself unreproved on the steps of the Temple of Athena, climbed up to the Acropolis and down to the stadium with its starting gate and was back in the stone streets with the drains beneath them before anyone else appeared to break the spell. I remain puzzled by the grandeur of so many municipal buildings in such a small space and by the size of the stones that composed them. How could so few people create and support such opulence? And what was life like there in its decline?

Ephesus was no less memorable, but for a more earthy reason. One cannot walk down the Arcadian Way to the dried up harbour where Anthony met Cleopatra without a *frisson*, but the restoration is so painstaking that there is a Walt Disney air about it. But my abiding memory is of standing high up at the back of the theatre and idly noting a stout American tourist down near the stage. Suddenly he whipped down his trousers, whipped up his shirt, bared his backside and, with a series of explosions, defecated. The noise was dramatic proof of the theatre's amazing acoustics. Romans, however, who enlarged the Hellenistic original, would not have been amused. They were particular about that sort of thing. Having provided conveniences for every bodily function – the baths of Scholastica and their attendant brothel were hard by – they would expect them to be used.

After seeing the splendid Hittite museum in Ankara I expected to find in the vast uplands of Hattuşaş and Yazilikaya monuments on an equally impressive scale, but the figures in the Tombs of the Kings, all in profile like Egyptian figures, are about half life-size. In the citadel were the usual little ragged boys selling bits of modern pottery they pretended to have excavated. '*Sprechen sie Deutsch*? Cigarette? Photo? Very old coins!' And these coins, I was told, they had judiciously, in order to achieve an authentically antique patina, 'passed through goats'.

Besides its headquarters in Ankara, the Council ran a Directorate, library and Anglo-Turkish English teaching institute in Istanbul. From my visits there it is not so much the mosques that I remember – there are beautiful mosques elsewhere – as the extraordinary mixture of monuments. In particular I was struck by the alien elegance of the former embassies of Holland, Russia and Sweden, and the grandeur of the French, German and British ones – all overshadowed, in streets that were full of holes and seas of mud, by spick-and-span new tower blocks. And within these blocks the lifts rarely worked, while in the foyers night watchmen cooked kebabs on braziers and slept on mats on the floor.

In the Protestant Cemetery the British section had beautiful tombs dating from the 16th century but the most recent Levantine-British ones sported photographs of their incumbents. One prominent memorial in white marble had an open book carved upon it and an inscription to 'Professor John Constable, Professor of Chemistry at the University of Istanbul'. I was told that he had left £3,000 for this memorial (which a faithful friend had had erected) and that for many years he had insisted on playing the organ in church – 'to the dismay of the congregation'. Could his academic distinctions, spelt out at length, compete with the inscription to Mohamed's standard bearer, Eyüp Ansari, also buried in Istanbul? 'Well did he know the end of this life, for he had been familiar with its beauties; thinking his appointed time yet another gazelle-eyed one, he said, "My dark-eyed love!" and followed it.'

After the embassies had followed Atatürk to Ankara their old buildings were either sold or demoted to consulates. As a mere consulate the classical Barry-inspired British Embassy, with its gloomy chapel, became a white elephant until the Council and its Institute joined the Consul there shortly after my arrival. This arrangement had its drawbacks, one being the perennial problem that bedevils a joint Council and FO building, especially if the Council is conducting English classes. The Council likes to be apolitical and open to all comers; an embassy or consulate has security requirements. In Istanbul students and library members had to be issued with passes to get them past the guard at the gate, which was awkward for us but understandable in view of the unrest in the country at that time. What I found harder to condone was the Embassy attitude to our library. It was housed in the magnificent ballroom, but when the Ambassador paid official visits to the city we were required to make the ballroom available for formal entertaining. Consequently, the bookshelves had to be rolled against the walls and camouflaged. It seemed to me that other rooms could have served almost as well and saved us from such a public exhibition of philistinism.

Outside the main towns roads were often hazardous. It was not unusual to come across stretches of major roads from which the entire surface had been bulldozed for many miles but no new one yet applied. I was introduced to the horrors of the Istanbul-Ankara highway when I went to fetch my car. I drove it back among the trucks going through to Iran and India, and at one point, going uphill in the twilight, met a large American car coming down on the wrong side of the road. I flashed my lights and it swerved past me and then skidded back, bouncing off a truck immediately behind me and disappearing over the edge of the road. The worst accident I ever saw was when I emerged from thick fog into a clear patch and found myself on a scene involving a coach, a truck, a tractor, a minibus and three cars. The coach had been sliced in half and fifteen bodies were laid out on the roadside, looking frighteningly uninvolved, as bodies always do. Coaches had a bad reputation for accidents due to the drivers' long working hours. No doubt many of them were also owner-drivers with relaxed ideas about their and their passengers' drinking habits. I was held up once on a minor road by a coach parked in the middle of it to find its male passengers relieving themselves along the verge and, more spectacularly, from the front and rear steps. The women stayed demurely, and I can only hope comfortably, in their seats.

Turks were fatalistic about accidents. The weather, for example, was something that happened as providence decided and was never prepared for. Gloves were seldom worn, even in the snow – though galoshes were (and for the first time since childhood I followed suit). When the first winter snow fell in Ankara it was as if snow had never fallen before: everyone set off as usual for the office, hoping for the best, with cars and buses sliding into each other, into shop fronts and into lampposts until everything had seized up. On Turkish planes, too, a safe landing seemed to come as a surprise to the passengers, for they always clapped the pilot vigorously. Having said all that, I have never failed to be offered help when in trouble on the roads, and notably when in a rainstorm one night I drove into a foot-deep hole in the middle of the Ankara-Istanbul highway and had a double puncture.

Ankara was better than I expected; at least it was less frenetic than Istanbul, and easier to get in and out of. But being in a basin at a high altitude it had a smog problem, and an acrid atmosphere compounded of coal, oil fuels and heavy traffic emissions seemed to impregnate the buildings at all times of the year. As soon as one entered a perfectly respectable flat or office one was assailed by a kind of Dickensian factory smell. One also had to learn to be fatalistic about power cuts, water shortages and other hazards. At least the power cuts meant relief from the music in restaurants.

When I first arrived I spent a few days in my predecessor's house before its lease ran out, and on the first night was awakened by machine-gun fire. A passing carload of Palestinian sympathisers had loosed off at the Egyptian Embassy next door to express their disapproval of Sadat's visit to Jerusalem. Next morning a bomb was found in our shared dustbin.

The flat I moved to was more cheerful, well up the hill in what was now the smart suburb of Çankaya, and above the smog line.

In Turkey it was often the juxtaposition of ancient and modern that pleased – Selçuk caravanserais in the middle of nowhere, Ottoman baths in the scruffiest village street, or, in the very centre of Ankara, the citadel with the gypsy-like life going on within its walls and country craftsmen in the narrow passages leading up to it, sewing and sawing and banging out copper and tin bowls and lethally-handled frying pans as if they were hundreds of miles away hundreds of years ago. Just over the hill from Çankaya tortuous lanes led to the simplest of farms and sparest of villages, and only fifteen miles away the Elma Dağ mountain with its tortoises, storks, snipe and herons, its winter snow and summer shepherds with their murderous dogs, seemed as distant as furthest Anatolia.

Çankaya, too, had been a comparatively remote village when Mustafa Kemal Atatürk moved his capital from the polyglot Istanbul to Ankara in 1923 and decided that this was the place for his presidential palace. Most other countries, on leaving their embassy buildings in Istanbul, had built afresh in what they conceived to be the most influential area of Ankara, its centre. But Atatürk had a soft spot for his friend and drinking companion, Sir Percy Lorraine, the British Minister. 'You come up to Çankaya with me,' he said, or words to that effect, 'and we can have jolly evenings together', and he presented Britain with a huge compound near his own. Acres and acres remained unbuilt over, notwithstanding the extra accommodation required for staff working for CENTO (the Central Treaty Organisation) – to which Iran under the Shah still adhered – in addition to the Embassy itself.

The compound included a light and airy chapel, which was the scene of a touching and remarkably ecumenical ceremony. One of the great sites of Turkey is Pamukkale (Cotton Castle), the ancient Hieropolis, with its cascading white limestone terraces and exotic warm pools. It also has all the other appurtenances of a classical spa town – a theatre, temples, and baths and altars and, to top it all off, a huge necropolis. Among the side-shows beside the Temple of Apollo is the Plutonium, with a gateway, then half walled up, opening into a chamber 3 metres square with a stream issuing from the rock at the back of it. Emanating from the steaming water are toxic vapours which, it is said, only the eunuch priests of the oracle of Cybele were able to survive. It was possible, with the help of a leg-up to the top of the wall, to sniff these noxious fumes. When a group of young teachers from Ankara went to spend a couple of nights at Pamukkale, two of them, from England but teaching English in a private school independently of the Council, announced that they were going to change their hotel. Consequently they were not missed when they failed to meet the others in the evening. The next day, however, their absence was apparent, and the others in the party, recalling their special interest in the Plutonium, went to see if they were there. They found a small boy standing by the gate who told them there were 'two deads in there', and, alas, there were. One of the teachers was Jewish and his parents arranged for his body to be repatriated for an orthodox Jewish burial. The parents of the other flew out for his funeral in the Embassy chapel, and it is that occasion that has remained so vividly in my memory. The chapel was crowded, not only with their son's fellow teachers but with his Muslim students, many of them openly crying, and on the coffin were two wreaths inscribed by them. I had been told that the 'infidel' part of the big Muslim cemetery was grim but I thought it a good deal more acceptable than the soulless cemeteries in Britain. The large eucalyptus trees looked beautiful in the spring sunshine and the Christian area, being confined to an outer wall, blended into the life of the huts beyond. Children sat on the wall watching, I suppose, this entrance to the gates of paradise and I found the normality of it all, the horses and carts and poultry and smoking chimneys and laundry hanging out, very comforting.

Unfortunately the ecumenical spirit displayed in this sad story was by no means universal, and political uncertainties were echoed by uncertainties in the Council's strategy. The Council Office and library in Ankara was in stark contrast to the vast Embassy compound, and was extraordinarily scruffy, especially compared to the Council building in tiny little Cyprus. The Anglophile Teaching Institute nearby was little better. It had recently been separated in Ankara (though not in Istanbul, where things ran more smoothly) from Council control, and handed over to a Turkish director. The Council's Representative remained on the Board but had no greater financial or professional responsibility than any of the other members. The other members were agreeable, but they had one terrible weakness – a decision reached at one meeting was often reversed at the next.

Much Council work that had looked alright on paper had proved impractical when put to the test of a shaky national infrastructure. There was an immense gap between efficient teacher-training schemes and village schools too primitive for trained teachers to put up with for long. There were many universities, but many in various stages of student revolt. There was a veneer of cultural sophistication. The National Ballet Company, started by nominees of Ninette de Valois, thrived; and there was an active School of Archaeology, besides the British and other schools. Concerts and art exhibitions were well attended. Sotheby's considered my office a worthy recipient of their lavish catalogues. But there were stories of professional and political incompatibilities and every up side seemed to have its down one. The ubiquitous army looked distinctly old-fashioned in its equipment, while the American bases, on paper a reassuring Cold War bastion on Turkey's eastern borders, were the subjects of endless wrangling and national touchiness. Above all, almost every enterprise was sooner or later hamstrung by warring unions of left and right.

The failure of one of our ELT training schemes to materialise resulted in a disaffected colleague having nothing to do. He was a gloomy character and I foresaw no solution to his predicament except a transfer to a more realistic post elsewhere. This and other uncertainties led me to propose to the two old friends in the London office responsible for my area that I should fly back in December for 'consultations', now that I had seen the situation on the ground. (I had last talked to them when on leave over a year earlier and had returned to Cyprus for nearly a year before going to Turkey.) By a happy coincidence, I added, my eldest son was getting married, so I would also be able to attend his wedding. They were so obliging as to see my point.

The wedding of Gus and Jane was a delight, but my 'consultation' was not so satisfactory. There was no post available at that inauspicious time of the year for my gloomy colleague, so I would have to put up with him.

From then on the gloom increased all round. Power cuts increased; so did sick leave among the local staff; student unrest and army retaliation grew more violent; bombs were frequent; at a personal level I found Turkish difficult to learn after Greek, and I was involved in an unsatisfactory love affair. Even a honeymoon visit from Gus and Jane did not escape mishap, for in Cappadocia the car-key-crisis struck again. We had parked the car at the edge of the Peristrema Gorge and reached it again after an exhausting scramble just as the light was going. Gus had last been driving and felt for the keys in what passed for pockets. No doubt he would have found them had jeans been built for convenience rather than effect. As we stood there in the middle of nowhere, 150 miles from Ankara, recriminations – mostly mine – flew round like the bats emerging from the caves. 'They must have fallen out,' said Gus, and he vanished to retrace his steps. As it grew darker and we thought of needles in haystacks, our spirits sank further – when, lo and behold, Gus appeared, poker-faced, to dangle the keys in our faces. He had remembered one particular rock from which he had jumped down with a bump, and that was where he had found the keys.

My distracting love affair did not help relations with some of my colleagues. In any case there were problems, for this was the first time I had had to work with the 'managerial' intake who were increasingly to dominate Council policy. Their interests fitted more easily into the management of overseas development funds and the sale of 'educational packages' than into the traditional but increasingly anachronistic fields of academia and the arts for which the Council had hitherto been known. One of my staff had been a management trainee with Sainsbury's and another with Clark's shoes.

'I joined the Council,' said Mr Clark, 'because I wanted to contribute to the development of disadvantaged countries.'

I thought at first this was a mundane, not to say pompous, thing to say, and then reflected that I had been just as bad in my attitude to the inhabitants of Colombia and Iran – 'lesser breeds without the law' who only needed good doses of Dr Johnson and Noel Coward to love us, buy from us and live happily ever after. Both approaches left open the question of how each attitude affected Council work in general and the whole man in particular. Messrs Clark and Sainsbury were admirably practical, but my difficulty lay in finding any intellectual interests in common.

With the Turks I had no such difficulty. There remained the conundrum that whereas Turks as individuals, whether urban sophisticates or simple country people, were helpful, hospitable and likeable, when acting together in groups – in political parties, unions, committees – they became utterly intransigent. This last trait was all too evident in our local staff's union negotiations. Just over half elected to join the most militant left-wing union. This was demanding 'representation on our committees', and supported a member of our local staff who had been suing us and was intercepting London mail in pursuit of evidence for his case. I was dependent on the Embassy Legal Adviser for advice over negotiations, but the Council's quasi-diplomatic status was a problem for him, and Embassy staff never seemed to grasp the fact that the Council no longer controlled the Language Institute. In any case, and not unreasonably, with their preoccupations with CENTO, Cyprus and local business contracts, the last thing they wanted was to get side-tracked by the labour troubles of a mere cultural organisation.

Throughout this deteriorating situation I received no guidance from HQ. My two senior contacts had been succeeded by younger men in the fast stream, whom I had not met. One of them, formerly in the Bradford wool industry, suddenly proposed a visit. It was just before I was due to go on home leave at the end of June 1978. The gloomier things became in Turkey the more I had looked forward to this leave. It was to start with a reunion with friends from Cyprus: John Cambridge on his first leave as Ambassador in Kuwait, was to rendezvous in Pisa, where John and Celia Turvey, from the English School, would collect us for a stay in their hillside cottage near Lucca. I was therefore not best pleased when I had to postpone arrangements to accommodate this last-minute visit by Mr Bradford. Nor was I reassured by his manner when he arrived. He was plastic man personified, and clearly bent on finding fault. He did not, however, take me into his confidence over his misgivings or discuss remedial options arising from them, but talked at length with the Ambassador, with whom he had served in a previous post – and while he did so I was invited to wait outside. He also talked at length with Mr Clark. He departed as uncommunicatively as he had arrived.

By the time I reached neat little Pisa my distrust of Mr Bradford and the austerities and anxieties of Ankara had dropped off my back like the burden in *Pilgrim's Progress*. I found John Cambridge in the Trattoria Bruno, reclining like a contented Buddha, well into the second course and halfway down the carafe. After he had aired his Italian and bonhomie to the waiter we emerged to walk round the *duomo* and leaning tower in bright moonlight and absolute silence.

When the Turveys collected us the next day the tourist coaches were pouring in and we were relieved to escape to the felicities of Lucca and, beyond it, the hamlet of Torigliano from which a rough track led up to the house. The house was far enough up the hill to have a panoramic view of such splendour that if the Turveys hadn't been so energetic I think I would have been content to sit on the terrace just looking at it, and John Cambridge would have been happy to learn his lines as the King in a forthcoming production of *Hamlet*. But they took us even higher up to meet the 'Shepherdess', a handsome weather-beaten woman of about sixty (or conceivably forty ... or eighty), with almost no teeth left, who liked a good gossip. She lived in a biggish house and had thirty-two sheep, with vines, olive trees and vegetables growing on the steep slopes. She shared the house with a crippled old man. His family had prevented them from marrying for many years, and when they did eventually join up they found that their respective flocks of sheep did not get on together. There was no electricity or water in the house and the winters must have been very hard, yet they seemed cheerful and contented. Whenever we walked past, dogs burst into song, but they were a welcome contrast to the sheepdogs of Anatolia – though not to John Cambridge who had an allergy to dogs, even the mildest-natured ones. He had many allergies, but for every allergy he had his addiction, and it was the spontaneous expression of his likes and dislikes that made his company so refreshing and endeared him to his friends: the fondness for old clothes and the gathering of flowers into nosegays; the striding out hour after hour and querulous argument about the path back; the negotiation of simple obstacles with oaths and whimpers and happy clambering up a vertical mountainside; the impatience when hungry and patience when cooking expertly himself; the confessed meanness and lavish hospitality; the insincerity of his compliments and candour of his self-mockery.

It was a marvellous five days, though the abandoned farms in the mountains were a sad sight and the armed guards at the banks suggested that the little towns were not as peaceful as they looked. Spa towns like Bagni di Lucca had clearly declined since the days of Byron, Augustus Hare, Lamartine and Heine. There was also a commemorative plaque to Charles Lever, and I was shocked, in my intolerant way, to learn that neither John had heard of him. On the last morning, as a bright sun dispersed the blue-green haze in the valley, the two Johns discussed a bath.

'No, no! Really! Don't bother with the geyser. I don't need a bath.'

'Nonsense! It's no trouble.'

'No, no, I insist. It's much too beautiful a morning to mess about with wood and matches. I can perfectly well do without a bath. After all, I shall be in Eastbourne this evening.'

'The wood's here; it won't take a minute. You can't travel dirty.'

'Yes, I can. Please don't bother. I can't impose on you like this. ... Well, are you sure? All right then. Let me at least get the wood. Oh, have you got it already? Now, where's some newspaper and matches? Oh, have you lit it? Really, John, how you do spoil me!'

I was leaving after John Cambridge, and he, who had brought his hosts no present from Kuwait, insisting that it would have been an insult to their hospitable instincts which deserved appreciative comments and compliments rather than mere presents which anyone could give, gave me twenty thousand lire (£15) to buy a present for the house.

'I think I shall buy a huge gnome. Tuscany is full of gnomes, classical gnomes and modern gnomes.'

'No, you will not! Buy a basket.'

'A super gnome. The John Cambridge gnome.'

'No, Stephen, now stop it!'

After days of such sunny living, London came as a sobering experience. I went with my daughter Clare through the pouring rain to see her heartthrob of the moment, Tom Conti, in *Whose Life is it Anyway?,* and looked forward to seeing the rest of the family.

Twenty-four hours later, summoned peremptorily by telephone, I found myself facing a kangaroo court at Council headquarters. Sitting opposite me were the plastic Mr Bradford and the older and embarrassed-looking Director of Personnel Department.

'We think,' said one, 'you should not go back to Ankara.'

'Why not?'

'You called the Turks,' said the other, 'barbaric.'

20
Indian Summer

'I DO NOT LIKE whispering campaigns,' wrote the only one of my Ankara colleagues to express regret at my departure. Evidently Bradford, Clark and company had pooled confidences; so much for family chitchat over the breakfast eggs! I was evidently not to be told the office gossip for fear that I might refute it; but it did emerge that our union troubles had indeed alarmed the Embassy who feared they might spread to their own locally engaged staff. I was thought too confrontational. 'Maybe my time in Cyprus had made me pro-Greek!'

Well! Put not your trust in princes! Why should I have expected support from a body that was itself the most sophisticated of trade unions, dedicated first, last and all the time to not rocking the boat? Had not my hero, Anthony Trollope, in *Dr Thorne,* summed up my feelings in Lady Arabella's words: 'A profession ... would degrade him; but to dangle at a foreign court, to make small talk at the evening parties of a lady ambassadress, and occasionally, perhaps, to write demi-official notes containing demi-official tittle-tattle; this would be in proper accordance with the high honour of a Gresham of Greshamsbury.' Demi-official tittle-tattle in Turkey had it that the Cultural Relations Department of the Foreign Office was particularly sensitive – with personal passions involved – to growing Russian influence in the Turkish Ballet. But in truth it was not thc Council but only myself I had to blame. I had chosen Turkey from the options offered to me in 1976 – and I had blown it.

For me Turkey triggered off the Peter Principle. If, instead of being fobbed off with years of 'acting' and 'temporary' promotion I had been promoted ten years earlier, I might have acquired self-confidence, tolerance, patience – all the things that grow with authority; I would have preserved a proper distance from colleagues, not favoured them with tactless jokes; I would have acted solely in a social capacity on the Boards of Language Institutes and left them to stew professionally in their own juice. I would have learned to rely less on embassies and more on Council HQ. Perhaps I would have had the clout to insist on, say, a six weeks' full-time course of Turkish before taking up my post. As it was, I was now asked to brief my successor, a likeable and obviously capable man much younger than me, who had worked in Turkey before and spoke Turkish. If he had been posted there in the first place no doubt things would have gone more smoothly. But the point is academic as the Turkish Army, as is its habit, took over soon afterwards, and union troubles together with many others were bundled into cold storage.

I, however, must always have been a square peg to fit into Personnel Department's round holes, or my promotion would not have been so wayward. No doubt my divorce had not helped, though it had never overtly been held against me. Accident-prone postings like Iran and Venezuela had been followed by therapeutic ones to Lebanon and Cyprus.

'Your file,' said an urbane Assistant Director-General, producing it with visible effort at my last interview, 'is one of our largest.'

'So it should be. It's been going a long time.'

'Others even older are less bulky. You have a history of contentiousness – some of it very lucid.'

This, however, was after the dust had settled from the first interview when practical attention was turned to its fallout. Various suggestions were put forward: perhaps I might like to retire early as I only had fifteen months' service to go? Or, there was a job in London available, which had recently been used for a similar casualty from overseas.

I did not intend to retire with such a bad taste still in my mouth, nor did I welcome the idea of a London posting which would have been both demeaning and disadvantageous to me tax-wise, and it would also limit scope for retiring overseas. I also sensed some anxiety that I might press for a post-mortem into my lack of guidance or official warning and the suddenness of my withdrawal, and when I held out for a slot overseas, any slot, to save embarrassment all round, I felt the official wheels beginning to turn in my direction again. Slots were scarce, I was told, but at last one was identified – in Madras where the Regional Representative was to be invalided home. His predecessor, too, had left early with eye problems. 'The Board would not like yet a third short posting to Madras,' said the ADG, but he would 'see if he could sell it to them'. At this my spirits rose immediately, for I had no doubt that his persuasive charm would sway any mere Board. Nor was I disappointed.

So it was that at the end of October 1978 I took off for Kuwait in a jumbo jet full of package tourists and Indians carrying cassette radios and tiger-skin-patterned blankets. At Kuwait I was delivered in style by an Embassy Jaguar to John Cambridge's shaded Residence for a few days convalescence before flying on to Delhi. Besides its swimming pool, the Residence boasted a collection of charming prints of red-coated marines skirmishing up and down the Gulf, with cannons discharging pretty red shells against crumbling forts.

At Delhi I was to stop for briefing at the Council HQ. The scene at the airport at 5 o'clock in the morning, with two jumbo jets landing together, was one of unbridled horror. With my allergy to queuing born of my POW experience I sat on a vacant desk, reading alternately *The Wonder that was India* and *Carry on Jeeves*, while the dawn broke round us and I waited for the queues to thin out. But before they did, yet more jumbos arrived. A party of climbers, including Sir John Hunt, suffered with me. They were en route for Darjeeling and Nepal for a 25th Everest Anniversary climb. 'It's fairly light-hearted,' said one of the women. 'They've even allowed us wives to come along.'

By the time I got my final luggage chit and emerged blinking into the sun, I had been in the airport for three hours and my fellow passengers had long disappeared. Everything was quiet; nothing moved. One or two people sat or squatted about, and ancient taxis – the notorious 1955-style BMC Ambassadors and a few Triumph Heralds and Fiat 800 models – were parked nearby. Of course I had taken so long to come through that whoever had come to meet me had assumed I wasn't on the plane. So I drove in, feeling aggrieved, at about 15 miles an hour along wide streets between large green gardens with little on the road in this part of Delhi except narrow-handlebar upright bicycles, pedicabs and Vespa taxis with Victoria-type cloth hoods and exhortations painted on the back: '*BE INDIAN BUY INDIAN*' (or sometimes '*BE INDIAN BY INDIAN*'); '*WORK MORE TALK LESS*'; '*MANY RELIGIONS ONE NATION*'; '*EACH ONE TEACH ONE*'.

I was received apologetically and hospitably by my hosts, Edge and Jean Semmens. Edge, Regional Representative for Delhi, was a late recruit from the Colonial Service and an inveterate collector. There was an electric organ in the house as well as a piano and a vast collection of tapes, while countless carvings, pewter vessels, paintings and brasses bore witness to bargain hunting in Africa, Malaya, Israel and now India. One of his regular suppliers of antique brasses arrived while I was there, asking about 250 rupees (£14) for each of the only three pieces he was interested in. Edge patiently beat him down to 50 each.

Representative for all India, also residing in Delhi, and presiding over the four Regional Representatives of Delhi, Bombay, Calcutta and Madras, was the side-whiskered, sardonic and drily amusing Bryan Swingler. He was obviously shrewder than his pose of puzzled world-weariness suggested or he wouldn't have achieved ministerial rank here with, I was told, Paris already promised as his retirement post in two years' time. He and his beautifully dressed Viennese wife, Herta, kept a splendid table and later on took me with them on a tour of Rajasthan. They also later on put up my son Ian on his way to stay with me.

The Rajasthan trip followed a Regional Conference, and I did just wonder, the further we got into it, whether the Council's set-up in India, where fast-track recruits were often posted and tended to be promoted *en poste* and catapulted up the line, was quite the jewel in its crown that it was claimed to be.

Bryan and Herta had planned to take me to Sariska game park on the way to Jaipur. As a special treat, rooms had been reserved in the former palace of the Maharajah of Alwar rather than in the Government Resthouse. Although – or perhaps because – we took a Council driver we ran out of petrol 30 kilometres from the nearest pump and were only saved by a passing Polish diplomat who siphoned off some of his own petrol for us. At first sight the palace was impressive. But as we drove up the drive to the twin-turreted Franco-Saracenic wedding cake of a building we saw that the gardens were a parched wilderness, the tennis courts and swimming pool were long disused and the tiger cage, from which the creatures used to be released for the maharajah to pot at from a balcony, was rusty and overgrown. The house was sparsely furnished, though the huge dining-room still had enough chairs in it for us to expect the arrival any minute of Miss Haversham, and the rooms were unlighted except for a few of the bedrooms which had one small naked bulb apiece. The water was delivered in a bucket by an ancient retainer, and there was no food available. We gathered that nobody ever stayed voluntarily in the palace; it was used only as an overflow for anyone unfortunate enough not to be able to get into the resthouse. When we went over there it appeared that we were unfortunate enough not even to get food because it was so full. We did, after Herculean arguments, persuade the staff to give us fried eggs and bread and jam before returning to our freezing, empty, dry, dark and haunted palace. The dawn could not come soon enough for us to sally forth and drive into the game park, where we saw absolutely nothing except some thin cattle and a shepherd or two. There was alleged to be a holy man who spent his life under one of the trees, but he must have knocked off for the night.

But the rest of the trip more than made up for this start, and included besides Jaipur the marvellously sited and decorated palace of Amber and its sky-high fortress. Bishop Heber, who was man of the world enough to know that the Lord might not always provide and travelled on camels with his own tents and food supply, visited the palace in 1824. He was thrilled by it and asks in his journal what Ariosto or Walter Scott would not have made of it.
As for the Sariska Palace, its fortunes were to be revived: in the year 2000 a British travel agency could offer 'MAHARAJAHS AND TIGERS – a seven-night stay at the delightful, comfortable superior medium-class "heritage" hotel, where peacocks strut on the swathes of manicured lawn, with jeep safari game drives and (available at extra cost) a short "Tiger Trail" night walk ... from £599.'

No one in India ever alluded to events in Turkey. Had London tipped off Delhi about my failings – or asked that I be treated tactfully as more sinned against than sinning? At any rate, Bryan and other colleagues in India became good friends.

Meanwhile, it only took a couple of days after my arrival before cracks began to show in the Delhi facade and I was treated as one of the family, entitled to hear the family gossip. Two married colleagues, I gathered, were having affairs with High Commission staff and two contract specialists in Hyderabad and one in Calcutta were teetering on the verge of divorce. As for work, India had always been the Council's highest spending area, and it was inevitable that bureaucracy would flourish and anomalies occur. The buzz word at that time from Judith Hart MP was that aid money should concentrate on 'non-formal' and 'grass roots' education for the underprivileged (shades of Ronald Adam's community development seminars for taxi drivers!). Well-meaning proposals had a rocky path through the vast centralised government machine, with everyone grinding an axe and taking a cut, and as the underprivileged were unreachable except in their own language (even missionaries only converted a few handfuls by educating them formally and equipping them for jobs) we jumped from one scheme to another, keeping visiting consultants spinning plans like jugglers' plates and taking in each others washing.

The only things that really kept growing steadily were the enormous libraries; a 'Resource Centre' for teachers of English was hardly used. Even the libraries were not without problems, as I was to find when I took over mine in Madras, Bangalore and Trivandrum, and opened a new one in Hyderabad. In order to prevent the Russians having too many outlets, the Indian Government had limited the establishment of foreign libraries and centres to cities with a diplomatic presence, in the British case the four Deputy High Commissions. The Council had therefore negotiated a tortuous process of devolving responsibility for other libraries to the Arts Council of India. The Arts Council was responsible for appointing and administering the Indian staff; we were responsible for supplying and running the libraries and for paying for everything. This was fine in theory but risky in practice. I was fortunate in having a first-rate staff – except in one library where we were lumbered with a lunatic whom we could not and the Arts Council, leaned on by friends and relations, would not discharge. He was still there, making the life of his Indian head librarian a misery when I left.

In Delhi the staff were unhappy with their London 'Controller', a management whizz kid like my own late and unlamented one. Closer to home, a cause of comment was a Ms Demeanour, PhD, who had been recruited as a potential high flyer and was destined for the fast track. She was certainly fast, enthralling one of the Indian staff who already had a wife and family. 'Either she goes or I go,' exclaimed one of her exasperated colleagues. 'The girl's quite simply mad. She's got this working class kink which makes her refer to all of us as "the snobs" and accuse us of living out of touch with ordinary people.' This accorded with her brisk refusal of Edge's invitation to lunch with a 'Lunch? No *thank* you!' and perhaps with her white overalls with 'US Army' embroidered across one breast.

Of Delhi itself I only had time to see the Red Fort, a sad, dusty, desecrated echo of Granada, and the pink Government building by Lutyens – almost immensely impressive but not quite big enough for its spaces and approaches.

In Madras, after banking above the 18th-century sea-girt Georgetown group of fort, church and government buildings, I landed with the lurches and bumps familiar to passengers on internal Indian flights and was met – although it was a Sunday – by both my British Assistants, a wife, an Indian Assistant and a driver. This was my introduction to the wonderful local support for my last year in office. As we drove in past the old Portuguese church on St Thomas Mount the damp heat settled down on me like a cloak, at once protective and threatening as though to say, 'Welcome, but don't try and buck the system!' Everyone kept saying that this was the coolest time of year, but that March and April were really hot.

The Assistant Regional Representative (or 'Educational Adviser' as we were officially labelled for reasons of political convenience) was Peter Moss. As a former teacher and married to Manoura (Norma) Mathai from Kerala, he knew far more about the educational scene than I would ever know. But these two bore their knowledge lightly, passed it on imperceptibly, and by the end of my tour, thanks to their tutelage, I felt that I had never learnt so much about a country in so short a time. Inevitably, though, our interests reflected the generation gap between us. Peter and Norma were interested in the future; I was interested in the past.

My other Madras colleague was Dr Penny Aspden, the Science Officer. Unlike the US Army fan in Delhi, she was a solemn Blackburn Quaker, big-boned, pigtailed and a serious cyclist. As a biologist from the Open University she was very 'committed' and a reproach to us all in the zealousness of her search for causes, projects and candidates for grants. Perhaps some of these were geese rather than the swans she saw them as because of their science degrees, and she tended to see herself as a martyr to interference from Delhi. 'Now you're being opaque,' she would write to senior colleagues there, and be surprised that they were annoyed. Her house had a strongly academic air, with posters taped to the walls, but her heart was in the right place for she hired a piano on which to take lessons, and she put Ian and me up while we were awaiting our voyage home.

The Council offices and library were very grand and presided over with great efficiency by one highly civilised Indian married couple, about to retire and to be replaced by another. There were queues to join the library, and we were clearly very popular, though perhaps more as a milch cow than a cultural organisation. However, being situated just behind the Deputy High Commissioner's office, we were once picketed by a militant women's group demonstrating against pregnancy tests for would-be immigrants to Britain. It is, of course, an anomaly of a Council presence in former colonial territories that with one hand we beckon our hosts in and with the other shut them out.

My own house, Balakrishna, was in College Road. It was a white mini-palace in a compound shaded by noble trees alive with tree rats. New garish villas were pressing round it and it was itself to be developed after my tenancy. The air of change and decay lent the scene a pleasing melancholy that suited my mood. The detached servants' quarters housed my bearer, Freddie, and his family, Mari, the ancient cook, and a gardener; I declined to appoint a 'bathroom wallah' as well, and despite the deprivation was ridiculously spoilt. Old Mari was a marvellous cook; he was as skilled with delicate Indian dishes as he was, for instance, with a supper of roast duck with new and roast potatoes, peas, bread sauce and tamarind sauce (instead of orange), and feather-light baroness pudding to end with. I could leave all arrangements for dinner or cocktail parties to Mari and Freddie. (As the state of Tamil Nadu was dry under the Janata regime my parties were very popular, though the guests had to keep an eye out for the Alcohol Police on their way home.) I soon got used to Freddie shaking his head when he meant 'yes'. (Indians don't waggle their heads when they mean 'no', because they never do mean 'no'. The nearest they get to it is to say 'No problem!', a phrase whose negative import only emerges later.)

Balakrishna and its indulgent staff was a haven for young friends and relations on the hippy trail. Clare came out for three weeks, and was seen through Bombay by my colleague there. On the way to his house she was dismayed by the sheer number of people in the streets, and by a driver bombarding her with remarks, like 'How much are you paying me?'. Unfortunately in Bombay she cleaned her teeth with tap water and was afflicted by the usual aftermath. The Swinglers in Delhi passed on to me Alexander Fyjis Walker, a mature and self-possessed 18-year-old (and future publisher of travel books), who had evidently been living rough, was in the same condition as Clare, and was waited on by the solicitous Freddie. Alexander knew his way round a South Indian menu far better than I did – but had suffered for it.

The Swinglers had also put up Ian on his way to me from Bangladesh, where Peter Evans – who had come to Caracas with him – was now in the Embassy. Having missed me with Clare, the car-key-crisis struck yet again – and for the last time – with Ian at Bangalore. It was I who had slammed the door with the keys inside this time and eventually we found a garage with a key that opened it. What was particularly annoying about this was that it happened just when I wanted to get away from a troublesome teacher. As it was, after bidding him a brisk 'Goodbye', I had to throw myself on his mercy. For another mishap on our travels Ian was himself responsible although I did not know it at the time.

In 1979, I had not heard of the Tamil Tigers and Sri Lanka was far more advanced than India – or at least South India – in tourist amenities. Penny Aspden, Ian and I made a threesome for a visit, hiring a car for a week there, and going from Madras by train and ferry in order to see the country on the way. The train was fairly rough and amazingly slow and in an upper bunk was an Aussie, also fairly rough and amazingly slow. Paul Theroux says somewhere that you know you have reached rock bottom in travelling facilities when you find yourself in the company of Aussie backpackers. I remembered his words when we found many of them on the boat from Cape Cormaran, stretched full length on the few available benches, leaving local mothers and babies (and, not for long, me) to stand. I had not paid much attention to the monosyllabic Aussie in our compartment but when we made a lengthy stop on the second day Ian, looking very pale and apparently running a temperature, said he felt ill and staggered out for some air. Awful visions of having to abort our plans and search for a doctor in a strange town, or of pushing on only to find Ian in a worse condition in the middle of nowhere, assailed me. But after a quarter of an hour, he said he felt a bit better and clambered aboard again. It wasn't until twenty years later that he revealed his indebtedness to the generous Aussie for his first experience of smoking pot.

We saw a fine variety of the sights and sites in Sri Lanka – Buddhist, Hindu, Dutch/Berger, British – but omitted the tea gardens, which I presumed echoed those in the Nilgiri Hills. I was intrigued to see in the Kandy Botanical Gardens the scene where 'The Bridge over the River Kwai' was made. Though infinitely cosier than the original, it was – when confined to the viewfinder – extraordinarily true to life. Certainly, after the beauties of Sri Lanka, Madras seemed flatter and more polluted than ever.

Balakrishna boasted a raised *porte cochère* that preserved the car from the monsoon rains that flooded the compound. In October I could step dryshod into the car in the morning and splash through the lake which by lunchtime would have dried off. In an effort to improve things I ordered a load of builders' rubble to raise the level of the path but was foiled by its delivery in a bullock cart – the entrance, of course, had a cattle grid to keep out wandering sacred cows. At Christmas I was well and truly marooned. Three days before it the carol singers got through to me ... at 4am. Thereafter it rained continuously, and by Christmas Day the water was 18 inches deep in the drive and within three inches of my carpets; I found the servants marooned on their beds, apparently quite used to it and adamant that they would not take refuge 'in Master's house'. I rang up Neville French, the Deputy High Commissioner, to say I was flooded out and couldn't get to his dinner party. (Had it not been designated 'dress lounge suit' I could have waded there in shorts and sandals.)

'Don't worry, old boy,' boomed Neville. 'We won't let you miss your Christmas dinner. I'll send the Land Rover for you.'

So I joined Sir Denis and Lady Wright, the German Consul and his English wife, and several Indian couples as guests for dinner which was followed by competitive party games and ended with progressive charades. Denis Wright was in Madras to deliver a lecture sponsored by Shell. We talked about our days in Iran and Turkey. He had been impressed by my prescience: the day after I had said what a mess Turkey was in it blew up. Neville, who had been an unhappy Governor of the Falkland Islands, was a tall impressive figure, which made visits by the High Commissioner, Sir John Thomson, a small donnish man, sometimes embarrassing. When they went on tour together Sir John was assumed to be of junior rank and tended to be left out of the conversation, which did not please him. He was already tipped for Washington, and the gossip columns were carrying items to that effect when Mrs Thatcher visited Delhi. It was said that she missed the attentions of Lady Thomson, who had elected to join a painting course at an art colony on the beach near Madras. At any rate Sir John went not to Washington but to the UN in New York.

Madras is as flat as a cow-pat and largely covered in it (and in water-buffalo-pat); women eagerly collect it all by hand to use as fuel. The place is also covered by man-pat and the stagnant rivers, prevented by sandbars from discharging regularly into the sea, stink with sewage. A *Murray's Guide* twenty years old claimed that there was excellent boating and sailing on the Adyar River, but when I saw the local rowing club tipping their cox into its scummy waters I thought that was carrying tradition too far. *Murray's* did, however, say that 'a houseboat trip on the Buckingham Canal is *not* recommended'.

I sometimes took an evening stroll along the banks of the noisome Coum River, averting my eyes from the citizens parking their Atlas bicycles and slipping secretively down to the weeds by the water's edge to add their contributions to it. Just below the Belgian Consulate was a relic of the hopeful town planning of yore, an elegant boathouse and pavilion on a stretch of bank that had been revetted and paved. I was passing this scene one evening with the poet Anthony Thwaite, a small solemn man who had been lecturing at a Ladies' Training College. As we walked I quoted Cecil Day Lewis's reply to Christopher Marlowe's 'Ode to a Shepherdess':

At evening by the sour canals
We'll hope to hear some madrigals.
Care on thy wanton brow shall put
A wreath of wrinkles, and thy foot
Be shod with pain; not silken dress
But toil shall tire thy loveliness.

Thwaite had never heard of it, which shows how quickly reputations fade as each generation embraces the newest academic fashion. I doubt if he knew the fifty years earlier 'Song of Madras' either:

Clive kissed me on the mouth and eyes and brow,
Wonderful kisses, so that I became
Crowned above Queens – a withered beldame now,
Brooding on ancient fame.

Robert Clive's stables were opposite the river pavilion and even more elegant. In lofty cream-coloured 18th-century Gothic trim, they boasted blind arrow slits and stuccoed brick pilasters, carved with pretty swags of flags, bunched gun barrels and neat pyramids of cannon balls. High archways opened onto the river, presumably for the horses to be watered. The stables were now education offices and not far away, in a park all by itself, was the little Victorian garrison theatre where I put on Ayckbourne's *Confusions*, but was myself confused, as in Guyana, to know how far one should adopt or adapt local speech patterns in metropolitan plays.

The street life thereabouts was in marked contrast to the wide empty avenues round Balakrishna. On the pavement were bicycle repairers with their puncture kits at the ready, trishaws with their oil lamps being lovingly polished by their riders, and shoe repairers – some of them so desperate for trade that they repaired even the flip-flops we consider expendable.

Then there were the motionless human heaps under rags in the gutter or slap in the middle of the pavements, swarms of children, mothers with babies and breastfed older children, boys leading blind beggars, and barely human creatures who waited by traffic lights to lollop across the road on all fours with India rubber limbs pointing the wrong way; people, people everywhere, and monkeys screaming in the trees, and carrion crows calling, and three-wheeler taxis darting about like dodgems, hooting incessantly. Skirting all this on quieter roads I sometimes saw ex-Queen Frederica of Greece bicycling with her daughter to study with their guru.

Madras is not a handsome town but there are handsome buildings in it. The Georgetown quarter is full of them, dating from the days of Clive and the Marquess of Wellesley, and St Mary's, the oldest Anglican church outside Britain, has good monuments. One is to Elihu Yale of Yale University, but a more remarkable monument to ecumenicalism is the inscription on that of the Danish missionary, Father Schwartz:

... Beloved and honoured by EUROPEANS
He was, if possible, held in still deeper Reverence
By the Natives of the Country of every Degree and every Sect:
the Late HYDER ALLY CAWN,
In the midst of a bloody and vindictive war with the CARNATIC,
Sent orders to his Officers 'to permit the
Venerable Father Schwartz to pass
Unmolested and shew him Respect and Kindness
For he is a holy Man, and means no harm to my Government....'

Government had long moved from Georgetown to the centre of town. We mounted an exhibition in the former Government House banqueting hall, a magnificently pillared and chandeliered room. It was opened by the Governor who arrived with his ADC in a Triumph Herald convertible. The portraits of past governors, including a Chinery and a Lawrence, had been replaced by hastily painted pictures of Indian worthies.

I attended the funeral at San Thomé Roman Catholic Cathedral of Sister Catherine MacLeary. A dynamic woman in her forties, she had cut herself off from her family when she left Liverpool eighteen years before to teach in Madras at Stella Maris Convent School. Switching to adult education for the poor, she built up a remarkable reputation and we readily co-operated in some of her ELT and other schemes. To do all this efficiently she bought a moped and was a familiar figure whizzing about among the trishaws and buffaloes and horses and carts – until she was knocked over and killed by a truck. The funeral, as was the custom, was on the next day, and was in Tamil. The large congregation included about 100 black and 20 white nuns, and the loudness and vivacity of it all helped to console us for our loss.

Inland from San Thomé was St George's Anglican cathedral, a handsome but rather heavy 1816 building with fine wall monuments by Chantrey and Durham, one commemorating Bishop Heber's short but sweet ministry in

India. The solemn congregation was not sure how to take the police band that augmented the carol service I attended. The initial pot pourri of traditional carols started reverently enough, but a thundering 'Jingle Bells' was followed by a jazz version of 'I'm dreaming of a White Christmas', and the band played us out with a *paso doble.* I thought Bishop Heber would have enjoyed it, though not perhaps the two parishioners commemorated on the tablets by my pew – a lieutenant who had died of cholera on the *Walmer Castle* on his way to the Chinese War, and his colonel who, while storming the fortress of Ching Ka Keou, was 'afflicted by a *coup de soleil* from which he afterwards expired'.

Not far from the Roman Catholic cathedral was the old Portuguese church of San Luz with its tombs of the De Vries family, but the one that everyone knows is the other Portuguese church, the one on St Thomas Mount, which commemorates the death of the saint at the hand, it is said, of a non-ecumenically-inclined Brahmin. The Mount is only 300 ft high but that is enough to command a wide prospect over the flat land surrounding it. I enjoyed the former army cantonment area nearby for being so spaciously designed and so sparing of people. This, I was to find, was also the case in towns like Hyderabad, Cannanore and Bangalore where the army did themselves proud and bequeathed the citizens a model of town planning. The Bangalore Cantonment was served by a pretty church whose cheerful atmosphere was belied by the fearful number of monuments to young people, particularly missionaries. One of the more ornate ones commemorated Lt Col Sir Walter Scott, Bart, who died aged 45.

Perhaps the most valuable land not yet built over in Madras, apart from its threadbare golf course, was the Adyar estate of the Theosophists, a private woodland on a peninsular dividing the town from the then undeveloped and endless beaches beyond. John Coats of the cotton family presided over the estate from his beachside house, and in a pavilion near the second largest banyan tree in India could be seen his Western guests – stout white women in saris and bare-chested pigtailed men in *longhis* sitting cross-legged at a lecture by an Indian lady with an old-fashioned Oxford accent. Dotted about in a Whispering Glades manner were temples and churches built in the style of various faiths. The Theosophists' own temple and museum contained statues of the prophets, magnanimously including Christ, and of Annie Besant and Madame Blavatsky and their subfusc menfolk. The literature lying about seemed to concentrate more on ecumenicalism than reincarnation.

Apart from some of its buildings, neighbouring attractions like Mahabalipuram and the old Dutch settlement of Sadras, Madras had little to boast of. But its general flatness and untidiness was curiously relieved by enormous hand-painted cinema posters. The Tamil Nadu film industry was big business, so big that (like Britain twenty years later) the media dominated not only the private but the public life of government and people. The Chief Minister, 'MGR', was a former film star, Maruthur Gopalar Ramachandrar, who had achieved stardom in the role of a rickshaw driver (more or less repeated in 135 films) and at sixty-one was desperately hanging onto his youth. He wore not only wrap-around dark glasses to conceal his wrinkles, and a wig, but also a fur cap with dark hair sewn round its edges. I only met him and his entourage once, and wondered how his heroines could bear to play opposite him, for he still liked to keep his image warm by appearing on screen from time to time, and always as the *jeune premier* of yore. But when he flew to New York in 1984 for a kidney transplant twenty girls committed suicide, and three years later twenty mourners were shot in the excitement of his funeral celebrations. It was not for nothing that he was regarded by the poorer people as a god.

21
Cities and Thrones and Powers

FORTUNATELY MADRAS was not the be-all and end-all of my bailiwick: we had libraries in Bangalore, Hyderabad and Trivandrum – and, in the first two, lecturers and specialists, as well as educational links in Mysore, Tiruchchirappalli, Tanjore and Cochin. Each of these towns had its fascination and the country between them was strewn with monuments to the ancient past.

Bangalore, a slow six-hour drive from Madras, was sometimes referred to as 'the garden city', though as India's techno-centre it has probably become unrecognisable now. Even then its fine bungalows and large gardens were fast disappearing, but the ample parkland was still presided over by statues of Queen Victoria, Edward VII and George V, and there was something of a holiday atmosphere in the air. It was much cooler, certainly, but more importantly the state of Karnataka was not 'dry' like Tamil Nadu. Unfortunately my favourite hotel, the beautiful old West End, all too often *was* dry – that is, of water. Its staff were immaculately dressed in traditional costume, the rooms were beautifully furnished and there was a swimming pool; but nothing worked. The water or the power was constantly cut off and the glorious beer, or the soda water one had to wash in, was at room temperature. A notice informed me that the bill included a service charge and I was requested not to tip the staff, but when I left the bearer appeared and introduced the cleaning woman, while three porters fought over two modest bags, and as I was stepping into the car a man appeared who announced he had cleaned my shoes.

Our library in Bangalore was well run by its Indian staff but things were running less smoothly with an ELT lecturer at a training college and with a visiting professor of psychiatry at a post-graduate institute. The ELT mismatch was a recruiting failure on our part; the visiting professorship, like many in India, fell foul of local politics. Whereas short academic attachments were welcome, longer tenure sooner or later aroused jealousies; reports and recommendations would be shelved and mysterious difficulties would arise over the renewal of visas. In this instance the personable incumbent was Morris Carstairs, former Vice Chancellor of York University, Reith lecturer, author *of The Twice-Born* and himself born in Mussoorie. ('He's a friend of Judith Hart,' said Peter Moss darkly, 'so be careful what you say!') If anyone could make a go of things Morris could, but though he went on to a second attachment at Chandigarh I think he felt his words had been graven in sand. He was accompanied by Nancy Hardin, a pretty young 'literary journalist' from Texas, whom it was understood he was to marry. I don't know what her journalism was like but, as Norma Moss wryly remarked, she had no trouble in turning the heads of all the men in any room she happened to enter.

When I made my last, 1,500 mile, journey with the Council driver, Venugopal, to open the new library in Hyderabad, Nancy proposed getting a lift with us from Bangalore to Hyderabad and back, taking in Dharwar (our most northerly university link), Badami and the Mogul monuments at Bijapur. But when we called to collect her Morris announced with a long face, but perhaps with relief, that she had had to fly suddenly to the States to see her ailing father. I don't think she and Morris ever did get married. Academics, if we are to believe Malcolm Bradbury and David Lodge, are more tolerant of each other's lifestyles than the rest of us. At a seminar in Hyderabad I met again Bob Lepage, whom I had last seen in Guyana, with Andrée, an amiable professor from Strasbourg, with whom, he said blandly, he often arranged to share seminars overseas. I foolhardily invited Bob and Andrée to dine with me but had made the mistake of trying a new hotel, the Bonjara. The lift was not working, buckets of cement stood about on the unfinished staircase with no banisters, the bar was unfinished and the air-conditioning only worked at full blast or not at all. It was all too easy in India to find a hotel that was either run down or not yet run in; the problem was to find one in-between.

On the outskirts of Bangalore is a suburb called Whitefield developed by the Ruler of Mysore at the turn of the century for retired civil servants. In this cosy Anglo-Indian nest of neat over-furnished bungalows and tidy gardens the L Ron Hubbard of Bangalore, Sai Baba, had laid his cuckoo's egg, a huge complex of shrine, hospital and guesthouse in purple and pink, and rumour had it that some quite respectable local academics were about to help him turn it into a university. All this had grown from his trick of materialising gold watches out of the air for prospective disciples. It was not to recruit a psychiatrist for Sai Baba that I went to Whitefield but to call on Leslie Johnson, a retired ICS colleague of my brother David. I called on the wrong Johnson first; he turned out to be a cousin, and over the shoulder of the girl who answered the door in hair curlers and jeans I caught sight of a cluttered room looking like the lounge of a Thirties golf club.

'Come in and have a drink,' said her father – a far cry from Madras where drinks were as scarce as women in jeans. Leslie also, when I reached him, was not long in offering me a drink. He was a dapper man who sounded very English; his wife, a placid Swedish missionary's daughter, was nursing a very Indian-looking grandson.

Leslie was bursting to reminisce about the good old days of Empire and the decline of India and Pakistan ever since. He had intended to retire to Dehra Dun but 'it hadn't worked out'. The Whitefield Anglo-Indian colony with its Anglican church, Anglo-Indian chaplain, equable climate, formal drives and big gardens was a good deal more attractive than many of the cold, trafficky places people like me were likely to end up in, but there was a deep melancholy about their situation – an atmosphere of simultaneous fly-in-amber immobility and impending break-up. Where, in their shoes, would we feel most at home – in India or in England? The most prominent Anglo-Indian I knew was the impressive Police Chief in Madras, a fine figure of a man; he was looking forward to his retirement – in Australia.

It was in Bangalore, supposedly the most go-ahead city in the south, that I first had to go to a government department in person, instead of sending one of our Mr Fixits as I did in Madras, and it made me wonder how far its present state differed from that under the Raj. The place was crammed from floor to ceiling with cardboard files and brown paper parcels, endless supplicants squatted resignedly on steps and in corridors, and the great panjandrum himself, Jarndyce in the flesh, played God with cups of tea.

One of the attractions of Bangalore was that it was near Mysore and on the way to Shrirangapattana. There were no beggars round the tomb of Tipu Sultan, which was clean and well-kept, but that of Colonel Baillie nearby was much scribbled over. From Ker Porter's painting of 'the storming' I had expected the fort to be on a hill, but it was rather Famagusta-like, flat with intricate double fortifications, redoubts, and moats with a water gate opening onto an animated scene of washerwomen in the river. The mosque was small but the summer palace was a fine one, with French pencil drawings of the Sultan's family and two huge murals of the battle. The isolated and overgrown cemetery of Swiss mercenaries was particularly evocative, and Father Schwart's little grey 18th-century church was still standing.

On my first visit to Mysore I stayed at the Old Residency, which had become a government resthouse. It was empty except for the usual posse of bearers, and the billiard and dining room were gloomy in the extreme. On the walls were portraits of the Maharajas and some Indian landscapes, but also *The Stag at Bay* and a Scottish house party scene by Landseer. Beside the entrance was a plaque: 'Occupied by Sir John Malcolm 1803-1807' and in the library was a bookcase of dusty books: *How Strong is Britain?* by Count Puckner (Right Book Club), Hakluyt's *Voyages*, *Everyone's Political What's What* and *In Another Girl's Shoes* by Berta Ruck. When I left I wondered if it would be insulting to tip the impressive major-domo, who was after all a government employee, and I asked Venugopal if he would be offended. He smiled.

'No, sir.'

'How much? Five rupees, or ten?'

'Five rupees will do, sir.'

I held out five rupees to the venerable figure and his hands enfolded them like the tongue of a chameleon round a fly.

Later I stayed at the Lalith Palace Hotel, the former Maharaja's guesthouse, which stood looking like a lost St Paul's a couple of miles out of town. The lawns stretched beguilingly down in four descending levels to ... nothing. The double staircase in marble was like the V & A's, there were vast tiled verandahs, a noble billiard room, well-appointed bedrooms with good carpets, swag curtains, mahogany closets, brass window fittings and prints of temples by the Daniels and *Hunting Jackals* by Captain Bonington. But there was no hot water. In the echoing ballroom I drank half my curry soup and abandoned the rest of my dinner. At breakfast a girl sat sniffing and blowing her nose in a corner while a babble of noise emerged from behind a screen. After five minutes I shouted, 'Is anybody serving breakfast in this establishment?' The noise reverberated round the chandeliers, the girl's head came up with a start, stopping her sniffs abruptly, and there was dead silence behind the screen. At last a bearer came in to take my order and ten minutes later, when the girl's mother, an American, entered, the noise was in full flow again. She walked behind the screen and I heard her say diffidently, 'Excuse me!', and the noise was turned off once more.

I overheard her again later, when she was leaving for her tour, talking to the receptionist.

'You know, that kitchen is not as clean as it ought to be. There's a lot of trash lying around. Now, will you get someone to clear it away?'

'Yes, madam. Of course, madam.'

'And you'll do it right away?'

'At once, madam!'

The most cheerful of the palaces was in town and had been shipped out at the turn of the century from Glasgow. It was a riot of art nouveau stained glass, mirrors, cast iron pillars and painted roof trusses and displayed a confidence and exuberance unthinkable today. I was given a guided tour with Donald Insall, the conservation architect responsible for the Wren Library at Trinity, Cambridge, who came out on a lecture tour for us. We were escorted by the Director of Archaeology, Najadraya Rao, who had recently been to Russia. He had not enjoyed the endless queuing for 'airport ogresses', the awful hotel rooms, hanging about for tourist buses and the agony of trying to get food that was fresh and suitable for a vegetarian.

Donald Insall told me his family had been in the luggage business in Bristol for three generations. 'I have got one of your products,' I said. 'I bought it second-hand for £11 from Skuse, the saddlers in Lower Redland Road, just before I sailed for South America in 1946.' And I brought out my heavy solid leather trunk, full of flaps and tongues and striped pockets and buckles and straps, with INSALL MAKER BRISTOL stamped deeply into the leather at each end on the outside and, on a flap inside in scarlet and gold lettering, 19 & 20 ST AUGUSTINE'S PARADE – W INSALL AND SONS – BRISTOL. I had had the trunk refurbished in Ankara, and when it eventually finished its travels with me I gave it to Donald as a family heirloom.

Another memorable place in Mysore was the Institute of Sereculture. Originally introduced, or at least encouraged, by Tipu Sultan to keep his Muslim women out of mischief (women fed the silkworms rather as farmers' wives do chickens, while the men looked after the mulberry trees), the industry greatly expanded during World War II, with the demand for silk in parachutes and maps, and also – with Japanese help – afterwards. Now India ranked fifth after Japan, South Korea, China and Russia for silk production. Unlike the highly mechanised and two-crop Japan, India had four or five crops a year, and tried to keep the industry labour-intensive. So far she had been successful but the factories were increasingly threatened by strike action. Happily the silk worms were not aware of this during my visit, and I could hear them munching away at the mulberry leaves in their trays, which were refilled every four hours. It sounded like rain pattering on a distant window pane.

Mysore is only 15 miles from the foothills of the Nilgiris. From the steeper Madras side one can ascend them on the little train; from Mysore the approach is through forests and lakes and wildlife sanctuaries, and I saw my first Toda 'tribals'. They were attractive to look at and made the same kind of patterned articles as South American Indians. In their villages higher up they lived largely with or on their buffaloes, and as they rubbed their bodies with buffalo fat and never washed they were not easily missed. As the road zigzagged up for an hour and a half, the scruffy overcrowded villages gave way to neat tea plantations with names like 'Prospect' and 'Lidderdale'. The patterns of the bushes seen from above looked like endless green tripe. Women wearing sacking and plastic bags to keep the rain off their heads picked the bushes in gangs, and I could hear their chattering coming across the valleys like birds in an aviary. At the top the scenery became very grand, with beetling cliffs and awesome views down through the clouds to the plain below, until – whoops! – suddenly I was round the last bend and over the pass into rolling green meadows, streams, pine trees, lakes, palaces, villas and a golf course. But Ootacamund, the Queen of the Nilgiris, was cold, wet and deserted now that the rains had started and the 'season' was over. At Ooty Club I was the only guest. It stands on a verdant slope at 7,440 ft where Sir William Rumbold built it in 1882, and it was here that Lord William Bentinck, who had rented it, received Macaulay. And it was here that the lonely bored Club Secretary, Colonel Appiya, and his wife received me and shared the dining room with me for three days of olde worlde comfort – except for the wet without and the dry within, for I was back in Tamil Nadu after the liberal regime of Karnataka. Yet I did not feel that we dined alone.

The ghosts of former members looked eager to emerge from their portraits, like the Murgatroyd ancestors in *Ruddigore*. In the bars were Ackermann prints of cockfighting (*Throat: O Mighty Caesar Dost Thou Lie So Low?*) and Cecil Aldin paintings of the Devon and Somerset Hunt and *The Card Game*. On the walls of the billiard room the mildew was beginning to attack *Scotland for Ever!* by Mrs (not yet Lady) Elizabeth Butler. Next to the cube-stand a framed 1939 letter from Colonel Sir Neville Chamberlain described how as a subaltern in the Devonshire Regiment he had invented and introduced snooker to the club in 1875.

In the lobby were an armchair weighing machine and height measurer, photo albums of the 1953 Coronation Ball, and the last Complaints Book dating from 1955:

> 'At dinner while serving chicken and boiled peas it was found that the peas contained live worms. This completely upset the apitite [*sic*] of the table. I am unable to understand as to how a club with such a good reputation for food can allow such a thing. K Rajagopal, Coimbatore.'

'The incident is very much regretted and the staff concerned have been warned to be more carefull [*sic*] in future. My apologies to the members for the unintentional annoyance caused. C R Campbell, 4.10.76.'

There were now about 150 club members, mostly Indians, who belonged 'for the sake of belonging' and only appeared during the two-month 'season'. The billiard table, still in perfect condition, was permanently shrouded; there was no riding in town, except at the races, and there were no dances. 'No activities,' said Colonel Appiya forlornly, 'even in the season. It is terrible, terrible!' Nor could the poor colonel drown his sorrows; Colonel Jago's Room only echoed to a discreet clink when the Committee met and brought their drink permits with them. At other times the Appiyas, who lived in the Secretary's house down the drive, were left to moon about the empty rooms watching the elderly staff polishing the brass nameplates and wiping the panelling, eat in solitary splendour, waited upon by the old retainer, or read four-month-old copies of *The Field*, *Blackwoods*, *Reveille* or *News of the World*. The only club member I met was a Scots tea planter named Duff who had driven down and up for four hours from his British Co-op estate on the neighbouring range of Annamalai hills to attend a committee meeting.

Neighbouring mansions were schools or hotels: the Maharaja of Mysore's palaces were in poor shape; in the Fernhill Imperial the family pictures were still on the walls – *The Meet of the Ootacamund Hunt at Fernhill 1939* – and a few Indian families were having whispery lunches in a huge ballroom where the curtains over the big windows were shredding away from their rings. At St Stephen's Church on Sunday morning you could have counted the congregation with one hand, apart from the girls of the Anglo-Indian St Hilda's School. The only 'white' school, Hebron College in Lushington House, was run by clean-cut missionaries from the white Commonwealth (who, as Baptists, patronised the Union Church). The school had oppressive texts posted all over the walls and twelve O Level boys had recently been expelled for sharing a bottle of beer in the town. The Council did not assist private or mission schools financially, whatever the colour of their pupils, apart from allowing them membership of its libraries. At Wellington not far away, and once the Sandhurst of South India, I visited a large English-medium school for Indian boys, but such schools were now considered elitist and, in clinging to old colonial curricula, misguided, and were not offered VSO teachers or equipment.

In Ooty it was difficult to reconcile the seigniorial appearance of the rolling meadows and lawns and lakes, the lodges and driveways and neat hedges with the scruffy figures walking miserably about in the rain and the tatty lower town with its 1952 Standard Vanguard and Vauxhall taxis. There was a similar dichotomy, as I was to see, in the smaller hill towns like Kotagiri and Coonoor, each with its little Church of South India (CSI) church and British chaplain. In Kodaikanal the small church of St Peter's, perched at one end of the spectacular cliff edge, 'Croaker's Walk', was more romantic outside than inside, where a liberal deposit of India's ubiquitous curse sat proprietorially in the nave.

The Planters' Club at Munnar was a humble version of Ooty. In the library was a shelf labelled BOOKS ON LOAN FROM THE BRITISH COUNCIL; it was empty. Kodai was smaller and quieter and the missionary hand lay heavily on it. I stayed at the Carlton Hotel, formerly British-run and still with an elderly stayer-on from the Midlands, 'looking after its books'. A cupboard contained its library of missionary memories, Pearl Buck and *Mr Wells Replies to Mr Belloc's Criticism of his Outline of History*, all lovingly bound, titled and numbered in brown paper long years ago. The houses in Kodai were grouped round a lake with the co-educational American Lutheran School bang in the middle of the village. 'We try to keep our girls away from the American School's pupils,' said Sister Cecilia, Mother Superior of the Presentation School. 'Drugs, you know; and there have been one or two pregnancies.' Sister Cecilia was Goanese. Her father had worked in oil camps in Abadan and Aden 'in the good old days'.

'Which way are you going now?'

'To Madurai.'

'On your way you must call on Brother James Kimpton at St Joseph's Boys' Village.'

So I did, and a very neat and busy place it was with its model farm of cotton, vines, loofah and mulberry trees all created by this deceptively ordinary-looking Salesian from Manchester. There was a school for village boys and he also worked with lepers. He looked like a rather fit bank manager or headmaster or perhaps a colonel of the RAOC, and had come here from Ceylon when his place was expropriated by the government. He wore smart trousers and shoes and a well-tailored silk shirt with a cross very faintly embroidered on the chest. British school-leavers and recent graduates would come out to help for a few months, and one rode past looking very happy on a locally made Royal Enfield. Brother James was completely unassuming and matter-of-fact but clearly had authority, was efficient and as patient as Job. He hadn't been home for ten years but had an occasional holiday with Sister Cecilia up the hill. 'She's Mother Cecilia really, but they are all called Sister nowadays.'

Was there more in that than met the eye? After all, what is the point of being good all the time if you can't enjoy an occasional well-earned sin?

And so back to Balakrishna and Freddie bustling out ('Have a good time, sir?'), old Mari beaming and salaaming in the background, the gardener twirling his drooping white moustache under the tamarind tree, Freddie's three children and Joseph's grandson lined up outside their quarters and saluting, Freddie's wife as usual very much in the background by the water tap, and two new ducks waddling about.

'Hullo, Freddie, are you starting a duck farm now that Joseph has made you get rid of the rabbits?'

'They were very cheap in the market, sir. So we'll keep them some time until they are worth more. Tonight it is roast pigeon and bread and butter pudding.'

My first visit to Hyderabad was to look at a prospective site for a new library. There was a devil-may-care atmosphere about the place that made a pleasant change from the muted and prim air of Madras. The town centre round the great four-minaretted Charminar mosque was exceedingly scruffy and very lively – four or even five children squashed into a rickshaw on their way to school was quite usual – while the racecourse, cantonment and university area preserved a dignified quiet. (It was there that I later attended a breast-beating and nit-picking seminar on E M Forster and Wordsworth, and wondered treasonably which of the two subjects was more inspiring for young India and which view of Forster to favour – his canonisation by the local lady lecturer or Simon Raven's description of Forster at King's as an 'idle, pampered, sanctimonious and spiteful old man, pathologically mean with money and forever sucking up to the working class'.) I was brought up short by an accident on the outskirts of the town in the chaos of bicycles, carts, trucks and rickshaws. An enormous ox stood patiently bleeding in the roadway beside a jeep that had run into its cart, tearing off one long curved horn at the root and leaving it lying like a severed limb on the ground. Elsewhere there were the usual admonishments to unheeding drivers: 'COURTESY COSTS NOTHING CARELESSNESS COSTS LIVES'; 'PLEASE HORN'; 'WE LIKE YOU BUT NOT YOUR SPEED'; 'NO HORNING'; 'BETTER LATE ON EARTH THAN EARLY IN HEAVEN'.

As it turned out we were a bit early in heaven with our *pujah* celebrations for the library site. Although the auspices were good, planning permission fell through and we eventually opened in another part of the town. Meanwhile we squatted in the selected corner, the south-east, towards which the walls must be oriented, and two *pujah* professionals decorated us with red powder on our foreheads and pinches of this and that elsewhere, waved lighted tapers about, demolished bananas and melons, squashed limes, murmured incantations and concluded operations by smashing open a coconut. Apparently workmen were apprehensive of starting work without such preliminaries. I watched a couple of drivers preparing their taxis for use at a wedding going through similar precautionary measures. Weddings could only be celebrated at an auspicious time, even if it was at 4am, on an auspicious day, and never on a Tuesday or Friday; limes were put several times under the wheels and the cars rocked over them; naphtha flares were passed over salient points of the exterior and inside on the steering wheel, door handles and gear lever; and finally a coconut was smashed open on the ground and small boys scrambled for the pieces.

Among the chaotic traffic was a sight that I would not have seen in Madras – a man cycling along with a box of meat on the carrier and, sitting on the box and tearing at the meat, two carrion crows. Further on, another bullock had collapsed in the shafts of its cart and sat immovably on the ground. A boy lifted its tail and lit a straw bonfire under its anus to get it going again. A hoarding proclaimed, 'AN HONEST WORKER ENJOYS THE ESTEEM OF ALL'. That week the Deputy High Commissioner was to present a £4,000 ambulance to the local SPCA.

At 7 o'clock one morning, before it got too hot, our ELT expert took me to Golconda, the old capital and fortress five miles away where the Qutub Shahis ruled from the 14th century until 1686, when it was betrayed to Aurangzeb. Its passages were full of kinks and maze-like dead-ends where attackers could be ambushed; a hand-clap at the city gates was audible in the citadel and from the Throne Terrace at the top the Sultan could hear his favourite mistresses, Taramati and Pemamati, singing in the pavilions a kilometre away. Everywhere there was a suffocating smell of bat.

At breakfast I met the ELT expert's wife, who had bare feet and rings on her toes, and at a drinks party that evening I found that bare feet were *de rigueur* with some of the FAO guests. One of these, working on crops that would give a better yield, was Rupert Sheldrake, a biochemist who was also gestating his theory of 'morphic resonance'. This purported to explain why simultaneous discoveries are made by scientists in different parts of the world unknown to and independently of each other. It later made headline news when applied to dogs. 'Morphic fields' inherited from ancestral memory, he claimed, radiated telepathy ('distant feeling') in them so that they sensed events about to affect their masters. They had presentiments and precognition; for example, they knew when a man left his office miles away and went to the front door to greet him at the precise moment he reached home.

I did eventually open the new library, but in part of an existing building. Long queues of hopeful members stretched down the street and round the corner. Later visits never recaptured quite the variety and at the same time the I-have-been-here-before feeling of that first visit. Indeed I can almost swear to having seen, as I sat on the upstairs verandah of Percy's Hotel in the witching hour, the spruce figure of Dr Aziz trotting his pony across the old racecourse.

Above me a ceiling fan creaked slowly round and now and again I heard a tinkle of glass, as a sparrow flew in and perched on the chandelier. Below me immaculately dressed Indians were playing cricket. Up the road was the cantonment arca, whcrc British troops had been ostentatiously housed to remind the Nizam of their presence. The Nizam's own troops were quartered in an early Victorian camp on the way to Golconda and the modern Indian army seemed to have expanded into both. Their shorts were even wider than I remembered them in 1942 and much shorter, and as they were rigidly starched they looked like khaki ballet skirts. Also up the road – and near the British cemetery – was the long, low, creeper-covered Hyderabad Club, which looked delightful at night but the worse for wear by day. I had dined there the night before with the vice-chancellors of two universities.

'I was sorry to see,' I said, 'the beautiful facade of Osmania University – "Indo-Saracenic" my guidebook calls it – covered with graffiti. I was a bit puzzled by some of the slogans: "FIGHT FOR SCIENTIFIC EDUCATION" and "WE WANT SCIENTIFIC EDUCATION". I thought they had all too much scientific education nowadays. What do they mean?'

'They mean they want "scientific socialism", that is to say Marxism; they want Marxist education.'

One VC was in a very jumpy mood because eight thugs had just beaten up three of his staff. As in Turkey, the student body was a very amorphous one: anyone could be a student for years and India didn't even have national service to curtail it, so students often enrolled for full and part-time courses, getting grants for both and thus deferring indefinitely the awful fate of returning to their villages.

While the Nizam's palaces – many of them open and looted – were rotting away, he himself was on his sheep farm in Australia with his Turkish begum. The Hindus said that the Muslims in the old days never did a stroke of work and life was very leisurely. Many noble old houses now languished under ignoble notice boards – Andhra Pradesh Fingerprints Department and suchlike – and perhaps none nobler or more ignoble than the former British Residency, now the Hyderabad Women's College. The size of the place, with its grounds and offices and barracks, made one understand how, for instance, Lucknow resisted the mutineers for so long. It was built for the first Resident, James Achilles Kirkpatrick, in 1802, in the Nash Regent's Park style: a gigantic Grecian portico topped a wide flight of seventeen steps flanked by two enormous Landseer-type lions, and a confident but slightly blackened royal coat of arms filled the architrave. Inside enormous circular stairwells ran round cream plastered walls under moulded ceilings, many of them domed. The durbar room was lined with mirrors from Carlton House and surrounded by a gallery for spectators. Two portcullises divided the core of the house from its flanking pavilions; the powder magazine was in the cellars. The Principal of the Women's College had studied mathematics at Cambridge and was a Communist, as was her husband. Outside in one of the niches in the wall under her office I noticed a small gravestone and, clearing away the monkeys that were playing king-of-the-castle on it, I read the following inscription:

MY BELOVED
FUIE
WHOSE TAIL STILL
WAGS IN MY HEART
ALISON LOTHIAN
NOV 24th 1946

I had brought with me to read at Hyderabad the slimmest volume I could find at a dash into the Madras library – *King Solomon's Mines.* I had forgotten what compulsive reading it was. 'Our dinners of giraffe steaks and roasted marrowbones were ready ... I know of no greater luxury than giraffe marrow, unless it is elephant's heart, and we had that on the morrow.' Alan Quartermaine is jealous of Commander Good's superb sets – he had two – of false teeth; yet Good is only thirty-one! And Haggard made good use of italics: 'The brute seized the poor Zulu, hurled him to the earth, and placing one huge foot onto his body about the middle, twined its trunk round his upper part and *tore him in two.*' I wonder what Haggard would have made of Hyderabad.

I went to Kerala to look at training schemes in Trivandrum with Peter Collister, the ODM Educational Adviser I had met in Cyprus. Peter Moss was also on tour in the area and we took a couple of days' leave to rendezvous at the Covalam Beach Hotel, then a pioneer in the infant tourist industry. Soon after Coimbatore, roadside notices had signalled the end of Tamil Nadu prohibition, 'TODDY SHOP' they read, 'TOADY SHOP', 'TIPSY HOTEL WINES', 'DRIVE-IN TODDY'. The houses boasted ornate wooden balconies and projecting eaves and steep tiled roofs, for this greenest of states was famous for its rain.

Everything here was more colourful than in the east, and there seemed to be every conceivable sort of church, the earliest dating from the 9th century Mar Toma Syrian Rite (with the Patriarch marooned in the ruins of Mardin in Turkey), through Orthodox, Jacobite, Anglican (CSI), Roman Catholic, Assembly of God, and Seventh Day Adventist. Huge 'cathedrals' of every persuasion and architectural style had Portuguese facades tacked onto naves like cinemas or garages, tall narrow towers like Big Ben picked out in chocolate and blue, domes and pinnacles in yellow and purple, spires in a peculiarly Indian bluey-green that left one feeling slightly queasy, tall shrines with silver figures of St George or blue Madonnas in concrete and glass. Free-standing towers or spires often served as a lych gate on the road, with a long path dipping and rising to the church well back on the hillside. There were also great Gothic English-medium schools – St Anthony's High School, The Good Shepherd Higher Secondary School, The Queen Mother School (which Queen Mother?) – for this most literate and thickly populated state supplied the Arabian Gulf with its work force. There were also hammers and sickles and anti-government slogans: 'NO DEMOCRACY WITH BANNED ENGLISH AND COW SLAUGHTER', and a hoarding announced 'PM 30 APRIL GORKY'S MOTHER DRAMA BY BRECHT'. The women seemed handsomer than elsewhere (except in Rajasthan where they look and dress like well-to-do gypsies). This may have been due to their slimmer midriffs or because there was so much time to observe them when held up by road works. They toiled on the roads, in gangs, pushing gravel about, using only their hands and baskets which they carried on their heads. It was painful to compare their graceful and straight-backed carriage with that of older women (but not as much older as they looked) working bent double, and often permanently so, in the fields.

The Covalam Beach Hotel was spectacularly sited and beautifully designed. The menu too was beautifully designed, but with promises that were unfulfilled: everything was tinned, the rice was cold and the coffee was stewed; rubbish was thrown into the garden, laundry was not collected, and morning calls were forgotten. The beach below the hotel was supposed to be reserved for guests, but the 'tourist police' were ignored and the locals, disdaining the miles of empty beach beyond, swarmed onto it and sat gazing raptly at the strange foreigners who seemed to like going into the water and sitting about half-naked. The hippies, too, had begun to discover this beach and I was waylaid by one of them who said he had been sleeping on the beach for three months but had caught hepatitis and cabled home for money.

When it finally arrived he had lost his travellers' cheques as he boarded a bus outside the bank. At least that was his story; he came from Wigan.

Peter Collister had had a gruelling schedule across the country, and later described our visit in a memoir:

> Afterwards I spent the weekend at a hotel beach resort where I was joined by Stephen Alexander ... It made a brave attempt to be like a beach resort hotel elsewhere except that our bookings had gone wrong and we were deposited in nearby cottages and instead of the fresh prawns and sea food advertised we were offered tinned pilchards. The last straw for Stephen was when our enclosed beach area was invaded by locals and he hurled himself at the tourist office in a few strides of his long legs ... I returned to Madras with Stephen who had become a friend and whose company and occasional short fuse I had come to respect.

I certainly respected Peter's old-world courtesy. In later years I bumped into him one day in the Mall as the Horse Guards were marching down it. As the colours passed he raised his hat. 'I always salute the colours!' he said. At Covalam we were sitting on the terrace one evening with some of the package tourists who had usurped our rooms when an elderly and not very spry lady had trouble with her deck chair. Peter Moss and I barely registered her predicament, but Peter Collister leapt to his feet, gave her an arm, adjusted the chair and resettled her. Evidently unused to such treatment from the (comparatively) young, she was touchingly grateful. (Perhaps, too, she had a professional interest in his behaviour; it transpired she was Ruth Glass, a specialist in Urban Studies and Social Science.) Collister's influence on the Council was invaluable. His judgement of educational projects was invariably sound and he was admirably free from cant:

> I was at times critical of our procedure until I got to know UNESCO, the EC and later, in a retirement job, the UN, when in retrospect our procedures seemed the acme of efficiency ... The work was always interesting and preferable to peddling the latest trendy-lefty educational concepts to long-suffering teachers, and to local authorities the virtues of structural changes in the name of egalitarianism. (Even HM Inspectorate, like the rest of the establishment in the Sixties, was affected by *the Trahison des Clercs* and communal death wish of which Matthew Arnold, the first of our predecessors, would not have approved.)

Cochin had much more to offer the tourist than Trivandrum and no doubt offers it now with aplomb. I found the hotels abysmal and it was particularly exasperating when, during dinner at the grandly conceived but run down Malabar Hotel on Willingdon Island, the lights kept going out yet one could see the blazing lights of ships anchored only a few yards away. I should probably have stayed at the old 'Dutch Palace' on Bolgatty Island, used as the British Residency after the Dutch were thrown out in the Napoleonic Wars. Like the best of the old Dutch mansions in Guyana, it was like a great white tent with generous square windows, elegant shutters, beautiful fanlights, enormous verandahs, a high-pitched roof and the interior divided up by dark wooden partition walls. The Dutch had taken over from the Portuguese in the 16th century and the old fort area still welcomes the traveller with the lovely sight of graceful counterbalanced fishing nets, like those in Macau. They swing out from the shore and then swing back again like giant swans taking off and – again and again – thinking better of it.

In the Church of St Francis, where Vasco da Gama is buried, the original hand-operated punkahs (as opposed to ceiling fans) ran down the length of the church, with mini-punkahs for the lectern and pulpit. Portuguese tombstones were lined up in the north wall and Dutch ones in the south, with inferior British memorials on the pillars. In the Dutch baptismal book a late 18th-century minister complains that a parishioner, instead of giving him the baptismal information in person, had handed it to his clerk, no doubt because he hadn't been near the church for *'twei jaaren'* and moreover had never brought his other son to church. 'What do you think of that?' he concludes in the margin.

The main tourist attraction was Jews Town. The trade of money-lending had passed to the Gujeratis and there were only about eighty pale and sickly-looking Jews left (the young ones having emigrated) who lived on as *rentiers* in the mediaeval houses and workshops, with names like Sassoon Hall, backing onto the harbour. A large dead rat was lying at the end of the cul-de-sac in front of the larger synagogue which belonged to the White Jews. Inside were lovely chandeliers, carved woodwork and a floor paved with Chinese tiles, none of them of quite the same pattern. A smaller synagogue belonging to the Black Jews, who claim to have arrived in 587 BC, was not open to the public. The Jews I spoke to had a courtly manner and spoke like well-educated northern Indians.

I splashed through the rain to a temporary straw theatre where there was a tourist show of Kathckali Thcatrc. Thc rcal thing lasts from 9pm till dawn, and this was just a demonstration of the conventions used in portraying the religious myths of Hindu culture, followed by a short duet. The men were dressed in skirts and stuffed brassieres (there are no actresses) and perhaps only Indians (or Indonesians, Chinese or Japanese) could have the patience, stamina and dubious taste to turn such conventions into a fine art (or vice versa).

In finding my way about I eventually learned to lengthen my fuse. It was no good addressing people too suddenly or saying something unexpected. Many Indians lived by formulae from which one must depart only in easy stages. For instance, instead of asking a bystander, 'Is that St Francis' Church?' and getting a blank look, one must first say, 'Good morning!'

'Good morning.'

'You OK?'

'Yes, OK.'

'What is that building?'

'That building is chirrooch.'
'Chirrooch?'
'Yes, chirrooch.'
'Ah! Chirrooch has name?'
'Yes, chirrooch name Sanfran Sees.'
'Ah! Sanfran Sees? Good! Thank you very much.'
'No problem.'

It is easy to make fun of Indian habits – the speech patterns, the admonitory notices, the caste system, the superstitions, the quaint Victorian ideas of right and wrong. It is not easy to make fun of the sheer fecundity of the place – the superfluity of human beings, with its poverty-cull, the seething mass of humanity frothing over into opulence and vulgarity, self-denial and half-being. Where do outsiders fit into all this? I think the British still regard India with a proprietorial feeling; we are all mini Kiplings and many still try – and fail – to become part of it. But long as our colonial relationship was, ancient ruined cities put it in perspective: between my four library towns were the ruins of Golconda, Gingee, Halebid, Hampi and countless more. Somehow women pushing little stones about have replaced them with the Tanjores, the Cochins and the Ootys of today. I could only peer beneath one of India's surfaces, which I was attempting to keep polished, but I think our proprietorial air is justified. If the French had colonised India, it might now be more fun for tourists but it would be less fun for the people. Today one senses that India always had a life of her own, irrespective of governments, and that she still has.

Cities and Thrones and Powers
Stand in Time's eye,
Almost as long as flowers
Which daily die:
But, as new buds put forth
To glad new men,
Out of the spent and unconsidered Earth
The Cities rise again.

22
Searchers

INDIA HAS ALWAYS been the happy hunting ground of Westerners looking for the exotic combined with a familiar infrastructure and low cost of living, and it is not surprising that I should stumble across some of them on the periphery of my official duties. A few scruffy British searchers after truth used our Bangalore library; they lived at an ashram and affected Indian dress. Others of a less contemplative bent started philanthropic enterprises with which they could attract charitable funds and build a little empire for themselves – and perhaps their partners. Then there were the missionaries, aid workers and British Council teachers who detached themselves from their governing bodies to set up on their own. The doyen of the holy men was Dom Bede Griffiths, who ran the Shantivanam Ashram on the wooded banks of the sacred Cauvery River near Tiruchchirappalli.

I had an introduction to Bede because he had been at Oxford with my brother Noel. After coming down, he and two friends, Martyn Skinner and Hugh Waterman, had formed a triumvirate to lead a simple life of contemplation, study and self-improvement. They rented a cottage on the Cotswolds and were supposed to be self-supporting while each pursued his own particular discipline. In fact they were saved from the worst privations of incompetent agronomy by Skinner patrimony (Sir Sidney was Managing Director of John Barker's) and the triumvirate soon broke up, Martyn to pursue farming and poetry seriously, and Hugh to become a schoolmaster. Alan Griffiths, however, moved from low church to high church and then to Roman Catholicism and finally – as Dom Bede – to a Benedictine cloister. After Prinknash he became Prior of Farnborough, where he was said to have become too charismatic to please the authorities, who sent him up to the far north. Meanwhile, having become fascinated by the tenets of Gandhi, Hinduism, pacifism and Eastern mysticism, he espoused the cause of ecumenicalism, provided of course that it was on his own terms.

'There is a hidden presence of Christ in every man,' he writes in his 1966 *Christ in India*, 'calling him to union with himself and this presence is active in every religion and indeed wherever reason and morality are to be found ... There is also a hidden movement of the Church going on in the hearts of men from the beginning, drawing men to Christ without their knowing it, in Hinduism, in Buddhism, in Islam, even in agnosticism and unbelief. It is only at the last day that the full significance of this movement will be revealed ...'

In the course of several books expounding Hindu philosophy Bede more or less concludes that Hinduism is almost the perfect religion and if only it acknowledged the godhead of Christ and the BVM it would be absolutely perfect, and we could all adopt it. The Catholic hierarchy were not much impressed with his reasoning, but he managed to get himself to an ashram near Bangalore in 1955 with a French monk and, after several moves, ended up at Shantivanam.

One of the people Bede attracted to his ashram was Rupert Sheldrake, who developed his theories on 'morphic fields' under Bede's banyan tree.

'Why,' I asked Rupert at a UN party in Hyderabad, 'don't you people staying at Shantivanam do any physical work? Why do you leave all the farming and cooking to paid villagers?'

'Oh, we do work. We have to work an hour every day peeling vegetables!'

The ashram was in a lovely spot with little thatched chalets dotted about among the trees and a chapel decorated with painted figures of Christian saints in Hindu costumes and attitudes (looking remarkably like something out of Walt Disney). Bede himself, then in his seventies, was a venerable saffron-robed figure with silvered locks, flowing white beard and deep-set eyes that seemed at once secure with inner belief and anxiously imploring one to share it. (An air of other-worldliness was weakened by a large bunion on one bare foot; I was reproved by Martyn Skinner for remarking on it.) He emerged from a chalet containing a chair, a bedroll, some holy pictures and a typewriter, and I salaamed – which I think he preferred – before shaking a soft hand.

'And how is Martyn Skinner? And how is your brother?'

But I and my Indian colleague had hardly removed our sandals and squatted on his verandah before we were interrupted by the arrival of the postman, genuflecting, touching his forehead and handing some letters reverently to Bede.

'You'll stay to lunch, won't you? It's only vegetarian of course.' We accepted gratefully and had just begun to talk when the noonday bell rang. 'Ah! That'll be prayers. We're having Sikh prayers today. Come along and we'll look at the library on the way.'

This was a little round building where a pale girl in a white sari was reading. 'This is Kirsten. She's from Finland so we're giving her some warm weather for a change, ha, ha!' Kirsten smiled faintly.

'It's a charming building,' I said, observing the uninviting books.

'D'you like it? Well, I designed it myself.'

'Who looks after the buffaloes?'

'Oh, there's someone who understands them. Well, here's the church.'

We made ourselves tolerably comfortable on mats on the floor, which were rolled up after the prayers and put away. One by one the congregation came in and lined up opposite each other, then bowed their foreheads to the ground before sitting cross-legged. There were four well-nourished Indians, one of them a nun from an ashram next door, and ten white people, all young and bearded and white-robed except one middle-aged executive-type with a coloured shirt over his longhi. He had the place of honour next to Bede who led the chants in English in a thin other-worldly voice. One of the Indian men took over for the Hindu chants, which everybody answered – *shanti, shanti, shanti!* – from a book of ecumenical prayers and chants; Bede read some Sikh prayers in English and we said a modernised psalm. The Indian came round with a flame from which we lighted tapers and Kirsten came round with red powder for our foreheads. There was only one other woman present, with her partner, both darkish and accompanied by a little boy of about four chattering in Spanish.

The middle-aged man was introduced as Father David, ex-Indian Army and now on a sabbatical from Stonyhurst. (When I reported this sea change to Peter Collister he said, 'Don't I know it! When army officers get religion they get it very badly!') Before lunch everyone lined up to receive their mail from Bede, and I was reminded of the old Bert Thomas advertisement, 'Who's been at my Eno's?'

While we scooped and dabbled our lunch from banana leaves, a shaven youth read, very badly, passages of a biography of a Brahmin. The last time I had dined in a refectory with monks, listening to someone reading during the meal, was at Monserrat, that great powerhouse of training, tourism and Catalan politics, with an Abbot as sharp as a razor and anxious to pick even my brains to add to his store of wisdom.

After lunch I asked if I could take some photographs. 'Oh, yes. I'll stand by the chapel. That's Our Lord in the Vishnu pose. Rather nice, I think, and done by our own masons. And St Paul with the hand raised in the Shiva position. And the Holy Mother at yoga...'

We chatted about mutual friends until I looked at my watch.

'I expect,' I said rising, 'that you usually have a siesta now, so we'll be off.'

'Well, yes, I must say that I do.' And flinging his robe shawl-like across his shoulders he accompanied my smooth, sceptical, Indian companion and me to the gate. As we bumped down the lane I saw his saintly figure, with a final gesture of benediction, turn back purposefully, and I expect with relief, into the welcoming and dappled gateway.

The ashram is only a few miles from Tiruchchirappalli (once Trichinopoly), with its 236 ft high Rock Temple ('Hindus only') and large 'tank' familiar from prints by the Daniel brothers. The huge Victorian Gothic complex of St Joseph's College and Jesuit Church is near the town centre, and not far away is Father Schwartz's Church of St John and the house of the judge where 'Reginald Heber, third Bishop of Calcutta was called suddenly to his eternal rest'. (What would Bede have made, I wonder, of Heber's remark that Anglo-Indians were so small because soldiers and suchlike who took native mistresses could only afford those of the lowest and therefore least well-nourished class?)

Father George Thottungal (a specialist on Thomas Hardy) had 3,000 students to look after at St Joseph's. He said ashrams were now fashionable and there was even one Jesuit with Bede, apart from Father David. Father Griffiths was well thought of and the Church was now encouraging ascetics;

he had gone a long way towards achieving the Sanyasi state. Father George was not sure whether the Indians at the ashram were Christian or Hindu, nor where the money came from – 'possibly from America'.

My Indian colleague, however, was dubious about the whole enterprise and took exception to the translations – or, rather, the transference – from Sanskrit. For example in the chants the Sanskrit *Kumari* had been used for the Virgin Mary. But *Kumari* was the South Indian name (*vide* Cape Cormorant) for the particular manifestation (there were many) of the only goddess to withstand the passion of Shiva (all the others had been done to death by the strength of his semen and only she had given as good as she got). Her name had come to be used as a courtesy title for girls, and today was equivalent to no more than 'Miss'. So whatever concept of the BVM the ashram was 'trying to sell', what it did actually sell must be very different to a Hindu and a Christian, and remote from either's religious experience. He considered that to encourage mindless belief by droning repetition of short easy chants merely compounded the sharp practice.

It would be interesting to see in 175 years' time which passage to India is remembered most – the three-year one of Reginald Heber or the forty-year one of Alan Griffiths.

On our way out of India together Ian and I called at Shantivanam to say goodbye to Bede but after a few minutes the bell from the chapel rang out and women draped in white with their hair in buns started wending their way towards it. Bede asked us to lunch but we parted at the door of the chapel and rejoined our car at the bottom of the lane as a bus from Tiruchi was disgorging what appeared to be the next package tour of devotees in dark raincoats carrying suitcases; as they made off purposefully to the gateway I could see in their faces that they were determined – once they had changed into their regulation kit – to get their money's worth.

Martyn Skinner was not amused by my account of Bede's regime, and I was only sorry that I could not share his faith in it. He, with a mind infinitely more sensitive and informed than mine, thought his old friend genuinely touched by God. I could only think him touched; or, if not touched, as calculating as Sai Baba or 'the Mother' at Pondicherry, or any of the other people playing God in this country.

Many other people in India had a knack for funding their places in the sun with contributions from charitable rather than religious sources. There were the corporate high-living players like the UN and Oxfam Representatives, but also the lone rangers. The former Oxfam Representative in Madras had set up a talent-spotting enterprise of his own, called SEARCH, near Mysore. I found his Oxfam successor, an American born of missionary parents, sanctimonious, secretive and jealous, and there was a similarly smug and ill-disposed girl operating near Hyderabad. So I cannot judge from my short stay how effective the Oxfam projects were. But I did visit some of the one-man (or woman) bands who might conceivably qualify for financial support from the Overseas Development Ministry as part of Britain's official 'aid to the poorest' programme. They were often operating in remote places which were near historic sites that I had no official excuse to visit on their own. So I included some of them on my 1,500 mile drive to Gingee, Bangalore, Anantapore, Hampi, Hyderabad, Vijayawada, Guntur and Vellore.

It could be argued that using foreign money to better the lot of small groups was hard to justify to the taxpayers who had involuntarily supplied it. The justification was that the Government of India would copy such pioneering methods on a wide scale in a programme of national and classless regeneration. But the government was suspicious of neocolonialism among missionaries and charity workers, and of the motivation that seemed to cause such rivalries between individual saints and saintly bodies, and tended to welcome initial investment but make things difficult as soon as local vested interests were in any way threatened.

On the way to Gingee we looked at the few remaining walls of the Wandiwash fortress taken by Clive (how did his redcoats survive the heat?). The ruins were in a flat and uninteresting landscape and did not prepare us for the dramatic crags of Gingee. The noonday heat was sizzling as we went a little way up the path of the 900 ft high fortress of Majagiri, dating from 1442. Then we went a little further up, then halfway up to where the climb was broken by a 'pleasaunce' with trees, a temple and a spring. Then we decided to keep going, with our trousers sticking to our knees, round the other side of the rocks and up round the walls to a final bridge over a chasm and onto the summit. A high wind was blowing, and we got a terrific feeling of exhilaration. There were granaries, a treasury, a clock tower, a cannon, a temple and more springs and huge cave-cisterns. Far below were temples, the royal stables, a 'Reading Tower', more granaries, an elephant tank, gymnasium and morgue, and about half a mile away a lower fortress crowned with similar buildings. There was nobody at the top with us except a rather simple boy of about twelve who showed us the springs and was anxious to be helpful. In a final bid for appreciation, nodding and smiling, he burst into song.

'Baa, baa, black sheep,' he bawled, 'have you any wool? Yes sir, yes sir, three bags full ...'

At Penukonda, between Bangalore and Anantapore, we had our first puncture mended – a lengthy business as an ancient banged away at the outer tube with a sledge hammer and a single spanner, his only tools. He reminded me of the handsome women in Kerala crawling over the road spreading gravel with their bare hands. Was this healthily labour-intensive or a prodigal waste of human resources? As usual, our white Ford Consul attracted gasps of admiration from local children used to Ambassadors and little Fiats of long ago.

Penukonda was a bleak, waterless, scruffy little place at the foot of a rough and ready fortress with nothing remaining but loose stones and dry-stone walls. Yet it was to this dreary spot that the Vijayanagar kings retreated after their defeat at Talikota in 1565, abandoning the fruits of their 300-year divide-and-rule, mercenary and bribe-defended empire, and all the glories of Hampi. And it was near here that I visited an experimental farm run by a lively northern Indian named Bedi and his attractive Sino-Dutch wife, with financial backing from Holland, Germany, America, and in Britain from

AID. There were a dozen academics helping them with various schemes of social improvement and living in comfortable staff houses, though there was as yet no electricity. Colourful notices invited the public to enter and inspect activities – or planned activities – and no doubt classes in social awareness were a necessary priority for illiterate villages. But the mere mention of audio-visual aids and flash cards sounded incongruous in the middle of a farm on which the staff themselves never seemed to work physically. Bedi had begun as a disciple of Father Vincente Ferrer, whom he'd met in America and who was to be my next port of call at Anantapore. He said that he was a Communist and had been thrown out of Rajputana, but had himself only just managed to settle his first strike and he thought his troubles would recur.

I walked in on Ferrer in the middle of a meeting about the possible purchase of land for an experimental farm. 'Come and join us,' he said. 'This will interest you.' The meeting seemed to me to have been arranged in order to persuade a Captain Ashok, the Chairman of the Trust, to accept a preplanned outcome without feeling that democratic processes had been flouted. Gaunt, fiftyish and dressed in a white singlet and black clerical trousers, Ferrer was addressed by everyone as 'Father'. Born in the Barrio Gótico of Barcelona, he had been disowned by the Jesuits. Ten years previously he had been visited in Rajputana by an English 'freelance journalist' and her brother. The brother had moved on but the girl had stayed as his 'secretary'. They had moved to Anantapore where a hospitable Collector had invited Ferrer to start his present scheme, and where they had the first of three pretty children. These, I was surprised to hear, they proposed to send to the Baptist Hebron School in Ooty. Ferrer, however, admitted that he never knew whether his visa would be renewed or not. He was a softly spoken man who radiated a quiet self-confidence, but I don't think I would have bought a secondhand car from him any more than I would have from Bede Griffiths.

D'Abrieu, an educational psychologist in Madras, thought Ferrer 'a very cunning fellow who can charm money out of a stone'. I said I classed him with Bede Griffiths as someone I felt I had to humour because he was not quite right in the head.

'Oh, much more dangerous than Bede Griffiths!' said D'Abrieu. 'And don't forget to call him "Father" next time!' (I had described the suspicious look he had returned when I had breezed in, airing my Spanish, with a *'Muy buenos días, Señor Ferrer!'*).

Hampi was another 70 miles through Bellary, with its fortresses refurbished by Hyder Ali and Tipu Sultan, and Hospet, where we stayed in comfort with the engineers of the dam. Hampi's huge spread of treasures, which included a temple on whose fluted pillars tunes could be played, were spoilt by backpackers squatting round the Ganesh temple complex. But our main concern in Hampi was where to stay.

The Travellers' Bungalow at Mahbubnagar had been taken over by the Electricity Board for its employees and we were directed to the Inspection Bungalow, which was booked for 'the Minister'; we could try the Collector's

Resthouse but it was closed and in darkness; a bystander directed us to the Municipal Guesthouse which was full, but a guest relaxing in his evening white cottons suggested the Railway Staff Resthouse which he declared was always empty – no, not the Public Retiring Rooms, the *Staff House*. Although it was dark and raining by this time, he came along to the station with us. We walked over recumbent bodies on the platform to the sub-stationmaster's office.

'It is full.'

'No,' said our new friend, 'it is never full.'

'It is not permitted.'

'Oh dear me, yes!' and voices were lowered. 'British High Commissioner ... stranger ... hospitality ... Madras.'

'Come back in an hour's time. I will seek permission.'

Our friend left us at the Qualitee Bar where we sat, in cubicles so small that they felt like privies, and ate fearfully spicy food; but at least there was beer to wash it down with. (I had learned by now to be very chary of the initial glass bowl of soup, which could be lethal, and even more of the final 'pan'.)

Returning to the station we found the official gone, but the aged bearer at the Guesthouse said he'd received the necessary instructions. The building, under enormous trees full of crows, was distinctly gloomy but cool and tolerably clean. I slept well and in the morning Venugopal appeared looking refreshed from somewhere behind the building, possibly the car – it was accepted that his arrangements were his own affair. Beyond the trees, loud now with the cawing of the crows, was an encampment of nomads. There was much busy cleaning of teeth with twigs, soaping of breasts, thumping of wet clothes and of course the usual adjustments to the internal economy. The wild-looking long-haired men were surprisingly gentle with their children. I paid the bill (well satisfied with my 30p's worth) in the back of the booking office and it was strange to see all the action from backstage: the old-fashioned banks of tickets, the date-stamping machine, the anxious faces at the window, the piles of change ready to hand, and the grasping hands clutching at tickets flung contemptuously down almost out of their reach.

My last visit on this trip did as much as anything could to dispel my scepticism over foreign missionary enterprise and one-man bands. David Horsburgh's school was in the lightly-forested Horsley Hills country of pretty beehive villages about 80 miles from Bangalore and 220 from Madras. Here he built a picturesque estate entirely of local materials, except for WCs, a septic tank and a water pump (mechanical in the absence of electricity). He had studied Indian languages at SOAS before teaching in India for the Council for eleven years. In 1968, rather than be moved elsewhere, he started his own dream school subsidised by royalties from his books which were widely used in private schools in India.

He was an immediately likeable chap in his fifties. Shortish, with long fair hair, straggly moustache, missing teeth and a slightly mischievous look, he radiated not only enthusiasm but also good sense, humour and a know-how not often present in visionaries. He dressed 'Indian' but in the sensible working fashion of loose shirt and *longhi*, not in the robes of a guru, but in spite of his practical bent it was obvious that to his staff and pupils he was something of a guru. Doreen, his second wife, daughter of a Ceylon planter, was patient, self-effacing and slightly deprecating about it all, but must have played a major part in his achievement. Their eldest son was about to join them after his probationary teaching in England, and there was never a shortage of local teachers anxious to work there in order to learn his methods. The school accepted only poor or deprived children and had about thirty, aged from three to nineteen, who all studied together.

As we were walking round the huts, one of his pretty young teachers came running down the path crying, 'Baba! Come quickly! Gopal is killing his wife. He has a knife!' Her breath came in gasps and her eyes were dilated with fear as she looked trustingly at David. He grasped both her hands in his and spoke soothingly in rapid Kanada.

'Gopal's always getting drunk and causing trouble,' he said. 'I'll have to go and sort it out.'

The man was the husband of a cleaning woman and father of a pupil. He resented the 'goings-on' in which he had no part and, like many villagers in these idyllic-looking surroundings, turned nasty when drunk and took it out on his wife. Although the women, who were as tough as old boots and, working in the fields or on the roads harder than the men, could easily hold their own against their usually rather scrawny husbands, they never attempted to do so. When attacked they went into a kind of trance and submitted passively to having stones bashed into their faces, heads knocked against door posts or stomachs kicked and bodies slashed. This particular man had to be manhandled back to the village, sat upon, sworn at and given a calming cigarette while being treated to a mixture of reasoning and threats.

Could this particular little paradise survive the loss of David's touch without being institutionalised or taken over by the Indians? Meanwhile, not the least of his achievements was to own three 1926 Austin Sevens, in one of which a few weeks later he and Doreen came rattling up the drive of Balakrishna to one of my parties, bringing to this humdrum Eastern scene the exotic air of Birmingham at the apogee of her creative art.

A much bigger and more dubious enterprise that I visited on another journey was the ashram of 'The Mother' at Pondicherry and its offshoot, Auroville, six miles outside it.

Most of Pondicherry is like any other Indian town, but the esplanade (from where I took a swim) was kept clear of beggars and squatters by Indian police in white uniforms and red *képis,* and was redolent of any French watering place. A statue of Dupleix stood in the garden of the French Consulate, French-style bars and a Vietnamese restaurant flourished, and by a special dispensation prohibition had not been applied in Pondicherry and the tourist trade profited accordingly. Several mansions of former French merchant princes belonged to the Aurobindo cult of The Mother; one of them was a shrine, another a library, and in both white-robed figures moved slowly about or sat meditating.

Before my second visit, however, the prohibition blow had fallen, and I found traders sitting hopelessly in empty cafés waiting for custom that would now never come, but not yet resigned to closing shop. The Government had promised compensation and retraining, but any salvation obviously depended on the fortunes of the Aurobindo cult, which owned not only property but half the town's industries. And at that time the auspices were not good. Funds from Europe were said to have been misappropriated for unworthy purposes, but between the entrepreneurs of God and Mammon accountability was no easy matter. There was a great divide between the businessmen who ran the shrine, ashram, guesthouses and enterprises like a biscuit factory in town, and the starry-eyed pioneers who invested in the back-to-the-land experiment in Auroville.

The ashram had had a chequered history. It was started by a northern Indian, Aurobindo Ghose. Educated in England, with a First in Classics at Cambridge, he entered the Indian Civil Service but became an activist in the nationalist movement. Jailed for a year for his involvement in a bombing incident, he escaped further arrest by taking refuge in Pondicherry, where he set himself up as a philosopher and guru. A French woman, Mirra Alfonsa, met him in 1914 and from 1920 onwards 'dwelt with him'. In 1926 at the age of 44 he withdrew from human contact – except, presumably, with her – and from then onwards she, 'The Mother', ran the ashram alone. She survived him by many years, so many that heretics alleged that she was propped up by her disciples for her last public balcony appearances, an embalmed and bedizened corpse. Her death was finally announced in 1973.

In the shrine to The Mother and Aurobindo were their tombs, covered with flowers and tended by women in white, and a room nearby was fitted up with some of their furniture and unprepossessing photographs. Pilgrims sat meditating or lay prostrate for as long as they could manage. I spoke to a courteous and slightly dotty psychiatrist who had joined the ashram eight years previously and been allotted a nice little house where he lived happily with his wife. In the ashram library a dozen or so youngish people, mostly European or American, were sitting in cane chairs on the verandahs with open books on their laps. The Bengali youth who showed me round had been at the ashram school from the age of eleven to twenty-three and since then had been teaching there.

'How old are you now?'

'Twenty-seven.'

'When are you going out into the wide world?'

'I am not thinking of leaving yet.'

'What's your subject?'

'Literature and drama, mostly in English. We do plays and readings.'

'Do you have the townsfolk at them?'

'Oh no! This is only for the ashram people.'

'How many are there?'

'About two thousand, I suppose, including the people in Auroville.'

'Do the people in Auroville have anything to do with you?'

'No. I don't think relations are very good at present.'

I went to Auroville to see a Welsh potter, Tim Reece, who had applied for ODM funds on the grounds that he would develop new cottage industries for the local villagers. When I enquired at the 'Information Centre' on the main road how to find him a well-laundered and benign Indian instructed me to go first to 'the centre of the city'.

'What? Back to Pondicherry? I've just come from there!'

'No, the city of Auroville.'

'Why do you call it a city? Surely there's no city yet, only a few houses?'

'It is a City of Mankind for Citizens of the World. Here are the plans for the three phases of development. Would you like me to explain them to you?'

'Thank you. Perhaps later? How do I get to the city?'

As soon as we turned off the main road we saw some of the citizens of the world – solemn, half-naked chaps in their thirties, bicycling about or leaning on fences in front of oddly shaped thatched huts. A gateway onto ploughed land in the flat and featureless landscape had a flowery notice reading 'THE GOOD EARTH'. In the distance the futuristic shapes of the Globe and Conference Centre reared up but were difficult to get to on the mud roads winding through native villages. When I did reach them they and the big Stadium proved to be only half-built and abandoned. The only visible work I saw in the fields was being done by villagers. The settlers from whom I asked directions were French, one repairing a tractor, two mending bicycles and three watching them do it. A middle-aged American on a racing cycle eventually guided me to Tim Reece's cottage. He was away, raising funds in Germany and America, and I was received by his assistant, Jocelyn Elder, an attractive girl of mixed race and impeccable English. She had two blonde boys from, I gathered, a Swedish former husband, and a current American companion of whose status I was uncertain. Her cottage, named 'Tranquility', was Japanese in style but she showed me two concrete Riviera-style holiday houses belonging to wealthy Germans. She said they were ill-designed for protection from the local bugs and mosquitoes, and were often burgled by villagers, whose homes had been engulfed in the real estate deals of Auroville. Another large concrete house belonged to the Indian 'Administrator', but he had made himself scarce when the financial scandals surfaced. The various communities – artisans, farmers, teachers, engineers – were supposed to contribute by their labour to the common weal. We visited the food store, run on a coupon and barter system by a mild-eyed woman called Margaret Stuttle ('Sradavan is my Indian name') and while we were there a Dutch customer came in with two angry black spots on her thigh. 'They've come back, I see,' said Jocelyn anxiously. Evidently, from the poor complexions around me, a vegetarian diet and traditional medicine did not suit everyone or cure everything. Jocelyn introduced me to some of her neighbours, gentle middle-class people from France, Holland and Sweden, and in every cottage – in 'Peace', 'Meditation', 'Resignation' – a portrait of The Mother's raddled face hung in the place of honour. Jocelyn herself talked quite rationally about the financial problems of the community, but even her voice would suddenly drop a semitone and assume a note of awe when she mentioned, in palpable inverted commas, 'The Mother'.

The parents in the community were worried because their children – as children, alas, do in even the most idyllic surroundings – were growing up, while the ashram schools were growing more and more impractical. What could I suggest?

(I could only suggest – but could hardly say – what the landlord of the pub at Cocklake had suggested when I put the same question to him. Two of us had timed our Mendip walk to land us at his pub for lunch. It was ominously empty except for three very local patrons who regarded us with suspicion.

'Can you do us some sandwiches?'

'No.'

'Oh dear! So what have you got in the way of food?'

'Nothing.'

'Nothing?'

'No. We don't do lunches.'

'Oh! Well, where do you suggest we go for lunch?'

'I suggest,' – long pause – 'you go 'ome – ha, ha, ha!')

As a matter of fact one thought had been going through my mind and that was one of regret that this pioneering community had chosen such a dreary bit of land and such a shady bunch of patrons for the investment of their dreams, their energy and their money. How much more romantic and useful it would have been had they chosen to restore the old 1616 walled town of Tranquebar down the coast. Its Rex Whistler arched gateway, surmounted by the Danish coat-of-arms, led into well-paved straight streets – King Street and Queen Street – of fine but dilapidated houses, with two airy and lofty churches. The Lutheran 'New Jerusalem' church had been recently and clumsily restored with German assistance, but the English 'Zion' church, with a bell dated 1752, was in an advanced stage of dissolution. Both churches had a catholic mixture of tombs around them – English, French, Portuguese, Armenian, Swedish, German, Dutch and Danish. The white-pillared British Collector's house was falling down round its present Indian inhabitants and a Siva temple was beginning to be washed away by the sea. The only sign of life in this atmospheric little ghost town was a women's training college. The Danes sold Tranquebar to the British in 1845 and the British let it rot away.

* * *

'If you're going to Mysore,' said Peter Moss before another of my journeys, and giving me a straight look, 'I think Yvette Kersey might welcome a visit.'

'One of our teachers?'

'No, very much her own woman. She runs a clinic cum cottage-industry at Scott's Bungalow. I don't think she has a husband at the moment.'

Scott's Bungalow at Shrirangapattana was mentioned in the guidebooks as the scene of an 'unsubstantiated' tragedy in garrison days before the army moved to Bangalore to get away from cholera epidemics. It was dead from cholera that the colonel was supposed to have found his wife and children when he returned one day from manoeuvres, and he was said to have drowned himself in the river. He must have had his work cut out to do so; it was a delightful river to swim in and I didn't see how he could have avoided fetching up against a rock sooner or later. The position of the bungalow, perched on its bank with a balustraded terrace hanging over the water and huge trees finishing off the scene like a Gainsborough picture, was idyllic. There was an air of timelessness about it and an enchantment tinged with melancholy. The word 'bungalow' in those parts did not imply a single-storey building and Scott's Bungalow was a substantial two-storey house with high ceilings, a fine carved staircase and, most unusually, sash windows. The clinic operated in a separate building, but in the wide verandah running all round the house about thirty women in saris sat twittering happily together as they worked on the well-designed tapestries, dresses, bags and shawls which sold for high prices in America.

When I first called, at about ten, Yvette was 'in bed' and I met only her son, Jamie, a dark boy in his late teens with a wispy moustache, and Peter, who was 'helping Yvette out for a few months' and seemed to be living in a cottage in the garden. Small, fortyish, with a Mexican moustache and shoulder-length hair, he 'couldn't stand bourgeois society and creeping bureaucracy' and had spent six months drifting about in Afghanistan and the Himalayas. When I returned a couple of hours later Yvette was up and dispensing tea. There was a good-looking fair boy present, the son of a neighbour. She was elegant with slim capable hands, short henna-coloured hair, green eyes, freckles – in fact with very much the colouring and evidently the capability too of some Jewish women I had known. She must have been striking when younger and was still attractive, but with the washed-out look that some women acquire when transplanted to the tropics. She talked composedly and with humour.

She paid her girls 75 rupees a month once they had learned to embroider to her standards. Now that she had begun to hive off the clinic she could do with a bit of capital and resented Oxfam not having helped her earlier, though they had now offered to do so. In her clinic she used traditional medicines rather than modern drugs.

'How did you know about clinics?'

'I worked here first on leprosy, so it was easy for me. What I'd like to do now is to dig a hole in the ground and build a house with what comes out of it. It's scandalous what architects build and how much houses cost. I've built dozens of houses and I know I could do this. And I also want to start a school.'

'What sort of school?'

'A school like David Horsburgh's.'

Yvette sometimes talked of 'we' as having done this or that but I didn't discover who 'we' were. Like Lady Hester Stanhope, she seemed to be flying higher the older and less robust she was getting. When I went upstairs to say goodbye after my swim, she was lying on the bed with the fair-haired boy beside her, reading.

'What are you reading?'

'*The Awkward Age* by Henry James. How is Madras? Have you met people yet? Do you know the Theosophist place? There are usually some interesting people staying there.'

I thought of the dazed drop-outs I had seen there, with beards or shaven heads, in sackcloth dresses or saris; and the earnest elders who seemed to run the place in great comfort; and the *kalakshetra* dance drama I had attended in their palm leaf theatre, with hideously uncomfortable cane-bottomed chairs, and dancing and music and *puja* which had gone on and on and on – the only mystery being how the men could dance at all with such enormous rice bellies.

I left Yvette reclining, like Lady Hester at Jezzine, on her bed under the high roof rafters once covered tentlike by a canopy ceiling. I crossed the verandah with its bright-plumaged ladies working on the floor, and drove off under the peepul trees with the gleaming Cauvery River dropping away on my right, then past the clinic and out onto the rough track lined with ant hills.

I wasn't sure if Peter Moss saw Yvette as a Sleeping Beauty to be rescued from her entanglements (or perhaps joined in them), or the whole Scott's Bungalow situation as one to be seen but steered clear of. At any rate my next visit was with my architect visitor, Donald Insall, and Yvette had welcomed the chance of professional advice over an alarming crack in one of the end walls. There were other disadvantages with the house: it had, for example, no running water or electricity – water was brought in from a spring and there was only an outside bathroom; nor was money wasted on toilet paper when torn up newspaper would do. Its peaceful situation was also misleading; neighbours were disputing the legality of the lease and for good measure had beaten up young Jamie. As if this were not enough, when I next met her in Bangalore Yvette had other preoccupations. I bought her an orange juice, which she promptly knocked over.

'I'm in such a nervous state. Can you try and get the Archaeology Department to declare the Old British Cemetery at Shrirangapattana a protected monument so that the locals stop pinching the gravestones for building material? I've already secreted some of them to save them from theft, but there's a systematic government trend to restore only Hindu monuments and destroy everything else.'

'I'm afraid I spelt your name wrong on my last letter,' I countered.

'It doesn't matter. Actually, I'm going to change my name soon, back to my maiden name, Lothaldar.'

'Is that Scandinavian?'

'Spanish, from the Basque provinces. It's Jewish.'

'Sephardic Jewish?'

'Yes.'

'And have you family ties there?'

'Not really, except my father's library which he made available to scholars.'

David Horsburgh, who was also in Bangalore, lecturing at the Training College where he used to teach, filled in some of her background. She had lived in Australia but the father of Jamie was a French doctor in Mysore.

Jamie had just finished his O Levels at Christopher Wren Comprehensive in London and not surprisingly didn't want to 'waste any more time there'. On his first day he had seen a master beaten up by a pupil and taken to hospital.

Nobody knew whose son the younger boy, Rupert, was but he was a bit of a problem; he had never had any proper schooling and David doubted if he ever would because he was an aimless and delicate creature who made the most of his infirmities. Yvette had not believed in marriage until she met Derek Kersey, a British Airways pilot. They had a son called Alexis, now at school in England and living with Kersey, who wouldn't let him come to India. Kersey was a nice chap, said David, but the marriage seemed to be over. He admired Yvette for her enterprise and generosity but whereas he could natter away with the locals in Kanada, Tamil, Hindi and even Sanskrit, she, like Bede Griffiths, appeared unable to speak any Indian language at all. He thought that was one of the reasons why she had never managed to be on good terms with her neighbours. Another was probably that in their eyes a woman had no right to live the sort of life she was living. It appeared that the Maharaja's agent from whom she bought Scott's – no doubt for a ridiculously cheap price – had given her invalid receipts before making off with a third of the Maharaja's property, and it was that legal weakness that her rapacious neighbours were trying to exploit.

The next time I called at Scott's Bungalow ('Do come and stay, Stephen,' Yvette had said, 'or send any of your friends. I trust you.') Peter had been replaced by Danny, a guileless young Australian who had mistaken the house for the nearby Travellers' Bungalow and stayed two months. There were now four flea-bitten dogs there; Rupert had just brought in the last one. He and the fair-haired neighbour were going to go to the school at Ooty, which practised some Horsburgh precepts. ('Yvette is obsessed with money,' said David, 'but she never keeps accounts. I hope she'll pay young Rupert's bill at the Blue Mountain School, which I got him into as I'm on the Board.')

Also at Scott's was one Susan and her companion, Hassan, a Muslim Palestinian from Kuwait in his final engineering year at Mandya. He had, he said, been a Communist and followed all the usual sects until he decided, after one of Sai Baba's lieutenants had made a pass at him, that all their followers were either mentally or sexually abnormal. Susan had also drifted from Pune, where European girls smelt you at the door to check that you weren't wearing perfume offensive to their guru, to a Buddhist monastery in Sri Lanka and was now travelling the world (thanks to private means) studying wood carving and batik printing. Jamie had got a job as interpreter with a company filming in Mysore. So things appeared to be looking up for Yvette. But evidently I was mistaken.

'You are extraordinarily fit for your age,' said Yvette, 'but my arthritis looks like finishing me – and at fifty-three! Of course it's partly psychosomatic because of the worry over this house. It's become a full-time job just to follow up developments in all these offices. I don't drive and I can't even ride a bicycle, so all these trips are exhausting. I must try and see the DC before he gets caught up in the state visit of the Chief Minister.'

Devaraj Urs, the Chief Minister for Karnataka, had recently split with Indira Ghandi, thus dividing the Party into 'Congress I' and 'Congress U', which did not simplify local politics, and Yvette and Jamie feared that their compulsory valuation had gone wrong and would land them with impossible tax arrears. Yvette still had her dreams. She wanted to 'do everything, absolutely everything'. She'd like to return to China (she'd always got on with the Chinese); not to America though (they wouldn't give her a visa because of her work for Indonesian refugees from the Dutch East Indies). She'd walked through Turkestan and Sikkim; she'd sailed round India on an Arab dhow, the only woman on board; the Australian bush was the most magical country she knew and she'd like to live there – if she could stand the rest of Australia. She'd never be able to stand Spain again; her only brother had been 'virtually killed' by the Civil War. And Rupert's father, who was a cousin, had been killed in a road accident. But at least she had saved Scott's Bungalow, restoring it to its original white beauty from its green and purple and puce. And why was I rushing home to Europe where it was impossible to live now, with people obsessed by all the wrong preoccupations?

The river was particularly beautiful that evening, with oil lamps glimmering in little shrines on its bank and the roar of the falls drowning the noise of distant radios. Two large black geese, a heron and some egrets were standing sentinel in the shallows, occasionally taking off for long sweeps among the encircling kites. But before the darkness hid them flecks of detergent showed in the whirlpools and I wondered what the effect would be of the hoarding I had seen higher up the river: 'HABIB'S INDUSTRIALS: SITES AVAILABLE.'

'We've never bribed anyone,' said Jamie, 'and we never will!'

'If only I knew *who* to bribe, 'said Yvette, 'and how much, and had the money to do it! Not one of my so-called friends would make me a loan when I needed it! And I've had such awful trouble producing evidence of the payments I did make. My husband refused to certify his payment on my behalf in England and a friend of mine in Fulham said she couldn't remember making a payment for me. When I asked her she wrote back – here's her letter – "Dear Girl, of course I'll give you an affidavit for anything you want only I can't actually remember anything about it. But you can rely on me to do the 007 stuff; send me the name of the man for the pay-off and I'll send him the cheque..." But I didn't like to send it to the poor old thing to remind her of it.'

'That friend in Fulham wouldn't have lived in Redcliffe Road, would she?'

'Yes.'

'I thought as much. That "Dear Girl" and "007 stuff" sounds very like her. It's Biddy Cook, isn't it? How did you come to know her?'

'I met her when I took a room in her house.'

Suddenly the whole picture changed. From the misty scene of Peter Moss's Sleeping Beauty, from the Hester Stanhope-Jane Digby-Isabella Bird world of the free spirit, I was decanted into my own backyard. Biddy was the school friend and confidante of one of my sisters. She became the always-abridesmaid-never-a-bride friend or godmother to the arty-crafty daughters of the Bristol plutocracy who kicked up their heels in the war and emigrated after it to London, where public jobs or private means preserved them from the awful fate of a bourgeois life. Biddy chose Fulham for her homes ('I will not live south of the river!') and they always looked like a cross between a Regency salon and an old clothes shop; even after years of her occupancy it was as if she had only moved in the previous day. No doubt the rooms that she let to other refugees from the provinces were more orderly. Her lodgers were engaged in painting, acting, script-writing, managing BBC studios, researching or even typing as long as it was in good old Whitehall; or, more often than not, being about to be – or to have just finished being – so engaged. In between were money-making schemes or liaisons or marriages that never quite came off. Biddy shared the general volatility, the do-goodery, generosity and slapdash intellectualism; the anticlericalism, winebibbery and flamboyance; while men – often of non-marrying disposition – came and went like shadows in the background. And Biddy herself – inevitably – had tried a spell with the Theosophists at Adyar.

And into all this Utopianism – notwithstanding my starry-eyed first impressions – the regime of Scott's Bungalow with its charm and insubstantiality fitted, I discovered, like a glove.

I departed through doors with their museum titles preserved on the lintels – 'MILITARY UNIFORMS', 'NINETEENTH CENTURY DRESSES' – down stairs overlooked by a Burne-Jonesey peacock and art nouveau flower piece, into the sitting room with white furniture and green cushions and trailing plants, through the dining room with murals painted for – or by – children and a shelf of books by Bertrand Russell, along the hall lined with travel trunks painted white and covered with flowers, down the balustraded steps and out to the car where a poker-faced Venugopal awaited me. We drove off under the great trees and out onto the track where the ant hills to left and right of us were picked out in the headlights.

'Those are full of snakes,' said Venu. 'When the ants move out the snakes move in.'

23
Whither, O Splendid Ship?

'Whither, O splendid ship, thy white sails crowding,
Leaning across the bosom of the urgent West,
That fearest nor sea rising, nor sky clouding,
Whither away, fair rover, and what thy quest?'

I AM GLAD to have lived before the full rot of air travel set in. My ships, on which HMG were good enough to pay the passage, were not as glamorous as those of Robert Bridges but I enjoyed them all, and not least because aboard them I was totally out of HMG's reach. My 60th birthday in October 1979 sounded the knell of my Council service and my successor in Madras arrived soon afterwards. Ian was still with me and as he had finished at Oxford and time was no object we decided to put the car on a slow boat to the Piraeus and enjoy a leisurely drive home from there across Europe.

MV *Hellenic Navigator* was a Greek tramp with a few cabins for passengers, sailing from Cochin; she would wander about the Indian Ocean and Red Sea calling wherever freight was signalled. There was therefore an air of inconsequence about the trip, of uncertainty, detachment and timelessness, with a lot of hanging about waiting for something to turn up. This reflected my own state of mind. Being the last voyage as a slave of the Council, this should have been the best. I was sailing into freedom – no more having to leave my family in England's green and pleasant land, no more management reports or monthly accounts. On the other hand I was also sailing into the unknown, no longer with an organisation behind me; I had no authority now and no one cared what I thought about anything. I had never remarried and I now had to face the problem of companionship in retirement. However for the moment I was not alone – I was with Ian and with Captain Papoutsidakis and his exiguous and scruffy crew.

It all started off well enough, thanks to the Krishnaswamis in the Office, who had made all the arrangements, and to Venugopal who had taken a week's leave to come with us and see us on board, taking in anything interesting on the way. After several false alarms the Hellenic prevaricator did at last dock in Cochin, and it was sad to bid farewell to Venu. He had been a wonderfully companionable human map of South India to me, and made my last year in the Council one of the best and most memorable of all.

The car was swung aboard by a Hungarian crane and we inspected our quarters. They were not reassuring. Until Colombo we were the only passengers but we had to share a cabin as most of the others were full of stores. Ours had no coat-hangers, a missing shelf, shower-rose and soap-holder, a cold tap that didn't work and a hot one that spat out gouts of deep orange water as soon as it sensed any laundry in the basin. The ship's library contained a couple of Alistair MacLeans, a James Hadley Chase, Maxim Gorky's memoirs, *Mrs Dalloway* and, the final hammer blow, several dozen works of English literature – in Longman's *Simplified Edition for Foreign Students*. Ian had brought *The Tin Drum* which I found even more impenetrable than *Mrs Dalloway*, and we also had *Anna Karenina* and *The Great Railway Bazaar* (reliable on Aussie backpackers; less so, I suspect, on child brothels in Madras). As we intended that I should revise my modern Greek and Ian should study Italian for use on the road home from the Piraeus, the distraction of a good library would, I suppose, have been a mixed blessing. We finally sailed on 20th November and, stepping out on deck in the fading light, I felt once more the euphoria brought about by a creamy wake, a gentle motion, conspiratorial ship noises, and colours like nothing on earth – fluffy clouds dappled with blue, pink, purple and grey.

It was clear that the menu was to be a change from spicy Indian food – bean soup, pasta, salad and mezés with Greek coffee, tinned fruit juice and beer (a great treat after Tamil Nadu prohibition). This last, and the odd bottles of whisky and retsina, were never charged to us because the steward was flown home to have his varicose veins operated on and Captain Papoutsidakis said he couldn't be bothered to work out the cost. We dined with the Captain and Chief Engineer, the former despondent and the latter taciturn. Papoutsidakis expressed surprise at seeing us at all as his sister ship, *Hellenic Sun*, was faster and more comfortable, with a swimming pool. Our ship could only do fourteen instead of sixteen knots because of barnacles acquired by her long stay at Karachi. We were to go wherever cargo beckoned, probably Port Sudan, Jeddah and Aqaba, but first to Colombo. And at Colombo we learned that travelling by tramp steamer was by no means plain sailing. We hung about for two weeks and watched the *Hellenic Sun* sail in and a couple of days later out again, and a President Line and French container ship do the same. Meanwhile coolies were loading an amazing mixture of cargo – cinnamon for New York, tea for Aqaba and soap cakes for Djibouti – yes, we were to call there too.

The ship's repainting programme was marginally advanced by a not over-enthusiastic Ian at the suggestion of our gloomy captain. It needed it, he said, because he couldn't get a crew of trained seamen any longer, apart from a few old ones; the young deckhands only came along for a few months to see the world, and half the ship's officers were unqualified and merely promoted ABs. He resented having to watch the crew all the time, doing other people's jobs and never getting any sleep. The founder of the Hellenic Line had died the previous year, aged eighty-six, and his daughter (the son having his own line of nineteen ships) had taken control. Certainly the crew seemed on the exiguous side. From time to time two Calibans emerged from the engine room to blink in the sun and a third deckhand liked to do a bit of fishing on the shady side of the ship.

When Captain Papoutsidakis said that we were to be joined by another passenger and her two children at Colombo, I wondered if fate even at this late hour had conjured up that not impossible she I had begun to look for more seriously as retirement loomed. 'Hope springs eternal in the human breast', but when Hope Savage came aboard this fancy was rapidly extinguished. Sarah, an attractive little girl of eight, was made much of by the crew; Jane, two years older, wore spectacles, was seasick as soon as we left port and got her own back by calling Sarah 'stoopid' all the time. Hope talked readily enough on general subjects – on the Moslem faith, for example, or how much she was enjoying George Sand's *Consuelo* (in French) but about her circumstances was less forthcoming. She had been staying at Mount Lavinia for six months 'in a friend's house on holiday' and had been six months in Goa and two years in Turkey. She herself came from South Carolina but 'it was a long time since she'd seen America'. In Goa, Sarah revealed, they had known 'David, who made door bells to catch thieves'. He was, she thought, English and they were going to Kyrenia to stay with his mother. Sotirias, the boatswain, didn't believe in beating about the bush.

'Where's your Daddy then?'

There was a pause.

'In Turkey.'

'Why is he in Turkey?'

'Because he is Turkish.'

And although we ate with them four or five times a day for a fortnight this was all we learned of this rootless little family with its simple clothes, second-hand school books from a mail order shop in Falmouth, and belongings carried in plastic bags. Slow in getting anywhere with the Savage family, we were equally slow with our journey. Eleven hours after leaving Colombo we were back in Tamil Nadu at Tuticorin. The new harbour was five miles from the former Portuguese and Dutch settlement, recently notorious for a fire in a travelling cinema, in which over a hundred people had died. These cinemas were built of bamboo and palm leaves to avoid tax as temporary structures, but they usually remained there until they fell down. It might be thought that an audience could simply force its way out, but this is to forget that the proprietor's first concern was to prevent people forcing their way in.

Five days later the Horn of Africa shimmered over the port bow and a couple of days later we anchored in Djibouti. The port area, two miles from town, was entirely French; with a roll-on-roll-off supply ship from Marseilles unloading supplies for four old-fashioned warships, one evidently a training ship for black crews. Fat white gendarmes in shorts and peaked caps waddled about busily, and among the yachts in the harbour I saw for the first time wind-surfers in action. We walked along a causeway looking at the sea birds on one side, where all the rubbish was, and at the French birds sunning themselves on the other. That was all we saw of Djibouti, but fussing round the ship were two tugs, named *Abubakar Pasha* and *Arthur Rimbaud.* I could not help regretting that British tugs no longer worked in Aden or Malta, or that if – under new ownership – they did they were unlikely to be called, say, the *James Elroy Flecker* or *Samuel Taylor Coleridge*. The tall thin dockers in Djibouti were the most slapdash and incompetent of the whole voyage. When unloading the crates of 'washing soap' from Colombo they persistently overfilled the nets causing the crates to burst open and the dockside was soon littered with bars of soap. Such accidents to such a commodity could scarcely have been intentional.

Captain Papoutsidakis bemoaned the departure of the British from our next port of call, Port Sudan, which had gone to pieces so badly that he never knew how long it would take to get anything done there. The whole area, he said, had been destabilised and Russian warships were much in evidence; there was one particular bank where five were always anchored. They did not appear on radar as they had effected a system of blanking their presence out. Radio communication between us and the owners in New York, however, now deleted Port Sudan and Jeddah from our programme and we made straight for Aqaba.

We passed through the Tiran Strait at night, being quizzed by the Israelis from 3 to 5am, and tied up next to a packed Saudi Arabian ferry from Egypt. While containers were shipped Ian and I snorkelled in marvellously clear water with the most spectacular fish I'd seen since leaving Venezuela. Departing through the straits we were raked by Israeli searchlights and in the Red Sea the climate itself became very unfriendly. At Suez, where the empty Lesseps pedestal stood among bombed buildings, it was freezing, and we joined a convoy of thirty ships entering the canal in the rain at dusk. The lights of the still neat Ismailia barracks revealed an incongruous Gothic chapel at the water's edge. Out in the Med the sun returned but not the damp warmth that in India one thinks, wrongly, one will never miss. Then one evening when I stuck my radio aerial out of the porthole to pick up the news after the ritual jargon on Khomeini, Vance, Vietnam, Rhodesia, Ulster and British Steel – sounding from the little world of the *Hellenic Navigator* like some esoteric media game – I heard of a grotesque accident to the Ballantraes. A tree had fallen on their car, killing Lady Ballantrae. After the dreamlike interlude in a Southern India still criss-crossed with steam trains and innocent of Tamil Tigers and atomic tests this was real news again, and near to home with a vengeance.

On 22nd December we reached a frozen Piraeus, and Hope and the girls went ashore, festooned with bundles. One broke away from its handle and dropped into the sea, where it bobbed about until fished out by a docker with a hook.

'Oh my!' cried Hope, 'It has all my diaries for the last five years in it. But I think they'll be OK. I wrapped them in cellophane paper.'

Whatever had been confided to her diary couldn't have been anything about Ian or me for she had shown not the slightest interest in either of us. Perhaps this blow to my self-esteem was a salutary one. If the voyage had been lacking in incident it had demonstrated that without the glamour of the

British Council behind me I had changed from a middle-aged member of the crew, for all my faults employable or at least employed, to just another boring ancient mariner; so when the *Hellenic Navigator* disgorged Ian and me onto the frost-bound quays of the Piraeus the only passage I could now look forward to was as a passenger in the Ship of State. So whither indeed, once splendid ship, and what her quest?

* * *

Once home, I attended a retirement course. Predecessors took the stage to talk about their experiences. We were disabused of any idea of frittering away our days enjoying ourselves. To a man, or more often to a woman, the speakers were 'busier than ever' on voluntary work or on courses of self-improvement. A young medical man told us to maintain a disciplined routine of regular exercise, modest diet and early nights. We were as old as we felt. Naturally we would find ourselves getting up more often in the night, and we should not try to resist this tendency by, for example, cutting down our liquid intake before going to bed. Were there any questions? Stifled by so much earnestness and such unromantic nightlife, I broke the silence. 'What about sexual activity? Did he recommend it?' There was a silence. Then the ladies laughed and the doctor, most charmingly, blushed.

I did do a little work here and there and attended courses in home maintenance and cookery, but my good intentions were soon curtailed. I met Ruth and, a few months later, impelled by a howling gale on the Roman Wall, proposed to her and – after a judicious interval – was accepted. My one regret was that this hadn't happened earlier; Ruth had lived in France for eleven years and would have enjoyed life overseas and been a stabilising influence in Turkey.

Happily and busily married, I had little cause to follow Council affairs, though I was happy to exploit them on our travels. We honeymooned in Morocco, where John Cambridge was now Ambassador, and visited Council contacts in Barcelona and Cyprus. When I retraced my steps on the Kwai we stayed with Peter and Norma Moss in their vast American-style apartment in Bangkok. We were nobly wined and dined by Bryan and Herta Swingler in Paris and in the spectacular duplex apartment on the quay at Agde to which they retired. Meanwhile Newsletters from the Council indicated seemingly conflicting trends, a drift to the left and what sounded like severe managerial overkill. One of the Council's trades unions brought Trevor Huddleston out from Donald Reeves's rectory to condemn Council work in South Africa, and Geoffrey Howe, on an official visit to Council HQ as Foreign Secretary, was booed.

* * *

With frequent changes in the government attitude to its cultural ambassadors, it is not easy to assess with hindsight the motivation and achievements of the

Council. In my time its policy varied between scattering largesse and handing round the begging bowl; between going its own way and calling in management consultants. Although the Council's cost effectiveness puts to shame the feather-bedded establishment of the Foreign Service and the profligacy of that cultural cuckoo in the nest, the Arts Council, it could be argued that if the entire Council budget had been spent on subsidising overseas schools British trade would have benefitted more than it has from piecemeal, pump-priming, aid-oriented and constantly shifting enterprises. Cynics have even suggested a conversion of the budget to a slush fund, perhaps to flood the world with British dancing-girls who would marry – or otherwise influence – VIPs everywhere. Others say it no longer matters because our national culture will soon disappear in the wash of a federal Europe.

The routine of Council work does not make for easy reading, with its weeks of examinations, its months of interviewing, and its years of planning. The Beaverbrook vendetta in the *Express* and *Evening Standard* that was still strong in the fifties, gave it a morris-dancing label that has never quite died and was never quite untrue; the Council has been sometimes twee, because Britain was twee. The British Travel Association had its Beefeaters and Bath buns; the Council had its Arnold Bax and *Tales of Beatrix Potter*, and it is oddities like these – if they can't get any real scandals – that newspapers look out for.

If scandals do occur, whether personal ones such as defections across the Iron Curtain or cultural bricks like showing Greenaway's *The Tempest* in Malaya, we should be frank and robust rather than apologetic in our press responses. Other nations, too, make mistakes. I have sat through films at Goethe Institutes that were embarrassingly pretentious and boring and *Alliance Française* evenings that were all too much the contrary: my French colleague in Cyprus had not previewed an amusing but risqué film about a libidinous salesman in Pont Aven, and the hush from his VIP and largely female audience was deathly; and in Madras a Tamil audience was flummoxed by the portrayal by two lesbians in velvet breeches of racy scenes from the *fin de siècle* Left Bank.

To defend gaffes of this kind – and the more adventurous the work the more gaffes there will be – an organisation needs to show punch and wit, and though there have been plenty of people in the Council with both, they have never been used to influence the media favourably. Public awareness of the Council's work may have been raised by new logos, annual reports full of sound bites and pretty pictures, and newspeak that announces a cuts-dictated relocation in Manchester from a prestige purpose-built office building to a few rented floors as 'Moving Forwards', but in the long term the Council's reputation rests not on what appears on paper but on personal experience of its work. For years journalists have enjoyed pulling it to pieces, but it has made many foreign and British friends among those who have used it. Even the dissident academic who once recommended closing it down altogether, and dividing its work between the Foreign Office and the Ministry of Education, 25 years later (as Baroness Blackstone) pronounced it indispensable. If the Council's role were taken over by Civil Service departments bureaucracy would surely increase and a valuable halfway house with its own ethos would be lost. The Council has bred a staff uniquely experienced both in seeing ourselves as others see us and in persuading those others to see us as HMG would like them to see us.

Inevitably, the man or woman representing the Council overseas today, so much more comfortably housed with his or her partner and his or her new car, must miss the independence of earlier years and be subject to more managerial harassment from a headquarters in instant communication.

'You can say what you like about the Council,' Germaine said to me one morning in Beirut in the fifties, 'but not every employer would let you slope into the office at half past nine in the morning.'

'Yes, but I was busy there until midnight blocking in *Romanov and Juliet.*'

'Who for, though? You or the Council?'

'Both – I hope.'

Hopes of this kind may be dupes but they keep up the cultural spirits in the face of the diurnal slog of less glamorous routines. For thirty-three years I was privileged to observe life overseas without the constraints of a diplomat or the long commitment to one area of a businessman. But it is simply not enough to be a good manager, communicator or aid worker; Council employees need an interest in the intellectual life of their own country and a conviction that promoting the best of it makes friends. In France the sense of *La Gloire* permeates all classes and survives all changes of government, and my German, American and Italian colleagues have all pursued intellectual interests of their own. Without this spark enthusiasm soon dies.

My involvement with our cultural history has been transitory but at least I have had time to reflect on it; others younger than me have not. David Horsburgh died only a few years after chugging up my drive at *Balakrishna*, and Neville French, who had rescued me from that same flooded drive, died soon afterwards. Both Cave Women died – Betty Hunter-Cowan in Cyprus and Phyllis Heyman back in England. Herta Swingler died in Agde, and Bryan soon afterwards while making a new home in Northumberland. Michael Glover died in his sixties after writing a dozen or so books, and Peter Collister in his seventies after five. Michael Pawley, after bravely leaving the protective wing of the Foreign Office to teach English in Poland, died of a heart attack at fifty-six. The unkindest cut of all came to Peter Moss, a Himalayan mountaineer, struck down at sixty-three while walking in Blenheim Park.

My colleagues and I worked to a brief that was instinctive rather than defined. Working abroad it was hard to appreciate how much things were changing in the corridors of power at home. To us, as the voice of the most charismatic of our founding fathers grew fainter and more out-of-date, something of its sentiment nevertheless remained. The visionary Lord Lloyd of Dolobran could be practical enough at times: 'All Orientals think extra highly of a lord,' he said to his wife in 1925, having demanded a peerage before going to Egypt as High Commissioner. In 1938, in an effort to ginger up Lord Halifax, he used a rarer and more old-fashioned language: 'There are worse crises even than war – a still worse issue would be if we were found morally too feeble to stand up and too cowardly to sacrifice ourselves for what is Right over what is manifestly evil and Wrong. It would be worse than war to be unwilling to be the champions of weak peoples or that we should, through a shrinking from suffering, fail in a task surely set us by Providence. This is the moment to play the man, to face clear-eyed what is coming, confident that we are capable of drinking the cup and that we shall not be left without the power to do so.'

To a managerial Council in a managerial Europe, Lloyd's visionary expressions are alien. His aid-dispensing and revenue-hunting successors cannot afford to take too high a moral ground. Some friends abroad find this difficult to accept, and especially patrons of Council libraries who see the minimal uses of literacy they are to serve in future. 'A couple of weeks ago,' write the Turveys from Cyprus, 'we received a circular letter addressed to members of the British Council Library, beginning: "We are changing for the better!" Each of us, reading this separately, realised that bad news was coming, and indeed, after mention of "an exciting new Information Centre", we were told that the library was to be closed down. Even the reference books are to go – only some teaching books to remain. A sale of books started on Monday.'

In Barcelona the cultural mechanisation has been equally dispiriting to Montserrat Pau i Pifferrer, who was my indispensable PA there. 'The Council,' she writes, 'has again problems. Apart from the teaching of English all other activities here are fading away. A restructuring in January will mean a reduction in staff. *En fin*, we have been lucky to leave the Council when there were still good times.'

Montse is not alone. Most of my colleagues – and especially those in our unglamorous Home Service – were imbued with a sense of what I can only call benevolent cultural patriotism and were a pleasure to work with. When I consider in what a disoriented state I was in 1945, and how ill-qualified professionally, I marvel at my luck in being welcomed aboard our pinnace of the Ship of State and (except for walking the plank in Turkey) being carried round the world to 'look at mankind instead of reading about them'. Certainly there were stormy times aboard, but for thirty-three years the Council was faithful to me in its fashion – and vice versa.

It may be that Montse and I and others will be confounded by a globalisation that makes cultural ambassadors redundant; it may be that a new and more splendid ship – a supranational scholar-ship? – will sail on a different quest. It may be that the quest will be grander than ours. I doubt if it will be more interesting.

'And yet, O splendid ship, unhail'd and nameless,
I know not if, aiming a fancy, I rightly divine
That thou hast a purpose joyful, a courage blameless,
Thy port assured in a happier land than mine....'

Appendix

The Athens of South America

The sun has set on Bogotá
And mist will soon reclaim the hill;
The cries and fading footsteps are
More eloquent when they are still.

The frigidaires with sour milk,
The Chibchas in their stetson hats,
The mourning girls in sheerest silk
And gasolineless diplomats,

The bulls and bells and bootblacks are
More eloquent when they are still;
The sun has set on Bogotá
And mist will soon reclaim the hill.

Now damp and ageing Romeos
Rehearse the chilly serenade
They later sublimate with those
More quickly won, more cheaply paid.

When neon-lighted cabarets
Are darkened, still the bars are bright,
Where poor portentous poets praise
Each others' verses through the night.

How faintly shines Neruda's star,
How dimly Byron's lordly skill!
The sun has set on Bogotá
And mist will soon reclaim the hill.

Do purple bishops in their sees,
Enthroned above this nether world,
Keep fingers crossed in blessing these
For whom Bolivar's flag unfurled?

'Bolivar ploughed the sea' – and still
They fantasise, nor care how far
The mist may curl around the hill
Or sun recede from Bogotá.

The country where 'his glory grew
Like shadows while the sun declined'
Disintegrates in patriots who
Have yet to liberate the mind.

How many dawns will leave in vain
The dreamers undisturbed, until
The sun has slowly set again
And mist again reclaimed the hill?

APPENDIX

Low Country 1948

The Hague in spring at six o'clock; the street -
Van Lennepweg with every cobble neat,
Swept of the fallen may-tree bloom, each tree
Trimmed back and sides, the once enfolding sea
Kept at a proper distance, but the air
A salty threat to embassies that stare
Through spotless, blind, incurious window panes
At empty flagpoles, sluggish weather vanes
And gates intact and gleaming in the sun,
Their modest diplomatic duty done.
And by the kiosk at the end a stream
Of bicycles give way to coupled, cream
And rubber-footed carriages. Each tram
Spills out dark coats. I watch from where I am
The well-fed batlike flitting forms deploy
Towards their redbrick mansions to enjoy
Beschuit and yoghurt, to denounce as false
The Jogjakarta Talks and sip their Bols.
Their Bols! Reminded, down white stairs, past prints
Of long-dead Wilhelms, flowery pots and chintz,
Batavian canals in photographs
And van der Wycks in kampongs and on staffs,
Descending, at the door below I pause
And hear within the bustle of in-laws.
Anon we're toasting, Bols in warming hands,
My sailing orders from their Netherlands
While in the distance, out beyond the dunes,
The ships above us breathe their mournful tunes.
These solid people, fragile with their years,
Sit – like the huge old press with chandeliers
Trembling above it – on the verge of tears.

Farewell, Van Lennep! In your sea-girt street
Three generations of the Indies meet.
So, as the setting sun moves on to rise,
Let's splice the mainbrace with our family ties!

Gilbert and Sullivan
(for a Beirut lecture)

After reading his libretti it is difficult to mingle
The life and works of Gilbert without lapsing into jingle.
A remarkable disparity divides his juvenilia,
And *Dan'l Druce* and *Charity* from farces even sillier.
While *Gretchen* and *Pygmalion*, though undoubtedly applauded,
Have never earned the praises that, for instance, *Pinafore* did.
Some early works were weightier – though possibly improper – yet
He only found his metier with Sullivan in operette.
To Gilbert's wit the other added musical precocity,
Collaborating brilliantly (in mutual animosity).

The major works of Sullivan are still obscured confusingly
By melodies that Gilbert wrote the words for so amusingly;
His early orchestration showed an admirable skill but
It lacked the inspiration that he later got from Gilbert.
He wrote when irritated by Gilbertian absurdities
One epic overrated, which as none today has heard it, is
Conclusive he alone could never London stage enliven; no,
He only bored the public with his grand but dreary *Ivanhoe*.
But Sullivan *and* Gilbert – to our lasting curiosity –
Collaborated brilliantly (in mutual animosity).

Performances sensational and lasting so delighted them
That, bowing to the nation, two succeeding monarchs knighted them.
For *Onward Christian Soldiers* and religious verse by Tennyson
Sir Arthur got in first in gaining Queen Victoria's benison.
But, having made the bloomer of encouraging hilarity
By disrespectful humour and political vulgarity,
Plain Mister Gilbert, writing for his public just as zealously,
Worked longer for *his* title – and he did so very jealously.
Inevitably both in the ensuing reciprocity
Collaborated brilliantly in mutual animosity.

In the course of a production William Gilbert was a martinet,
Interpreting his lines to every person with a part in it,
Dictating every gesture from the point each actor started from
So rigidly that even now his rules are not departed from.
Yet Sullivan, revolting from his role of a minority,
Once gave him quite a jolting by asserting his authority,
Refusing to compose, despite Gilbertian bravado,
Except for what he chose – and what he chose was *The Mikado*;
Then, gratified at Gilbert giving way to his ferocity,
He collaborated brilliantly in mutual animosity.

APPENDIX

Although completing quickly any score he'd once embarked upon,
Poor Sullivan was sickly and nostalgically harked upon
The plot that he was after – something grandiose and dignified.
Now Gilbert, for whom laughter was the only thing that signified,
Was naturally unbending but, unmercifully badgered, he
Obliged him with an ending of quite unGilbertian tragedy.
The audience, astonished at an opera so marred
By morbid histrionics as *The Yeomen of the Guard*,
Preferred *The Gondoliers* with its wonted virtuosity.
They collaborated brilliantly in mutual animosity.

In vain they separated to escape from their vendetta;
For neither one was fated to write better operetta.
In hopeful emulation many later pairs have written –
A P Herbert has with Ellis, Eric Crozier with Britten.
The immortal situations that their authors gave a handle to
Are still unique creations others cannot hold a candle to;
The wild extravaganzas made by Sullivan believable
Had scores where only fancies such as Gilbert's were conceivable.
For they, where others only shared a fond impetuosity,
Collaborated brilliantly in mutual animosity.

Index

INDEX